HUNTING
THE
SNARK

HUNTING
THE
SNARK

A COMPENDIUM
OF NEW POETIC
TERMINOLOGY

Robert Peters

FOREWORD BY WILLIAM PACKARD

PARAGON HOUSE

NEW YORK

First edition, 1989

Published in the United States by

Paragon House
90 Fifth Avenue
New York, NY 10011

Library of Congress Cataloging-in-Publication Data

Peters, Robert, 1924–
     Hunting the snark : a compendium of new poetic terminology /
Robert Peters.—1st ed.
         p.   cm.
     Bibliography: p.
     ISBN 1-55778-052-8
     1. American poetry—20th century—History and criticism—Theory,
etc.—Dictionaries.   2. English language—Versification—
Dictionaries.   3. Poetics—Dictionaries.   4. Poetry—Terminology.
I. Title.
PS323.5.P49   1989
811'.009—dc19   88-30122
                                                                                              CIP

Manufactured in the United States of America

The paper used in this publication meets the minimum requirements of
American National Standard for Information Sciences—Permanence of Paper
for Printed Library Materials, ANSI Z39.48-1984.

"It's a Snark!" was the sound that first came to their ears,
　　And seemed almost too good to be true.
Then followed a torrent of laughter and cheers:
　　Then the ominous words, "It's a Boo—"

Then, silence. Some fancied they heard in the air
　　A weary and wandering sigh
That sounded like "—jum!" but the others declare
　　It was only a breeze that went by.

They hunted till darkness came on, but they found
　　Not a button, or feather, or mark,
By which they could tell that they stood on the ground
　　Where the Baker had met with the Snark.

In the midst of the word he was trying to say,
　　In the midst of his laughter and glee,
He had softly and suddenly vanished away—
For the Snark *was* a Boojum, you see.

　　　　　　—LEWIS CARROLL, "The Hunting of the Snark: Fit the Eighth"

We sit around the campfire and sing songs of snark-hunting. One of us has been to Africa and knows the dangers of what we seek. Our colors and our smells glisten in the smoke toward the waiting flock.

What we have said or sung or tearfully remembered can disappear in the waiting fire. We are snark-hunters. Brave, as we disappear into the clearing.

—Jack Spicer, "The Hunting of the Snark,"
The Heads of the Town (p. 165)

Contents

Journals Cited

For further information on any of these journals, the reader is invited to consult either *Directory of Poetry Publishers: Second Edition,* ed. by Len Fulton & Ellen Ferber, Dustbooks, Box 100, Paradise, CA 95969, or *Poets Market,* ed. by Judson Jerome, Writer's Digest Books, 9933 Alliance Rd., Cincinnati, OH 45242.

Abraxas, 2518 Gregory St., Madison, WI 53711
Agni Review, Box 660, Amherst, MA 01004
Alcatraz, 354 Hoover Road, Soquel, CA 95073
American Poetry Review, 1616 Walnut St., Room 405, Philadelphia, PA 19103
Antaeus, 18 West 30th St., New York, NY 10001
Blue Light Review, Box 1621, Pueblo, CO 81002-1103
Bogg Magazine, 422 N. Cleveland St., Arlington, VA 22201
Caliban, Box 4321, Ann Arbor, MI 48106
Columbia, 404 Dodge, Columbia University, New York, NY 10027
Connecticut Poetry Review, Box 3783, Amity Station, New Haven, CT 06525
Contact II, Box 451, Bowling Green Station, New York, NY 10004
Crab Creek Review, 806 N. 42nd., Seattle, WA 98103
Croton Review, Box 277, Croton on Hudson, NY 10520
Electrum, 2222 Silk Tree Drive, Tustin, CA 92680
Field, Rice Hall, Oberlin College, Oberlin, OH 44074
Georgia Review, Univ. of Georgia, Athens, GA 30602
Graham House Review, Box 5000, Colgate University, Hamilton, NY 13346
Helicon Nine: The Journal of Women's Arts and Letters, Box 22412, Kansas City, MO 64113
Hudson Review, 684 Park Ave., New York, NY 10021
Iowa Review, 308 EPB, Univ. of Iowa, Iowa City, IA 52242
Ironwood, Box 40907, Tucson, AZ 84717
Long Shot, Box 456, New Brunswick, NJ 08903
Louisville Review, Univ. of Louisville, 315 Humanities, Louisville, KY 40292
New Letters, Univ. of Missouri, Kansas City, MO 64110
New York Quarterly, Box 693, Old Chelsea Sta., New York, NY 10013
Open Places, Box 2085, Stephens College, Columbia, MO 65215
Paris Review, 45-39 171 Place, Flushing, NY 11358
Pearl, 3030 E. 2nd St., Long Beach, CA 90803
Poetry Box 4348, Chicago, IL 60680
Poetry East, Star Rt. 1, Box 50, Earlysville, VA 22936
Poetry/LA, Box 84271, Los Angeles, CA 90073
Poetry Northwest, 4045 Brooklyn NE, Ja-15, Univ. of Washington, Seattle, WA 98105
Poets On, Box 255, Chaplin, CT 06235
Prairie Schooner, 201 Andrews Hall, Univ. of Nebraska, Lincoln, NE 68588-0334
Quarterly Review of Literature, 26 Haslet Ave., Princeton, NJ 08540
The Reaper, 325 Ocean View Ave., Santa Cruz, CA 95062
Shenandoah, Box 722, Lexington, VA 24450
The Southern Review, 43 Allen Hall, Louisiana State Univ., Baton Rouge, LA 70803

Southwest Review, Southern Methodist Univ., Box 4374, Dallas, TX 75275
Sulfur, English Dept., Eastern Michigan Univ., Ypsilanti, MI 48197
Temblor: Contemporary Poets, 4624 Cahuenga Blvd. #307, North Hollywood, CA
    91602
Triquarterly, 1735 Benson Ave., Northwestern Univ., Evanston, IL 60201
Yellow Silk, Box 6374, Albany, CA 94706

Anthologies Consulted

Most entries are preceded by abbreviated titles employed in "List of Primary Works and Authors."

21 + 1: 21 + 1: American Poets Today, ed. by Emmanuel Hocquard & Claude Royet-Journoud.

Bread: The Bread Loaf Anthology, ed. by Robert Pack, Sydney Lea & Jay Parini.

Controversy: A Controversy of Poets, ed. by Paris Leary and Robert Kelley.

Darkness: Carrying the Darkness: American Indochina—The Poetry of the Vietnam War, ed. by W. D. Ehrhart.

Generation: The Generation of 2000, ed. by William Heyen.

Geography: A Geography of Poets, ed. by Edward Field.

Halpern: The American Poetry Anthology, ed. by Daniel Halpern.

Kennedy: An Introduction to Poetry, ed. by X. J. Kennedy.

The Light From Another Country: Poetry From American Prisons, ed. by Joe Bruchac.

Men Talk, ed. by Elliot Fried.

NAP: New American Poets of the 80's, ed. by Jack Myers & Roger Weingarten.

New: The New American Poetry: 1945–1960, ed. by Donald M. Allen.

New Poets of England and America: Second Selection, ed. by Donald Hall & Robert Pack.

News: News of the Universe: Poems of Twofold Consciousness, ed. by Robert Bly.

Open Poetry: Four Anthologies of Expanded Poems, ed. by Ronald Gross & George Quasha.

Pattern Poetry: Guide to an Unknown Literature, ed. by Dick Higgins.

Poetry Loves Poetry, ed. William Mohr.

Postmoderns: The Postmoderns: The New American Poetry Revisited, ed. by Donald Allen & George F. Butterick.

Poulin: Contemporary American Poetry, ed. by A. Poulin, Jr.

Streets: The Streets Inside: Ten Los Angeles Poets, ed. by William Mohr.

Vendler: The Harvard Book of Contemporary American Poetry, ed. by Helen Vendler.

Voice: The Voice That Is Great Within Us: American Poetry of the 20th Century, ed. by Hayden Carruth.

YAP: The Morrow Anthology of Younger American Poets, ed. by Dave Smith & David Bottoms.

Preface

Anyone setting forth to hunt the snark, until the very conclusion of the voyage, believes he will succeed. So the critic who pursues the magical beast of contemporary poetry imagines that the creature has William Blake's face, the tail of Christopher Smart's cat, the scales of Elizabeth Bishop's fish, the beak and croupy voice of Poe's raven, the udder of R. L. Stevenson's cow "all red and white," and the claws of Tennyson's eagle. As the critic approaches the Emerald Isle (Manhattan) where the beast reputedly dwells, he hears siren sounds mixed with raucous cawings. A deceptive Jub Jub bird poised in a plastic banana tree regales him with mock carolings to decoy him. *There is no snark! There is no snark!* My own snark, I realize, as I look back over my book, is as elusive as any other critic's.

My method is denotative: by examining hundreds of poems by twentieth century moderns and post-moderns, as well as poems by a vast representation of living poets, and by arranging them into types, I hope that a totality emerges, a creature however beruffled, deplumed, anemic or plump, and noisome.

For most categories, I present examples of both failures and successes. My thesis is that gifted poets transcend pitfalls disastrous to lesser poets. While hacks write dismal self-pity and ego poems, a few poets write superb ones. I have tried to be as specific as possible in deciphering both negatives and positives. I give text and verse, and quote passages as well as whole poems. While more people than ever write and publish verse, much of it is flaccid, conservative, and moribund. Writing programs with their academic overtones (most poets who teach in these programs have professorial appointments) spawn poets who follow sanitized norms of language, style, and theme and who then secure teaching sinecures in other writing programs. Publishers of journals and various trade and quasi-trade presses foster such safe writing. Throughout this book I shall name names.

At the same time, while I lament the domination of current poetry by conservatives (see recent panels awarding NEA grants), I celebrate a host of independent poets (and publishers) who keep working, believing that they just may prevail. I highlight these folk, as a means, I hope, of gaining them something of their due. *Snark* is intended to break new ground as well as to review the current and the old. Most of the giants of modernism appear here, along with currently fashionable poetry prizewinners and fledgling and obscure writers. I have quoted generously from poets whose work has either not yet been published, or is inaccessible in libraries and bookstores—and less generously from work that is either in the common canon or can be easily obtained. The complete bibliography will assist readers in further trackings and exploration.

Above all, I hope that most readers will find *Snark* challenging and entertaining, and that young poets will find something to guide and stimulate them. Librarians also may find the book useful for making choices of poets to acquire for their collections. This book has allowed me to assemble much that has deeply concerned me over the past twenty-five years as a poet and critic. My illustrious masters all wrote criticism with iconoclastic flair and great readability: Jonathan Swift, Thomas Carlyle, Algernon Charles Swinburne, D. H. Lawrence, Ezra Pound, and Kenneth Rexroth. I should like to think they would be pleased with these results. In our own time, Robert Bly's encouragement has been crucial to my work, as has the example of his critical essays, particularly those written as *Crunk*. James Dickey, of *The Suspect in Poetry*, has also inspired me. Thanks too to Tom Montag, founder and editor of the much-missed *Margins,* who invited me to write for him; to William R. Eshelman, formerly of Scarecrow Press, who launched both my series of *Great American Poetry Bake-off* volumes and the *Poets Now* series; to Pamela and Charles Plymell, of Cherry Valley Editions, for publishing the first *The Peters Black and Blue Guides to Current Literary Journals;* and to Len Fulton for inviting me to write a regular review column for *Small Press Review.* I have also had special assistance from Charles Hood who read the entire manuscript and made seminal suggestions for topics and for poets. Some of his own words, indeed, appear in the entry on war poetry. He also suggested the category of the "five-minute sonnet," and provided several examples. Eloise Klein Healy and Wanda Coleman advised me on lesbian and black poetry respectively. I have greatly appreciated the first-rate editorial care *Snark* has received from Paragon House. Its superb copy editor, Peter Borten, has saved me weeks, if not months of time, and I am lucky to have been in the good hands of Ken Stuart, Ed Paige, and P. J. Dempsey. Further, that the publisher assigned the making of the huge index to a professional indexer, again saving me numerous hours and errors, is appreciated more than I can say.

I realize that in so encyclopedic a work some categories are slighted, and for this I apologize. Black poetry, for example, is so complex and rich a topic, that to treat it adequately would require a book. Also, Latino, Asian-American, and native American poets deserve a more thorough, and, perhaps, more sympathetic ear than I have provided. I should like to think that my omissions will stimulate other critics to correct me and to carry on where I leave off.

At last, a word about some of the categories which readers may find worrisome. My aim has been, as Swinburne's was, to scrutinize poetry "under the microscope." I find much that would have offended readers a generation or two ago. The truth is that new freedoms of language and sexual expression in society at large are reflected in much current poetry. Nor do these poems appear only in alternative, or counterculture, periodicals; they are beginning to grace the pages of some of our most staid journals. To omit these categories would be to falsify the real nature of poetry today.

Much is being written these days about a pervading "cultural illiteracy." We bemoan the fact that teen-agers think "Genesis" is first and foremost a rock group, and so on. Younger poets do indeed lack the grounding in traditional culture once considered the norm. For better or for worse, Marilyn Monroe, Daffy Duck, the Beatles, Mickey Mouse, Madonna, Sylvester Stallone, and Dolly Parton provide immediate frames of reference for our entire citizenry. Once, perhaps, the works of Shakespeare, Tennyson, Dickens, or Longfellow were common fare—today bright university undergraduates may never have heard of Walt Whitman, or, if they have, can't say whether he was a poet or a robber baron. We can no longer count on the old cultural frameworks. Whether as a result of this shift our literature is diminished or enriched, I leave to my readers to decide. My aim has been to take a broad, deep, and unflinching look at American poetry, to categorize what I find, and to judge. Poetry does matter, and matter greatly. That the snark may not exist is immaterial; the pursuit is what counts, and I sincerely hope that my readers, even when I may irritate them, will find my quest useful.

ROBERT PETERS
Huntington Beach, California

Note: I am grateful to Scarecrow Press for permission to reuse the following entries, which first appeared in *The Great American Poetry Bake-Off* series:

"Baseball Poem," "Dedication Syndrome," and "Opening Lines."

Other entries, all much revised (among them "National Treasures," "MacDonald-Eddy Syndrome," "Mock-Heroic Poetry," and "White Poetry") appeared in the *Bake-Offs*.

I express deep thanks also to Cherry Valley Editions and to Dustbooks for allowing me to develop many terms which first appeared in my *Guides*.

Foreword

With this remarkably funny, sane, and enlightening book, Robert Peters emerges as the John James Audubon of contemporary American poetry, indefatigably collecting and collating and cataloguing the various types of birds to be found in our literary shrubbery and underbrush. And like Audubon, Robert Peters provides us with flawless ornithological portraits of each species, complete with a description of habitat, the shape, hue and number of nest eggs, characteristic mating cry, nutty migratory patterns and feeding habits, even the unique tilt of the tailfeathers.

Hunting the Snark includes every sort of bird on our contemporary American poetry scene. There is the foolish confessional poet loon; the ego poem whooping crane; the dimwit academic sleaze turkey; the lyric skylark poetaster; even the quaint Poetry Society quail that gets skittish if anyone looks too close. Like the trusty ornithology guide that he is, Peters goes on this wonderful wild poetry goose chase, so he can flush out the assorted dopey, boorish, crass, absurd birds that are lurking there in the thicket. We even get an occasional glimpse of an authentic bird, now and then, here and there, flitting across the forest floor or perching from twig to twig.

Hunting The Snark is a hip guide to the colorful aviary of versifiers who are around us today, inhabiting our chapbooks, little magazines, and slim volumes of poesy that may even make it to the major houses. What a gargantuan amount of reading Peters must do, to be able to present us with such a prodigious range of contemporary American poetry! As I have to plough through some 50,000 poetry manuscript submissions every year for *The New York Quarterly,* I'm well aware of the various types of tit-willows and ding dong dodos that are out there in our great outdoors. Take it from one bird-watcher about another, Robert Peters has his birds down pretty well, ranking them neatly in order of unimportance according to their unique plumage.

We should be grateful for the bird-watchers among us: the way Poe paid attention to that raven, the way Coleridge made amends for that albatross, the way Yeats made his swan song in "The Tower." Yet I remember beginning a NYQ editorial talking about a mythical bird, the phoenix, "The odd thing is that Herodotus seems really to have believed that such a bird actually existed; in his *Persian Wars,* Book II, Section 73, he reports of the Egyptians:

> They have also another sacred bird called the phoenix, which I myself have never seen, except in pictures. Indeed it is a great rarity in Egypt, only coming there (according to the accounts of the people of Heliopolis) once in five hundred years, when the old phoenix dies. Its size and appearance, if it is like the pictures, are as follows: the plumage is partly red, partly golden, while the general make and size are almost exactly that of the eagle. . . ."

Whether these bird watchers be historians like Herodotus or painters like Audubon or poets like Peters, we desperately need our expert bird-watchers to help clarify our landscape.

Hunting The Snark is an extraordinarily well-informed, joyous encomium to poetry itself. It displays the variety and diversity of our contemporary American poetry scene.

WILLIAM PACKARD

ABC Poems

The ABC poem grew from the *Abecdarium,* a gathering of Latin words arranged according to letters of the alphabet. One of the earliest dictionaries in England, the fifteenth-century *Promptorium Parvulorum,* was translated as "Storehouse for the Little Ones." It was intended for pupils, and compiled by a Dominican friar known as Galfridus Grammaticus (Geoffrey the Grammarian), in Norfolk. He listed about twelve thousand words. In 1500 came the *Ortus Vocabulorum,* "A Garden of Words," printed by one of Caxton's assistants, Wynkyn de Worde. The first authentic English dictionary was the *Abecdarium Anglico-Latinum pro Tyrunculis,* compiled by Richard Huloet, in 1552. Huloet defined both English and Latin words, the total running to twenty-six thousand entries. The book was so expensive that only the rich could afford it. This fact led to briefer works, one of which appeared in 1570 and contained nine thousand items—it was called *Manipulus Vocabulorum,* "A Handful of Words." The Abecdarian form is obviously related to the acrostic (see *Princeton Encyclopedia of Poetry and Poetics* for a complete history). ABC primers satisfied the desire to acquaint children with basic vocabulary. Kate Greenaway's nineteenth-century *A Is For Apple,* though written for children, continues to amuse adults. The ABC poem itself is an improvisation on the primers, devised by poets seeking a fresh form.

Among poets writing ABC poems are Denise Levertov, "Relearning the Alphabet," from *Relearning the Alphabet;* Antler, *Factory;* and Paul Vangelisti.

In Paul Vangelisti's series of twenty-five eight-liners, each poem is devoted to a single letter of the alphabet. The poems are occasional, in that each is written to a specific friend, several of them being fellow poets. This friend is a painter:

> does it strike at all unfair I mean
> don't you find it irritating to be born in
> Dallas and translated to San Diego by a name so
> doubly verbal? or maybe names
> draw very little from a painter unless
> darling in that hush the riddle of her ·
> dolphin face once staked you to?
> Don, has your name always been a verb?

Here he addresses another poet:

> ride one's humor into the ground and
> ridiculously enough one has satire or catharsis
> rid of purity or the singing voice or the odd
> risk of someone's spittle in the mouth
> riddle it anyway you must you
> ring *satura* [satira] mixed dish, medley

I

right on to *satura,* full or sated
Robert, was it satire or satyr you asked me about?

This is for a teenage son:

that fathers and sons disappoint
that our *own little worlds* are disapproving seems
the least we can allow
to outlive such platitude undertakes
the rage fathered in you or the bitterness or
the reflection you must have found in my eyes
Tristan, you are written after all the rest
to admit the abyss we blame each other for

The whole of Vangelisti's sequence appears in *Temblor* (Summer 1987).

Academic Sleaze

This monster defaces most literary journals and assumes three primary forms: the lugubrious literary phrase, often echoing Shakespearean turns or chock-a-block imitations of Yeats at his worst; easy allusions to writers/poets read in undergraduate literature courses; generalizations of a metaphysical sort passing as profound, designed to satisfy fellow academics who like dredging around in poems for Heavy Mystical Momentosities.

The Southern Review (April 1982) is clotted with academic sleaze. Not a poem is touched by anything transpiring in American poetry since the 1940's, when the "Fulbright" or "academic abroad" poem was in, and poets chose motifs dear to their professors—from the Greeks, Shakespeare, and sights seen while on sabbatical. Charles Gullans is "so filled to utterance" he propounds "divinity from sacred texts/Of brow and lips." Sounds good, doesn't it? At least his tomorrows don't creep in petty paces. In another poem, when Gullans declares that "Something is surely coming to an end," his pontifications induce us to hear clumping echoes of Yeats's "violence upon the roads, the violence of horses." We turn the page expecting more, and better.

Opening lines overtly Shakespearean in their orotundity, pretentiousness, and elevation echo like exercises intended for a typing class. These examples are chosen anonymously from *The Southern Review*: "The recent storms' detritus banks the dune"; "How many times I've dreamed you here, the black"; "Ascent is simple where the tourists are"; and "A center of the world: in power once."

Among the literary allusions in *The Southern Review* these will be recognized as dear to world lit classes: Ulysses, the Sirens (they appear in two poems), Caligula, Orpheus, Kirkegaard, Zeus, Hymettus, the Nereids—offerings all, on the altar of academic sleaze. One poet, David Middleton, knows his Tennyson pretty well: his "Sirens" is an impressive echoing of detritus from Tennyson's more flamboyant monologues: "swooning awake," "unshrouded wisdom," "essential night," and "murmuring time." Even a fine writer like Joyce Carol Oates warms up over old Robert Browning. In "High-Wire Artist," she echoes that old fart of a Bishop ordering his tomb, one of the most admired (and taught) of all personages in nineteenth-century poems. Here is Browning: "Hours and long hours in the dead night, I ask / Do I love, am I dead?" Here is Oates: "Nights of getting through nights. / Often I forget: am I dead now, or still alive." Pick the better effort. Oates concludes with this bit of bathos: "It is not God that beckons, only the sawdust."

The Threepenny Review also fosters academic sleaze. In one issue (vol. 4, no. 3) nearly all the poets are professors: Florence Verducci, U. C. Berkeley; Dan Goben, U. of Cincinnati; Daniel Mark Epstein, Harvard; Paul Lake, Arkansas Tech; Howard Nemerov, Washington University; Miller Williams, U. of Arkansas. Yes, I do admit that not all professors or writing program poets write academic sleaze. Yet the editors of *The Threepenny Review* apparently prefer verse that assumes a superficial name-recognition of things cultural. The entries below appear in poems by the above poets:

> 1. Kronos eats his children. Rhea feeds him a stone. Zeus shears off his genitals.
> 2. Moon-seas: Serenitatis, Nectaris, orchestrated by W. B. Yeats's "unsounded gong."
> 3. *Madame Bovary, L'Education sentimentale*, Homer, Horace, Baudelaire, Mt. Helicon, and Berkeley, California.
> 4. Briseis, Achilles, and the latter's youth-lover, the dead Patroklos.
> 5. Paolo and Francesca.
> 6. Dante, Beatrice, and Gemma.

The Hudson Review is also rife with academic sleaze. An especially noisome spread occurs in vol. 24, nos. 3 & 4, in Alicia Ostriker's "The Pure Unknown," where lugubrious literary phrases clank in their chains like the Ghost of Christmas Past: "the immeasurable feel," "the system of the world," "the virtue of the pure unknown." She compounds the malady by showing off some of the books she's read: *King Lear, Crime and Punishment,* and Thomas Aquinas.

George Hitchock, in numerous poems in his *The Wounded Alphabet: Poems New and Collected 1953–1983* gives the lie to practitioners of academic sleaze, those poets who rift their poems' small ore with easy allusions cultural and literary. Hitchcock, one of our most-gifted non-academic poets, is as well-read and as well-traveled, and as any professors of world culture. What makes him special is his vision of contemporary life as a disaster: he is one of our finest political poets and employs the past to sharpen his doomsday themes. He himself, in "Lessons in Alchemy," provides this warning to academics abroad: "Exchanges will not be honored. / There will be no rebates. / The Kingdom of Heaven is permanently closed / to tourists wearing stilts."

"There's No Use Asking" concludes with a frightening image of Corday ready once again to strike Marat's fatal blow, seen in the context of a current Christmas of failed machinery and cultural death:

> look, the politician's watch
> has stopped an embolism attack
> the Christmas tree its ornaments
> glitter and go out the mannequins
>
> have lost their motors and stand
> motionless in the empty shop-windows
> in the museum of wonders
> the woman with the wax knife
>
> stands ready to strike her fatal
> blow while Marat naked and pustulent
> squirms in his four-legged tub
> he is ready to enter the black house
>
> he is already rehearsing the secret
> code-words I promised to show you

Hitchcock's "Western Civ.—(a short course)" devastates mindless adulators of past cultures. His encapsulation of Western Civ. courses in 4 biting stanzas must set academic teeth on edge:

> 1.
>
> A
> ristotle influenced
> Thomas Aquinas who
> swayed Car
> dinal Newman who
> was thought poor
> ly of by Thomas A
> lva Edison.
>
> 2.
>
> Avocados
> and almonds are di
> lecious. William E
> wart Gladstone took
> God very serious
> ly. La p lume de
> ma tante est.

3.

Thomas Jefferson
Hogg slept
with Shelley's
wife the poet
approved his
daughter-in-law
never spoke to
Hogg who
survived
them
both.

4.

There are no
longer any
lions on Mt.
Ararat go
forth and pro
create the Lord
commanded/ the
world is full
and tigers
too.

Thomas Meyer, one of our brilliant lyricists and love poets, writes almost always in a non-Surrealist mode, inspired by ancient Greek culture. And he's never pretentious. His readings of the past always serve some sensitive, intellectual framework appropriate to the mid-twentieth century. In his preface to *Sappho's Raft* (1982), explaining that Géricault's famous nineteenth-century painting "The Raft of the Medusa" provided a vision recalling the Greek poet Sappho. Meyer seeks to transcend a simple academic reading of the seminal canvas. The painting

> encodes for Art History—a passionate yet scientific obsession with the human body focused against pathetic, modern circumstances in total belief the heroic were still possible. Then too, we've been told in darkened auditoriums, that lantern slide smoldering on classroom screens, that 'the appearance of this canvas marks the beginning of a struggle between the classicist and Romantic movements.' Sappho has always felt to me like just such an upheaval, the ache of indifference, the ecstacy of embroilment. While she provides a raft upon these boiling waves, her raft is but a *rideau,* a "curtain" which when raised to the rafter lets in the vision of shipwreck. So in this private drift of associations, it was a scarf or shawl, the gift of a goddess, that once kept Odysseus afloat. And Mytilene, an island in a sea, home to all bright manner of things under Sappho's sun, is, I pretend, the

cartoon painted upon that *rideau* hiding from me, at times, the scene about to be discovered.

In his long "Love's Dial" Meyer suits Sappho's feelings to his own. His raft sails on difficult seas: can the ancient poet's lesbianism provide the courage he, Meyer, needs to write of his love for men and openly "address that god your song / arose from, for whose sake / you bade it / take new strength. . . ." Around him birds (cowbirds, finches) are at a feeder, small creatures evocative of similar creatures that might have pleased Sappho. The pain of unfulfilled love for another male is eased by recalling Samothrace where "men bid / Love enter them" and "bring them home/ to stroll the garden / of themselves safely." Meyer then adorns his poem with graciously expressed evocations of the past, simple yet telling accoutrements from Sappho's world:

grappling for that light
grape, stock and tendril
are
nodes, shades

of in their
ache
for
that urge that

drives wood
green and
flesh
into desire

and reined
would draw
Love's chariot
beyond

Love's destination
larkspur forever
adrift
on an ocean. . . .

When old pro Stephen Spender reviews his days with Auden, in "Auden's Funeral," he seeks a traditional pastoral consolation and Auden has become a

. . . marvellous instrument of consciousness
With intellect like rays revealing
Us driven out on the circumference
Of this exploding time.

Phyllis Thompson, in *What the Land Gave,* writes meat-cleaverish rhythms drenched in stiff draughts of literary geritol, cadences of the stentorian sort one imagines that ancient Queen Bodicaea must have used on her troops before she was tied to four horses and driven madly off in all directions. She strums Purcellean, Rilkean, and Yeatsian lyres. She avoids concrete imagery, preferring vague leaves, berries, and "everlasting" mountains. While she seems to have copulated much, she treacles erotic moments o'er with too much sweetness, eschewing sweat, mucus, and other glandular excretions fair or foul. In a poem to a friend, to accommodate her inflated feelings, she inflates nature. The dear old Susquehanna River has an "onwandering way"—so "onwandering" that "it can be thought of as common speech." That's strained literary pirouetting, ill-felt and forced. We get carp, not trout. Towards the end, safe and sentimental, she pulls out the organ stops, wafts her abstractions and smoking censers, and loads on an embarrassing allusion to one of W. B. Yeats's more famous lines:

> Of all men I know, John [Logan], yours is that voice
> I can call to mind anywhere from my deep heart,
> The serious and the ordinary
> Plainsong that grows out of but beyond weeping and triumph,
> Diminishes guilt, and can reduce even heroic love or failure
> To the same unasking simplicity of clear music
> As of river water lapping weeds on a low shore. . . .

Jane Hirshfield, in "Alaya" likes appearing as a Ceres of poetry—her title "Alaya," a Sanskrit term meaning "the consciousness which is the store house of experience," is, she says, "a place where seed-grain is kept, held for the next season's crops—as the way experience travels forward in time." This seriousness is most leaden, alas. Big Thoughts spew forth; and Hirshfield favors cultural references from college courses: Hermes, Proteus, Vermeer, Urdu Poetry, Troy, Stonehenge, and the Parthenon.

Robert Kelly, in various poems scattered through *The Alchemist to Mercury,* has a gargantuan appetite for lit-crit allusions. His alchemist craves to transmute the dross facts of life into art, via allusions. His juxtapositions of the mundane and the erudite are uncanny: eating clams in New England engenders thoughts of the Enlightenment, Dostoyevsky, and Gurdjieff. A fantasy of feeling up the dank posterior of a lesbian cab driver through a tiny hole in the cab is creamed over with allusions to Charles Ives, Shakespeare, and a "tantric text." Occasionally, an effect is downright horrid: when he washes his hands in cologne he's reminded of a cathedral (in Cologne, Germany?), and busies himself cleaning his nails with a cathedral spire. I'm much more impressed by all of the *drosseries* Kelly rams down our throats than by his tarnished and facile allusions. He's best when he stops acting as a world lit schoolmarm.

Duncan, almost alone, is able to translate allusions and borrowings into something vital. The breadth of his reading in texts both original and theoretical is awesome; and his singular intelligence enables him to transmute whatever he borrows. In his early poem "Night Scenes," *Roots and Branches,* a tripartite lyric on the stages of a young homosexual's coming of age, a recitative in celebration of the bliss of male sex is enhanced by numerous allusions to medieval and Renaissance poetry. These phrases, "green lovers" in a "fearful happiness," evoke moments from Elizabethan love lyrics. The "Prince of Morning" opens "a door of Eros" for the lovers. Their copulations, seen as the Beast, create Beauty, i.e., male and female transcendant. The lyric mode Duncan employs is the ancient aubade: "maiden hours" dance, "circling" the lovers' ecstasy. Archaic, semi-medieval allusions borrowed from Provençal love poetry and from Shakespeare's *The Tempest* suggest timelessness. Morning "steales upon the night." Darkness dissolves. The lovers' "rising sences / Begin to chace the ignorant fumes that mantle / Their cleerer reason." A Shakespearean innocence blesses the lovers—the Cowslip and the Sucking Bee. The nurturing flower is the lover. Duncan's youth enters the flower—"Where the Bee sucks there suck I." Semen-honey swept up the stamen, primal, as "the mothertides of the first magic," Adamic, where Adam, as yet alone, discovered masturbation, and flowers, and the mystery of generation. Duncan's beaker bubbles over. Brain zephyrs waft bubbles along the moon's track, towards the golden harpstrings of the sun.

By Part Three of "Night Scenes," the youth is no longer the closeted homosexual, and now pursues courageous sexual confrontations in the streets, released from guilt and fear. He no longer requires medieval or Shakespearean escape motifs. A modern poet, André Breton, supplies the youth with clues. Breton's *parvis,* or forecourt, of the poet's imagination/temple, stimulates a fresh vision of male lovers. A mystical Byzantine Queen of art is now essentially sterile: Penises are no longer glowing tapers, nor are the gorgeous flanks of strong men lion-flanks. Sexual cravings are not now diluted into mystical feelings, imagery, and literary fantasies imported from earlier, exotic literatures. The Queen is now a Zolaesque queen of the belly of Paris—a "temple of produce" is her palace "of transport and litanies." This is where rough trade, hustlers, hang out. In the Queen's Outer Court seminude men mount and dismount trucks (and one another). The Queen (the poet Duncan?) savors that primal beauty (music) engendered by the loins of men loving men. In these thoroughly modern environs, the poet is at home, unshackled, free. His heart "smokes." His fumblings through the zigzag streets reach the moon. What an incredible interweaving of allusion, fantasy, realism, and art!

Acrostics

This venerable form, usually relegated to warm-up exercises in beginning poetry workshops, is not much used by serious poets. Psalm 119 is a most elaborate early example. The twenty-two letters of the Hebrew alphabet, in order, form the initial letters of every other line of the twenty-two stanzas of the psalm. In our own time, John

Malcolm Brinnin published a book called *The Sorrows of Cold Stone*, made up entirely of acrostics, each spelling the full name of a different friend. The most fascinating of all such recent poems is W. D. Snodgrass's "Cock Robin's roost protests from (W. D.) (Mr. Evil)," in *Word and Image:*

COCK
ROBIN'S ROOST PROTECTS
W.D.   FROM   MR. EVIL

C ome to my arms, my fine young friend;
O vercome this cold resistence; we
C an't bring our differences to an end
K eeping our grounds so distantly.
May this spell, hold us as we **R**,
This ring of force we're parted by—**O**
Impassable, firm-fixed and far **B**
Twixt the likes of you and **I** .
N o doubtI'm not so very handsome;
S ome judge by one's appearance, so
M any a man condemns me, and some
A re far more like me than they know.
May this light house's N R **G**
Reveal your features bright as day; **I**
Trust by this gleam men may **C**
No Real Good in you for **A** .
L ight cast out on the faults of others
B linds men to their own faults. We
A lso share drives, all men being brothers;
R elinquish this proud enmity.
Our blood alliance shall B **R**
True shame, a defect in the **I**
Your double-cross-eyed poli-**C**
Would dwindle and waste D O **A** .
D rop such d-fences; we'll double you, De.
Only across Styx, Mr. **E** .

Adam-Consciousness Poems

The American poet as Adam was initially proposed by the critic R. W. B. Lewis. Whitman was the major Adamic poet—only when he had absorbed the American universe through his own mind and senses could he achieve grace. His obsession with his body and the flood of impressions (messages) received through the conductors he imagined glued all over his person produced mystical insights.

This motif is visible everywhere in current poetry. The ubiquitiousness of the "I" or Ego poem is directly Adamic: A poet's personal history is valuable, no matter how commonplace it may seem to others, because it is *his*. These poets avidly share their insights, emotions, and personal histories with readers, and feel readers care.

Lew Welch's "Wobbly Rock" is an elaborate Adamic discovery poem. At the outset, Welch examines a rock, decides (no God informs him) that it is "a real rock / (believe this first)," resting on real sand at the surf-edge. He names the spot: "Muir Beach, California." Though "someone else" had once pointed the rock out to him, he "found it" by himself. More discoveries: Adam/Welch observes that this huge rock, the size of "the largest haystack," actually "shudders" as waves clobber it. Like the original Adam, to see a miracle you must "sit real still." You may then even see the object move in "a good gust of wind."

Welch's poem winds on, developing various motifs of discovery—other rocks, the "EYE," differences between rocks and "the spaces in between," boyhood recollections (here he closely resembles the young Walt Whitman on the Paumonock shore):

When I was a boy I used to watch the Pelican:
It always seemed his wings broke
And he dropped, like scissors, in the sea . . .
Night fire flicking the shale cliff
Balls tight as a cat after the cold swim
Her young snatch sandy . . .

He continues to wait and observe: a girl in jeans splashes in a creek. "Feeding swallows dipped down to pick up something ran back to / Show it." Fishing with two others in a boat. A small cove. Again, the Seeing of Discovery:

Below us:
    fronds of kelp
    fish
    crustaceans
    eels

then us:
    then rocks at the cliff's base
    starfish
    (hundreds of them sunning themselves)
    final starfish on the highest rock then . . .

He stands on a scarp looking over the ocean, and in good Adamic fashion declares: "*I think I'll call it the Pacific.*" As he waits, he's wet through with salt water, and like Whitman in his cradling sea, Welch too is cradled and "rocked."

Note: It is not surprising to find the original Adam himself in poems. *The Norton Introduction to Poetry* (3rd ed.) has such a section of poems, including a snippet from *Paradise Lost,* A. D. Hope's "Imperial Adam," Francis Sparshott's "The Naming of the Beasts," John Hollander's "Adam's Task," Linda Pastan's "A Symposium: Apples," Christina Rossetti's "Eve," Richard Wilbur's "She," Nancy Sullivan's "The Death of the First Man," and Robert Frost's "Never Again Would Birds' Song Be the Same."

Alliteration Sleaze

The following examples will suffice to represent this ubiquitous instance of failed writing, often appearing when the poet loses his emotional drive. Charles Fort (*Georgia Review,* Spring 1982) contributes these typing-exercise lines:

> . . . how your own
> proud heart might someday come to painful
> poise. . . .

Robert Penn Warren, thinking of bees, types this: "The unhived lead hums happily honeyward." (*Chief Joseph of the Nez Perce*).

Walter James Miller's "He Thinks on Bowling" is lavish with what could be called "alliteration sleaze":

> Ten tenpins
> Temptresses attempted
> Ten potential
> Seriatim, nearly
> Simultaneous. . . .

Emily Grosholz (*Southwest Review,* Summer 1986) tarnishes a good poem, "On the Untersberg: *Salzburg,*" with overwriting sweetened with alliteration goo: She observes the ammonite and coral embedded in rock "left by a vanished ocean's vast reversal."

Alphabetty Poems

"Alphabetty" poems resemble that old farm kitchen delight Apple, or Brown, Betty. Poetry alphabetty is mixed with letters of the alphabet and individual words arrayed on the page often without any discernible connections with words coming fore or aft. Pure alphabetty poems written by e. e. cummings remain unsurpassed despite the poeticules scrambling up Olympus threatening old e. e. c.'s supremacy. The umbrella term designating such poets is "Language Poets," the nucleus being clustered near the base of Mt. Tamalpais in San Francisco, and consisting of such expatriates from New York City as Charles Bernstein, Barrett Watten, and Bob Perleman.

First, a glimpse or two of the impossible model cummings set. In the opening stanzas of poem 262 of the *Collected Poems* he seems to be taking an utterly cross-eyed look at a stripper: his eyes don't match up, so neither do his words. Considerable semantic agility is required of the reader to decipher a form of anagrams rather than poetry, an exercise in dyslexia:

sh estiffl
ystrut sal
lif san
dbut sth

epoutin(gWh.ono:w
s li psh ergo
wnd ow n,
          r
Eve . . .

The translation: "she stiffly struts all ifs and buts/ the pouting who No/ she slips her gown down (he)r/Eve". . . .

This more or less makes sense.

Poem 263 is even more outrageous. Punctuation itself spins and pirouettes in the midst of fractured words lip-burbled (as if one were strumming one's lips with one's fingers):

'
t,
;d
;:a:
nC.eda:Nci;ddaanncciinn

(GlY)

These maneuvers are a panegyric to Ruth St. Denis's dancing, and cummings explodes the words so as to evoke his excitement over the whirl/swirl of the famous dancer's motions, maintaining sufficient hints of the literal, i.e., words with recognizable meanings, once those words have been recombined from their scattered syllables and elisions.

Another of cummings's famous fractured alphabet poems is this simulation of a grasshopper making one of his more flamboyant leaps (poem 276):

r-p-o-h-e-s-s-a-g-r

who

a)s w(e loo)k
upnowgath

PPEGORHRASS

eringint(O-

aThe):l
    eA
      !p:

S   a
                        (r

rIvInG   .gRrEaPsPhOs)
                                                to

rea(be)rran(com)gi(e)ngly
,grasshopper;

This all makes lovely sense, both visually and semantically—once you have unscrambled the letters (the ingredients of this alphabetty) to their normal order.

One of the purest and finest contemporary writers in this mode is Dick Higgins. His recent *Poems Plain and Fancy* is a smorgasbord of alphabetty forms, some seemingly inspired by cummings, others by Gertrude Stein. Still others reflect Higgins's scholarly interest in "Pattern Poems," as they have been written in all languages, a specialty of Higgins's. He recently published a definitive study of the genre *Pattern Poetry: Guide to an Unknown Literature.*

In "friend, what's going on here?" (p. 29), the diaresis and the exclamation mark, in various arrangements, constitute the entire poem, charting the excitement of a first meeting, proceeding to a deflation of that excitement, and moving to a second, shorter stanza, where exclamation marks express intense surprise (and possibly outrage, with sexual innuendos) as the meeting becomes something very different from what it seemed at the start:

friend, what's going on here?

!

!
‼
!!!
!!!!
!!!!!

milwaukee
11.ii.77!

A five-part piece, "How the abbott trilled with his lady easy yet," starts off with stanzas that appear to be automatic writing ("rotary yarmulke, under randy yore / melt try yes sam muddier ram/ mad mouldy yams zilch check came / mountain nattyyouth thought trim"), proceeds to five combinations of many of these words in lists (with indentations) that seem about to slip off the page, and then focuses on the principals: the "natty youth," the "trill lady / trilllady," and the trim and natty "trimmountain." At this point, sexual innuendos occasion much tripping through amazing alphabet/word flowers of joyous randy play:

> mountainnatty nattyyouth
> easyyet
> trimmountain mountainnatty nattyyouth
> nattyyouth
> thoughttrim trimmountain
> rammountain mountainnatty natty youth
> nattyyouth
> thoughttrim trimmountain
> rammountain mountainnatty nattyyouth
> nattyyouth
> thoughttrim trimmountain
> trilllady
> easyyet. . . .

As with "friend," "Supra," a love-narrative, slides implicitly through consummation and release, suspiring in this final cummings-esque exploded alphabet poem:

> m
> ou
> n
> t
> (i)
> n
> a
> t
> y
> (oo)
> th
> (aw)
> r

Yet another use of the alphabetty poem, as a reflection of a cultural moment, appears in Harry E. Northup's "Listening to Savoy Brown at the Santa Monica Civic". Northup tells me that he aimed here to show via the hesitations suggested by the individual words a drug-culture youth of the early 1970s (the poem is dated August 21, 1971), stoned, trying to enter subliminally into Savoy Brown's jazz:

```
if
if i if i
if i can      can get
     can get      into     in-
   to the rhy
          rhy
          rhy  th
rhythm of this
of this
of this


        of this song
```

```
if i can get into the
   rhythm of this song
if i can get
     can get
     can get
if i can get into the rhythm
if i can get into the rhythm of
                   this        of this
              of this song
if i can get into the rhythm of this song
               there is
               there is
               a possibility.
```

Northup's poem stresses one of the inadequacies of language—its inability to evoke music directly. I have no sense here of what jazz Northup was hearing; nor was Northup seeking to convey the specifics of Brown's riff: the state of mind of the aficionado trying to move his consciousness into a higher state, and enter the realm of music, is the theme.

Most writers of alphabetty, alas, are nowhere as adept as cummings, or Stein—or Higgins, or John Weiners. The latter's *Behind the Statehouse,* while it is an alphabetty treasure, too often results in automatic writing, larded o'er with all the weaknesses such writing is heir to. If the mind producing this writing is vapid, the writing is vapid. This awful truth remains obscure to many poets, and this is nowhere clearer than in a new anthology, *21 + 1 American Poets Today,* edited by Emmanual Hocquard and Claude Royet-Journoud (Montpellier Cédex, France), which features a generous smorgasbord of "Language" poets. That the volume originates in France also underscores the influence of such currently fashionable French semanticists, literary theorists, minimalists, structuralists, and poststructuralists like Derrida, DeGuy, and Lacan, among others.

In Frank Samperi's hands the minimalist alphabetty form owes something to Tarzan talk:

    rain not last day
    recalled today
    this blue sky day
    striking pool lake
    generates in
    definite spheres. . . .

One has the feeling that Samperi got caught in the woods near a lake when the urge to write a poem hit him. Either he had only a tiny scrap of paper available, or grabbed off a small piece of birch bark, and let the pen flow.

Charles Bernstein's "Type" does seem to have been composed on a typewriter on a narrow strip of paper. The pretentious words "egregious," "machinations," "mesmerized," and "crisscrosses" sit in their skinny lines like dull toads waiting to be prodded by a princess stunned on crack. There's little or no lyric music. These two lines seem constituted of suet chunks: "manner embrace / mesmerized by. . . ." So with Michael Gizzi. Here's an anorexic moment from his "Avis": "Seldom / But like / This / I list / In a cage/ Glazed / In a / Pearliness / *Persona oscura*." Robert Grenier does pallid homage to Gertrude Stein's "A rose is a rose is a rose." Here's Grenier: "grass // there is grass // grass // here is grass // grass // grasses. . . ."

Susan Howe employs alliteration to pep up some nonsense writing: "Right or ruth / rent / to the winds shall be thrown // words being wind or web. . . ." What I read here is that if we were to "rent" *right ruth,* i.e., negotiate with a realtor to take them home for the day (perhaps an image of renting a VCR casette for home viewing might be more apt) we could then play with them, throwing them to wind and/or web. Or, if "rent" means to cut them up, then we can scissors them into their syllables and throw them into the alphabetty of our next poem. I'm perplexed, and as I contemplate the possibilities I hasten back to the rental place to return the words.

And so it goes. These poets are part of a considerable, and apparently growing, school of poets. One admires their energies, and, as Erato knows, American poetry needs some freshening of the stagnant voices represented by the conservative writing programs and the trade presses. My guess is that the novice would find far more excitement and mind-expansion reading 21 + 1 than either the Smith and Bottoms *The Morrow Anthology of Younger American Poets;* the Myers and Weingarten *New American Poets of the 80's;* the Heyen *The Generation of* 2000; or Vendler's Harvard compendium. Some of the best poets associated with this group are Leslie Scalapino, Jerry Ratch, Charles Bernstein, John Yau, Keith Waldrop, Michael Palmer, Michael Davidson, Rosmarie Waldrop, Dennis Phillips, and Paul Vangelisti. Among journals featuring their works are these: *Temblor, Sulfur,* and *Caliban.*

Anachronistic Jig

The "anachronistic jig" occurs when a contemporary poet dances his tune according to some literary figure from the past. He or she writes in the mode of that figure or incorporates work from past journals and poems in a pastiche or collage fashion.

Amy Clampitt in *The Paris Review* (Spring, 1984) visits the English Lake District and, for some 150 lines, inhabits Dorothy Wordsworth's psyche. The subject is Dorothy's incestuous feeling for her brother William. Rather than attend his marriage, she stayed behind on his bed weeping. Clampitt performs an anachronistic jig, finely tuned and set to Dorothy's own journals. When Clampitt writes in her own voice, she still manages to evoke Dorothy's. This erotic passage is a good example:

> . . . birds singing; the sacred stain
> of bluebells on the hillsides; fiddleheads
> uncoiling in the brakes, inside each coil
> a spine of bronze, pristinely hoary;
> male, clean-limbed ash trees whiskered
> with a foam of pollen; bridelike
> above White Moss Common, a lone wild cherry
> candle-mirrored in the pewter of the lake

In the same *Paris Review,* Andrew Motion's "A Lyrical Ballad," rife with Wordsworthian connections, is an exercise in sprung pentameter quatrains in a bucolic mode. The occasion for the poem is domestic, a wretched marriage; and, since it is painful, it is un-Wordsworthian—at the outset. He visits relatives and is left to "wander alone" amidst the daffodils and lonely clouds of his imaginings. On one excursion, he meets an equivalent for Wordsworth's old leech-gatherer (my parallel, not Motion's), a hippy in a tartan shirt, with tangled hair, who leads him up to a minor Ararat and shows him an abandoned ark. Like figures in Wordsworth who turn up, change one's life, and then disappear, this one too vanishes, "politely, running his hand in silence / over the salty prow." The anachronistic echoes contribute to an already glossy poem. Motion is too self-obsessed (like Wordsworth?) to give either nature, the Canadian relatives, or his wife a fair shake.

A fine use of the anachronistic mode is Alfred Corn's sequence (also in *The Paris Review*) from his *Notes From a Child of Paradise*, a set of fourteen poems of fifteen lines each, which form a homage to a neglected Victorian poet, George Meredith. Meredith's magnificent sequence of fifty sixteen-line "sonnets," *Modern Love,* published in 1862 and characterized by sardonic wit, self-probing, and a fresh conversational tone, anatomized the sufferings of a marriage on the rocks. Before Meredith, this subject was nonexistent in poetry, unless one includes the difficulties of Milton's Adam and Eve at the time of their expulsion from Eden. W. D. Snodgrass, in *Heart's Needle,* was the first contemporary poet to write at length about a failed marriage.

Corn's story is of two students whose love goes awry—"children of paradise." Alfred is a poet, Ann is a literature major. As a "linesmith" obsessed with verse, Al allows the "animal magnetism" between himself and Ann to fade. As things get worse, they actually discuss *Modern Love*, "Meredith's obsessive / Jamesian antiromance." In fact, while she's at home, absorbed in reading Meredith, Alfred walks over, touches her shoulder, and waits

> . . . ten counts until you lift a face
> Still vaguely fogged over with the trance of reading.
> "Hm?" you ask; and eyes answer full voice.

Eventually, I am sure, some informed critic will examine the uncannily exact reflections of Meredith's tone, style, phraseology, and metrics found here. On the surface, Corn's poems might seem to be tours de force. The opposite is true: his poems are his own, the subject matter personal and contemporary. Yet Corn lovingly and intelligently reflects his origins. How pleased Meredith would be. Most twentieth century poets who are aficionados of earlier poets content themselves with merely borrowing a few "tags." Seldom has a poet worked so much from the marrow outwards.

Among our more visible traditionalist poets, Judson Jerome is one of the most tenacious and prolific. His *The Village: New and Selected Poems* proves again what followers of his career have known all along—that he takes great delight in pouring the events of his own life into old wineskins—his family, his loves, and his views on communal living, his aging and his art. Only a few of these poems are written in free verse. Most of *The Village*, however, is end-rhymed in an array of forms. Among the most impressive pieces is a sequence of some fifty sonnets, called "Homage to Shakespeare," all written in a deft Shakespearean manner. There are dramatic monologues, some richly humorous, in the voices of Romeo, Juliet, and the Nurse, and of our primal parents in the Garden of Eden. Many shorter poems on sexuality, the passing of time and beauty, and acute observations of the natural world, all breathe easily inside the various traditional forms Jerome selects for them. Reading him, one feels that these traditional patterns are thoroughly alive—he's never artifactual or self-consciously archaic.

Art-Notion Poems

One of the most egregious of these, by Laurence Lieberman, appears in *The American Poetry Review* (January 1982). A Japanese tilemaker caps his thirty years of crafting with a temple built on a bluff. He's the "impresario of the hill, / the happy tile-Czar" who directs a protégé on the heights. So far, so good. What damages the piece is a sudden irruption of clichés: "he breaks new ground . . . he takes risks . . . his eyes glow." Lieberman can't make up his mind whether to be the tilemaker or the observer. And he keeps intruding facile allusions to art. The tilemaker evokes this apostrophe: "Ah, slowly he creeps into his roof- / walker's second skin of an artist!" His disciple "may carry / into the future" this man's "Cézanne skill." Lieberman fancies that the old man spent years in France, as a youth, and discovered the French painter, who became "his patron-saint."

Lieberman isn't content to ravish painting for images, he turns to dance, an even clumsier forcing of art-notions: the tilemaker now "infuses into body language of his delivery hand-wafts / of dance choreographer, / lilted gestures of band conductor on his podium, or opera / scenarist molding stage sets / (he has studied their styles in theatre rehearsals). . . ." This is awkward and cluttered. It's as if Lieberman has weighted the old man's jockstrap with heavy stones, thereby impeding his attack on "his canvas / the many-layered sweep of hill slopes."

Asafetida

"A yellow-brown, bitter, offensive-smelling resinous material obtained from the roots of several plants of the genus *Ferula,* formerly used in medicine . . . smelly, fetid."

—*The American Heritage Dictionary.*

In literary parlance, the term refers to editors who claim to print the best poetry and prose around, and to editors of anthologies purporting to print the best poetry and prose appearing in literary journals over a given year. Of the first order are the editors of *The Paris Review;* then comes Jonathan Galassi, one of the editors of *The Paris Review* who is also editor of *The Random Review,* an assembling of most conservative choices. Another editor to note is Bill Henderson of *The Pushcart Prize VII: Best of the Small Presses,* assisted here by Gerald Stern and Carolyn Forché as poetry editors. Many of these same writers also appear in *Random.*

I've never understood that old cliché "tongue in cheek." If you thrust the tip of your tongue against your right cheek, does that carry less of an onus than if you thrust it against the left? In either case, I suppose, you convey an unspoken signal of being had, or taken in—or that you are about to "have" someone, or take them in. That's how I feel after plowing through a *Pushcart* collection. True, there are minimal nods to minority writers, gays, and obscure presses. But their favored magazines are *APR, Poetry, Antaeus, Iowa Review,* and *The Yale Review,* all journals that have held chloroformed hankies over our faces for too long.

Two presses that publish much asafetida verse are Atheneum and Black Sparrow, one a considerable trade press, the other not—though

Black Sparrow in fact falls somewhere in between a trade and a small press. For years, Atheneum has published one of the most visible of all poetry series—"privileged" in the sense that once the series was set going the editorial policy was to add no new poets to it. The Press is the very image of East Coast elitism. Though the Atheneum editors have not always held strictly to the closed list policy, they have informed poets who wrote inquiries that they are closed. The series had indeed become, with few exceptions, geriatric.

Black Sparrow is also pretty much a closed house not particularly known for its daring—although, bless John Martin (Black Sparrow is a one-man show), it has published tons of Charles Bukowski over the years. I am told that Bukowski keeps the press solvent. While Martin's long list is crammed with deadwood, it does include Diane Wakoski, Wanda Coleman, a complete Jack Spicer volume and the collected poems of John Weiners.

Asian-American Poems

Asian-American poetry seems to lack a driving center, a focus that would give a national scope similar to that enjoyed by black, gay, and lesbian poets. One vast social injustice suffered by Asian-Americans was, of course, the internment of Japanese-Americans in detention centers during World War II. The degrading treatment of Chinese laborers imported during the late nineteenth century as cheap labor for railroad, mining, and lumbering interests in the Far West also had devastating effects. Mitsuye Yamada's *Camp Notes* treats her and her family's lives in one of the largest of the World War II detention centers. In this poem she is a child being deported with her family to a California center—she later saw herself, smiling as she is marched away, in a photo on the front page of the *Seattle Times*:

Evacuation

As we boarded the bus
bags on both sides
(I had never packed
two bags before
on a vacation
lasting forever)
The Seattle Times
photographer said
Smile!
So obediently I smiled
and the caption the next day
read:

Note smiling faces
a lesson to Tokyo.

Yamada's most recent book, *Desert Run: Poems & Stories,* amplifies
the themes of *Camp Notes.* Nelly Wong writes of her mother's difficulties
in coming to this country to be with her husband, and of the ruses
necessary to thwart the inhumanity of the Immigration Service. In this
poem, "Poem for a Woman Who Has Fallen," from her *Dreams in Har-
rison Railroad Park,* she writes again, as she has earlier, of being afraid
of physical intimacy with her mother. She seems to distance herself by
focusing on an old street woman. The questions she raises seem as much
about her own mother as about the other woman:

Are you someone's grandmother?
Are you hungry?
What do you keep in your string shopping bag?

Cathy Song, in *Picture Bride,* though she bears too many Workshop
Poem trademarks and was a Yale Younger Poet, writes effective mono-
logues. In the title poem Song imagines her Korean grandmother arriving
at the Waialua Sugar Mill camp to meet a husband she has never seen. In
the ensuing poem the diabetic mother has aged and the daughter is ill.
Some of Song's power results from her subdued, almost prosy writing.
Here, though, as the daughter bathes the ailing mother, she reaches
beyond placidity. In her bath, the old mother makes

. . . jokes about her great breasts,
floating in the milky water
like two walruses,
flaccid and whiskered around the nipples.

Ronald Tanaka, "The Shinto Suite," writes what many Asian-Amer-
ican poets write, trivia seen in a clichéd Oriental manner—tiny details
with a porcelain or floral twist, pastel understated delicacies. He also
sprinkles his poems with enough Asian words to give a further sense of
authenticity:

i want to make you
breakfast.

raisin muffins on
gray shino

garnished with a
fern from

the windowbox, and
coffee, my

famous blend of mocha
java and dark french.

if you like you could
bring flowers.

the vase is egg shell
stoneware—from gump's.

Deborah Lee consciously writes Poem Calligraphy to render a senti-
mental coy image of her daughter, in "Haiku for Leah." The concluding
image of mother and daughter as tulips is embarrassing.

Numerous Asian-American poems are family-centered. Richard
Oyama writes humorously, if slightly, of his mother's buying oval rice
cakes and then teasing him for eating too many: "You eat too much
mochi! / One of these days you're going to / turn into one big mochi!" Joy
Kogawa curls her mother's "fine white hair" with a "new mist curler iron"
bought for her eighty-first birthday. Shirley Lim writes an original poem
on her father with overtones of poverty, love, and health:

Pigeons

Grey and white, they littered the doorways
And verandahs. Strutting in hot mornings.
Metal chests puffing in hot mornings.
Or limp feathers afloat in our
Water-tank, they stank as we washed,
Half-awake, for school. Father ate pigeon
When he was sick. "Pigeons bring good luck,"
Father said. We thought of money thumping
Like claws on zinc roofs, good money
Fluttering in to buy shoes, and toes
Like blind worms blunting heads against
Tight rubber. Pigeons gobbled fat maize
As many sacks of golden grain they came.
Ten, twenty, twenty-five, till we gave up
Counting. Our feet continued hurting.
We tasted their dark potent: thighs like
Baby fingers, masses boiled with fungus,
Bark and splintered horn. Skulls dissolved;
Mists steamed towards cots where they flurried.
A spoonful dense with meat—good as a week
Of New Years—filled us all afternoon.
But father ate pigeon only when
He could no longer work: Pigeon
Was too rich for daily eating.

Chungmi Kim's *Selected Poems* juxtaposes romantic and tragic fam-
ily experiences, the loss of much Korean heritage, and painful conflicts

between Asian and California mores. In one moving poem, "The Color of My Dress," a branch evokes a memory of a silk dress her mother once made for her to wear at a harvest festival. She wore the dress once only, for "the war like a wind / came and stole everything." Behind many of Kim's delicate and powerful poems is the motif of the traditional exploitation of the Korean woman.

By contrast Jessica Hagedorn (in *Pet Food & Tropical Apparitions*) seems jazzed-up and trivial. As one review observed, Hagedorn suffers from "terminal cuteness." The reviewer quotes these passages:

you slip a hand
into my dress
tenderly fondling
each breast
as if
i didn't know
about those claws
pulled back
inside the fur.

("The Leopard,")

king of the lionmen
come dancing in my tube
sing, ming, sing . . .
blink sloe-eyed phantasy
and touch me where
there's always hot water
in this house

("Ming the Merciless")

Garrett Hongo (in his widely reviewed first book *Yellow Light*) writes of his Japanese ancestry and attempts to resolve numerous personal frustrations by considering moments of delicate primary color: he abandons his usual introspection and meditates on whatever it is "that flowers from itself," shaking forth "the yellow dust of thought / onto the red cloisters" of his heart and passions. Bitter lemons ripen on his window sill.

The title poem, "Yellow Light," opens with a pastiche of Asian-American urban life in Los Angeles, focusing on a woman returning home from shopping. On one arm is a "tar-black patent-leather purse"; in the other is something for dinner: spinach, mackerel, Langendorf bread. After descending a city bus, she passes schoolboy gangs, a Korean grocer's wife, apartments beginning to steam "with cooking / and the anger of young couples coming home / from work, yelling at kids, flicking on / TV sets for the Wednesday night Fights." Yellow moonlight informs this book, and by focusing on such an image, traditional and at the same time material, Hongo manages to blend his cultural heritage(s) with contemporary life, in an impressive harmony of contrary themes and images.

John Yau's *Corpse and Mirror*, chosen by John Ashbery for the American Poetry Series, is a surreal meditation on death as an image for life. Yau has death watching a movie called life, while life returns the favor by watching a movie called death. With Yau the issue of Asian origins seems to matter little. He's a thorny poet, deriving much of his inspiration from painting, particularly twentieth-century work—the title of his book comes from Jasper Johns. His style is not lyrical; in fact, it seems consciously deadened by a series of slapped-down bits of prose which may or may not have logical connections between them.

Baseball Poems

". . . baseball's their game
because baseball is not a game
but an argument. . . ."

—George Oppen, *Of Being Numerous* (p. 18)

From Aristotle's day to this, intellectuals have argued about the nature of poetry and the influences on it—influences from the poet's unconscious as well as from the tangible daily universe. Today the American literary establishment is characterized by a fatuous split between baseball addicts and despisers of the game. Towards resolving what is probably a tempest in the shower drain, I have solicited the opinions of a handful of well-known poets about the sport, arranging them in alphabetical order to avoid tantrums of envy. Following the interviews I shall examine a few representative contemporary poems on the theme, some fair and some foul.

I dedicate this chapter to Jonathan Williams, an aficionado of baseball who eschews the team effort in poetry and largely goes it alone, whacking balls into the stratosphere with great zest and abandon, all the while performing linguistico-boogies on the names of players and teams, and on arcane lore relative to the sport. We further supply this bit of window-dressing by way of prelude from the folk-wisdom of one of my old aunts: "I like baseball 'cuz that seam down the back of the player's pants always lies true to the crack of his ass." (Aunt Bobbie Lustall, Spring Green, Wisconsin, 1939)

John Cinderberry:

First of all, I don't know. I never thought of myself as having much of a relationship to baseball, or baseball players. Every hour of my life is surrounded by a lot of things that don't add up to anything, and these sprout up as part of a situation I'm writing. I prefer skating to baseball. I begin with the figure of a baseball arcing through the air, on an only partly explicit trajectory. I end now with a figure eight cut starkly in a cake of ice, by a skate. This may be a geography—if you want to call it that. But you'll have to forgive me. I'd rather write on the hollow handle of a paper knife, or on one of the last Czar of Russia's ornamental Easter eggs.

Robert Really [Read in a clipped Projective-Verse mode, in a monotone]:

I wouldn't feel much at ease playing baseball with other poets, or writing poems about baseball, unless doing so would result in something like a whole experience with LSD. Yet, the free-running player winging into home plate, or dashing between bases (the idea of stealing bases has possibilities) is the unexpressed question mark some poets (including myself) love. A poem has to be an echo of something, if only an *if*. And *if* there's a baseball team upon your roof reciting Chaucer and waiting to fuck your nagging wife, that's fine with me. To be insistent, rather than make an accumulating statement—an inning, after all is a kind of canto, isn't it?

James Hickey [Read with a thick southern accent, crescendoing]:

I'm against it. It's for sissies, and suggests to me a faggotry of the poetic art. You do a series of dances in your baseball uniform, you play with a ball about the size of a dog's gonad, and when you sock a ball into that baseball mitt, it whunks almost as if you've rammed home a sodomic thrust. I'm for football. There's more beef on the hoof in football. And when those bodies collide! It's the stuff of cavemen jetting ever greater poet republics!

Allen Ginseng Satsang [Chant, accompanied with Hindu temple finger-bells]:

My data is [sic], as always, half-conscious; yet it serves as a cosmic flashlight for my nubile-baby, pubescent-navel-quest introspections, Himalayan and western. The game, I think, lacks any Hebraic ghost-presence however, is hardly a trip to impel you out toward the cosmic spaces very far, or very fast. *Om, Om, Om*—!

Donald Vestibule [Adopting a chummy, casual, mid-Western tone of mild self-amazement]:

I have a wicked self, and that self loves baseball. A baseball game is runic, as a poem is, in the sense you can't flatter it. I feel especially wicked when I am being runic; was resident in England, where the persona (myself) seemed, I am sure, awfully insular to the British because of my preference for baseball over cricket. Where would American poetry be without poets to share baseball? There'd be nobody to put in my anthologies but women.

Richard H. Morpheme:

If you catch the lagoon of my drift, or attempt to paddle about on limpid waters propaedeutically, you will sense that baseball, a noun, requires an adjective *steamy*, in solution, en gelée, even when, of course, those who struggle adversely with their balls (poems) turn their distaste into Chautauquas of distress. New men. New methods. The locus of baseball, an impenetrable patina of pretty things, and hence of verse, is a refusal of, a languid wrestling of, or at least an insistence on, encouraging moisture to stream along the deepest and most noisome body trenches, flooding the poems with anti-human acceptations—the fans in the stands, towards a logorrheic fungoid growth, having both furred tongue and speech. I remind you of Thomas Aquinas's proposition that Willa Cather was never at home except with muskrat bites. I don't mean to have bad manners, rather hope to formulate an implication, a bravery of attitude, a valorization of baseball separated by an anacoluthon full of despondent sailors.

Erika Aging:

I resent, with a mastiff bitch's anger, baseball. Women are mere contraries here, and are seldom allowed to stretch their *queyntes* over those well-placed diamonds. To my calme observation (do please mee believe), too many American male bards now approaching middle age affect cute baseball caps whilst allowing their poems (and miserable shrunken codpieces) to dangle toward and a-down their trencher side. Their scribblings often sound as if they were strummed on a single high-stretcht lute string—no more. These ambitious bawds have greatly reduced testosterone levels, faint lecherous humors, are woefully shy before all women (except their mothers), and pursue strange meats. I have done!

Galway Firth[To be read in some existential distress]:

Unless you are playing the game—it doesn't matter in what position—and are in enough pain to make you grit your teeth, to test your limits; and unless at that endurance peak, you don't exclude animals, plants, and tones from your interior life, a connection resembling the one a skunk or a porcupine has for another skunk or porcupine, baseball won't affect your poetry much one way or the other. Yet, now that I think of it, if, at the end of a long, hot game, poet-teams could be persuaded to throw their sweat-drenched jockstraps, caps, and uniforms into a heap, at the edge of a woods outside some New Hampshire hamlet, the porcupine, skunks, and bear who'll appear to drink sweat-nectar might suffice to generate a whole new school of totemic animal poems. It's a thought.

Diane W. Koski:

The "team sense" irritates me. I've always wanted to read my poems to a baseball team of poets, right after they've finished a game: Iowa 7,

New Hampshire 3. Since baseball is so matter of fact, it fits my matter-of-fact sense of poetry very well. Also, when you were young, game-playing was a good way of starting poems. Neither George Washington nor the King of Spain played baseball, or even knew of it. Well, if I, naked, wearing only oranges, diamonds, and peaches around my neck, walked into a team's locker room, they probably wouldn't look up—they'd be so stuck on one another. That's when I'd scream at them to stand there jocked while I showed them some real poetry! I'm sure they wouldn't be so contemptuous of women when I was through with them!

Adrienne Poor:

I refuse to answer the question, since so far as I can tell, a male asks it.

Three very different poems about baseball are Philip Dacey's "Wild Pitches," "Lesson I" by Joel Oppenheimer, and Jonathan Williams's "O For a Muse of Fire." Dacey gives some tough advice to his son: pitching at life is like pitching a baseball—don't hold back, and stop aiming the ball. Let your animal fly. Joel Oppenheimer's "Lesson I," extols the power of coaching for any team, dirt-lot or big league:

> Without coaching the base runner is caught off his base
> the runner is kept from the plate without coaching
> Runs do not go up on the scoreboard
> runners make no advance under flies
> the rallies are squashed inning and inning
> from the first, even till the ninth
> The Giants are not without coaching
> Neither the Yankees, both first.

Jonathan Williams is a poet of the democratic urge who respects folk sources and popular culture. He seems to imply that if a poet ignores these sources he is severely diminished. Without such roots there can be no vital literary language. "O For a Muse of Fire!" defies any ordinary definitions of poetry. It commemorates Stan Musial's three thousandth hit, on May 13, 1958, and is an arrangement of the details, almost as if they were presented as a fact sheet. At the beginning, when he lists people born on that awesome day, he permits himself a bit of esoteric humor: the birthdays of a prize fighter and an empress—and the execution date of a Dutch statesman, reputedly one of the best Holland has ever produced, who was injudiciously eliminated by arrangement of his political enemies. The latter event is sufficiently esoteric that one can be sure the ordinary reader, and certainly the typical baseball fanatic, will never have heard of it; moreover, chances are that no reference book in their homes would contain Barnveldt's name.

In the phrase "the Muse muscles up," the word- and sound-play Williams loves appears. There follows a patch of found material and some announcer's lingo in quotes; *"It felt fine!"* has the effect of a refrain, and via its understatement evokes Musial's modesty. Any reader wanting to examine the way Williams plays rhythms against each other will be surprised to find how much originality there is. I reproduce the entire poem:

O FOR A MUSE OF FIRE!

Date: Tuesday, May 13, 1958—
        a date previously memorable in history for the birth of
        Joe Louis (1914)
        the Empress Maria Theresa (1717)
        and the beheading of
        Johan Van Olden Barnveldt (1619)

Place: Wrigley Field, Chicago, Illinois

Time: 3:06 p.m.; warm and sunny; breeze steady, right to left

Attendance: 5,692 (paid)

Situation: top of the sixth; Cardinals trailing the Cubs, 3–1: one out;
        Gene Green on 2nd

Public Address: "Batting for Jones, #6, Stan Musial!"

The Muse muscles up; Stan the Man stands in . . . and O, Hosanna, Hosanna, Ozanna's boy, Moe Drabowsky comes in

2 and 2
"a curve ball, outside corner, higher than intended—
I figured he'd hit it in the ground"

("it felt fine!")

a line shot to left, down the line, rolling deep for a double . . .

("it felt fine!")

Say, Stan, baby, how's it feel to hit 3000?

"Uh, it feels fine"

*Only six major-league players in baseball history had hit safely
3000 times prior to this occasion. The density of the
information surrounding the event continues to surprise me,
rather belies Tocqueville's assertion that Americans cannot
concentrate.*

North Atlantic Books has published a series of anthologies devoted to baseball, all of which feature poetry as well as prose. Among the titles are these: *Baseball I Gave You All The Best Years of My Life*, edited by Kevin Kerrane and Richard Grossinger; and *The Temple of Baseball* and *The Dreamlife of Johnny Baseball*, edited by Richard Grossinger.

Bent Genes Poems

Various artists have taken the motifs of the monster, the mentally handicapped person, the schizophrenic, the carnival freak, and the sexual outcast as a vivid, sometimes brutal means of shocking us into perceiving truths about ourselves. Bosch and Brueghel were early models, as were the great Cologne masters of the Middle Ages. Their inspirations were religious, their pictures intended to prepare us for eternity after the coming apocalypse. Many later artists were also fascinated by the abnormal and the grotesque—Flaubert, Hugo, Constantin Guys (aquarelles of monsters and devils invading Paris by night), Fuseli (of the nightmares), James Ensor (great tableaux of masked skeletons and masked carnival figures), Soutine (mad humans and flayed fowl and beasts), Francis Bacon, and the photographers Diane Arbus, Richard Avedon, and Joel-Peter Witkin.

Four contemporary poets specializing in the motif are David Fisher, Laurel Ann Bogen, Cynthia MacDonald, and James Bertolino.

David Fisher, winner of the first Poetry Society of America's William Carlos Williams Award, devotes much of *The Book of Madness* to terrifying poems on his own bout with madness in 1972. No poet has ever written quite as searingly on these themes. Fisher sees his initial illness with some of the tender lyricism reminiscent of Christopher Smart or William Blake:

> There is angel strife in the poet's eyes,
> o little lost poet with
> many fine doctors and one celestial pillow.

Hallucinations torment him. He runs a razor across his throat. As the blood flows, someone borrows a dime for him to make a phone call. In another poem, "I cut my throat with an easy motion," he is harrowingly specific:

> my intent had been to blot out the fake green
> leaves of the plants, complete to the last serration,
> my intent had been to submerge the boat
> that rides the green hills of the Blue Ridge Mountains.
> > But by now it was winter in Munich,
> and my God, I was crying, and the beams of my lamps
> had caught the gold eyes of a fox.
> I followed the fox across the frozen snow.

Here is "Electroshock":

> O rubber mouthpiece
> o tremor that brailles my heart
> the frail gymnastics
> of my jigging limbs

Desire, the tiger,
rolls in the flame of the cord . . .

I lie on many hills
the doors swing open
birds are screaming
History is mercifully lost—

and fresh headlamps have come to comb my wall.

His torment seldom eases: his mind "which would be bright/ and smooth /
is a shipwreck of horses."

Laurel Ann Bogen explores schizophrenia. In "Mr. Jasper," a vision-
ary satanic figure grips the speaker's wrists: "I am his: / do with me / what
you will." Taking out his scalpel he asks if Bogen wants power, magic, or
tears. He has them all, and will display his "minarets" and teach her
"tongues." Another visitor, a Spanish lover, enters her unlatched win-
dows at night where she lies naked, and plays her "like a gold-toothed /
gypsy / on his violin." The ecstatic union produces blood.

Bogen's sense of personal injury is heightened by bizarre images
fashioned in a mind that seems barely able to perceive what is real and
what is not:

I do not want
to hurt you, he said,
as 6 miles of lace were wrenched
from her stomach,
crayfish spewed forth,
ken dolls appeared.

Even as a child Bogen's persona loathed herself; she was fat, fuzzy-
haired, myopic, and clumsy. She dreamed of a "discerning tapeworm"
who would eat the fat from her hips, waist, and thighs. She yearns for her
father to put her in his bed and crush her to death, reducing her to
"crumbled shards" to be placed in an urn, and later reassembled when
"you" (father, or God) "have a more charitable eye."

"27 Years of Madness" is written by the occupant of a mental
hospital. The speaker reveals that the wish to maim, present for
27 years, remains:

it is in the face
in the mirror
that you want to smash
for telling you lies
the eyes for falsifying beauty
the mouth for voicing fraud
the ears that were prey to every con man

The doctors woo her by treating her as a child: "Darling Laurel / Good Laurel / Gifted Laurel." They strip her, open her skull, and peer inside.

Bogen is not always grimly realistic. In "I Eat Lunch With A Schizophrenic," humor appears, and the conclusion is wise. Here is the poem:

I check for gestapo agents
under the table
there are no electronic bugs
in the flowers
we talk freely
about jamming devices
and daredevil escapes
The waitress asks
if everything's OK
I tell her fine
except for the two SS officers
sitting drinking rob roys
pretending not to watch us
They slip a secret message
on the check—
Please pay when served—
Dollars or marks
I ask.
She says just pay up
and spits out her gum
on the napkin
Her nametag says Barbi
I don't want to make a scene
so I pay the bill
and glance at my jr. hypnotist watch
Large segments
of the world's population
have been converted by this time
saving machine
I strap to my wrist
disguised as a timex
I turn it on the SS officers
They think nothing's changed
but we know different
We know the allies
are going to bust
in here with tear gas
and submachine guns
looking for nazi jew-haters

The problem's not in the hamburgers
chili
or cokes
I explain
the problem is in being susceptible

Diane Arbus, the photographer, seems to be an important influence on, or an inspiration for, Cynthia Macdonald's *(W)holes*. By evoking freaks, hermaphrodites, and carnival figures, Macdonald acknowledges the photographer's vision. The result is an homage to, rather than a slavish imitation of, Arbus. Macdonald's earlier books, *Transplants* and *Amputations*, make clear that her world is a vast carnival of dwarfs, cripples, hunchbacks, and variously smashed persons. She seems to trap us in our own snickerings. Who are the real freaks? It may just be that we are. She can be bizarrely funny: "siamese sextuplets / heroic couplets." An ice storm creates a "frieze" on a building.

Her "All Mouth" is just that, a ravenous mouth possessing an attached "rudimentary bag." All Mouth finds itself pregnant—it seems hermaphroditic. Soon "All Ear" is born, moving All Mouth towards self-completion. Twenty years elapse. All Ear is lonely, so he wills himself to create another being from himself, as he had been created from All Mouth. He decides against an All Nose, because he thinks he couldn't stand the smell (har, har). So from a drop of his blood, he births "All Eye." All Eye ("All Poet"?) sees past the edge of self on into the darkest quarters of experience.

"The World's Fattest Dancer" stuffs herself with chocolates and "larded guinea hens" before regaling the public with dances. Her mouth is so tiny no one can kiss her. In "Celebrating the Freak" Macdonald sets "the freak-flags flying." "The Siamese Sextuplets" is grisly and hilarious. "The Kilgore Rangerette" squeezes her grandmother too hard right after the latter's surgery, and winds up as a bag lady. "Florence Nightingale's Parts" is a brilliant tour-de-force on the famous angel with the lamp. Nightingale's rigid, compulsive hair-parting parallels the rigidity of her Crimean hospital-keeping. The poem, of course, also refers to her sexual parts, and her starved life. Disorder, to her, is a form of death. Parting life into severe halves allows her to reject and to accept decisively. When her hair falls out during her final illness at age ninety, it makes no difference, Macdonald writes; she simply "parted her skin." Another poem reports the birth of the ultimate human freak—Hermaphroditus, offspring of Hermes and Aphrodite. There is also a twelve-foot statue of a hunchback, carved by an Austrian in 1520, an image for rebellious women who pick babies full of holes.

Through various poems laced with a Grand Guignol brand of arsenic, celebrating various mutants and otherwise maimed folk, fetuses, and beasts, James Bertolino proves that he is tough enough for the 1980s (see his chapbook *Are You Tough Enough for the Eighties?*). X-rays of teeth, possibly his own, crowned with decay are meant to provide a mood of sanitized but ruthless rot, a premonition of what we are in for. Bertolino provides us with a new savior, a "genius mongoloid" to lead us to a "new world." He's the special creature of a new and appropriate mythology, a goat-footed turtle, as he describes himself, epitome of the mutants produced by our DDT sprayings, gender confusions, and mindless hormonal injections. In the mongoloid poem our beloved creature, a "red-faced genius," comes "like the balloon / of no karma" to save us.

In Bertolino's "French Kiss" (*Precinct Kali and The Gertrude Spicer Story*), a man with a cleft palate has sex with a girl who is apparently turned on by him. Fearing that she will tell her mother, the man kills her:

French Kiss

Her tongue in
my cleft
palate
a finger playing the ridge

.   .   .

I couldn't let her go she'd tell
her mother
threw it in the crick
i didn't lose
my way back over the baby toads
ankle-deep
that year

I lied they didn't
like my nose
mouth I talk funny &
hate
your tongue slut

Elsewhere, Bertolino discusses poetry at a meeting of an "Artificial Limbs Club." Afterwards, members surround him, "flexing their fixtures," glancing with sunlight. Jeanette—her forearms and fingers "nude"—has intelligent eyes. The other club members worship her, and they ask Bertolino to write a poem about her, which he does.

Some readers may find Bertolino unbearable. Who wants to meditate on the X-rays of someone else's caries? Isn't poetry supposed to deal with "the higher things of life?" Bertolino grabs our attention, and I suspect he's right in seeing the mutant in us. He provides rare memento moris for these times.

Other poets writing potent "bent genes" poems are C. K. Williams, Thom Gunn, Lucien Stryk, and Paul Zimmer. Williams in "From My Window" is drawn by the coming of spring to gaze out on the street towards some budding sycamores, "the thick spikes of the unlikely urban crocuses" breaking through "the gritty soil," and surveyors with their tripods measuring for spring building. People appear: a girl jogging, kids playing hooky, and the paraplegic Vietnam veteran who lives down the street in a partially converted warehouse with his "friend." The latter pushes the vet in the chair, weaving, as the chair lurches. He's seen them before on their way to the "Legion," where they often go. They talked to Williams once, and both were drunk. Williams asks himself how they stay alive—"on benefits?" Are they "lovers?"

As they approach Williams's house, the chair tips over. Both men "tumble, the one slowly, almost gracefully sliding in stages from his seat, / his expression hardly marking it, the other staggering over him, spinning heavily down, / to lie on the asphalt, his mouth working, his feet shoving weakly and fruitlessly against the curb. . . ." The friend trying to haul him back into the chair, manages to pull the other man's "grimy jeans" off. His thighs are shrunken and blotched, and "the thick, white coils of belly blubber, / the poor, blunt pud, tiny, terrified, retracted, is almost invisible in the sparse genital hair."

The friend stares up at Williams who wonders if the man remembers that Williams had seen him the winter before, pacing, almost running for many hours in the fresh snow, fashioning perfect figure eights. He "lost the race," for the snow was falling so fast it covered his designs almost as soon as he made them. In the morning, no traces remained.

There are at least three dimensions to this poem: the pathos of the paraplegic war vet with no place to live; the vulnerable and maimed physical body, and the maimed psyche of the friend in the snow. Then, of course, there's the "normal" poet watching the saga of these unfortunates from the security of his room, behind his window. He's not thoroughly safe, however; for there are hints that what he sees are images of himself. Spring hardly delivers more than a promise of maimed rebirth.

Thom Gunn's "Sweet Things," from *Passages of Joy*, is as much about his own need to be loved as it is about a "mongoloid Don" he meets in the streets. Don, seated on the steps of a laundromat licking chocolate ice cream from "the scabbed corners of his mouth," sees Gunn and runs over "with the mannered / enthusiasm of a fraternity brother." He asks to be taken across the street—his request "part / question part command." Gunn holds "the sticky bunch of small fingers" in his as the pair "stumble" across the street. There Don demands a quarter, which Gunn does not give. Why? Because the "seven-year-old mind" never recognizes "me, me / for myself, he only says hi / for what he can get."

In "As Expected" a group of retarded men come to life because of the ministrations of a conscientious objector to the Vietnam war, Larry, who works with them. Until his arrival they lay "knocked out by thorazine," had sheared heads, and some were brutally washed off with hoses:

> They looked like ninepins.
> But he found that none had head-lice
> and let them grow their hair.
> they started to look
> as if they had different names.

One invents a game and teaches it to "the unteachable." One learns to eat by himself, another becomes toilet trained. Eventually Larry's duties cease, less humane keepers arrive, and once again these "ninepins" return to being "unteachable, / as expected."

Ai's "The Kid," in *The Killing Four*, is a chilling portrait of a teenaged murderer, seen from inside the skin. He observes his sister's cruelty to her doll—she rubs its face in the mud, then climbs into an old truck through the window. She ignores her brother, who circles the truck, slapping its flat tires with an iron rod. He hears "the old man" tell him to hitch up the team. He keeps on circling the truck, banging harder than ever. When his mother calls, he flings a rock at the kitchen window, but misses.

He walks over to his "old man." When the latter doesn't look up, the kid splits his skull open with the iron rod. When his mother runs over, he lets her have it across the spine. In need of better weapons, he grabs a rifle from the house:

> Roses are red, violets are blue,
> one bullet for the black horse, two for the brown.

He's so intent on murder he bites his tongue bloody. He remembers "the one out back," and shoots her as she climbs from the truck. Her doll flies to the ground. In his madness, he rocks the doll in his arms, boasting:

> Yeah. I'm Jack, Hogarth's son.
> I'm nimble, I'm quick.

Lucien Stryk's "Amputee," in his *Collected Poems: 1953–1983,* is the portrait of a man who goes piece by piece to a grisly death, making of it much cheer and a pair of sick jokes. Failing circulation of the blood results in the amputation of his legs. The victim laughed that his "unwilling heart" caused the problem. Soon he'd lose his arms:

> "Now you see it, now you don't,"
> he quipped. They
> told us he died laughing under gas.

Finally, Paul Zimmer's "Zimmer Guilty of the Burnt Girl" is a modification of the "bent genes" poem. It portrays a girl damaged by accident rather than birth. The telling motif is of the boy Zimmer's mix of distaste, pity, and fear for the disfigured girl, feelings, it appears, that his mother also shares, although she does buy the girl's burnt sweet rolls, rolls she is selling to "mend" her face. During these weekly appearances, Zimmer recalls that he would hide behind the piano as his "unflinching mother" made purchases only to drop them into the rubbish later. Up to this point the poem is deeply felt. In the third and final stanza, however, *writing* takes over as Zimmer does some facile editorializing. I don't believe that Zimmer, whenever he has fevers, sees the girl again and (in a fractured grammatical twist) is "guilty for her and of her." Nor does the equation of his own burning with fever adequately correlate with the girl's tragedy. Was this send-off necessary?

Billy the Kid Poems

(*see also* Celebrity Poems)

J ack Spicer was enamored of Billy, and in *Billy the Kid*, wrote of him with great originality. The Kid was to Spicer what Adonis, Childe Harold, Alastor, and Werther were to the nineteenth-century Romantics. He is prettified—Spicer forgets the fact that Billy was an idiot, a moron, a sadist, and incredibly naive. He's made into a symbol for the outlaw poet who opposes the bad guys of the outside world for whom poets are "faggots" or worse. Billy's body is so pure he never needs bathing—no jockey shorts beneath his tight, worn jeans. And, yes, he's out there confronting vast panoramas of nature: the Western landscape is Spicer's equivalent for Byron's Alps or Shelley's Euganean Hills. Billy even represents the poet as Christ, since Billy has *stigmata:* bulletholes, three in the groin and one in the head, "dancing right below the left eyebrow." Billy has a touch of the comic-book character about him. Spicer writes a kaleidoscopic poem, or, rather, to use a word he himself chose to characterize this work, a *collage*—a collage constituted of "hell flowers" resembling gold leaf, flat strips of wrinkled wrapping paper ironed out smooth by an electric iron. The result is a "painting" of Billy's death; or, at least, the picture informs Spicer of that demise. Heroes, Spicer says, "really come by" colors that are "flat." Once, though, we appear to *see* a collage, we don't *see* it, for we are in "memory," and our Billy is Spicer's invention. The bullets are not real, the death is irrelevant, and the swatches of paper and cloth so meticulously arranged do not really constitute a collage. Clear, isn't it?

Spicer is rather mindless in loving butch Billy, expressing his feelings with the subtlety and directness of a mash-note valentine. Yet, there is one special moment, in homosexual parlance, a reference to "honey" in Billy's groin, i.e., his sperm:

> Billy the Kid
> I love you
> Billy the Kid
> I back anything you say
> And there was the desert
> And the mouth of the river
> Billy the Kid
> (In spite of your death notices)
> There is honey in the groin
> Billy.

Spicer was sufficiently touched by Robert Duncan and Charles Olson to appreciate the fact that various romantic myth-motifs could be helpful in his own work. Among them are the eternal river, the holy grail, and the poet portrayed as a shaman figure and sensitive plant. Let's examine how

Spicer employs the river image: Billy the Kid reaches the river where he is to die. Dry grass and cotton candy appear at the river's edge—death motifs, possibly, of the real world (grass) and of a fantasy world (cotton candy); the latter is the essential and fluffy material of the imagination, derived from natural fact, for the look of cottonwood trees from a distance resembles cotton candy. Ahem.

As he approaches the river, Billy, aware of his doom, meets his Romantic double, his secret sharer, Alias. Billy tells Alias that "somebody" wants him "to drink the river / Somebody wants to thirst us." Alias says it's not the river that desires their deaths, for no river cares to trap a man. Rivers lack malice. The youths remove their shirts, a sort of courtly / knightly exchange with homosexual overtones. Billy declares:

> I was never real. Alias was never real.
> Or that big cotton tree or the ground.
> Or the little river.

Exploring sophisticated neo-Platonic Shelleyan notions of the Real and the non-Real, Billy opts for a way of driving deep into the perplexed brains of despised Philistines the inference that art/poetry is the true Reality and that all else is illusion.

Billy's most controversial appearance was in Michael McClure's *Jean Harlow and Billy the Kid* which fuses the two legendary figures in a scenario full of posturings, fun, and sex. Like Spicer's Billy, McClure's is both raunchy and idealized, and in Harlow Billy meets his match. As he does frequently, McClure loves conjoining legends, often writing them as though they were two-dimensional figures in pop modes. Their remarks often seem suited for comic-strip balloons. At the same time, he writes with great sophistication, borrowing stylistic devices and even language from Shakespeare, Shelley, and Walt Whitman.

McClure's notorious verse play *The Beard*, based on these poems, remains controversial, as it was in the 1960's in San Francisco and Los Angeles when its actors, producer, and director were repeatedly arrested. Few works in our time have had the impact of McClure's play in broadening sexual mores and insulating daring writers and artists from legal and societal persecutions.

An elegant treatment of the outlaw is Thomas Meyer's *The Bang Book*, "an erotic cowbody ghost story in verse." Part of the fun is in the homosexual overtones, in the older and the younger man pairings. Billy is both lover and protege of Wild Bill Hickock, who is, surprisingly, very feminine:

> His hair
>   flowed to his shoulders
>   & his hands delicately drew
> ivory pistols from his holster.
> he wore small tooled boots on his almost
>   effeminate feet (a *badde*
>   man or *baeddel*)

Billy, one of a dozen kids spawned by Herm and Freda, was gang-banged early: "he was so pretty / there in the / waters of Abilene." Hickock visited him one Christmas in what resulted, apparently, in some magical sex:

> Bill's silver spurs rang
>   like bells
>   every
>   time he came
>   to the shack
> at night.

The Kid's first gun was a gift from Wild Bill who advised him to sleep with a woman, although "no one ever supposed / he was straight." Eventually, Jack McCall shot J. B. Hickock dead, so he had to visit Billy as a ghost, in ghostly fellatio sleep time amours:

> A ghost went down;
> The Kid next to him.

Wild Bill remained the Kid's mentor, calling for him to "Shoot love. Mark 'em, make 'em / all kid, with the / gun you are." Just before his final departure, the ghost handed over a gold bullet stamped "LOVE." Billy, indoctrinated into sex and love by his older friend, strengthened and hardly wise, was ready to leave his boyhood behind.

Black Poems

(*See* also Asian-American, Native American, Gay, *and* Lesbian)

Like most contemporary poetry, that written by blacks can be divided into conservative, radical, and middle-of-the-road sub-groups. Further, the poets' geographical spread, from New York City to Los Angeles and San Francisco, complicates the issues, and in so brief a piece as this, much about black poetry will remain to be described and defined. An authoritative treatment would include black writers from other large cities as well, particularly those in Detroit and Chicago. I am greatly indebted to Wanda Coleman for assistance in arriving at the groupings that follow. I hasten to add that the final determinations are mine, and I am responsible for any inaccuracies and omissions.

The conservative poets—Coleman calls them "safe"—those "least threatening to white people's reality and assumptions," are usually identified with colleges and universities (most predominately white) where they teach creative writing. Their publishers are apt to be the larger trade houses and literary journals. Writers like Michael Harper, Gwendolyn Brooks, Nikki Giovanni, Quincy Troupe, Sonia Sanchez, June Jordan, and recent Pulitzer winner Rita Dove fall into this group and seem nearly indistinguishable from hosts of white poets spawned by a white literary tradition. Brooks, I hasten to add, is larger than her limitations, and for years has written powerfully and lucidly about the plight of blacks in a racist society. By winning a Pulitzer Prize in the 1950s, Brooks gave a precious new visibility to black poets. She is a true ground-breaker.

Quincy Troupe (a college professor and editor), as Michael Duff remarked recently (*Contact II*, nos), writes "poetry filled with attitude." In *Skulls Along the River,* Troupe "strides across the continent catching in rhetorical language the chaos, destruction and fierce determination for a better life that is characteristic of the Black community of which he is a part. As with most rhetoricians, Troupe's voice is bombastic." His spelling mimics black speech and his tone echoes such jazzmen as Coltrane and Parker. Here is a passage from "River Town Packin House Blues":

> Big Tom beat his wife after killin all
> day
> his six chillun too,
> eye say Tom beat his wife after killin
> all day,
> his young chillun too,
> beat em so awful bad, he beat em right
> out dey shoes

This is from "Impressions 8":

> slick hop stylin spirits
> of the greased way highsign
> give high fives of speech
> step the low road
> strut bojangle
> their words in motion

He writes what appears as unrevised, first draft matter. Troupe seems to relish both a rhapsodic rhetoric and his sizeable ego:

> anyway, ey'm here, with my deck full
>   of metaphors
> songs, my phone book filled with
>   poetic
> court jesters, my bitch of an ego,
>   hanging around
> like the wind, outside everyone's door
>
> ("Here Eye Am Again")

Calvin Forbes, who teaches at Howard University, seldom moves past what sound like workshop poems. His work is feisty and a bit crude. This patch from Forbes's "The Other Side of This World" sounds cooked up to appeal to a white person's stereotype of an old black "jiggerboo" beggar with missing teeth:

> I cried as many tears as I have teeth.
> And I only got two in my mouth. Son of the
> Sun look out: as you get black you burn.
> Is everything in its place except me?

He might have said "mouf" instead of "mouth," and "cept" instead of "except."

Rita Dove, who was born in 1952, teaches at Arizona State, and has an M.F.A. from Iowa, writes utterly safe workshop poems. The assignment in "Geometry": take a commonplace image, say, a house, and see if you can make it fly. Use a coy image from nature to lock it all in. A touch of the pathetic fallacy is always recommended. And be sure to use a big abstraction and some facile personifications. Dove sets out to "prove a theorem" and manages to expand a house: windows "jerk free" and "hover near the ceiling." The ceiling gives a "sigh" (the pathetic fallacy again) as it floats away. Abstraction emerges from an easy personification: the walls "clear themselves" of all "but transparency." Dove is "out in the open"—where, we don't know; she leaves that nicely vague. She sees windows hinging "into butterflies." Here's a neat bit of workshop glitz: sunlight at the intersection of the windows. The windows (symbolizing visions?) spin off "to some point true and unproven."

Another poem, "The Fish in the Stone" again makes use of the pathetic fallacy. In "Dusting," a maid named Beulah, "patient among knicknacks"—this sounds liked hoked up Dylan Thomas, right?—dusts, bringing "a grainstorm" of light to the objects "her gray cloth" brings "to life." She makes "scrolls / and crests gleam"—obviously she is polishing objects. Her mind wanders, thinking of a "silly boy" who kissed her in the rifle booth at the fair. Up through her "wavery memory" (slick workshop sound echoes) she recalls rushing into a snow-filled parlor, finding a pet goldfish frozen in its bowl, thawing the little creature, etc., etc.

In "Planning the Perfect Evening" Dove keeps a date waiting. She pauses to admire her nails ("such small pink eggshells"), then proceeds, with an ego-ridden fatalism, down the stairs where the lad is standing "penguin-stiff," in a room that's so quiet "we forget it is there." She teases him, with a frost of malice, asking him what the lump is "below" his "cummerbund." If it's his erection, Dove is too genteel to say so.

A second group of poets, those falling between safe and unsafe include Ismael Reed (a dynamo of energy, who has founded journals and publishing houses devoted to black writers), June Jordan, Jane Cortez, Etheridge Knight, Sonia Sanchez, Don L. Lee, Lucille Clifton, and Kamau Daoud. The more radical black poets, those most threatening "to white people's reality and assumptions," include LeRoi Jones (Amiri Baraka), Ted Joans, and Etheridge Knight, who along with hosts of black jazz artists, have inspired impressive younger talents. Among the latter are Wanda Coleman, Jayne Cortez, Essex Hemphill, and Yusef Komunyakaa, and the still younger Michelle Clinton and Nathaniel Mackey.

One poem by Jones, "For Hettie," is in the voice of a young buck who sees his wife's left-handedness as "a fierce determination . . . to be different," and is more than a little puzzled by it. Jones's language makes no concessions to white norms, particularly educated and literate ones—which intensifies the paradox: his dude is almost too concerned about appropriateness, that his woman "rite" right:

> I sit
> patiently, trying to tell her
> what's right. TAKE THAT DAMM
> PENCIL OUTTA THAT HAND. YOU'RE
> RITING BACKWARDS. & such.

He doesn't get very far. She persists: "left-handed coffee, / left-handed eggs." When she comes in at night from work (she seems to be a stereotype, the generic employed black wife of an unemployed black husband), she offers him her left hand to kiss.

As Amiri Baraka, Jones further purifies and rarifies "black talk," employing it in one poem in a devastating, unsubtle slam at Secretary of State Henry Kissinger. Baraka signals that he no longer writes for a white audience, as more conservative black writers do: his language is meant to abrade the sensibilities of those, white or black, who believe in good norms of diction, usage, and tone. An effective example is "Horatio Alger Uses Scag."

By comparison, Nikki Giovanni's "Revolutionary Dreams" is tame. Giovanni is too gentle and unabrasive; she once dreamed of being mili tant, of "taking / over america to show / these white folks how it should be / done." Now, however, she's decided to use her "perceptive powers / of correct analysis," not on dreaming that she can "stop the riot and negoti-ate the peace," but on being "a natural / woman doing what a woman / does when she's natural. . . ." Also see Raymond R. Patterson's 26 *Ways of Looking at a Black Man*, for a noncontroversial treatment of some of the same issues that so disturb Baraka and produce his rage and lack of willingness to compromise.

Ted Joans, slightly older than Baraka, lives in Africa (according to reports), and writes amazingly energetic riff poems with overt social implications. In "Knee Deep," he relishes his black body, imagining that he can plunge tongue and forefinger into any of his orifices and can kiss his armpits and elbow his way "down into my own spread legs":

> I lying naked uncovered with nudity wanting everything I can give myself
> I opening and closing pushing and shoving giving and taking breathing
>   hard and shaking rising upward fast tumbling down so slow
> coming into my one and only self gasping and gasping hanging on banging
>   on until the cool calm
> narcissistic self satisfying ego ridden climax flows gently all over my
>   beautiful body
> and I drown
> in my own
> juices
> of
> joy

In "Zoo You Too!" Third World animals caged in zoos are images of European and American blacks. "To Fez Cobra" is a short poem of threat, in which the revolutionary image of a cobra prepares to sink poisonous fangs "deep into you." Joans's rhythms boogaloo and snap along, as pleasures in themselves:

> After he strikes you'll
> turn blue   what usually
> happens when cobra does his bit
> Usually most people—just shit!

Of the mavericks, Wanda Coleman's work is among the best. Her language has a black flow, her poems a chant quality, as though they should be recited to jazz. Her voice has a sound indigenous to Los Angeles black poets; in fact, her reading style (it has been likened to "gospel incantation") has influenced several other Los Angeles writers. One of the most gifted of these is Kamau Dauod, who orchestrates poems as taped pieces. He belongs to what Coleman calls the "cosmic niggah" style of writing—"as if Zen mated with Soul." He, like Michelle Clinton, derives from Baraka.

In this passage from Coleman's "Eyes Bleed Pictures/Tales of a Black Adventurer," the rich internal rhymes (*3-memory, jazz-caresses, skids-kid, gone-on*) dropped at intervals seem to mark a kind of syncopation:

> jazz notes of 102.3 & billy holiday as he caresses a memory
> how he fucked her once or twice when she was on the skids
> he was almost a kid & she was far too gone
> on heroin for him to use

Coleman's theme is of a black woman who can't resist loving a "black adventurer" who is bad news: she sees him as one of those men "who hate beyond hatred / who think women are to be ground up like mulch / flesh to feed egos." She can't trust him, and knows his kind inside and out:

> i smell cells of folsom on his breath
> bodies of hundreds of men cast in to die
> mindless in their fury
> knowing life outside means everything

He boasts that Billie Holiday gave him public blow jobs, and about how she feared he would cut off her money and hence her supply of heroin. Images of marching legions of black men and women "claiming heritage so long denied" float past.

In the same poem Coleman stands with this lover on a beach where white blond boys surf, near a southern California town, one of the most exclusive and bigoted on the entire coast, and reveals how blacks react to their exclusion from so seemingly ideal a life. The two fantasize that they can live there and "be somebody": "you breathe better here. the air / is pure. we can rent a house off the beach":

> satin slate pelicans perch atop the lamps
> that dot the pier. charcoal and enamel gulls dive
> for fish. small gray-brown pipers scuttle
> back and forth ocean side
> the cream white crests of waves crash
> along the most unspoiled beach i've ever seen . . .

She's just told him that this is "a tougher lily white town" than the one she comes from, "and i don't swim." He sees the point. As the waves roar, she picks "sand stones / to carry home."

In "6 AM & Dicksboro," Coleman provides a glimpse of one world blacks must often endure, a dangerous and rickety old hotel. A black woman (a prostitute?) and her lover need a room; and as she waits in yet another ravaged hotel, she imagines the battered children, rapes, and murders that take place inside. There is a sense, almost naive, that the woman's "love" can right matters. She and her male are "erect wind machines" for clearing the air: "love. any kind of love. but love." Each corner turned in her life, she sees, "leads to / a new soft and fading carpeted heart / a corridor of occupied rooms / accessible by key. . . ."

A vivid poet of a different order than Coleman, tougher in her language and the life she writes of, is Michelle T. Clinton. "Ain Bout Nuthin But Some Toast" celebrates the speaker's love for something as basic in life as toasted bread:

> He (I think) is a real gourmet, and
> when the kitchen all cold & black,
> cat snorin, roommate out chasin pussy somewhere,
> jess gime some Wonder bread, 'n I'll be cool,
> gimme three cigarettes, jet fuel coffee finna perk,
> & steam risin offa my hot buttered toast.

"Star Dust" is spoken by a young woman in a fleabag hotel who, while the other women are selling pussy and giving cuts to pimps, gives it to her "old man," who has no money, "for free." Even in such dire circumstances, there are things to be proud of:

> Though I have been known to fuck more than one man
> at a time, get slapped around, free base,
> & steal shiney things from middle class bathrooms,
> I am a decent woman:
> I don't shoot dope, never had to take a righteous
> ass whippin, & ain't never sold no pussy,
> So I don't have to look at them. I prefer
> to sit behind the haze of limp curtains
> & wonder at the center of the white flowers
> on my broken lamp painted wih red nail polish.

She declares her decency again, as she listens to the whores selling themselves in the rain, and cursing. She hallucinates on "unwound hangers" (for performing abortions?) her

                              man brings me wounds
    wound in a taut penis, the newspaper
    folded & creased, with red circles around
    want ads. We eat chicken McNuggets
    with our fingers, drink Jack Daniels
    from the bottle.

    I am a decent woman: My old man
    never has no money, so I fuck him
    for free.

Jayne Cortez, in *Coagulations: New and Selected Poems,* writes with power and reach. She incorporates very few touches borrowed from mainstream American writing, but when she chooses to do so the result can be vivid and special. As she says below, "i imitate no one." Note the physical, earthy, harsh imagery in "I Am New York City":

    i am new york city of blood
    police and fried pies
    i rub my docks red with grenadine . . .
    this is my grime my thigh of
    steelspoons and toothpicks
        i imitate no one

In "Do You Think" she lashes out at the hostile world of violence and rich exploiters of herself and her people:

    And my chorizo face a holiday for knives
    and my arching lips a savannah for cuchifritos
    and my spit curls a symbol for you
        to overcharge   overbill   oversell me
    these saints   these candles
        these dented cars   loud pipes
    no insurance and no place to park
        because my last name is Cortez

Nathaniel Mackey, in "Ghede Poem," writes brilliantly (and offensively) of love and his own randy, quasi-threatening mystique. At the outset, he warns the conservative reader he is in for an energetic romp. Are his angels hustlers?

        They call me Ghede. The butts
    of "angels" brush my lips.

The soiled asses of "angels"
touch my lips, I
kiss the gap of their having
gone. They call me Ghede, I
sit, my chair tilts, shin across
thigh.

A litany of selves accretes: Ghede-Who-Even-Eats-His-Own-Flesh,
Ghede of the Nasal Voice, Ghede of the Many-Colored Cap, Ghede-Who-
Gets-Under-Your-Skin, Ghede-Who-Beside-The-River-Sits-With-His-
Knees-Pulled-Up-To-His-Chest, etc. His dick is "medicinal" and is

so erect it shines, the slow
cresting of stars astride a bed
of unrest gives my foreskin the
sheen of a raven's wings,
the
untranslatable shouts of a previous church my
school of ointments, my attendants
keep a logbook of signs.

As he sits there, legs drawn up against his chest, someone throws a
"swill" of rum sloshing between his feet, while in his "horse's face whole
boatloads / of assfat explode."
He's something of a kinky-sex dude waiting in the slime showing his
face smeared with angel-ass smell, a funky piano player, and an implicit
threat to white values as well as an image of death:

hands
heavy with mud.
Hands heavy with the mist of your
own belated breath, as you come up
you feel your mouth fill with graveyard
dirt, the skinny fingers of dawn
thump a funky piano, the
tune three parts honky-tonk, two parts church.

Yes, they call me Ghede of the Many-Colored Cap,
the Rising Sun. I make the hanged man
supply his own rope, I gargle rum, the
points of knives grow more and more
sharp underneath your
skin.

Bodily Functions Poems

Antonin Artaud, who smeared the walls of his mental hospital room with *merde* might be seen as the most fecal-obsessed writer of his age, or perhaps of any age—except, perhaps, for Jonathan Swift. Swift wrote an excremental disquisition of an amazing order, so much so, that critics speculate on the nature of Swift's own peculiar morbidities: was he feces obsessed? His Yahoos delighted in discharging excrement on Gulliver's head. Gulliver boasts that he managed to escape pretty well "by sticking close to the stem of the tree"—the filthy creatures are up high among the leaves, although he was "almost stifled with the filth." He endures this ignobility more than once.

In our own day, "feces" (particularly the four-letter synonym) is still used as a badge of rebellion against a smug status quo in the arts. True, some poets parading *the word* sound more like obstreperous children asking that their mouths be washed with soap. Others, though—and Clayton Eshleman is one of them—inspired by Artaud and Jung and Reich, develop a fecal view of life as a way for poets and artists of encompassing hitherto neglected aspects of the psyche of the whole man.

In Eshleman's "Coproatavism" a primal dream occurs in which he (as a child) rises in the night, defecates, and arranges his feces "in pieces" around a "sleeping roommate's head." He performs a primitive ritual dance, chanting that he wants "Jimmy" to die. When Jimmy remains sleeping, Clayton tries again, "like I did when I was a Scout, / hopping about him, going woowoowoowoowoo, / waahwaahwaahwaah." A drastic shift back in time, and the dreamer is a cave man performing a ritual in a cave, making "turds" from "left-over clay" and tossing them at the wall. When Eshleman imagines himself crawling into Lascaux along "an umbilical cord of light," his fingers turn into "little fangs" tearing through an entrance to a chamber where "a fabulous coupling" takes place, which seems fecal and gummy:

> all brown, and runny, with eyes
> gleaming through the powerful brown stream,
> one hairy bearded dragon mounting a beardless one,
> or about to mount, its pink bloody saber
> braced to cleave. . . .

In a companion poem, "Cuitalocoche," excrement seems the earth matter leading us down into our subterranean selves. Such "'sleeping excrement'," Eshleman writes, is "the inversion of ripeness," symbolized in solid form as the fungus on corn. Such excrement lies dormant within the self until age forty-six or so, when it "begins to wake," eventually generating "minute interlocking flames," spinning us, via our perceptions, down to our primal psychical path, where "lion-masked gods / garbed in their own vermillion hair" crouch.

Eshleman's "Seeds of Narrative" whirls with "fecality" as theme and subtheme. Even the soul has its "fecal nature," offering berries to a mystical bird, a bird that picks seeds of life from an assortment of six rhino turds, seen as "semaphoric pairs" drawn on the Lascaux cave wall. These "black manganese turds" have lain there for fifteen centuries, the seeds, or berries, still intact. In order to confront our paleolithic selves, we must, like the ancient bird of narrative, take these turd seeds in our mouth and chew them. Or, like other bird figures on the great cave walls "perish / on a sausage of excrement emerging from a headless / reindeer's anus and kiss, or make love / talk on this tiny writhing hill of our hunger. . . ."

Jack Spicer employs fecality, far more playfully and briefly, as a metaphor for poetry. He declares to a lover that he "would build a whole new universe" around himself, then hastens to assure the lover (who seems to have said "You're shittin' me?") that what he's just declared is poetry, it's not shit. Because, he implies, so much of life is shit, *shit* must enter our poems. To elevate his effort, he introduces the ghosts from the Odyssey who feast on ordure.

Maxine Kumin's "The Excrement Poem" meditates on matters coprophiliac, noisome, animal, and human as she shovels up those "risen brown buns . . . fresh from the horse oven, as it were." As the manure pile grows, sparrows pick grains from it and inky-cap coprinus mushrooms spring up. She thinks

> of what drops from us and must then
> be moved to make way for the next and next.
> However much we stain the world, spatter
>
> it with our leavings, make stenches, defile
> the great formal oceans with what leaks down,
> trundling off today's last barrowful,
> I honor shit for saying: We go on.

Edward Field in *New and Selected Poems,* writes a suite on the joys of defecation. Of all the body's excretions, he hymns, this is "best of all." He loves bathrooms since they are devoted to one's being "blissfully alone / with the elegant movement of our bowels, / with our assholes and our cocks—/ a bathroom door that locks." On the theory that "knowledge" might accrue as the sphincter loosens, he tries learning Japanese, preparing for an oriental vacation. The theory fails: "Not a word sank in with the outward flow— / and I didn't go." A healthy evacuation is a religious experience: "Praise Jesus," an old "colored man" used to exclaim when he was done, commemorating the act—as "religious Jews and rabbis" have always done.

In "The Queen" Field pulls out all the fecal stops, fantasizing on the discipline of, say, Queen Elizabeth II, who must retain "it" during state occasions. "Spincter control" must "guide an empire, after all." Plain to see, Field says, examining Her Majesty's facial expression, she is someone who would enjoy a good crap. When she's lucky, and "gets the chance," a lady-in-waiting stands by waiting for "royal plop and splatt," ready to pull chain and supply "paper roll, swan's neck, terry towels . . . and congratulations." With her example, the entire realm, "surely on awakening moves its bowels / beautifully, in concert, as a nation."

While many poems mention men and beasts urinating, few focus on the act itself. A memorable poem about beasts relieving themselves is Maxine Kumin's "The Grace of Geldings in Ripe Pastures." A clever piece on humans is Sharon Olds's "Five-Year-Old-Boy" from *Satan Says*. Gabriel is a talkative lad with busy hands. He's standing on a porch, peeing into the grass when he's distracted by a bird flying around the house. He mis-shoots, watering the front door. In a reverie, his face glowing with "intelligence," he "twangs his penis." Long after the final drops have landed on the thirsting grasses, he keeps "gently rattling his dick," puckering his "white, curved forehead" (his glans?) in "thought."

Phyllis Koestenbaum relates urinations to a difficult adolescence. The implication is that she doesn't wish to know that her mother is human:

> When the thunder came I swore I would be good.
> When it went, I shuffled into the bathroom
> and peed
> then listened to my mother
> peeing.
> The next day I was bad.
>
> ("Blood Journey,")

Eileen Hennessy, in an untitled poem on the theme (*The New York Quarterly,* Spring 1987), observes that her urine turned the color of water poured over a teabag. Soon the color darkens as if the bag had been "sitting in it." Then

> red things started passing, bits of red peppers fried
> too long till they got dark and shrunk up. Next came shreds
> of stuff like meat all grey and wrinkled from standing in water.
> What my body is doing I think is it's making more body and
> pieces of it are breaking off. And fresh meat bleeds
> when it's cut.

Charles Olson advised that we *micturate* (as boys, not as girls) on a "dirty" world, to purify it and show our love for the moon, which despises such sullyings:

Avert, avert, avoid
pollution, to be clean
in a dirty time

      O Wheel, aid us
      to get the gurry off

You would have a sign. Look:
to fly? a fly can do that;
to try the moon? a moth
as well; to walk on water? a straw
precedes you

      O Wheel! draw
      that truth
      to my house

Like pa does, not like sis,
on all detractors, piss, o advertised earth!
And you, o lady Moon, observe my love,
whence it arose

Whence it arose,
and who it is who sits,
there at the base of the skull, locked
in his throne of bone, that mere pea of bone
where the axes meet, cross-roads of the system
god, converter, discloser, he will answer,
will look out, if you will look, look!

Cancer Poems

Cancer is to our time what consumption (tuberculosis) was to the Victorians. Victorian poems on the latter disease were written by William Ernest Henley who suffered both from tuberculosis and a resultant gangrenous leg. His "In Hospital," in those far less clinical days, was shocking—for he dared to write verses about the surgery which left him crippled though not legless, thanks to the great Dr. Lister's methods of sterilizing operating rooms. To write of such matters was considered offensive. Henley, an early British Whitmanite, found models in the great American poet for expanding English verse.

In our day few taboos exist, although the sanitized poem is still preferred by poetry journals and writing programs. The vast attention paid to poets' relatives dying of cancer suggests that while the messy details of the disease are seldom treated, the theme itself flourishes. Most such poems, like those I call "ego poems," are generally sentimental, self-pitying, and ring with a sameness indigenous to the experience. There seem to be two possibilities: you either muster the courage to face up to the ordeal, or you whine, cringe, and suffer ignobly. Perhaps there should be a moratorium on these poems.

Occasionally good ones appear. In "The Funeral," Norman Dubie, at an aunt's funeral, recollects standing with her naked in a brook one day while minnows nibbled their toes. Now, at her funeral, Dubie hears his Uncle Peter say that "cancer ate her like horse piss eats deep snow." Holly Prado writes of her mother's "suicide of cancer" in "By Seasonal Odor." She deflects her own pain through the image of a brown bear, a childhood toy but also a creature with totemic powers:

> my mother's suicide of cancer
> though she loved gardens loved sweet fruit
> brown bear brown woman honey on the paw
>
> sometimes there is nothing I want but fur
> as a child I'd pray but find myself asleep
> a recurring dream of animals who licked a magic bone
> who never had to cry again
>
> twenty-five years of grief
> midwinter it is time to mate
> today I have a body
> oh bear the larger heart
> bear
> wisest in healing
> will dig herbs will set bones
>
> if I have lost my trust because one woman died
> because I had to be a man too young because I have not made a home
> dark nest bright cave
> then it is time to bring the forest back to life
> if the wound is deep enough it's clean
> I was born in spring an animal
> daughter of mud
>
> the bear stands in its own smell in the smell of its young
> the bear's claw passes its power to the sick
> I crouch I growl low in a dream
> my shadow insists that I'm the sex I've always been
> this shaggy coat gives me my shoulders the tension turns to
> muscle the muscle turns to heat I left myself
>
> ancestors those young girls who dressed to worship artemis as bear
> blood under the pine tree

be innocent begin in mud
I wash vegetables in the sink
such skins I wash this morning
the man I love and winter blankets
he kissed me he licked me awake

cancer means the cells as aberrations
too much eats nothing but itself
what was in my mother's heart
she gave me
fear
what is loved dies
that's what I thought
the man watches me take a bath I know he won't hurt me he likes
to see me warm clean naked
I do not cover myself from him

today I have a body
hot fat yeasty
something close to the one I may grow
if I refuse nothing
the upright stance the growl
the lightning paw that reaches out to stare to understand

brown earth brown fur brown
weeds the memories be
patient
brown
the eyes of the bear look back at me

Canine Poems

One of the truisms of human life is that a boy and his dog are never parted, and that most dogs earn the name "Faithful." No painting better sums this up than an old Victorian genre picture called "On Guard," in which a grieving dog rests with its head on its drowned master's sailor hat. And just as there are well-groomed, pedigreed dogs, so there are well-groomed, pedigreed poems about dogs; and as there are unkempt curs, mutts, and hounds, so there are unkempt, burr-ridden dog poems.

The seventeenth-century poet Robert Herrick's "Upon His Spaniel Tracy" is an example of the former, and owes something to Roman stele poems written to commemorate the recently departed:

Now thou art dead, no eye shall ever see,
For shape and service, spaniel like to thee.
This shall my love do, give thy sad death one
Tear, that deserves of me a million.

Thomas Hardy's satiric "Ah, Are You Digging on My Grave" gives the
lie to the myth of canine devotion. Alternating stanzas are spoken by a
lass lying in her grave and her former pet dog who is busy digging above
her. She thinks it's her loved one, or her "nearest dearest kin," or a former
enemy repenting her hate. When the dog declares himself, hoping that
his "movements" have not "disturbed" her rest, she exults that she knew
that a "dog's fidelity" outruns all human fickleness. With a vast irony, the
dog responds:

"Mistress, I dug upon your grave
    To bury a bone, in case
I should be hungry near this spot
When passing on my daily trot.
I am sorry, but I quite forgot
    It was your resting-place."

Jim Daniels' "Digger Gets a Dog" begins *ab ovo*, so to speak, with the
dog as a permanent addition to a cozy home. Without consulting his
family, Dad decides to bring home a pup. J. D.'s daughters are enthusi-
astic; his son "looks interested"; his wife "makes faces." He sneaks the
dog in while his wife is shopping. The dog pees on the rug. The kids
won't clean it up, and fight. Family solution? Make a chart and tack it to
the fridge. As for naming the dog, J.D. sees that his family prefers "King,"
so he opts for "Clint." It's a matter of who's boss: "Trying to dethrone me?"
thinks pop. He eats his jello, while his stomach churns. The resolution?
After the cheery meal, pop announces that the name will be Clint. The
girls run off crying, slamming doors. The son smirks, and dad gives him
one of those men-against-women closed-fist salutes. The poem ends with
dad holding the dog to his chest, thinking: *At last / we've agreed
on something.*

Paul Mariani's "Lines I Told Myself I Wouldn't Write," reverses
roles—the dog rather than the human is dead, or presumed dead. When
Sparky disappears, Mariani promises himself he won't "get soft over one
fleabag / arthritic half gone in the head." Since it is spring, the family
assumes that Sparky has taken his "prunewrinkled groinbag" out after
females. He doesn't return.

Sparky now inhabits Mariani's dreams, and "battered and nettle-
flecked," plunges in and crosses the river to reach his folks. He springs
forth, his red coat glistening, his tail whacking back and forth:

As in an Aztec
mound painting caught in the flickering gleam
of the torch, the eyes shift, blend into one.
The lips have curled up. The bright eye shines.

William Matthews also commemorates a lost dog. In "Loyal," he recalls the boyhood horror of having his pet put to sleep. Thick with "love" and "longing," he wished for his pet "to live forever," as he "wanted to live forever too." He both craved company and wanted no one. He wished to know exactly "how they trash / a stiff ninety-five-pound dog," yet he paid them not to tell him. He didn't want to weep in baby "gulps and breath-stretching / howls, but steadily, like an adult, / according to the fiction / that there is work to be done, / and almost inconsolably."

Sidney Lea's "Old Dog, New Dog" is detailed, original, and compassionate. The old dog services a young brood bitch, showing her

> the way sex still explodes
> like a double barrel into the blanking winter
> of a life. His ears were blanks, his eyes—
> those snowy bays of cataracts. His nose
> remained, and the gleaming pinkish member.
> They locked, the high-blood nervous white-and-liver
> dame and he. He couldn't hear his howls
> that shook the kennel roof and shocked her
> there beneath him.

He dies. The speaker buries him, with more than a modicum of grief, wincing as the shovel clanks on rock. He does some weeping, but is too macho to admit it, preferring evasion.

Later, one of the old dog's pups takes his place, and seems adept at flushing "hosts of starlings, grackles / from the meadow into hardhack whips and popple." When a grouse chick rises, "bee-like," the pup pursues, stiffening for a moment, as a good bird dog should. When the entire brood erupts, the pup is confused, and when the grouse hen "clatters out" to decoy him in another direction, he follows her. There's hope though—as the cocked ears, erect nose, and wide eyes indicate. The speaker is pleased as he follows the pup downhill, "half blind" with his own laughter.

A most moving canine poem is Anne Sexton's "Your Face On The Dog's Neck." Here Sexton observes a "darling" asleep with his/her face against the fur of an "infectuous" dog. Though Sexton is not clear, the person appears to be a child, probably male, with thin arms. Sexton seems jealous of their intimacy, and speculates on how she will behave once the person awakes and opens his eyes "against the wool stink of her thick hair, / against the faintly sickening neck of that dog." She fears his remoteness, his "dark and leaden" eyes, ones that have "played their own game / somewhere else, somewhere far off." At the merest hint of his interest in her, she will pirouette, or, if the message is not inviting, she will "fall." She seems to lose, averring that she will crouch and place her own cheek next to his, and will accept "this spayed and flatulent bitch you hold, / letting my face rest in an assembled tenderness / on the old dog's neck."

Kate Braverman's "When the Dogs Bark" equates dogs and men, to the advantage of neither:

Men are like dogs.
Pet them.
They will crawl into your lap.
But never let them smell the fear,
hot and intoxicating.
They can snap limbs.
You cannot sing to them.
They will bury your bones in an alley for a rainy day.

Feed them.
They will stay with you.
Bellies bloated, yes red
listless in a thick sleep.
But in their dreams
they are stalking dark streets,
pissing on lampposts
howls ripping their throats. . . .

Case History Poems

Ezra Pound's "Moeurs Contemporaines" sets something of a standard here. The crucial word is "case," for the poet must be fascinated by the inner workings of some eccentric figure, male or female, who may be either larger than life or much smaller, though not caught somewhere in between, in the neutral or the pallid. Furthermore, the poet must provide details from these lives that explain them, and must either implicitly or directly suggest why they behave as they do.

Pound's central figures Mr. Styrax and Clara are of the *haute monde*—rich, cultured, stylish, blue-blooded, and beautifully mannered. Styrax climbed mountains, had huge muscles, remained a virgin until he was twenty-eight, and married, proving so inept a lover that he drove his wife "from one religious excess to another." He was, Pound says, with devastating candor, "lacking in vehemence."

At sixteen, Clara was "a potential celebrity" with "a distaste for caresses." When she left Styrax and joined a cult (she became its "high-priestess"), divorced, remarried, and then found that second marriage impossible (the second husband refused to divorce her), she entered a convent, where, Styrax reports, she writes of an "obscure and troubled" life:

She does not desire her children,
Or any more children.
Her ambition is vague and indefinite
She will neither stay in, nor come out.

And Styrax:

> After years of continence
>   he hurled himself into a sea of six women.
> Now, quenched as the brand of Meleager,
>   he lies by the poluphloisboious sea-coast.

T. S. Eliot, in his earlier years, wrote case history poems, the most famous being, of course, "The Love Song of J. Alfred Prufrock." See also his "Portrait of a Lady," "Aunt Helen," and "Mr. Apollinax." James Merrill's "Lost in Translation" and "The Broken Home" are other examples, as well as Allen Ginsberg's moving death poems on his mother, father, and grandmother; James Wright's "At the Executed Murderer's Grave"; Adrienne Rich's "Paula Becker to Clara Westhoff" (rendered in epistolary form); Michael Harper's elegy for John Berryman, "Tongue-Tied in Black and White," and Kenneth Pitchford's "Aunt Cora."

Madeleine Beckman's "Rosie" is a flamboyant, case history poem. Rosie, a former English literature professor, a specialist in Charles Dickens, throws over her career to become a whore and dresses in Frederick's of Hollywood crotchless panties. Bored, she eventually takes a fresh turn, another life change:

> When she swalled
> the ammonia   it burned
> her insides out   but
> not thoroughly
> she went blind.   Paralyzed
> from the neck down
> and her faithful customers still come.

Thom Gunn's "At An Intersection" presents two cases of lost souls screaming their rage. One is an old witchlike woman in San Francisco. She first rages at a pair of "plump young cops" who drive off laughing in their "upholstered police car." She then seeks out other objects for her rage:

> At the bus stop she came against
> a young bearded face: it
> fixed her with a long pitying look,
> which fed her.
> She discovered an empty pop-bottle,
> she danced in front of the traffic
> stopped at the red light, waving it,
> and smashed it on the asphalt.

(pp. 67–68)

On another occasion, the speaker is in a room with a man who tells him not be be "upset" by what he is about to do. The man then pulls a pillow over his face, roaring "long muffled belches of rage." Such releases are temporary—it seems that we can smother the causes for our anger, but we can't. The cause returns, as does the cry, "out of control."

A variation on the form is provided by poems in which poets present their own case histories. The Asian-American poets Mitsuye Yamada and Nellie Wong have written moving examples (see Asian-American Poems). Yamada's *Camp Notes* details her life with her family and other Japanese-American detainees in camps during World War II. Nellie Wong, in her poem "When I was Growing Up," writes a harrowing and spare account of what growing up Asian in Oakland, California was like:

> . . . I felt ashamed
> of some yellow men, their small bones,
> their frail bodies, their spitting
> on the streets, their coughing,
> their lying in sunless rooms,
> shooting themselves in the arms. . . .
>
> when I was growing up, I felt
> dirty. I thought that god
> made white people clean
> and now matter how much I bathed,
> I could not change, I could not shed
> my skin in the gray water. . . .

Catalogue Poems

I limit this category to actual poems made up of named objects, rather than of simple lists of words as they would appear in what I call "concrete" poetry.

Walt Whitman, the father of the American catalogue poem, scattered catalogues throughout *Leaves of Grass*. The fifteenth poem of "Song of Myself" contains one of Whitman's longest and best. These figures appear, each with an appositive or some indigenous function, creating a sense of the teeming wealth of American life: A contralto, carpenter, pilot, mate, duck-shooter, deacon, spinning-girl, farmer, lunatic, jour-printer, surgeon, quadroon girl, drunkard, machinist, policeman, gate-keeper, young express-wagon driver, half-breed, marksman, immigrant, "wooly-pate" hoeing in the garden, dancer, squaw, connoisseur, deck-hand, "one-year wife," Yankee girl factory worker, paving-man, reporter, sign-painter, canal boy, book-keeper, shoemaker, conductor, performer, religious convert, drover, peddler, bride, opium-eater, prostitute, President, cabinet Secretary, fisherman, Missourian, fare-collector on a train, floor-man laying a floor, mason, tinner, ploughman, mower, pike-fisher, squatter, floatboatman, coon-seeker, and patriarch.

Allen Ginsberg has made the catalogue a trademark of his poetry,

particularly in *Howl* and *Kaddish*. Both are assemblages of named ob-
jects, persons and things. A trip across America in a VW bus becomes an
elaborate conglomeration of details of place and event. At its best, as in
"Sunflower Sutra," Ginsberg's cataloguing has the force of a chant
or mantra.

Gary Snyder's "Hunting: 13," from his *Myths and Texts,* is a poem
made entirely of names of foods, a veritable list of survival foods growing
on Western mountain lands. When this catalogue is read aloud, subtle
interplays of sound and syllable occur. Like Whitman intent on display-
ing and celebrating a variegated American life, Snyder too celebrates,
almost as though he were composing a hymn to the fertile Western
landscape. Implicit also is the sense that to name an object is to receive a
talismanic power from that object, while at the same time returning
power to it. The gesture is somehow primitive, a connection with aborig-
inal man and the landscape Snyder extols. One can easily imagine
Snyder on his haunches near a manzanita bush in the northern Califor-
nia mountains, reciting his catalogue as a prayer. Here is the list:

> Mescal, yucca fruit, pinyon, acorns,
> prickly pear, sumac berry, cactus,
> spurge, dropseed, lip fern, corn,
> mountain plants, wild potatoes, mesquite,
> stems of yucca, tree-yucca flowers, chokecherries,
> pitahaya cactus, honey of the ground-bee,
> honey, honey of the bumblebee,
> mulberries, angle-pod, salt, berries,
> berries of the one-seeded juniper,
> berries of the alligator-bark juniper,
> wild cattle, mule deer, antelopes,
> white-tailed deer, wild turkeys, doves, quail,
> squirrels, robins, slate-colored juncoes,
> song sparrow, wood rats, prairie dogs,
> rabbits, peccaries, burros, mules, horses,
> buffaloes, mountain sheep, and turtles.

(p. 31)

In Antler's "Factory," catalogues of objects produced by a factory
underscore the dehumanization of workers. This passage forms a ram-
pant ABC poem, a catalogue with powerful overtones. Like Snyder,
Antler arranges the words carefully:

> O awls, axes, adzes, augers,
> Barrels, bearings, bellows, brads,
> Crowbars, corkscrews, crucibles, calipers,
> Dumbbells, dollies, dibbles, drills,
> Exhausts, excelsior, forceps, faucets,
> Gauges, gouges, gaskets, goggles,
> Hammers, hammocks, hangers, hoists,
> Irons, icepicks, jewels, jacks,
> Keels, kilns, levels, ladles, lathes,

Mops, muzzles, mattresses, microphones,
Nails, neon, napalm, ouija boards,
Pistons, pitchforks, pliers, puncheons,
Quivers, quoits, ratchets, rounces,
Radar, roachclips, scales, scalpels,
Snorkels, stencils, shovels, shoetrees,
Squeegees, tweezers, trophies, trocars,
Tampons, trampolines, uniforms, umbrellas,
Vises, valves, wormgears, wrenches,
Wigs, wire, yardsticks, zippers—

I know where you come from!

(pp. 43–44)

Another poet who is fond of catalogues is Carolyn Stoloff. Her painter's eye values detail more than an ordinary poet's might. She seldom allows an assemblage of names to stand entirely alone—she reshapes them and inserts brief spots of commentary. In "Leaning," she employs a serial technique, using repeated words or phrases to provide a symmetrical visual order. She appears to be in a plane, banking before it takes off in its direct flight path:

Leaning against wooden bins
        against dresses swinging from rods above them
        leaning against empty dresses
Leaning against headless horses beside smoking holes
        horses that get you no place
        leaning against stiff horses that give
        like righteousness   not toppled but shifted
Leaning against the sound wall
        growling jets
        steady drops large as onions
        emptiness hammered in
        anguished farting and groaning
        as the crammed beast rises
Leaning against the hard hollow growth
        spreading on earth's skin
Leaning against this factory
        its crucial bird heart
        its electric lace
        its frantic metabolic hunger
I look to land that recedes like an ocean
        I look toward land

My catalogue poem, "Christmas Poem 1966: Lines on an English Butcher-Shop Window" (*The Sow's Head And Other Poems,* 1968), was written during a visit to Cambridge, England. In the streets one afternoon, I happened to find myself standing behind an open butcher's truck in which all manner of freshly killed animals were hanging—hare, sheep, beef, pheasants, ducks, etc. Directly opposite was the shop into which the driver was carrying all the carnage. The shop window was crammed with animals and fowl, rabbits and chickens and geese, all with their heads, fur, and feathers intact. On trays were elaborate patés fashioned in oblongs with the glazed heads and feet of the birds stuck in at either end. The window seemed to scream "death." I realized how different England (and the Continent) is from America—our supermarkets have neatly wrapped and sanitized our meats so that we are removed from death. In England, to walk into this shop and buy a hare was to buy a creature that was recently alive and that still bore the trappings and outward manifestations of life. I felt that I would be buying death. Various nebulous Christmas thoughts rushed in, as I recall, and once back at my rented house I set to work writing the poem that follows, wanting the catalogue to be something of a good-spirited litany. I loved the creatures named. Also, I chose the antiquated manner of the interjection so favored by the Romantic poets:

> O beautiful severed head of hog
> O skewered lamb-throat, marble eye of
>   duck, O meadow-freshened hare
>   suspended
> O lovely unplucked pheasant
>   ripening in the gloom
> O gracious suckling pig upended
> O twisted tail erect
>   and pinkish gouged-out hole
> O graceful nub of sow tit, merry xylophone
>   of fractured ribs
> O rib ends smarting where the saw
>   has severed you
> O pleasant rind of fat and rosy spume
>   along the incision sliced
>   from genitals to snout
> O livers tumbling, O clattering
>   jewel of pancreas and
>   ligaments of stomach wall
> O golden brains emplattered
> O calf-goin hacked in two
> O carcass spiked, with legs
>   encased and tied about
>   with paper, hanging on the wall
> O sheep form, severed shoulders,
>
> O ham string of ox, O whitening lyre,
> O steer loin pierced, O haunch,
> O ribcage disembowelled
> O glorious trays and juices, heaps of
>   lambhearts, chicken livers,
>   gizzards, claws
> I see you all!

Catatonic Surrealist Poems

Catalepsy, says the dictionary, is "a condition of suspended animation and loss of voluntary motion in which the limbs remain in whatever position they are placed." If we substitute "brain" for "mind" for "limbs," this definition is useful in describing a kind of poetry much written these days. Among its practitioners are Victor Contoski, James Tate, Bill Knott (as Saint Geraud), Andrei Codrescu, and Paul Trachtenberg.

Writing "catatonic poems" goes something like this: dissociate your head from the rest of your body; imagine that you are utterly suspended, almost as if in a blissful out-of-body experience. Now, remove as much furniture from your mind as you can; in other words, remove the tables, chairs, potted plants, and chrome ashtrays from the ballroom. In this pristine space, let figures, images, and symbols freely appear. Eventually, invent a narrative, no matter how slender, to accompany the surrealist scenes playing themselves out against the scrim in your mind. And the scrim is important, for it is here that the irrational and the bizarre materialize, almost without your willing them into life. All the while, you remain vaguely stunned, deprived of a general sense of your body's physical being—the ingrown fingernail stops smarting, the sinus ache behind your right eye disappears, the underwear stops chafing. Oh, glorious *tabla rasa* of the imagination! A cataleptic creative state originates your poem, which you now twist and anneal for optimum effect.

In "Salt," Contoski combines a cataleptic dream-vision with a fairy tale. Salt spilled on a wooden table enters the grains of the wood and "will never bloom again." A butcher dries his bloody clothes in the sun: "Salt turns them white." People in a park are "honoring salt." A princess works for a witch and makes "salt with her tears." Each day she fills a pail. Salt, lying deep underground, is excavated by "dirty men" who "stand amazed by its beauty." Religious statues are carved from salt and left for centuries. Finally, the poem comes round to the personal event: Contoski recalls his first communion, when "far down under the earth / someone placed on my tongue / a pinch of salt."

Paul Trachtenberg's book, *Short Changes for Loretta*, a fantasy-romp, combines rich surrealism of a catatonic kind with images recurring from old cartoons he loved as a child. The poet invites reruns of old shows to play on the split screen of his mind. A word about Loretta: she tries hard to be a saint in three acts, and when that fails, does estimable credit to Gertrude Stein's Ida in her quest for all manner of lovers, animal, vegetable, and mineral. She also has some of the class of her namesake Loretta Young, and borrows an occasional gesture from Mae West resplendent on her velvet couch. Her dash through life is incredible. In "Loretta Drives the Elves Crazy," as Loretta makes love in front of the picture window downstairs, elves and other fairy tale creatures are turned on. Even old Grandma, once she's burned a few elf throats with her hot brew, decides to join the sexual dance, and glues on her wooden shoes. Loretta's lover comes down from the roof and makes love to Loretta. Here is the poem:

Romancing near the window panes
And on the roof attracts the elves.
They're jigging and bringing goods
down the chimney into the old farm-kitchen.
Grandmother's brewing. They get throat-blisters.
The elves who follow after know better.
Festivity comes.
The cat and the mouse dance, so do many
forks and spoons. Grandmother glues on
her wooden shoes. My loved one's on the roof
with the birds, lilies, frogs and rocks
of romance. He comes down.
We make love in front of the downstairs
picture window.

Traditional surrealist poetry is far more cerebral and designed; the poet's psyche seems too alert to allow its being inscribed upon or covered by shadow images.

A recent poem by Bill Knott, "Childhood: The Offense of History," while it seems surreal, reads like a set of doodlings, and is an instance of catatonic surrealism gone flaccid. Here is the first stanza:

Scraping a poised enough patina of voyeur
From your eye I spread peanut butter on my
Groin and let the ocean waves wash it off—
Hey, nice cosmic microdots. . . .

I guess he doesn't like being stared at, so once he scrapes off "the patina of voyeur," he proceeds to smear his groin with peanut butter (with the same knife he scraped off the patina?). Once this excitement concludes, Knott proposes that they memorize all the Smiths in the phone book, and then "try to hump Empty Dumty [sic]."

Ivan Arguelles writes in a traditional mode. Here is how "Shafts of Agony" begins:

to escape cerebral comprehension of the collapse of the world
a nightmare with luminescent colors descriptive of the gods
twilight orders of submerged aviaries distance of colons junk sperm
where will the rivers four hundred of them nameless flow?

Yes, there is automatic writing here, but the general drift focuses on one issue: "the collapse of the world." Escape into verbal play may be an antidote. As the poem meanders, and certain key notes of sorrow, heart-break, freezing, threat, and disease prevail, Arguelles never once submits to any received matter from outside his own brain. He remains firmly in control. His reason orchestrates his imagery.

Arguelles's "Nikki I Am Still Talking to You" is a passionate elegy. In fact, several poems in *bone-text* are built out of what Arguelles calls (in "Teenangel can you hear me") an "obsession" with drugs, disease, love, and death: "I am obsessed with the venereal shape of the great deaths / with the corruption of abject love in the sands of the old testament." The lengthy poem to the dead Nikki reads as an enormous rush of grief: "Consonants bilabial conjunctions a spoonful of sugar to dose the fucking pain / how can the discrete sentences of the perfect paragraph isolate you so?" he exclaims to the lost girl. Left without a succoring ideology, he fails to believe, as the faceless street-man does, that after death our "last thought" will continue on "into some eerie universe without vowels." He's exhausted and forgets her room number in heaven:

> it must be a motel somewhere in the paradise we never invented where gazelles
> run amok looking for the absolute verb of water I don't know I collapse on this THING
> they say it is an enigma it should never mean anything music is everywhere
> how did Love enter that fine mass of nerves? why did plato seek dionysius?

Celebrity Poems: Film Stars

"Celebrity poems" are numerous. Political figures inspire them— a book of poems about the assassination of President John Kennedy appeared; the poems written about Che Guevara and the current mess in Latin America would fill volumes; satirical poems on Nixon and Reagan are staples; and memorials to dead poets abound, primarily to suicides (Plath and Sexton top the list), martyrs (Akmahtova, Lorca, Neruda), and father figures (Whitman, Pound, Williams, Olson).

The celebrity poems I shall consider are of two kinds: those inspired by film and television stars, and those having to do with jazz, rock, and pop stars. I shall select and comment on a few examples in each category—and they are legion. Poems to Marilyn Monroe run to dozens.

What is fascinating is that such celebrities should dominate our imaginations, as well as our hair-styles, mannerisms, and dress. Some of these celebrities are poets: Patti Smith, Joni Mitchell, Bob Dylan, John Lennon, Exene Cervenka, and Paul Simon. Others, like Leonard Nimoy, Richard Thomas, and Susanne Shutz, pass off wretched versifying as poetry. The trade publishers chew up millions of trees for these dismal books, depriving deserving poets of publishers.

Poets seem to find in celebrities certain aspects of our culture visible nowhere else on so grand a scale. Rock stars condition all areas of our lives—we make love to vivid rock numbers; we drive our zippy cars faster if the stereo blasts sounds that stimulate adrenalin and incite strong antisocial feelings; yuppies take values from John Denver and Barbra Streisand; rebels foment rebelliousness by worshipping raunchy punk groups. As Andy Warhol knew, the faces of celebrities are as omnipresent as Brillo pads or Campbell soup cans. In Warhol's serial paintings of Marilyn Monroe her face is almost as common as Washington's is on dollar bills.

Edward Field's *Variety Photo Plays* was a pioneering volume of Hollywood poems, first published by Grove Press in 1967. Field's "portraits" of Joan Crawford and her "scumbag" life, the Cat Woman, She, and Frankenstein and his Bride are both affectionate and satiric in their exposure of our foibles as magnified in these stars. Frank O'Hara is another significant poet who has published considerable work in this vein, dedicating poems to James Dean, Billie Holiday, and the "Film Industry in Crisis."

John Wieners includes poems on film personalities in *Behind the State Capitol: Or Cincinnati Pike*. He adores Alida Valli, best remembered for "The Third Man"; as well as Barbara Stanwyck, Greta Garbo, Jean Harlow, Marlene Dietrich, Linda Darnell, and Marilyn Monroe—the last three are figures he says he'd like to imitate in drag.

"While Miss Marlene Dietrich Was Singing" blends Wieners' sense of the actress's desperation with his own. He detects "seven oceans of sorrow" in her voice as he has her appear in guises suggested by her films: she's a girl covered with sequins and men's hands; she walks a bridge and observes how the moon glitters like "sunken diamonds"; she's a party girl sitting on the floor under a lantern, singing farewell to a lover.

In *Celebrities: In Memory of Margaret Dumont, Dowager of the Marx Brothers Movies*, I've written poems to Robert Mitchum, Gertrude Stein, and Marlene Dietrich. The Dietrich poem is a bitter take on the impossible demands we make of our celebrities. An aged Dietrich, continues to perform to maintain the myth of the throaty-voiced sex goddess. A problem: the arthritis in those magnificent legs is so severe she has had them amputated, and before she goes on stage, a male attendant straps on plastic legs that shake like human flesh. Her attendant is upset when she confuses him with Eric von Stroheim, etc, etc. "Porgy-platform" refers to the board on wheels Porgy used for spinning along Catfish Row:

Marlene Dietrich

He helped Marlene
snap her beautiful legs in place,
into the greased aluminum sockets.

She pressed a button
which caused her legs to glow
from the inside—hairless,
pink plastic.

"They're warm now," she said,
seated, extending the legs
from her black mannish shorts.

"I'm ready to go on stage."
The plastic muscles
bunched and shook, as sexual
as when she was thirty.

She tapped her black cane
on the floor. She had closed
her maquillaged eyes.
He was rubbing off against her.
"Eric von Stroheim," she purred.
"Oh, Eric, Eric."

Offended he rammed her porgy-platform
through the window so that
it fell thirteen stories, losing
all its fluff, paint, and ormolu
in a crush of souvenir hunters.

"I'm 85," she cried, "and dying,
and you leave me disastrously,
without wheels."

He threw her legs through
the window too, leaving her in a heap,
still wearing the top-hat as a memory.

Michael McClure's "The Sermons of Jean Harlow & The Curses of Billy the Kid" provided the text for his controversial play "The Beard." McClure's Billy is the American frontier man, youthful, paranoid, sexual, condemnatory of all he detests. He stomps on children. "GOD DAMN THESE FUCKING BASTARDS / WHO KILL!!" he exclaims, apparently blind to the violence in his own person. Harlow chants a masturbatory prayer: God is her lover, and she loves Him "WITH OR WITHOUT THE PAINT" on her lips. Her "reality" turns on ankles clothed in blue or cream. As she "gives" herself to God, she boasts that not even a strap of her slip is broken—she has been squirming on the hallway floor.

The Kid rants on: dark brown and black are his colors. He loathes blue, and all figures of the imagination—elves and fairies. He exclaims that although he's torn the wings off his skull, he'll raise himself "in the blaze" of his eyeballs. He sees his defiantly volcanic self overwhelming and dominating, with his face "A YELLOW MASK OF FURY!!!!"

The pair meet, grind, shout sexual ecstasies: "OH, / AHHH / OOOOOOOOOOH, / a rhinestone kiss for you . . . / A beaded bag . . . /A satin slipper. . . ." The Kid will reform, cooling his shotgun "with a slice / of sheriff's life! HO HUMMM!" So "the Love Lion and the Lioness live! Let's rejoice over "Platinum fur and brass revolver! . . . . sweet dust of gun and white neck."

Paul Trachtenberg's Mae West is the haloed image of a sex-Christmas tree, heralding an "eternal holiday":

Mae West

A glitter snow-night
a tree strung with diamond bells.
The carolers at their best
adore her with noels
lay tinsel at her feet.
Caviar and nog enhance the fete
along with frills and sunset hills.
Not a creature is stirring
when her majesty mellows
her snowflake solo.
There is a halo—
an eternal holiday.

Laurel Speer's "A Movie Script of Paradise Lost" is a sardonic look at Hollywood entrepreneurs. She assumes the voice of a tacky producer delineating the pitch and casting for a popular version of *Paradise Lost,* "something the public can relate to like / Spartacus; nothing too high tone. People / have to sit and eat popcorn, drink cokes / and suck milk duds through this. We want / them uplifted, not overawed."

Casting? For God, an overvoice. Charlton Heston is Adam—"full body makup" can cover his aging sags. Faye Dunaway is Eve. Eve can't be "too innocent. / None of this Primavera wonder teen first time / out of the shell shot." She's to look somewhat "ravaged and corrupt / before the snake goes for her." Joan Crawford as the snake: "I know she's dead, but we / can dub old clips." We'll cover Satan's fall with music. Satan is a "Peter Lorre type transformed into Mommie Dearest." Modernize the garden of Eden: A lush overgrowth / with mists like Lost Horizon." The climax? The expulsion, of course:

Jump to the worst slum in Detroit;
kids in torn t-shirts with switchblades and dope;
drunks in doorways; graffiti, race riots, bombs;
maybe throw in a clip of Buchenwald. Hold
language to a minimum, so we don't diminish
the visuals. No lecturing or debates.

Alex Gildzen, poet, archivist, and a thoroughgoing aficionado of old films, is inspired to set his own "old Hollywood fixative." He's perusing a book called *A Pictorial History of the Talkies:*

above Groucho's leer
                    Lois Wilson leans
                                     over her autograph
her eyes frozen daiquiris
                         in the scandalous Hollywood sun
it's 1931
         & she shares the top of the page
         with Sylvia Sidney & Lila Lee

under the brothers
                   in their kippered herring barrels
a quartet of "Promising Personalities"
the smiling blonde at the end
                              Bette Davis
(this is the year she plays Lois' daughter in "Seed")

at the bottom of the page
                         a pair of Lois' pals
     Gloria Swanson
                    gives Melvyn Douglas the eye in "Tonight or Never"
     Ruth Chatterton
                     looks icy under her lacy hat in "Once a Lady"

the ladies of 45
                 radiant in their agelessness
help us remember hours in the dark
                                   learning the new mythology

               Lila was our Leda
               Lois our Hera
we swooned when they came down from Beverly Hills
to match the gambol of Charlie's Pan
or watch the revels of W. C.'s Silenus

               & like the ancient deities
               who will die only when poetry does
               the ladies of page 45
               will live as long as light

Charles Bukowski, in a brief elegy entitled "for marilyn m.," compre-
hends the ephemerality of celebrities—though their memory lingers,
they are eventually forgotten, and the incredible renown they had while
alive is really only momentary. That he reduces Marilyn's name to lower-
case letters is of course significant.

Bukowski's tone is affectionate, as it is in most poems he writes for
and about women. Even those who do him dirt have his respect. His
Marilyn has slipped off into "bright" funerary ashes. Once the "target of
vanilla tears," her "sure body . . . lit candles for men / on dark nights."
Now, her night is darker than any candle's reach. We shall forget you,

Bukowski tells her, and though this is "not kind," we'll turn to "real bodies." Then he turns to us. We should love this "flower," he says, for she "brought us something, / some type of small victory." "Child, child, child," he says, and raises his drink in toast.

In Suzanne Lummis' "Death Rings Marilyn Monroe," the "heavy breather" is Death, dialing his obscene call. When the call ends and Monroe finds that all the figures on her dial are zeroes, taking pills seems the way out:

DEATH RINGS MARILYN MONROE

He was like all the others,
a heavy breather,
but when he called nothing rang.
The phone glowed like precious metal
a blacksmith had pulled from a flame.
She touched the receiver to her ear
and heard something
like "hold me," or
"let go." She imagined phones
at the bedsides of many women.
After the last bar has closed
and the sober are unable to sleep,
and the drunks sleep in their only shoes,
old men thumb through the phone books
in third class motels. They search
for the perfect initial.
She imagined the telephone lines
crossing the city to the thin
back streets, where the windows
are opaque as blackboards
and there's no sound except
for the drifting litter scraping
the pavement, or one pair
of footsteps closing in on another.
Then she noticed her own phone,
how it had changed.
On the dial, each of the ten figures
read zero. With a phone like this
one could call heaven,
if there were a heaven.
The receiver burned for an answer.
Baring a satin sheet, she lay down.

Celebrity Poems: Musicians

Here, too, there are categories. For decades poets have celebrated jazz musicians. In the forties, Kenneth Rexroth read his poems to jazz accompaniments in San Francisco. Lawrence Ferlinghetti and Kenneth Patchen also contributed to the link between jazz and poetry, especially in the course of the Beat Movement. Jazz performers were seen as outsiders, flowerings of an elite underground culture, rife with dope, short on cash and middle-class amenities. Until the advent of Bob Dylan, Joan Baez, the Beatles, and the major rock groups, jazz was the music of social angst and protest—an influence largely lost once rock music flourished, generating songs for flower children and Vietnam protesters.

Michael S. Harper's well-known "Dear John, Dear Coltrane" segues along in verse rhythms suggestive of Coltrane's music. Harper reviews the circumstances of Coltrane's childhood and youth, his departure from the South, when lynchings ("genitals gone or going") were commonplace. Coltrane's theme was always *a love supreme, a love supreme.* In the "electric city" (New York) he riffs "the thick sin 'tween / impotence and death." The tenor sax, the horn, the instruments of "heart, genitals and sweat" cleansed him. The gist of his miraculous playing: I'm black "cause I am"; I'm funky "cause I am"; I'm sweet "cause I am"; I'm *a love supreme, a love supreme.* His death from a "diseased liver" left his followers aching for the song he'd "concealed" with his own blood—a final song, pure, pumped by his "inflated heart . . . the tenor kiss, / tenor love: *a love supreme, a love supreme— / a love supreme, a love supreme—.*

Yusef Komunyakaa in *Copacetic* dedicates poems to jazz greats Thelonious Monk and Charles Mingus, and reflects scat rhymes, short-line riffs, and a language characteristic of black jazz. In "Copacetic Mingus," Mingus' playing bleeds together life and art. Thumping the "wood heavy with tenderness," Mingus dogs "the raw strings / unwaxed with rosin. / Hyperbolic bass line. Oh no! / Hard love, it's hard love."

Billie Holiday haunts John Wieners. In "Gardenias"—the flower was, of course, Holiday's trademark—Wieners sees the ravished singer's life in terms of his own. She is a "poetess," Wieners's female self. He too has lived years "of drunken futility" blended with much "fealty to beauty." What produces the loneliness rife in her songs, and in Wieners' life?

> is it jazz, or late-night musing by the harbor,
> unemployment with an empty head in the library
> merely only poverty, or could it be inability
>
> to hold a man, or woman as my own property?
> . . . . it's a womanish heart
> growing old alone above the city, parallel horizontal
> to the snow
> wrapping herself up in the dreams of other men. . . .

One of Frank O'Hara's best-known poems is "The Day Lady Died." He underplays his grief by recounting the humdrum events of that day— he gets a shoeshine, thinks of a dinner party he's to attend with people he doesn't know, swelters in the muggy New York City weather, eats a malt and a hamburger, and buys an "ugly" *New World Writing* "to see what the poets / in Ghana are doing these days." He goes to the bank, buys a Verlaine illustrated by Bonnard, recalls Richard Lattimore's translation of the Hesiod and Brendan Behan's new play, thinks of Genet's *Les Négres*, buys a bottle of Strega, and sees Holiday singing in the "5 Spot," whispering a song to Mal Waldron "and everyone and I stopped breathing."

Jessica Hagedorn writes, performs, and has a band, The Gangster Choir. Though her origins are Tagalog and Spanish, she too has absorbed something of Billie Holiday's subtleties, Jimmie Hendrix's power, and Bob Marley's reggae sounds. In "I Went All the Way Out Here Looking for You, Bob Marley," she recounts her dismay on reaching Jamaica one Christmas to find Marley gone.

Clifton Snider is inspired by the Beatles, and in "George Practices the Sitar," focuses on Harrison's mysticism and his lingering over his music until the cacophony becomes harmony, wafting him away from the heat and grime of India. Another poem, "John Lennon's Erotic Lithographs," is critical of Lennon's and Ono's public self-displays.

Michael Lally's "Lost Angels" reads in part like the personal history of a youth steeped in rock music who comes from the East to Los Angeles / Lost Angels to launch a career in acting. Like hosts of others he is one of a new Lost Generation, "angels" who feel they have nothing new to do or say. As Billy Idol sings, they push on, trying to be honest about the feelings of others while suppressing their own. Idol's expression "thrillsville" sets the tone—sex with a teenage "woman."

"Rocknroll" music connects these angels, perhaps spoiling them "for joy & / hope & honest bullshit." Their desire to be movie stars "forever" remains; and they see that music, dope, and their beat attitudes prevent them from finessing the "classic heroism" required, a classic heroism possessed by "idols of the / silver screen we injected / directly into the limelight / of our brains and hearts." Though rebellious, they wish to be free of "assholes," of all establishment authority figures.

Chant Poems

"Chant poetry" overlaps another category, "mantric poetry." Among memorable chant poems are Allen Ginsberg's *Howl*, *Kaddish*, and "Witchita Vortex Sutra." In this last poem Ginsberg, riding on a bus through Kansas, feels a Whitmanesque energy: "I am the Universe tonite," he chants, "riding in all my Power riding / chauffeured thru my self by a long haired saint with eyeglasses." Memories of both personal and universal significance whirl through his brain: visions of flat Kansas itself, recollections of the towns and cities he has visited, flaming factories, Apaches, bombing ranges, Salinas High School, Vietnam, youths anxious to meet and sleep with him, the force of language delivered with gusto and chanted, himself as the universe in all its power; along with the stupidities of President Johnson and all political and military leaders, the deaths of Marines, media hype, Asian flesh "soft as a Kansas girl's . . . ripped open by metal explosion," and the fear everywhere over the coming nuclear holocaust, and his own role as restorer of something like a faith in peace:

> I lift my voice aloud,
>> make Mantra of American language now,
>>> pronounce the words beginning my own millennium,
>>>> I here declare the end of the War!

Gary Snyder's frequent shaman songs are efforts to arouse American and world opinion against the despoiling of the natural universe. Jerome Rothenberg has made a career of writing about primitive cultures. In the pages of *Sulfur* (no. 10) he continues his labors, alerting us through a "Blood River Shaman Chant" to Finno-Ugric tundra folk. This chant, Rothenberg says, was performed by a shaman who worked himself into a trance while slashing his body. Maurice Kenny, who is part Mohawk, writes chants steeped in the lore of his ancestors. Anne Waldman's *Fast Speaking Woman* is an extended chant on lay-themes made famous through Waldman's slinky, funky performances.

Childhood Poems

Ever since Wordsworth declared the child the father of the man, Walter Pater wrote his mandarin *The Child in the House*, and Whitman celebrated his own youth romping barefooted on Paumonok Beach tuning himself to the stars, the ocean, and a sorrowing brown bird, American poets have written reams of childhood poems. These fall neatly into two categories: poems of a wretched childhood, and poems of a benign childhood.

Three writers who belong to the first category are David Ray, Diane Wakoski, and "La Loca." Ray was orphaned early, and Wakoski's father was almost continually absent. Ray's pain is evoked in "Orphans." In another poem, "Vincent," Gaugin's abandonment of Van Gogh symbolizes Ray's father's abandonment of his son. Here are the concluding lines:

> And he left
> for me as if he were
> my father
> (and my father had

left me something)
one blossoming
twisted tree
I found
in Manchester
when I went in
from rain when
they had no use
for me and it
was there, a gift
from Vincent,
in brotherhood.

A brief "Note" from Ray's "Gathering Firewood" reads like a footnote to
the poems above. The son as a grown man asserts he has resolved his
father-pain:

Dad,
have no feeling for you anymore
can lay your snapshot on the table
and not be moved to tears
your ancient mustache
and the plaid of your sport-coat collar
your slick tie with the wings of herons
I am unmoved

Brian Swann's *The Middle of the Journey* contains several poems on
childhood. The best is "Home Movies." In this excerpt he recalls his
grandparents:

& refusing to use
school toilets & arriving
every other day at
the backdoor
pants full
crying
& my grandmother hosing
me down on the scullery floor
& on hot days
when the scent of hawthorn
made me think I had
lived somewhere else many times
she'd hold my wrists
under the ice-cold faucet & still
today I can see everything
in the house where I was born
as if I had never left it

Diane Wakoski frequently writes of an unfulfilled childhood. See
particularly the *George Washington Poems* and *Greed*, Part V, "The

Shark—Parents and Children," an expansive concerto on motifs of parental failures and her own experience of putting a child up for adoption:

> Forget all this. The bad bad parents.
> Are there any good ones?
> My grief is old and ugly.
> The wounds on my belly
> > —like them
> > ugly wrinkled old lines

Unable to forget, she frames this sinister conclusion:

> We are all sharks.
> The only question will be
> > whose flesh
> will we strip
> bloody and raw
> from the bones?
> will it be our children's
> or our own
> or some poor stranger who comes by
> when we are hungry
> and it is time
> for another cold meal?

"La Loca" (Pamala Karol) recalls a childhood spent watching TV while her sexually frustrated mother prepares herself to receive a "grisly simian" washing machine repair man grasping his "tool." The mix of childhood fears, cartoon figures, and a mother's lust is unforgettable. While the girl can always turn off the TV creatures if they turn ominous and violent, she can't control the mother's visitor. Here is the entire poem, which will appear in a book of La Loca's poems to be published by City Lights:

KIDDIE SHOWS I USED TO WATCH

> My mother lashed me to the
> screen
> where everything was Black&White
> and she turned it on.
> Captain Kangaroo had a lap
> like a department store Santa.
> I was left alone on the couch with
> Mighty Mouse and Crusader Rabbit.
> Roadrunner, Daffy, Felix, Bullwinkle, Bugs & Rags
> leaped into the living
> room with soft paws and falsettos while their
> villains, forever penned, leered through the incandescent

cage, gnashed their teeth and growled.
I could black it out with a button.
Meanwhile
my mother bellied by
in spike mules and a
snippy bikini
to answer the
door
for some grisly simian
who came to fix her washing machine.
He looked like that scary caricature of a
"stranger" thumb-tacked on the
wall of my kindergarten.
They open their car
door
and offer you pomegranate suckers but you
mustn't get in with them.
Through the carefully left
open
crack
in the kitchen
door
I could see my mother posing on a
step-ladder and chirping and pointing
the painted toenails of one foot
at her busted wringer;
her spring-o-later dangling mid-air by a strap,
her instep bobbing it
articulately.
I could also see a three-fingered hand
with enormous knuckles,
covered with hair like rusty nails,
grasping a tool.
Porky and Goofy,
beardless and puffy,
stood at the loosed
gate
of our harem,
with red lollipops in their mouths.

Several poems in Nancy Shiffrin's recent collection *What she could not name* mix the motifs of the benign and the wretched childhood. One recollection is of a harsh grandmother who berates a grandchild for wasting paints to create a picture she thought the woman would enjoy ("Rosa Monstrosa"). In "Rapunzel" the witch is a mother. During a hot love session (she's busily nibbling nipples and lapping up sperm), the poet flashes back to the ugly child she was:

streaming hair, black hat, veil,
eyes hollow, cavernous, stomps,
whirls, a schoolbus arrives, she
climbs in, bumpy ride.

Her large breasts frighten and perplex Shiffren ("Shopping for Bras")
when at age thirteen, before a mirror, she shivers as she tightly cups
those "alien protrusions." In "Cousin Murray's Bris" she reports her
childhood mix of envy and relief that she can't be circumcised as cousin
Murray is about to be:

I have seen a penis. They are small and rosy. They flop.
Because they have penises, boys can pee outside.
Because I don't have one, I always have to wait.
Sometimes I wet a little.

What I have there is dark and soft.
Once I put my finger deep inside. My mother caught me—just as I
was pulling the blankets up. "It's normal," she said. A book she is
reading says all children touch themselves there and shouldn't be
frightened or told they'll get pimples or go crazy. That's what
Howard's mother tells him. He's my other cousin.
"But don't tell anyone else," Mother says,
"Other people don't think the way we do."

If anybody ever tried to cut me there I'd kick and scream a whole lot
more than Cousin Murray.
I'd kill them.

Thomas McGrath commemorates his father and a rare, blissful
childhood. In *Letter To An Imaginary Friend* (Part III) he creates an
elegantly Whitmanesque, cinematic threnody on the boyhood joys of
riding on a small sled tied to his father's larger bobsled over a frozen
North Dakota road:

I ride in the jingling wake, my small sled tied to the bob,
Jinking along at the back in the field-bound hayrack's furrow
In the deep snow of the river road . . .
                              hearing the thrum
Of the cold guitars of the trees and, distant in the deadstill air,
The rumbling of afternoon trains, the shunt and clang of the boxcars
Hunting their sidings in faraway towns at the ends of the wide
World of the winter . . .
                      and beyond the jingle of the harness bells,
And the hiss and hush of the runners cutting the deep snow,
As we crossed the river, came the long and compelling call magic
Of the whistling distant engines—
                         interrupting my father's tune.

The chore he and his beloved "Da" perform is to fetch hay for the animals; the excursion is enriched by visions of Santa Claus, prophets, the Holy Land, and Christ. His worlds are "Up" and "Down," the former the magical world of fantasy and imagination; the latter the practical, earthbound world. The father forks open the "ziggurat" strawstack:

> —And my Da beats down the snow and rams a pitchfork in
> And the stack-side opens like Adam to the glow of the inner soul
> So august-cured and pure . . .

He recalls summer and the excitement of building the stack, when he danced

> In the hayrack, building the load, as my laboring darling Da
> Lofts up the forkfulls of raw-gold straw like the aureate clouds
> Left over from summer.
>   And I, trading my fancy fandango,
> My turkey-in-the-straw, while he shouts and laughs and half buries me
> Lifting the last of the past year's light—the two of us singing
> In a warm winter fable of our summer's work.
>   And done at last
> I latch my sled to the right rear bunker and we run for home.

There are unmistakable echoes of Dylan Thomas's intoxication with words and his boyhood: see his "Fern Hill" and "Poem on His Birthday."

One childhood poem that does not fall within either of my categories is Richard Wilbur's "Boy at the Window." From the warmth of his home, a sensitive child listens to the wind readying a "night of gnashing and enormous moan," and observes a snowman (one he built?) outside in the yard, staring at him, and grieves.

In a lovely, balanced turn (the poem is in two eight-line stanzas), the snowman, though not desiring "to go inside and die," is moved by the boy's weeping for him:

> He melts enough to drop from one soft eye
> A trickle of the purest rain, a tear
> For the child at the bright pane surrounded by
> Such warmth, such light, such love, and so much fear.

Wilbur's empathy for the boy, who from the secure interior of a warm, loving home still feels fear, is apt and moving.

Chintz Poems

Chintz, like the cloth from which cheap curtains are made, refers to those flat, sprawling, pretentious, enervated phrases dropped into poems, giving the illusion of intellectuality, culture, and charm. Robert Pinsky sometimes writes chintz poems. His "The Unseen" lacks discernible, convincing emotion, and comes off as "writing." The piece is designed in flashy triplet stanzas, much as a miser's guineas might be arranged in piles of three. The rhymes seem fashioned rather than felt. A riff on *air* scampers throughout the first four stanzas, accompanied by much fancy diction, diction easy to see through, like chintz. Warmed-over Keats? Shelley splattering the guests at Crotchet Castle? Among the phrases are these: "menu of immensities," "a formal, dwindled feeling," "the single power of invisibility." Pinsky inserts a touch of fancy cinematic violence, "fire and blood." He drifts off to sleep. (Snore, snore.)

Jane Miller drapes yards of chintz. Among her profundities are these: "I've come to love the light," perhaps an echo of Robert Frost's platitude, "I've come to love only what I have to do." Flowers are embarrassingly prescient: "the daisies the iris called upon so often so kind . . ." "Tenderness in distance / is the death in distance / shared" sounds like a tepid Pythagorean theorem of life. Here is yet another: "even among the few we know / how many we are." Finally, just try reading this for rhythm and sense: "funny Southern vowels elegy to / part of me knows you." Miller seems to have dropped cut-up words on her carpet, then pasted them on the page without caring much about either syntax or sense.

Christmas Eve Poems

James Greenleaf Whittier's winter saga of American rural life, *Snow Bound*, with its depiction of an intimate, cozy family scene rich in small details and portraits of family members, is an excellent Christmas poem. The outstanding British lyric on the theme is Thomas Hardy's "The Oxen," in which Hardy's own craving to believe in the miracle of Christ's birth is reflected in his use of the myth that on Christmas Eve farm animals kneel down in their stalls to adore the Child.

Thomas McGrath's ongoing "Letter to an Imaginary Friend" contains a superb Christmas section. In its present version, the poem appears in *Passage Toward the Dark*. Most of the poem is a recollection of the McGrath family's journey via sled to midnight mass; it interweaves past and present, evoking the experience on that wintry Christmas Eve in rural North Dakota through images both religious and secular.

In a preface, McGrath describes his technique not as collage but rather as analogous to the cinema. Time, he writes, is the determining factor: "In any section there will be a general narrative time—the past. But the poem, like some films, makes use of flash-backs and flashes forward, 'replays,' 'subliminal cuts' (phrases from earlier passages or ones which will be developed later on), etc., etc. It would be easy to push this analogy too far, but there are, I think, equivalents of dissolves, fades, etc." As a result, his "narrative line" is often interrupted by "other time-lines" up to the present, since the composition of the poem itself is "*also* part of the subject of the poem." The narrative voice can also be interrupted by a recollected quotation, or by the voice of some "identified character." Even the voice or persona of the speaker can change, shifting suddenly from a serious tone to one that is "a satirical or fantastic view of the same material." There may be "elaborations to the scene, or language that is very distant from the point of view of the telling a few lines back." Soon the poem returns to "the initial narrative line." McGrath deliberately confuses Lisbon, Portugal with the little town of Lisbon, North Dakota. McGrath's Christmas Eve contains conscious echoes of Dylan Thomas' "Christmas in Wales":

> And out to the field at nones,
> At the ninth hour of winter song in the falling afternoon light,
> Under a sigil of snow and over the december-sintered roof
> Of the little river, lifting and lofting our cold voices—
> Poor gifts but breath our spirit—calling our holy office
> In to the black white of those fields' now-lost pages
> To bring the gold of the summer home for the créche and crib
> And to line the rack of the sled for the trip to Midnight Mass. . . .

Here energetic dissolves of object and time, and of intoxicated language, conclude with a yokel's eye view of the three wise men going to Bethlehem:

> Gentle Reader: Once upon a Time, in the Anywhere that is Dakota. . . .
> You can imagine about what it would have been like out there:
> Lift the window on Canada and let in a little snow—
> *Some cyclonic widdershins here, if you please*—and some of that cold
> That sent Sam Magee to the furnace with Shadrach, Meshach and
>   Abednigo,
> And a bit of smell from the lignite that burns in the pot-belly stove . . .
> And the woman, working, of course—milking the cow, maybe,
> Or making butter (best to have her inside here) or cooking
> (What?) Praties, maybe. Or if they're Norwegian—lefse.
> Not a bad angle there. *Cut.* Through the window we see her
>
> (*That dreaming farmwoman's face*—SHE IS IRONING CLOTHES: I
>   KNEW IT!)

Thinking of sunny Trondheim and the troll that took her virginity
(Make a note back there somewhere that she's pregnant and near her time)
While Sven is reading his newspaper: *The Scandinvian Panther*
And we see in LONG SHOT: HER POINT OF VIEW: away down the
    coulee

These . . . well . . . *kings,* sort of, mopin' 'n' moseyin' along
Towards. . . .

Coastless Poems

There exist numerous poetry worlds locked away from any view whatsoever, except on television, of either the Atlantic or the Pacific oceans. Towards these worlds, poets in New York and in San Francisco are either totally indifferent or patronizing. They even subscribe to theories that New York and San Francisco are blessed with special ions, a sort of crazy magnetic soup that affects all poets living there, vivifying them, charging their brain cells and hence their art in a way never experienced by poets in Milwaukee, Lincoln, Cincinnati, or Pierre. "Coastless poets" are American heartland poets much-influenced by James Wright and William Stafford.

Two of our significant loner poets, Robert Bly and Thomas McGrath, choose midwestern isolation for their work. Although Bly may give one the impression that he seldom stays at home, his Minnesota retreat in an isolated forest is where he does much of his writing. While Bly's frequent travels for workshops, seminars, and reading lend him much visibility, McGrath (who seldom travels) might be better known if he circulated more. A marvelous poet, Lorene Neidecker of Wisconsin, was largely ignored in her lifetime, probably because of her midwestern isolation. Only now, years after her death, through the enthusiastic efforts of Jonathan Williams who has published her collected poems, is she gaining the readers she deserves. Other fine poets who stay home and write are Nebraskans Ted Kooser and Greg Kuzma.

Vigorous poetry centers like those at the Universities of Cincinnati, Toledo, Michigan State, and the University of Wisconsin, Milwaukee; the poetry center at the University of Kansas (which collects poets with beat or counterculture connections); and the maelstrom of performance and poetry activities in Chicago, are positive signs that important poetry exists in the heartland. Alone in influence and power, the Iowa Writing Program is a huge morning glory vine impossible to eradicate, which sends forth vast root systems all over the United States. If one were to create a map of all writing programs, writing workshops, and poetry editors in the country, the numbers of Iowa City alumni in these positions would be astonishing. The reason for Iowa's prominence is probably as simple as this: when the Center was started, most colleges despised poetry and fiction workshops, declaring them pointless both as developers of writers and as legitimate intellectual disciplines. Slowly but securely the Iowa M.F.A. established its toehold, and when English departments, worried about student unrest in the late sixties and early seventies, decided to curry favor with students by giving them a curriculum they liked, writing workshops were in, and they've flourished ever since. When the Easterners and others finally chose to look, coastless Iowans had claimed much of the turf.

Comic Book Poems

These poems derive largely from the fifties and sixties, the Marshall McCluhan years when the funky and the minimal merged. The leading underground comic-book artists were R. Crumb and S. Clay Wilson, who appeared in *Zap Comix*. Mr. Natural, Angelfood McSpade, and Honeybunch Kaminski became seminal counterculture figures. Richard Brautigan, in both poems and prose, was regarded as a major, if flashy, writer. Much of this work was starkly and raunchily sexual. One of the tamer outgrowths in the seventies was Richard Morrice's series of poem comic books, where well-known traditional and contemporary poems were illustrated and reduced to captions.

Edward Dorn actually published his *Recollections of Gran Apachería* in comic-book format. Others of his poems could easily serve as texts for comic books. "For the New Union Dead in Alabama" is one such poem. I can easily visualize these opening lines divided into strip balloons:

> I lost in the tortured night
> of this banished place
> the phrase
> and the rose
> from wandering
> away, down the lanes
> in all their abstract directions. . . .

This moment from "La Máquina A Houston," from *Recollections of Gran Apachería*, would suit frames in which a somewhat dissolute, honky Western type rides on an old train and witnesses the approach of some Apaches:

> The Apache are prodded out into the light
> Remember, there are still dark places then
> Even in the solar monopoly of Arizona and Texas. . . .

"Anarchist Heart," by Jeru Hense is in the sexy, funky spirit of old Mr. Natural and his cohorts. I divide the poem easily into frames:

[Frame 1] I've danced with a nun,
            not many can say that.
[Frame 2] And afterwards bayed at the moon.
[Split frame 3/4] I've jerked off in a tin cup
            and drank it.
[Frame 5] The romance of chaos
            was my only hope.
[Frame 6] The cussedness of objects
            has driven me insane . . .
            [draw old car that won't work; a broken TV set]
[Frame 7] and so I lick the lap
            of doom.

A similar strategy could be designed for Wayne Allen Sallee's "What I Saw From My Window," which reads like a fairly inspired punk-rock lyric condemning ravaged Big City life and the poet's own failing inspiration:

while leaving Manhattan.
first I saw the journeyed
walls of mind then spit
dribbled from the mouth
of 98th and Park Ave,
unreadable ads and Christmas
lights, echoes of transient
sleep, alien graffiti broken streets,
Hell's Kitchen and Saul's Deli,
the runes of neon complete,
a long intersection
at the writer's block
left me staring at my haggard face,
sweating soon awakened
from a life-long dream.

                                                            (Ibid., p.29)

Poetry Motel, a randy mimeographed journal, adorned most of its pages with far-out comic-book drawings of a whips-and-chains gaminess. The poems could easily shape themselves into balloon graphics. P. W. Faulkner's "Medieval" has a mix of death, rot, and comic-book violence, presided over by Satan:

Lucifer, his hair sparking
like static wire
descends on a horde
of grateful angels.

Murderers' bodies
rot on cartwheels
stuck on poles.

Men-at-arms
in rusty chain-mail
rush towards the Good Thief
and crowd the sky
with frantic spears.

Eric Gardner's "He Has A Noose" is graphic and meditational:

He has a noose in his room—it is
Rare and regulation, almost a
Collectable in its thickness, its
Chafing roughness. People find it
Morbid; they shiver or try to laugh; ask—
"Did you buy that thing new or
Used?"
It hangs from his curtain rod; mostly,
He just looks out the window through the
Rope's maw and wonders. He is very
Careful when the wind makes it
Sway softly back and forth.

Cope-and-Mitre Poems

Poets here strain after the ecclesiastical, the pompously mystical, and are usually much encumbered—if we see the shape of the poem itself as an archbishop's cope, and the pretentious and ornate phrases as so many semiprecious stones suitable for an exalted poet-ministrant's alb.

When Phyllis Thompson proclaims that "writing a poem is an act of praise" shortly after having announced, in verse, that she has "always been a church-goer," we have a pretty good example of the "cope-and-mitre" mode. When Thompson detects the "flow of low bells" downstream "ringing singly," jangling into a "plainsong of water," more organ stops emerge as a jubilate, not to God, but to poet-friend John Logan. Thompson's world is prayer-book palatable, and as she wafts her abstractions and censers, she crams in an allusion to one of W. B. Yeats's more obvious lines:

Of all men I know, John, yours is that voice
I can call to mind anywhere from my deep heart,
The serious and the ordinary
Plainsong that grows out of but beyond weeping and triumph,
Diminishes guilt, and can reduce even heroic love or failure
To the same unasking simplicity of clear music
As of river water lapping weeds on a low shore. . . .

Michael Blumenthal has a special corner on the mode, mixing an unseemly *olio* of the sacerdotal and the profane. "Today I Am Envying the Glorious Mexicans" embarrasses us by stereotyping Mexicans as "napping beneath their wide sombreros / beside the unambitious cactus." "In Assisi" is essentially an adorational poem for his wife (will she be pleased to be seen as a man?):

> This morning, in Assisi, I woke
> and looked into my wife's face
> and thought of Saint Francis:
> how he explained to Brother Leo
> that Perfect Joy is only on the Cross,
> how he told him that, if they should come
> to the Convent of Saint Mary of the Angels. . . .

To Linda Gregg femininity is a "sickness" forcing her to a clear vision of the meaning of her life. Miraculously, she is able to proclaim herself "whole." She claims the "fish" of her own "spirit," and belongs to no one. Like a creature "bred for slaughter," she lies naked on a sheet in "indifferent" warm sunlight. At the "center," where she suffers "exactly," there are "no clues except pleasure."

Edward Hirsch combines the cope-and-mitre style with the "small creatures" poem in an embarrassing mix. Obviously Hirsch takes Christopher Smart's poem "Wild Gratitude" seriously, since it provides the title for his own most recent volume of poetry. He's been reading Smart's poem to his cat Jeoffry, and hopes to outdo the earlier poet without actually going crazy himself. I accept his sticking his fingers into his cat Zooey's (where is Franny?) "clean" mouth. But when he turns sentimental and rubs the "swollen belly that will never know kittens," I want to throw kitty litter in his face. She's a cute cat who, pleased with the attention, emits "solemn little squeals of delight."

Rubbing the cat reminds Hirsch of Smart's desire to kneel down and pray ceaselessly along all of London's "splintered" streets. (Were London streets made of wood? I thought that in Smart's day they were paved with stones.) Adjectives dropped in at monotonous intervals seem to be plastic apples from which Hirsch can't turn aside. Here are some particularly dull adjectival phrases: "sad religious mania," "wild ingratitude," "grave prayers," and "great love."

A few more details, already known to anyone familiar with Smart, segue towards a teflonesque attempt at merging the two poets. Remembering that Smart liked to hear "the soft clink of milk bottles" reminds Hirsch that he likes hearing the same thing. And that night, as Hirsch sticks his hand into Zooey's "waggling mouth" he recalls that Smart saw his Jeoffry as a mystical cat, "the servant of the Living God duly and daily serving Him." A tall order for a cat!

With touches barely skirting the maudlin, Hirsch recalls that Smart took a coy delight in seeing his puss delay springing on a mouse. Now, in fine cope-and-mitre fashion, Hirsch gives us a pablum sermonette: Jeoffry and Zooey by "purring / In their own language," teach us humans "how to praise." Moroever, it appears that these are cats straight out of the mystical fiery furnace of God, for they have managed to wreathe "themselves in the living fire."

Erica Jong exfoliates genteel Buddhist mysticisms in "The Buddha in the Womb," using short, free-verse lines that trip over their thickened ankles. She can't be content to let an image carry its own weight, but must apply exaggerated cope-and-mitre trappings, larding in ever more concentric, Saturnate whirls of momentous meanings:

> Meditating, I can see my skull,
> a death's head,
> lit from within
> by candles
> which are possibly the suns
> of other galaxies.

When she meditates further on death, light, and life, I find myself groaning for surcease: she knows "that the horses of the spirit / are galloping, galloping, galloping / out of time/ & into the moment called NOW."

Yusef Komunyakaa appears to be writing a cope-and-mitre poem, until frustration and anger at finding himself, a "crazy nigger," in mostly-white Orange County, California, overwhelms him. He's on a beach, observing the waves. By stanza two, anger stains the beauty of his and "their" notions of God:

> To them I'm just a crazy nigger
> out watching the ocean
> drag in silvery nets of sunfish,
> dancing against God's spine—. . . .

He reassures Miss Newport Beach, "Miss Baby Blue Bikini," that he is neither the Redlight Bandit, Mack the Knife, or Legs Diamond returned from the dead. There's just enough echo here of streetwise lingo to suggest Komunyakaa's power. He's not about to be intimidated, though any black *out of place* (italics mine) in such an area of Orange County is suspect, and may be hassled by cruising police and beach guards.

The concluding stanza is cryptic, and transforms any earlier hints of the cope and mitre into a violent sense of a black man's status in a closed white society.

Another contemporary poet who transmutes the risky cope-and-mitre poem into gold is Michael McClure. His many poems and plays celebrate life in all its manifestations, both fleshy and spiritual. A recent poem, "April Arboretum," featured in *New Directions* 49, seems to reflect the joy, intensity, and faith of a St. Francis among the creatures.

The contrast that fascinates McClure is between "manicured" nature and wild nature, the former a step nearer "inertness" than the latter. He observes a noisy killdeer; and a group of grackles peering through a heap "of pruned branches / with glint-yellow eyes / that see nothing"; a swan preening near a rhododendron; rabbits, bluejays, mallards, and quail. The "consciousness" of the grackles is "as innocent as a haiku / abandoning form / in mimesis of imagined experience." A jay stuffing a crumb into some humus for later eating, "creates an Osirian / recycling of remembrances / for worms, nematodes and beetles." McClure has been reading, using as a bookmark a postcard depicting a Serengeti waterhole. Uncannily, that scene of unmanicured nature is a perfect foil for the actuality around him. He returns to his "Detritus of Joy," observing four pigeons and a squirrel. The birds "have no interest in the squirrel / whose skinny ribcase / resembles that of a slender / nine year old boy." There are overriding themes—the greed McClure sees preventing us from absorbing more exalted spiritual experiences and our spiritual blindness.

Cowboy Poems

Cowboy poetry seems to be enjoying a new vogue. Poems written by authentic cow-pokes are recited at a yearly competition in Elko, Nevada. No one pretends these efforts have the literary qualities, say, of Ed Dorn's "Gunslinger" poems; yet they obviously have a popular appeal that more sophisticated poems do not. Over generations these have changed little, and owe much to the traditional ballad of rhymed quatrains, of which Robert Service's Yukon verses are the best known. Cowboy poems stand quite apart from works by true poets writing of the same figures; see Michael McClure's, Jack Spicer's, and Thomas Meyer's poems about Billy the Kid, Annie Oakley, General Custer, and the Indian Wars.

The cowboy poem developed among isolated punchers (largely Anglo-Saxon). Each man spent hours alone riding, often at night, engaged in work that absorbed little of his attention. To provide social diversions around the chuckwagon, or in going up the trail, they sang and recited ballads, inventing new ones, the result being a large body of folk songs and oral poems.

Most of these verses and songs are doggerel, and are of more interest as human documents than as art. They reveal conditions of frontier life, of the cowboy's round—the monotony and the fun, the heroes, love affairs, and dangers of the long, epic cattle drives overland from Texas to Montana. Refrains are often adapted to common cattle cries. There are simple and incremental repetitions.

The *Los Angeles Times Magazine* (July 5, 1987) paid homage to *Poets of the Purple Sage,* a mini-anthology of current cowboy verse, assembled by Jessica Maxwell. A three-volume collection of "the best of both traditional and contemporary cowboy verse," edited by Hal Cannon, founder of the annual Cowboy Poetry Gathering held for the past three years in Elko, Nevada, recently appeared. Maxwell quotes Cannon: "This year we invited more than 200 cowboy poets from 17 Western states and Canada. . . . All of them selected by their state's folklorists, and they're all genuine cowboys or ranchers—that's a prerequisite." The audiences, Canon reports, are also made up of cowboys, "not tourists."

Among the best-known of these dudes is Waddie Mitchell, who hails from Nevada. He's fairly young—thirty-six—has appeared on the Tonight Show, and unofficially hosts the Cowboy Poetry Gathering. Baxter Black, known for his "sideways sense of humor," with Nyle Henderson (both live in Colorado), are among the few such men who make a living with their oral and written art. Black confesses that he is "a better cowboy poet than a cowboy." Gibbs M. Smith Inc., a firm based in Layton, Utah, seems to specialize in publishing this verse. Two examples follow: "The Cowboy's Dance Song" by James Barton Adams and "Cowboy Logic" by Baxter Black.

The Cowboy's Dance Song

Now you can't expect a cowboy to agitate his shanks
In the etiquettish fashion of aristocratic ranks,
When he's always been accustomed to
    shake the heel and toe
In the rattling ranchers' dances where
    much etiquette don't go.
You can bet I set there laughing
    in quite an excited way,
A giving of the squinters an astonished sort of play,
When I happened into Denver and was asked to take a prance
In the smooth and easy measures of a high-toned dance.

When I got among the ladies in their frocks of fleecy white,
And the dudes togged out in wrappings
    that was simply out of sight,
Tell you what, I was embarrassed
    and somehow I couldn't keep
    from feeling like a burro in a purty flock of sheep.
Every step I took was awkward
    and I blushed a flaming red,
Like the upper decorations of a turkey gobbler's head.
And the ladies said 'twas seldom they had ever had a chance
To see an old-time puncher at a high-toned dance.

I cut me out a heifer from that bunch of purty girls,
And I yanked her to the center to dance those dreamy whirls.
She laid her head upon my breast in a loving sort of way
And we drifted off to heaven
    while the band began to play. . . .

When they struck the old cotillion on that music bill of fare,
Every bit of devil in me seemed to bust out on a tear;
I fetched a cowboy war whoop and I started in to rag
Till the rafters started sinking and the floor began to sag.
My partner she got sea sick, and then she staggered for a seat,
And I balanced to the next one
    but she dodged me slick and neat.
Tell you what, I took the creases from my go-to-meeting pants
When I put the cowboy trimmings on that high-toned dance.

Baxter Black has been called "a combination of Ogden Nash and Festus" and says he represents the "lunatic fringe of cowboy poetry," which describes his humor.

Black gave up a career as a veterinarian to write verse. Raised in Las Cruces, N.M., Black graduated from the University of Colorado. He lives on an 18-acre spread in Brighton, Colo., with his wife, Cindy Lou, and their daughter, Jennifer, 8. Though he does rope and ride, he says: "I'm a better cowboy poet than a cowboy." Black writes a syndicated newspaper column, "On the Edge of Common Sense," which he says is "mostly humorous, occasionally political and accidentally informative." Here is his "Cowboy Logic."

One morning bright and early
    we wuz goin' down the road.
The night before I'd missed my steer
    and Donny Boy got throwed.
But we wuz feelin' better
    when ol' Hard Luck bummed a ride.
He climbed up in the camper shell
    and settled down inside.

The pickup bed was fulla junk, our rodeoin' stuff.
But Hard Luck never said a word
    'cause there was room enough.
The sun rose in our rear view on I-20, headed west.
And Hard Luck dozed then fell asleep.
    I guess he needed rest.

Then somewhere on the freeway we almost hit a bus.
I hit the brakes and skidded nearly killin' all of us.
Ol' Hard Luck's head bounced off the back,
    it sounded like a shot!
Like someone threw a bowling ball against a cast iron pot.

"You reckon we should check 'im, Don?"
    "Nope," was all he said.
"He hit that sucker awful hard, I think he might be dead."
A look came in his beady eyes, like I had hay fer brains.
His logic was pure cowboy.
    While I listened, he explained:

"There ain't no point in stoppin' now.
    No reason on this earth.
If he's alive, he'll be okay until we reach Ft. Worth.
And if he's dead as Coley's goat, he'll sure be hard to lift.
He'll be a damn sight easier to move when he gits stiff!"

Curse Poems

These poems, though rare, have hoary origins in early Celtic runes, charms, and magical poems. Victor Contoski's "The Liar" is a notable example:

I

I give you my word.

He lied in his teeth
in his front teeth and his back teeth
in his crowns and his roots and his gum sockets
in his incisors and canines
his bicuspids and molars with their gold fillings
and in all the spaces in between.

He lied in his wisdom teeth
lying crooked in his gums.

He lied in his gums.

He lied in his tongue
in the front of his tongue
and the back of his tongue
in the tastebuds at its sides
and in the soft underside.

He lied in his uvula.

He lied in his jawbone
and the hinges of his jaw.

He lied in his beard
in the short hairs
and the long hairs
in the sideburns
and the chin hairs.
He lied in the hairs in his nose.

He lied in his lips
that he puts to the lips
of those he loves.

He lied in his mouth
in the floor of his mouth
and the roof of his mouth
in his upper palate
and his lower palate.

He lied in his throat.

In the air he breathed in
and the air he breathed out
he lied.

2

Like the rubber band
a farmer places around
the testicles of his ram
so they will shrivel
and drop off

may these words
wind around his balls.

Daphne Poems

A "Daphne poem" appears whenever a poet writes of a human being becoming, or wishing to become, a trée. Daphne was a Greek mortal loved by Apollo and Leucippus, the latter a mortal who disguised himself as a nymph to be near her. When for her benefit—so he thought—he flashed his sex while bathing, a gaggle of nymphs tore him to pieces. When Apollo pursued the lovely Daphne, alarmed, she prayed to Agea for assistance, and was, on the spot, transformed into a laurel.

Ezra Pound, enamored as he was of the Greeks, writes directly of this myth in "The Tree." The speaker has "stood still" in a wood, become a tree, and thinking of Daphne and "that god-feasting couple old / That grew elm-oak amid the wold," is content, understanding much now that hitherto seemed "rank folly." In Pound's "A Girl," the transformation of human into tree seems to have occurred very recently:

The tree has entered my hands,
The sap has ascended my arms,
The tree has grown in my breast. . . .

Branches extrude "like arms." The second and final stanza confirms the transmutation: "You," says Pound addressing the tree, "are violets with wind above them." A child—so high—you are, and all this is Folly to the world.

Robert Duncan's "Madrone Tree that was my mother," one of "Four Songs the Night Nurse Sang," is sung by a Shelleyan poet, "the wind's brother," and sired by a "shadow." His mother, a madrone tree, resembles the Germanic tree goddess Ygdrasil or Hertha (see Swinburne's "Hertha"). The madrone, native to the American West Coast, grows to heights of 125 feet, and has luxuriant green leaves, nearly white on their undersides, with clusters of flowers and bright red berries. Of the various types, the Pacific madrone is noted for its vivid brick-red bark. Duncan's poet feels isolated from other humans, and seems, in fact, invisible to them. He requests that his mother, the madrone, cast him "a cloak as red as your flower," and feed his soul from her "thirsty root . . . as if it were your fruit." He seems to crave more substance than the "truth" the wind bestows: "Cast down splendor out of the air. / My story has only the wind's truth." The song concludes cryptically on the theme of death, which "came," says the singer, "when he was born."

A subtle lyric by Robert Kelly, "To Her Body, Against Time," translates the animistic force of "tree" into human aging. The tree is reft of leaves, except for that Tennysonian "last red leaf" twirled away by the first winter tempest, utterly denuding the tree, instilling it with far different magical properties than it has during its bosky season. The "white-faced sky" now bestows "flesh to branch," a lean visual design, "simplified / of images," for "old age." The concluding brief stanza has an Oriental simplicity and understatement: the "form," the aging of the woman's body, is predicted in the image of the stark tree, as clouds break with rain.

Jack Spicer inserts a fascinating quartet of poems on the animism of trees into the middle of his "Fifteen False Propositions Against God." One seems to parallel Duncan's poem above. Spicer says that his heart "aches" when he observes trees in spring putting forth green leaves, trying to "look like real trees." In November, bare, drenched in cold fog, leafless, we see the "heart's / Timber." In the next poem, the trees speak their truth: "us trees" are on a "final" cliff-edge above the ocean, and eat salty air, fog, and rock; while humans bother their "fuzzy heads about God." Say the trees: "Gee / God is not even near your roots or our roots / He is the nearest / Tree."

A tree solaces Spicer after he has lost a lover, a "bitter experience." What shall Spicer do? Turn to trees, the tree advises, to "Slippery elm. Birch / that knows no thankless nights. Oaktrees and palm / Ready to start a revolution." Just stay where you are (like Daphne?) rooted in the ground, and wait for "whatever water" comes your way. In the final poem, Spicer recalls William Carlos Williams's grandmother on her back on the way to a hospital: "Trees," she said, "Those fuzzy things?" Though Spicer does not quote the poem exactly, he says that beauty, love, and the fact of death itself become "fuzzy / Like a big tree." He promises to chop down all blurred trees and people, even his own "eyestalks," whatever blocks his vision. The animistic tree must remain lucid, or it loses its magic.

Dazzle Poems

The "dazzle poem," like the "dazzle story" (as written by John Updike, and earlier by John Cheever), and the "dazzle art-song" (as written by Ned Rorem), seeks to amaze its audiences with bravura. Too often this is at the expense of emotion and ideas. The dazzle poet may show off a cute tone, and a twirling of forms akin to elaborate piano finger-exercises having little content or authentic emotion. He may fashion poems that seem humorous and take you in with brilliance and flash. He may write a "poetry yum-yum" of such surface richness and elegance it resembles a Bavarian mousse piled high with mounds of sweet *schlagsahne*. It tastes wonderful, but there's no guarantee that once you're finished eating you will feel satisfied. Even the best mousse does not stick to your ribs.

One of the great dazzle poets was Ezra Pound. His renowned "Ancient Music" ("Winter is icummen in, / Lhude sing Goddamn") reflects his uncanny ability to write in all kinds of flamboyant verse forms, from all manner of cultures—Oriental and Occidental, Anglo-Saxon to late Victorian. Here in two amazing lines, he parodies avant-garde art, c. 1910: "Green arsenic smeared on an egg-white cloth, / Crushed strawberries! Come, let us feast our eyes." His various "Come, my songs" and "Go, my songs" poems are derived from French medieval *chansons*, intended to stun us with their brilliance.

Wallace Stevens, too, produced a dazzling style at will. "The Surprises of the Superhuman" contains these end rhymes: "chambermaids / colonnades" and *"Übermenschlichkeit"* and "would soon come right." The sixth section of his seminal poem "The Comedian As the Letter C" begins this way:

Portentous enunciation, syllable
To blessed syllable affined, and sound
Bubbling felicity in cantilena. . . .

In "A High-Toned Old Christian Woman" Stevens fashions a bravura style to denigrate poets bound to a mindless pursuit of traditional forms. These gross "flagellants" whip themselves, believing they produce art. A moment of true dazzle concludes the passage via a brilliant dance of alliterative sound:

This will make widows wince. But fictive things
Wink as they will. Wink most when widows wince.

A recent poet, John Hollander, though skillful, never approaches Pound's or Stevens's inventive genius. His "Hidden Rhymes" entices us to poke our pink little snouts through the word-roots and ferret out all the semiconcealed rhymelets (truffles). It's fun. We feel we've snouted a fine poem. Like most dazzle poets, Hollander tries for momentousness: "the heavy / Burden of the tune we carry" hums us "to the grave." You can't fail with death as a theme, no matter how ill-felt the lines are which lead up to it. Ivy-smothered poems like this give a magazine class.

Ted Berrigan wrote dazzle poems with great flair. His brilliant technique blinds us to the deeply felt and serious elements behind his funky humor. In "Ann Arbor Elegy," the easy end rhymes dance and swirl, suggesting that the poem is not an elegy but something spirited and joyful. We attend an all-night party in dull Michigan. Morning comes, with the breakfast we love. Ho hum—another day, another issue of the *Ann Arbor News:*

> Last night's congenial velvet sky
> Conspired that Merrill, Jayne, Deke, you & I
> Get it together at Mr. Flood's Party, where we got high
> On gin, shots of scotch, tequila salt & beer
> Talk a little, laugh a lot, & turn a friendly eye
> On anything that's going down beneath Ann Arbor's sky. . . .

Kenneth Koch's 182-liner (approximately) "Sleeping With Women" dazzles with its ceaseless repetition of variations on the title, each striving after brilliance and originality and often succeeding, the whole pastiche much-kissed by the thin lips of Gertrude Stein. The serial technique is a parade of Koch's European travels. Here is a pretentious moment, and one not entirely complimentary to the woman in question:

> Bees, sleeping with women
> And tourists, sleeping with them
> Soap, sleeping with women; beds, sleeping with women
> . . .
> Sleeping with women: a choice, as of a mule. . . .

The conclusion is pure Gertrude Stein:

> The time and again nubile and time, sleeping with women, and the time
> now asleep and sleeping with them, asleep and asleep, sleeping with
>   women
> asleep and sleeping with them, sleeping with women.

Constance Urdang, who works impressively within an ornate style crammed with literary devices, is a Gustave Moreau of verse. Here is the ending of a poem written to a girl called "Lizard:"

> My lively, my lovely, my jewel-eyed,
> Cloisonné-mailed, cloth of gold,
> Field of a thousand flowers,
> Lizard, you have illuminated.

Urdang is adept at simple styles as well. In "A Little Elegy" she blends the two. What could be simpler than this passage?

> She was one with the mothers
> Whose children have disappeared.
> All they have in the world . . .

Yet, the poem concludes with some unfortunate dazzle style posturing:

> Let rain be her requiem.
> The steady unemphatic drizzle
> That drenched the mourners on the pale hillside
> Where they lowered her ashes into the sodden earth:
> The monotone of dull rains of December.

Here are some dazzle lines chosen at random from Olga Broumas' *Pastoral Jazz*—lines too typical, I fear, of her book: "Polygynous plethoric no thought thought," "Anger axial eye atrocious," "orgasms of the earth oneiric / deja-vus for you these healthy portions," "Syllabic melismatic pulse / To set the temp with handbells / The gift is eaten in silence."

Few poets write dazzle poems as consistently and as well as Thomas Meyer. Every page of *The Umbrella of Aesculapius* scintillates with intelligence, beautiful language, and an esthetic mix of ancient myths and modern goings on. Right off, Meyer snags us: ancient Greeks with umbrellas? I thought they kept what little rain falls in Greece off them with fronds, consorts, or huge leaves. In this simple lyric (there is no title) of breathless cadences, consonance, and assonance, the ancient instrument, the sistrum, protects all those who hear its tones and dance:

> Her sistrum shook:
>
> let joy & love attend
> this toilet.
>
> > Enter
> cosmetic mistress,
> merriment & music,
> sovereign of
> > song & dance.

Meyer has an uncanny skill (a dazzling one) of simulating ancient Greek epigrammatic poetry. Here he commemorates the Lupercalia, the origin of our custom of sending Valentines, in which Cupid shafted his arrows through actual hearts, lovely boys led to the altar:

Up to Luper's altar
they led
    the boys

& touched their brows
with bloody blades
& wiped dark's mark away
with milk soaked
        wool wads.

More ambitious is the lengthy projective verse poem "Liber Hermis."
"Part II" is a finely balanced mix of ancient and modern motifs, including
a passage of collage and a verse commentary on Charles Olson on myths
relevant now to poetry. Few poets manage such disparate elements with
Meyer's ease:

Poseidon's arm reaches
        inward
        down the Hudson,
the river is still salt
       at Kingston . . .

Semele dances on Hudson's waters.
Her son sports
      a Corinthian crown of wild celery.

   (Pindar tells us
   Corinth was a polis
   known for splendid youth.)

Mother & Son sailed from
      Crete, home of
        ancient hours,

     to the Empire
     state, New York.

Dead Semele, a shade beside the boy

     receives her son
     in Annandale,
        off the Hudson
& up Riverroad
      from Barrytown.

Abraham & Isaac
Olson said
was a much better

myth, or example of
the pharmakon

(than those three
Persian boys. What was the state
of Bacchic worship during those odd
twenty years?)

Drive out the plague,
the result of the
female-beast; our lady
of the riddle. She
guards the gates & eats
the city's men.

Al Poulin, Jr., ringmaster of a conservative poetry anthology and series of books, lets much of it hang out in a pair of raunchily dazzling contributions to *Outlaw* (1984). In one poem "Cock Man" becomes a morning crower. The transformation occurs after a good drinking session, when the poet, clothed, sleeps the night away in a barnyard. His face (the sun comes up) is "a pink pig's"; his toes are "chicks scratching in the grass." The wind off? A purple passage of much dazzle celebrating his purple-shafted cock, an image, of course, for old Chanticleer's crowing neck.

Purple neck, plumed gold and red
in the blazing sun, perched
on the fence of my open zipper,
my cock crowed and crowed and crowed.

Few poets outshimmer Lee Hickman for dazzle. His lengthy "Tiresias: Great Slave Lake Suite," is one of the most ambitious poems of growth, masochism, and sex ever attempted by an American poet. A father's whippings seem to have damaged a son's psyche. Throughout the suite, the youth seems to take intense pleasure in being beaten. At one point Hickman's mandarin rush, energy, and sexual fervor are on full display. An enormous sex "lion" overwhelms the youth, who "in /shitsong in self wallow I / beg you beat me let me swallow you. . . . abject we go, / daredevil Lee & Lion tailgating, los feliz western in brea gardner, scatter / my limits, boundspreadeagled, drunken, druggd, gaggd, home." The Lion fuses, I think, with an older male wearing a necktie, another aloof, inaccessible sex pleasure-giver and tormentor.

Reading Hickman requires an unwavering focus—assuming one is caught up in the writing. In this passage, for example, dazzling words and phrases pile one on the other and the whole moves toward a kind of self-exorcism:

forlorn in a severance rain from root.
then to slave austerely to wail down insanity into my singing

rages
    pleading stop stop me enthralld
by avidya's big boot death grum fugue death dry fountain death

pig pouf
    turdblossom cringing anonymous slurp I
beg trappt braying hate me dont hate me this is my song. . . .

Hickman can also write ineptly. In "He Who Delights in Signs," from a recent issue of *Sulfur*, not only is the talismanic grammar of the title pretentious, but the writing itself creaks and fizzles. Here are the opening lines (*tilphussa* is a spring from which Tiresias "must drink and so die"):

tilphussa without to drink thee
both tilphussa within

as when suckt about poet into poem's
more ruin in flame my deathmost

tilphussa of his goddess's juices
as of her serpent's tongue in my ears a
tiresian upwelling voracious not yet gone luminous down on honest
    as early as
sign as down on a
child's rift, rift of her portions fresh in. . . .

Harry Northup, poet, actor, and wild language "explosioneer," tumbles and jumbles words and ideas with the abandon of a skyrocket of flashing colors, a madly spinning storm of syllable and word neutrons and protons. The result? Lengthy poems expressing flamboyant psyches in flames, fast knives flipping through fire, hip-hits, film-land schlock-flocks, exorcisms (particularly of such hallowed institutions as Jesus Christ and Mother), eroticisms, sperm, and always poetry. This sample (untitled and dated 5/2/76) reflects the kaleidoscopic thoughts of a Hollywood teenager who is violent, troubled, and driven by funky rock music:

blush loss wash drive run cross throw burn keep cross
overpass underpass
through lights of a fence
i hear him & her watching   steals rhubarb
beast, anxiety, honesty & guilt, 1 & 2.
form less sense
hip & funky & bad & now teenage garbage, its nothing bad
keep the music loud so they don't hear the machine

drag main spike chalk
slightly ajar   oh & forgot, promise lust, love
& covered, with her right hand, luxury,
tires, screens, slashing tires.   out where i go.
watch course.

propositions young girls on their way to hollywood high.

Robert Phillips' "The Persistence of Memory, the Failure of Poetry" dazzles in lesser ways. Its opening image of a severed hand fluttering on the subway track "like a moth," is calculated to astonish. Next, Phillips informs us that the hand is sentient: it "knows" that it is *a severed hand.* Here is a cute riff in the Humpty-Dumpty manner, without any of the lyric zip of the original:

And all the king's doctors
    and all the king's surgeons
put hand and stump together

again. Fingers move,
    somewhat . . .

Unfortunately, all the hand can do is scratch and claw: it is "a mouse / behind the bedroom wall." At 4 A.M. it "remembers" and creates "intricate musical / fingersings, the metallic / feel of the silver flute." This ending almost works: the hand is aware in its deeply private moments, when the world sleeps, and plays gloriously fingered "music"—paradoxically, since it has no lips, tongue, or air with which to activate the flute. Perhaps if Phillips had opted for less dazzle in the first five lines and had shortened them, the poem would be better. As it stands it merely does cartwheels to amuse the poet's friends.

Andrei Codrescu is another master of the dazzle poem. Turn almost anywhere in his *Selected Poems* and you'll find tour-de-force writing filled with stylistic pyrotechnics. Reading Codrescu one must always be on guard for unexpected surprises—what seems to be a scintillating romp-poem will suddenly zap you with some profundity you hadn't observed lurking in the corner. When such a poem works, grenades explode amidst the rockets.

In "Us" Codrescu summons food items in a refrigerator to "stand up" and "turn on the light." They must assert themselves, since they and "all beasts" are "growing hungry from a fast" in us—in humanity. In "Body Blues" he talks kitty and puppy talk to his body in an effort to get it to tell him what it wants. Nothing seems to work; the body remains dissatisfied. What dazzles us here is the writing itself, which is pop, sensible, funny, and real, in the sense that most of us react to our body's demands by being either punitive or rewarding:

What do you body want? Food? Food?
Here, body, have some food. What does
the body want? Coffee? Coffee? Here here
body have some coffee! Outside? Outside?
Let's go! Inside? Pussy? Pussy?
Here body have some pussy! . . .

Ron Koertge's kinky poem "Adults Only!" riffs on inflatable male and female sex dolls. He visits the Victorville museum of Roy Rogers and Dale Evans, and considers all their adopted kids—why didn't the couple have kids of their own?

Implied answer: Roy was too busy riding the range; or else he was sterile. Dale never nagged Roy, "hoping that / some buckaroo sperm would hogtie the / wily egg." Koertge finds an "Intimacy Corner" and hopes there, for an extra fifty cents, to see Roy and Dale in "the Wonder Position." No luck. He continues on to Vegas, thinking of their lives "measured by golden horses, always the same." In the Apple Valley dark, he imagines Roy finally, after being rid of sidekicks and animals, trying to get it on with Dale, who, "for the first time," says, " 'Roy, don't.' "

John Ashbery, in "Daffy Duck in Hollywood," dazzles us with a thoroughgoing example of poetry yum-yum. Here are some of his yummy ingredients: an opera singer warbling something from *Amadigi di Gaula;* a gathering of old commonplace collector's-item objects—a can of Rumford's Baking Powder, a celluloid earring, "a sheaf of suggestive pix on greige, deckle-edged" paper of the sort popular in the 1930s; a fantasy Hollywood intersection called Pistachio and Highland Fling; a few lines spoken, apparently, by Daffy and sweetened by the French word *déconfit;* a heavy "magnetic" storm gathering over Elmer Fudd's garage; and an "emerald traffic-island."

None of this adds up to much except great visual and tonal zaniness. Ashbery's intelligence races along making puns ("happy-go-nutty / Vegetal jacqueries") and tossing in a pop song ("Up the lazy river"). A vision of Anaheim (home of Disneyland West) may or may not be burning; Anaheim "has the riot act read to it by the / Etna-size firecracker that exploded last minute into / A *carte du Tendre* in whose lower right-hand corner / (Hard by the jock-itch sand-trap that skirts) / The asparagus patch of algolagnic *nuits blanches* Amadis / Is cozening the Princesse de Cleves into a midnight micturition spree. . . ." The loading-in of French phrases ups the dazzle calorie count enormously, and puts Ashbery's yummy dessert well up front in the Gourmet Cookbook. The presence of Amadis of Gaul, that medieval personage, in his urination session with the Princess (Ashbery also implies that Amadis is an "algolagnic," one who likes to be whipped, especially by women) suggests a vivid time/ culture warp appealing to those of us who may be culture snobs and know "the old story." Will Anaheim go up in time/smoke? Oh, dear, where is our chivalric hero Amadis when we need him?

As we continue our feast, Ashbery guides us through a contemporary Hades, complete with Tophet, Stygian activities, and allusions ("stygian velvet"), designed not to frighten us but to complicate our already rarefied gustatory pleasures. In the middle of the poem, Ashbery pauses to examine what he is up to, and, perhaps without knowing it, provides a credo for poetry yum-yum:

> While I
> Abroad through all the coasts of dark destruction seek
> Deliverance for us all, think in that language: its
> Grammar, though tortured, offers pavilions
> At each new parting of the ways.

Keep all allusions nonthreatening and, if possible, fey. Hint at esoterica only the initiated would know—references to obscure literary works, singers, such medieval trappings as "pavilions" and dueling-pistols, and low froufrou tonalities—"pastel ambulances," aqua skies, expressions of hauteur towards new brutal standards in life and art. This is a truly chic moment: once the storm has passed, the lady Aglavaine discovers that no one she knew had ever heard of Amadis, nor of "stern Aureng-Zebe, his first love." Was Amadis bisexual, or was he totally gay and in love with Aureng-Zebe, the great seventeenth-century mogul, subject of John Dryden's last and best rhymed tragedy? Difficult doings, right? Amadis of Gaul, the hero of a thirteenth-century Portuguese chivalric romance, with a lover in the seventeenth century? Poetry yum-yum is allowed to take liberties with facts, as long as they sound right and are sufficiently esoteric to dissuade readers from going off to their cultural histories for verifications. Poetry yum-yum prefers the select, initiated, well-cultured audience, the ones who know smatterings of French and European culture. No sweaty Whitmanesque streetcar conductor, brawny road-builder, mechanic, or charwomen readers here.

Deathbed Poems

This term is generic for all poems commemorating deaths in a poet's family, particularly of aged relatives in extremis, complete with attached "life-support" systems, or, as they should be more properly known, "death-postponement" systems. American poets love deathbed poems, both the messy and the sanitized. Implicit behind them all is the notion that the deaths of a poet's relatives are of moment to the literary world, no matter how ornery, vapid, and anonymous those relatives were. The poet's ego assumes that since all poets are valuable to the state, relatives, no matter how distant, are of interest.

Contemporary writers of the deathbed poem are probably unaware of a Victorian poem, possibly the common ancestor of them all: A. C. Swinburne's elegy on the death of Baudelaire, "Ave Atque Vale." Unique among traditional elegies for its tone, the poem presents Swinburne standing in grief beside the corpse of the just-expired French poet. The immediacy is uncanny. It is true, of course, that news of Baudelaire's death was premature; this merely adds to the uniqueness of the poem. It is also true that Swinburne refused to write about visceral death and its messiness, classicist that he was. He steps round Baudelaire's final quakings and tremblings, evoking those moments when the corpse is stilled and the winding sheet is drawn up beneath its chin, the undertaker has stuffed the chops and nares with cotton, and the cosmetologist has gussied the cheeks with rouge.

One of the most famous of American deathbed poems is William Carlos Williams's "The Last Words of My English Grandmother." One may regret that Williams, as a general practitioner, did not include more medical details, viz., the old lady's temperature, exudations, and pustulences as she was wheeled on a stretcher to a waiting ambulance.

In contrast is W. D. Snodgrass's "A Flat One," in which "Old Fritz" lies for seven months on his rotating bed, dying:

> Unfit to move, shrunken, gray
> No good to yourself or anyone
> But to be babied—changed and bathed and fed.

His bedsores require pads, and prior to meals, and twice at night, his catheter tube is shut off so he can be turned. This is accomplished by bringing in a second "canvas-and-black-iron" frame in which Old Fritz is clamped, frightened. He is washed, covered, and, as he dines, each bit of meat must be cut:

> We watched your lean jaws masticate
> As ravenously your useless food
> As thieves at hard labor in their chains chew
>   Or insects in the wood.

In David Galler's "Meyer Levine" a "gentle, witty eighty-four-year-old" grows increasingly senile and is shuffled off to a nursing home. Like most families, his rationalizes the move, saying they've found him "the best old-age facility" possible. They visit him often to let him know that they "care for him, and more." The family is confused and torn as they observe his failing:

> Strapped to his chair, of which he'd made a mess
> (One broken leg), shoving it toward a fray
> With the roommate, he then caught sight of us
> On our way in, and named each with a smile;
> Then begged carfare to go to his job for a while.
>   He looked angry, forlorn.

Kate Braverman's "Cobalt Blue" portrays a dying father through the eyes of a small daughter who is learning her colors. While cobalt is blue, the father's blood is red. Friday, snowy, is white and black "by the railroad tracks." A nasty neighbor boy, "vying for the gold star," tells Kate that her father is dying. The family moves in with neighbors next door. Life goes on—raking leaves, swinging rag dolls in the back yard, going to monster and atomic war movies, seeing "worlds where all things were scarred, / like a knife criss-crossing / someone's father's throat." The mother, "preparing for the inevitable," cancels Kate's piano recital. There's a sale of household objects. They move.

Jorie Graham's "Erosion" commemorates her grandpa's "stiffening." Since he was a house painter, he sees death as a "tapping" of "the paintbrush against the visible, / tapping the mind." (I may be wrong in thinking he was a house painter; if he were an artist on canvas he'd show more originality, wouldn't he?) Graham herself doesn't want to become "a higher intelligence," for then she might miss the "sequence," might grow too "fat with unqualified life." As she runs beach pebbles through her fingers, flesh-atoms rub off, "evolving into / the invisible." This brings her to "erosion," which evokes a memory of her grandfather on his death bed, "learning / to float on time, his mind like bait presented / to the stream ongoing. . . ." Ugh!

Dennis Schmitz writes of old Uncle Lucien who stank. But then so did life. And old Grandma, with stiffening fingers, created a tree-of-heaven quilt, placing her own fetal image between her parents' shapes. She waited tidily beneath her Oxydol-iridescent sheets for Death. Daniel Halpern, in "Summer Nights," a childhood reminiscence, recalls his mother's painful childhood (the doctors wound her "poor legs" in wool and tar) and a visit she made to see a polio-stricken friend in an iron lung. Michael Blumenthal, in *Sympathetic Magic,* addresses an old dying woman urinating in the night: "You would go to pee— / the bedpan held between your shaking limbs, / a tired old plumber, / a wind-up doll / on its last rotation."

A most sentimental deathbed poem is Rodger Kamenetz's "Southern Crescent: In Memory of My Mother." The mother's slow dying, cell by cell, is compared to the slow passing of a freight train uncoupling its cars. The equation is forced and unfelt—as is the sentimental wind-off in which Kamenetz imagines he hears his mother, in "a little girl's voice" calling "Grandfather." Listening hard to the resolutions in some of our great traditional elegies—"Lycidas," "Adonais," "In Memoriam," "When Lilacs Last in the Dooryard Bloomed"—Kamenetz settles for the transcendental image of the eternal star; only here it's an image formed by a train, "The Southern Crescent," sent on its route out of the valley by red signal lanterns.

James Reiss's dying old man in "Something Like an Apple" envisions himself as a boy fading off, growing "paler" as he disappears into "whiteness", i.e., death. I admire Reiss's attempt to freshen the deathbed poem. Unfortunately, the language, which seems to come from a school primer ("Once an old man was an only / child who lived in a tiny apartment"), fails; any bright kid hearing it would feel disgust. Also, the point of view is confused. On the one hand, the old man seems to be having a vision; on the other, we stand in the room looking over at the old codger who is watching the "ghostlike boy" standing behind the bed. As one might expect, the boy has "thin arms" and "buck teeth." Then, when the bedpost turns into a tree for the boy to shinny up, and "across the yard"—a switch in place that doesn't work—a girl wearing a 1920s dress appears, Reiss loses this reader. The final phrase "the tree of evening" is a touch of academic sleaze, and the apple the old man plucks evokes facile echoes of Genesis.

Occasionally, deathbed poems are memorable. In "A Death Wish," by Roger Finch an old woman is found naked and dying, curled in fetal position on her kitchen floor, her hands and legs

> folded up sideways, embryo-fashion, locked
> tightly enough to cover the sex we issued from.
>   Her still-live, half-warm
> body was so wilted the head was too large,
> as a baby's head is large. . . .

She was apparently beaten by her husband who was rocking in his rocker when her children found her and saw "the blue-black rosettes / the shape of fists spoiling her back and her arms / and her breast. . . ." Even worse was a large myelocele on the back of her neck, which exuded an odor, "the flowers of incontinence" blooming "about her nestfallen bird's back." Finch concludes on this harrowing note:

> . . . my only thought now was that though her death
> from this moment never could come soon enough,
>   his would come too late.

Another powerful poem is Gregory Orr's "Gathering the Bones Together." With a few spare details he recounts a boyhood deer-hunting expedition during which he accidentally shot a younger brother:

> A gun goes off,
> and the youngest brother
> falls to the ground.
> A boy with a rifle
> stands beside him, screaming.

The boy is, of course, Orr, and the understatement hurts. The poem spins on, treating the theme of a youngster only vaguely comprehending the tragedy he has caused:

> I was twelve when I killed him;
> I felt my own bones wrench from my body.
> Now I am twenty-seven and walk
> beside this river, looking for them.
> They have become a bridge
> that arches toward the other shore.

George Looney's "The Last Vision of Light," is another vigorous poem. Looney's young brother, accidentally shot while hunting, lies beneath a respirator. A desperate need—there is still hope the brother will live— prompts Looney to "want to put my / hands on his shoulders and / shake him back; I want to / recover my brother from this accident." The brother dies.

Poignant also is Geoffrey Young's "Elegy." This lengthy piece, part meditation, part memory, commemorates an exceptional father and his messy death (one assumes it is from cancer). The strategy is non-narrational; very few lines refer directly to the father's demise. His final days are embarrassing: he cries while watching TV, and at night his "strange fuzziness" reminds one of "light sliding across the surface of a blimp." He hears voices from the past—he's been rock hunting, he's looking after someone (Young as a child?) who has food on his chin. "To hold love in one hand, and vomit in the other," Young writes, "is to have the story well under way."

A unifying motif in Young's poem is *language*. Death and love are constituted of "small accents, of waves stared at, of tiny prayers" fed by words. The "logos" of death is "broken down and distributed / into the typecase one letter at a time." Memories themselves are bits of letters in a font, to be drawn from the typecase and set, in homage to the departed father. Recollections struggle for air, as the old man struggled on his "diet of morphine, shallow air, blind ravings." News of the death comes as slang over the phone: " 'Ballgame's over' / there was just a plate, a fork, a chair, an empty room."

Edward Butscher grieves over the loss of a young stepdaughter in "A Suite For Amy," from his as yet unpublished *Child in the House*. Butscher has also written critical studies of Sylvia Plath and Conrad Aiken. His poems to Amy are marked by a subtle beauty; his grief is enhanced and intensified because he distances the event. His elegy is universal in a far more timeless way than if he had smeared the page with raw anguish:

> Here is the stoppered heart shaped by pure idea
> to bell the porpoise
> joy a princess flickers,
> jet flame refleshed in willful feather flights
> like a mother's veil dance
> for her daughter's dive
> into molten seas where black sails billow lies.
>
> Amy it is who spins and swims down the stairway
> of a hurricane's
> illuminated eye,
> two syllables, she laughs, webbing silence like glass,
> twin loaves of honey
> where darkness hives,
> one air, twice sung, to clasp hemispheres whole.

Here is the cortex that curves in a horizon
of liquified suns
above Dante's wood
as a little girl leaps from thread to ragdoll thread
like multiple stars,
loving herself from toe to limb to splash of hair,
keeping light alive.

Occasionally poets will fantasize about their own deaths. Randall Jarrell did so frequently. "The Woman at the Washington Zoo" closes with an apostrophe to a vulture:

When you come for the white rat that the foxes left,
Take off the red helmet of your head, the black
Wings that have shadowed me, and step to me as man. . . .

"Next Day," though spoken in the voice of a housewife intent on sorting out her pantry, is as much about Jarrell as the woman. When young, she was "miserable" though pretty, and now that she has aged, her thrill comes with her "womanish" wish that the box boy putting her groceries in her car will "see" her. He doesn't, and she is bewildered. "For so many years / I was good enough to eat: the world looked at me / And its mouth watered." She recalls a funeral:

My friend's cold made-up face, granite among its flowers,
Her undressed, operated on, dressed body
Were my face and body.

Andrew Glaze faces the knife in "A Masque of Surgery." The preceding weeks, waiting, have seemed "like trucks, loaded at both ends." He descends into a cave "that must be gone down into," an experience of bizarre humor and horror. Here Glaze describes the surgeon at work:

He pries between thumb and big toe,
forcing a truth out by impossible wedges,
parting knee and thigh, groin and plexus,
with sweaty wrist and shimmering pliers,
rocking, delving, prosecting searches
deep in secret attachments,
loosening like flux the last attached fibers,
lifting, prying up, holding like a
loving bloody cup or trophy of loss, *the thing*—
making our desolation his profession.

Ruth Whitman, in "You outlive all your diseases except one," imagines herself on her final hospital bed, in awe, and most anxious to please the doctors. The nurse asks for whatever she has of value—"watches, rings, teeth, whatever / is removable, also your eye, leg, hair / no I said and there are no / hairpins on me either, nothing, / nothing. . . ." Strapped beneath the arc lights she sees a "dark doctor" who says he writes poems in Arabic. She sympathizes with an anesthetist who can't locate her veins. She cheerfully *halloos* her own doctor "who like santa claus / with a black goody for me sends me / raw, split, sailing into cushions of mercy."

In John Logan's "The Dead Man's Room," the poet literally speaks from the bed in which a man has recently died. He clicks on the man's lamp to reveal various objects: a dictionary, Ovid's Latin, an encyclopedia, the photo of a mother and child mounted in cardboard, a milk glass candy dish, a ball point pen, a ceramic box, a finger nail file, an 1896 silver dollar, keys, a magnifying glass, a flashlight case, measuring tape, screws and nails, paper clips, a silver comb and brush, drugs, tiepins, some family plates, a nude "luscious Renaissance girl," a naked statue of a classical youth, and, finally, the dead man's picture when he was young and muscular, wearing undershorts. The poet rises, and sees in the mirror "only the contoured back" of his own head—an intimation of death.

The merging, though seemingly clear, remains mysterious.

Dedication Poems

Poems are written to commemorate friendships and loves, to borrow luster from more established poets, and to evoke the memory of some departed parent or other relative. Occasionally, poets appear for whom dedications are an unhappy addiction. For the sake of delicacy, I shall not name names; but recently I saw a book of some fifty poems— all but ten bore dedications. All of us who write, at one time or another, have published pieces for members of our families, for famous people, and for persons of no particular distinction other than that they are acquaintances.

Most of the time these poems lock the general reader out of the poem—he/she is spying at sentiments meant for one, and only one, person's eyes. In my more iconoclastic moments, when I do come across these poems, I stifle the impulse to send them back, complaining that the authors presume too much. If a poem carries an intimate dedication, why publish it in the first place?

Well, I won't play stupid; there are several reasons for such behavior. The chief one is probably vanity. When a poet publishes a poem signed to John and Jane Doelicker, to show appreciation for a groovy weekend in the country, or to Carolyn and Fred Anonymous for letting the poet rock Fred Jr. to sleep, or to Barry X-ray for that splendid fishing trip, or to Michael, Grace, or David, one-night sex stands lacking last names but so vivid in bed they deserve commemorative poems—when a poet publishes poems to such folk he displays his vanity by assuming that he is making them immortal.

Isn't all poetry, once it's published in even the most obscure journal, possibly immortal? One hundred and fifty years from now, when Fred and Carolyn, John and Jane, etc., are little more than bones or hanks of hair, some enterprising graduate student hot for a dissertation topic may unearth these poems and once more expose their fragile contents to the light. Moreover, if the poet has become famous, the most obscure dedicatee becomes worthy of inquiry and footnotes.

Obviously, though, vanity isn't the whole explanation. Whereas other mortals say "thanks" with a pint of homemade jam, an afghan, a birdhouse, or a coffee-table book on James Ensor's art, the poet gives what he is best able to craft—a POEM! Affection and social decency prompt his dedication.

Yet, while jam passes through your bowels, afghans wear out, and birdhouses come unglued and smeared with bird offal, the poem, once it is printed, may persist. And since poems belong with "the finer things of life," they have a possible lasting power beyond the fragility of the single words they contain. So, dedicatees are thrilled to see their names in print. Many even mount a copy of the poem in their bathrooms.

There's another kind of dedication, one a bit more suspect than these I've been discussing. Here a certain self-seeking strikes the gong of hoped-for success. Included are those battalions of poems dedicated to prestigious poets (some personally known by the authors, most not). The dedicator may be hoping that his dedication of a poem to James Wright, James Dickey, or Anne Sexton (even the dead ones get into the act) will help him get his poems published, eventually in book form. What editor, I ask you, wouldn't look twice even at a lousy poem, if he saw Galway Kinnell's or Jonathan Williams' name attached to it? To be fair, a young poet may simply be acknowledging a debt of gratitude to a writer who has inspired and influenced him. Swell! Too often, though, these dedications amount to mere namedropping.

Often, dedications are made to non-poets—dead politicians, victims of social injustice (Che Guevara, for example), famous actresses and actors (Mansfield, Monroe, and Dean), and dancers (Duncan). I have less quarrel with these dedications than with those to family and friends, and to famous poets. I don't discern the same self-seeking motives.

To help clear the air, I make this modest proposal: Have a committee of concerned poets, sponsored probably by the more alert membership of the Poetry Society of America and those poetfolk in Boulder, draft an agreement, to be signed by all publishers of poets, and by all poets listed in the Poets and Writers Directories, that there be an agreed-upon ratio of dedications to the overall number of poems published by any poet in any given year. Perhaps, as a rule of thumb, no more than one dedication should occur for every twenty poems. Another possibility: create a tradition whereby the final page of a book contains all the dedications crowded together in a single paragraph of small type. Friends and lovers can still find their names and be thrilled. The Committee (supra) may also want to restore that wonderful old nineteenth-century practice of the anonymous dedication: "To _____."

Disney Poems

(*See also* Celebrity Poems and Comic Book Poems)

Few pop phenomena have so permeated our culture as the incredible gaggle of creatures invented by Walt Disney and his studio. Very possibly, Mickey Mouse remains the premier citizen of the world, better known in more obscure corners of the globe than either Ronald Reagan or Mikhail Gorbachev. In Southeast Asia, I am told, "Disneyland" is street pidgin for "wonderful, very good." The current Disneylands on both American coasts have taken on the character of hallowed shrines: you haven't seen America until you've been there. Once you arrive, you leave your frowns behind—everything in those parks is designed to make you smile: workers in Pinocchio, Minnie Mouse, Winnie the Pooh, and Pluto costumes wander through the crowds; the grounds are sanitized— a dropped gum wrapper or popcorn kernel never remains unswept for more than a few seconds; and the "worlds" themselves are designed to elicit good cheer and fun. In exchange for their gifts, the Disney folk assume you will dress conservatively and behave accordingly. No topless men or women, no holding hands between men, no outrageous costumes, no bizarre behavior of any sort, no alcohol, no dope. Unobserved but ever-present are the Disney security people who have been known to cart off "suspicious" persons for scrutiny. During the 1960s the Anaheim park became notorious for having turned away the Beatles—their hair was too long.

For poets, Disneyland and Disney characters are fair game. Some have been used for satiric purposes, some not. Stephen Kessler's "Elegy Written in An Orange County Amusement Park" pays satirical homage to Walt himself. The "I weep for you" harkens back to the ancient Greek elegists Theocritus, Moschus, and Bion. The end-rhymes, suggesting the banality of some of Disney's films, also echo the tradition. The closing couplet and final alexandrine, and the old-fashioned "sluttish Time cannot deface" are, of course, borrowings from Shakespeare, Pope, and Byron. Residents of Anaheim, California will not appreciate Kessler's reference to *The Waste Land*. The first stanza concludes with a parody of James Joyce's *Portrait of the Artist*.

> I weep for you, Walt Disney: you are dead.
>   Your legend, planted skillfully, shall grow
> Like sugarplums in every tiny head
>   Across the land—a visionary glow
>   Which any young American may sow.
> Who would not weep for Walt? who in the Waste
>   Land built the smithy of his Studio
> And forged what sluttish Time cannot deface:
> The hyperanimated conscience of his race.

To build Disneyland, 160 acres of orange trees were leveled. People thronged to see the place, "the Ark / Of the Apocalypse." Walt, speaking biblically, as if he is God creating a universe, says: " *'We're selling corn. And I like corn.'* "

Kessler weeps "melodious tears" as he sits beside the freeway and has a vision of "Walt on the Eternal Stage: / More than a star among the Great Dead of his Age":

> James Dean and John F. Kennedy and God
> > And Santa Claus together couldn't hold
> A candle to his brilliance—he who shod
> > The feet of Cinderella, he who told
> So many lovely tales.

He finally reaches the park itself, and watches the funeral procession:

> > > Guides in candy-stripes (with due
> > Respect—note half-staffed flag—the show goes on)
> > > Precede the mourners, chanting, as they strew
> > > The hearse with long-forgotten film clips, who
> > Of public interest may be in the crowd:
> > > Mickey and Minnie Mouse, of course, the two
> > Whose birth marked the Creation; waddling proud
> Behind them, Donald Duck, whose nephews sing aloud

> > A dirge of *When You Wish Upon a Star;*
> > > *Fantasia,* Snow White, Seven small old men,
> > Zorro and Davy Crockett (with the b'ar
> > > He killed in infancy), Pinocchio, ten
> > > Of Hollywood's most famous Indians, then
> > All of Walt's animals, and then a band
> > > Playing—as guides name all the names again—
> > Some songs from *Mary Poppins.* Now, as planned,
> All cross the Old Frontier, into Tomorrowland.

Disney's final resting place is not in the shade of a "dead orange tree," but in a space capsule ("this soul's space-tomb") impaling the evening sky, appearing now as "a twinkling scar" of "everlasting Light." Kessler closes with a sort of pastoral consolation:

> > Sleep well, Beauty's Producer, who could see
> > > Life as cartoons of multicolored cash
> > Streaking the darkness of reality
> > > Till Fate dismantled the projector. Crash:
> > > The—happy—End. For, even as the trash
> > Is being swept up by your dutiful
> > > Employees (after hours), some other flash
> > May yet redeem the darkness: pull the wool
> Of Fantasy from eyes that saw Death beautiful.

Douglas Blazek's "The Factory at Bensenville" refers to Pluto and Mickey to emphasize the dehumanized conditions of workers laboring in an old factory. The setting is claustrophobic: walls, chimneys, and heating pipes clatter, bang, and fold in. Washrooms, dropped cigarette butts, scuffed shoe marks, piles of scrap metal and coal. Most of the workers, who are Catholic, suffer injuries: "the sorrow / of gauze in Catholic hospitals." Men in the mahogany board rooms and the file cabinets filled with "index fossil" are the nerve centers, the factory's true body.

The "other body" is constituted of the workers: near it you "hear more / backs than bedsprings / creak." Near it you "suffer the eyes / of Pluto and Mickey Mouse / as they stare / out punished glass." In other words, if I interpret the passage correctly, managers staring with dead, plastic eyes through plate glass facades down onto the works appear as Disney figures—harmless, but at the same time frightening. The Disney motif sharpens Blazek's empathy for the workers, a use that Walt D., I'd guess, would hardly have admired.

Robert Phillips, in "Vital Message," sees a parallel between the daily strapping-on of his heart to his wrist, and a Mickey Mouse watch. He strums a variation on two clichés: "wearing one's heart on one's sleeve" and being "open-hearted." The heart, outside his sleeve, "ticks / away the Mickey Mouse / of my days." Some people look off, others touch it, and find it "warm as a hamster." One "open-hearted" friend tries to give him a transplant . . . which won't work. Mean folk diminish it: a critic tries to give it an acid bath—it shrinks "smaller than a chicken's" heart. A girl breaks it open; vulnerable in love, the heart crunches open, "a Chinese cookie" lacking any fortune inside. Another girl wins it, and keeps patting it, "a regular Raggedy Andy." Phillips is his Mickey-Mouse-watch heart's worst enemy: he keeps chewing away at it, an impulse he shares with all "nail-chewers." For the heart, sitting there just above his wrist like a purple plum is too tempting. Once Phillips sinks his teeth in, most gently, of course, the heart "bursts with a juicy sigh." Sweet skin. No seeds. There's still more than half of it left to eat.

Among Ron Koertge's poems inspired by Disney are two on the Seven Dwarfs. The first, "The Seven Dwarfs," (12 *Photographs of Yellowstone*) relates what the dwarfs were like before Snow White appeared. During the day, they hung around film studios hoping to be hired as Munchkins. Nights they spent drinking double scotches and dreaming of females "big enough / to make two of them." They moved "into the hills" together, each then having "someone to hate beside himself." They "fought over who was shortest." Once they discovered a gold mine they could "despise the ore" that purchased their elevator shoes. They found a dog ("Shorty") and "lived on snacks." Then Snow White appeared:

> She cooked their
> geese, cleaned for them and worst of all best of all
> after dinner she danced. She thundered and strode,
> revolving mightily and they saw her immeasurable legs.
>
> Their nights caught fire again, massy visions of her
> hams, the slabs of her thighs. If she hadn't died, they
> would have killed each other.

But she did and remained somehow desirable. So each
was her paramour. Satisfied, they returned to work,
routine, sharing the same dream, tiny fist to tiny cock.

Then, alas, the Prince appeared, and Snow White rode "out of their lives,
straddling the fortunate horse." Doc first reached into his chest, curious
to see if his heart, that "hollow, relentless organ" was reparable:

The rest envied his expression of vast relief, and just
as they had followed him over hill and dale singing,
they followed him again, tearing at their barred hearts.

This time they worked in silence.

Koertge's second Disney poem, "The Seven Dwarfs, Each on His
Deathbed, Remembers Snow White," is kin to the controversial poster of
the fair maid being gang-banged by the notorious seven, a poster that
Disney Enterprises took to court and was able to suppress. Koertge's
poem is made up of seven short prose poems, one for each dwarf. Sleepy
always tried, he says, to get her "into the feathers . . . but just to snooze."
She wanted more: "Always the raised eyebrow and wagging finger."
Dopey confesses that by playing "dopey" he avoided lots of work. He was
sure that Snow White wouldn't stay long: "When she fell asleep like that,
I knew it wouldn't last." Grumpy, in character, grumbles that he barely
remembers the lass: "I believe she danced, but you couldn't prove it by
me. Every night I was in bed early, doubled up." Doc cared for her health,
and gave her weekly physical exams: "Of course a woman her size and
complexion was exciting, but I soon got used to it." Here's Bashful: "We
didn't have a t.v. so the others used to / turn off the lights and make me
blush. She / could make me beet red, just like that. Or / at first she could.
After a while she had to / get downright bold. And she liked saying / those
things too, I could tell." And Happy: "She made very little difference to
me. I was / always happy. I was then, I still am. Even / now. I imagine I'm
ill. Mentally ill, I mean."

Paul Trachtenberg devotes a good third of his recent *Making Waves*
to his experiences working in Disneyland as a candy man and pickle
seller. He recreates the feel of growing up in Southern California amidst
the surfing, fast cars, semi-nudity, and cheeky Disney animals. There are
dark themes—isolation, loneliness, and a troubled sexual identity.

He satirizes the Disney fetish for cleanliness: the "hunt for spilled
popcorn" is "a must performance in Everyland." An early poem, "The
Magic Kingdom," provides a swift overview:

The key unlocked
wax pirates with real souls
who pillaged Walt's subterrane.
Kegs & casks, and mechanical alley cats—
fixtures of this Caribbean inferno.

The French Quarter filled
with filigrees and fritters.
Mint juleps and a creole trio
strummed blues, furnished
the Quarter's cobbled roads.
Blue Bayou cafe complete
with Walt's animated fireflies.
"A swamptown Lady" spirit.

Easy thrills arranged by Disney technology amazed and startled him: "All
the transporters: capsules, trains, / boats, utopia cars, ragtime firetrucks,
etc. . . . / disseminated fairy dust in the Merry kingdom." Walt's "con-
tinuum" yoked the boredom of visitors' everyday lives to "exotic pros-
pects" lurking within dark corners:

There were real plants: impatiens, bottlebrushes,
flax on Tom Sawyer's Island,
banana plants & philodendrons
inhabiting Jungleland.
Petunias & marigolds designed
Mickey Mouse's face.
California oaks & varieties of acacias—
the Chumash spirit. . . .

Topiaries were everywhere,
mainly in fantasyland.
Stiff green giraffes,
elephants, bears & seals
intrigued visitors waiting
to board the Small World.
Only the privets and boxwood
felt mistreated and misshapen.

Beneath the facade of good cheer and almost overdone amiability
other matters seethe: a contretemps between Donald Duck and Minnie
Mouse occurs in public. Cameras flash. Ugliness is deflected only by "the
intermezzo and costumes." Virgin monorail girls lose their virginity.
Pinocchio "made hay" with the dwarves and "nosed the bottoms of tour
guides," while Dopey "varnished his wood into flesh." Very kinky!
Trachtenberg confesses that he "became a Disney character," loved
being Mary Poppins' pal and drinking beer with the Three Little Pigs. He
was startled to find, through Mickey, that both Alice and Snow White had
"been around." He had an affair with Lular, a lavatory matron. Rudy the
ragtime pianist, "like Tinkerbell," flitted dust over his favorite boys, and
dressed as an "humongus berry," sang "Life is A Breeze in this Merry
Kingdom." He invites Trachtenberg to be one of his fauns.
For two years Trachtenberg labored in the Merry Kingdom. He fell in
love with a lollipop girl: "She was bronze with rosy cheeks, / delicious in
her candy pink dress." When he began to drink too much, Toni left him

"stuck" in molasses. Sea gulls shrieked at him to "Leave Disneyland," which he does. Through his father's contacts he launches "a real job" in an Alpha-Beta warehouse. His horizon now includes Laguna Beach in Southern California, where "the gay boys lay."

Another poet of considerable verve who writes poems inspired by cartoons is Billy Collins. His *Pokerface* contains a suite called "The National Looney Tunes Portrait Gallery." "Bugs" succinctly sums up the wacky rabbit's prowess and acumen:

> There he leans:
> wisecracking
> biting his orange carrot,
> bugging the world.
>
> speed demon
> ventriloquist
> and master of disguise
> he is everywhere at once.
>
> buck-toothed
> and spectacularly eared
> he is armed with dynamite.
>
> he is the only one who
> really knows what's up.

Porky the Pig appears in another poem. He is happiest in his garden alone, far from his "terrible stammering," and from Petunia who nags and teases. Resting on his hoe, "unembarrassed," he "contemplates / the blue background / of his flat world: / a Zen pig."

"Daffy" captures the manic, driven spirit of the famous duck:

> he tears across the landscape, blabbering
>
> in lunatic flight
> from those who would
> pluck his jet feathers
>   wring his stem of a neck
>   twist his yellow bill
>   flatten him under cement rollers.
>
> his brain is a gumball: and with it
> he tears across the landscape, haywire
>   jabbering and amok
>
> outdistancing clouds of dust.

Elmer Fudd is the human prototype of the absurd and the ridiculous:

The mailbox in front
of the neat cottage
spells out the unfortunate
                    name

This morning
the homebody is humming
in his sunny kitchen
dum-dee-dum, waiting
for the tea water to boil.

Later he will have his nap.
The enormous pink head
will roll on the pillow
dreaming again of the wabbit,
the private carrot patch.

Waiting by the bed is
the shotgun
and the ridiculous tiny hat
for he
        is the human.

Disquisition Poems

Disquisition poems are written in journal form; in snatches of autobiography in plain, nonpoetic language, or in letters to friends filling them in on the mundane events of one's life. Here is the opening of William Wantling's "Sick Fly":

It was Tuesday morning
I was flunking out of school
The February sun was hazy
I went to bed with 2 jugs of white port
to drink myself asleep
but I kept flashing back to the day before
. . . but I kept letting my dog off her chain
& she kept running out in the road to
chase the gasoline tanker. . . .

The dog is crushed, but, still alive, she gazes up "with shamed surprise / as if she'd got caught shitting on the rug." This poem seems generated by the poet's wish to share the news of his life.

At their worst, disquisition poems celebrate events as mundane as having breakfast or sitting on the john. The poet may be picking his nose, hungering for a lover, eating toasted muffin crumbs, observing a hummingbird at the red-syrup feeder, waiting for the mail, or drinking a fourth cup of coffee. *The Newspaper of the Poet's Life* unfolds.

A contemporary master of the mode is Allen Ginsberg, who has sought intensity in hastily accumulated life-details, set down with the speed of scribbled telegrams. In *The Fall of America* he is incredibly prolix as he reports his journey across, around, through, and over "these States." The reader begins to feel the juices of AAA strip maps in his veins. More Refreshment, Gasoline, Spirit-, and Bladder-Relief Stations are needed along the way. Ginsberg's references to Oroville, Nespelem, Dry Falls, Lincoln Air Force Base, Riverside, Ruby, U.S. 80 near Big Blue River, etc., remain dull places on the map. Yet, there are times when the poetry is compressed, visually provocative, and symbolically alive:

> At Dry Falls 40 Niagaras stand silent & invisible
> tiny horses graze on the rusty canyon's mesquite floor.

I like that. But in another passage the attempt to elevate the commonplace is strained. The disporting of the final line as three staggered phrases moving across the sky is sleazy. The cannon image is forced:

> Moss Landing Power Plant
>   shooting its cannon smoke
>   across the highway. Red taillight
>   speeding the white line & a mile
>   away
>
> Orion's muzzle
>   raised up
>   to the center of Heaven.

The method works when Ginsberg allows himself time to develop an object in the poetry's landscape.

The anthology *The Streets Inside: Ten Los Angeles Poets* is rife with such writing. The most blatantly journalistic of this group of writers is Deena Metzger. Her poems read like prose chopped up to resemble poems, and contain much commonplace information, generally with a sentimental twist ("The women I know are so soft. . . ."). One of her devices, and one indigenous to the genre, is the simple stringing together of numerous thoughts with *and*s. *And* overused reflects a boring child's mind, a child who speaks a kind of continuous babble. Here is Metzger: "But you have lived almost a year in one house and have another year to go in it and have two cats you hate but they live and require food and that is important for all of us to remember that creatures live and require food and that we feed them and. . . ." If I suggest that this be drastically edited, I'll be damned as pedantic. Throttle the *and*s by their skinny throats and feed them to pussy along with her Meow-Mix! Metzger talks too much—talks *at* me. Some fine poetry is talk, to be sure—Whitman, some of Wordsworth, Williams; but such writing, to be effective, must have concision, imagery, inventiveness, insight, and originality.

Another Los Angeles poet, James Krusoe, realizes that inventiveness and poetic skill keep readers alert. His style is taut and lyrical, and when he writes a disquisition poem (most of his poems, however, are not of this genre) he is full of surprises, closer to the tabloid newspaper than to the daybook or personal journal. Here are some of his moments: "Joe loses his stomach; it comes out in bits / through his throat." "Bill loses twenty years of Christmas calendars, / His teeth in a bar, loses jobs, more jobs." "On Saturdays I watch cartoons, / The rabbit cuts the fox in half, / I buy a knife."

William Heyen's "The Berries" proceeds from journalese to senti-mentality (winter air forms "ascending souls" from his breath) to a facile contrast between picking the raspberries that made the jar of jam he has in his pocket and sterile winter, to the absence of God from his adult life. It's a contrived performance.

Diane Wakoski returns consistently to the disquisitional mode. In "Whole Sum" such material comes in late. Her observation of lithe youths swimming laps in a turquoise pool segues into her own obsessive love for food: "shimmering red heaps of sliced tomatoes / and translucent white slices of onion, / the picnic worship of salt, / the fruity granulation of sugared teeth." Yes, the swimmers leave the pool, their shoulders "drip-ping in jeweled elegance," and rejoice in frosty drinks, their mouths "ready for a summer feast." Suddenly, the poem turns formidable: eating is a metaphor for death, disease, and decay; things are "shoved into the mouth. Each bite / an attack on the liver. Each / sip an assault on the / kidney." The theme? "We eat in communion with waste / all we / eat is mud. The / swamp fills our mouth." Yet, the gorgeous July morning returns her to her "scrubbed" table, the croissants, the golden butter, the perfect egg, the mythic tea—all lovingly recorded as in a journal. Yes, the paradox remains: "each beauty, each / pleasurable sensation / is my death."

Lyn Lifshin also twirls the disquisition poem with éclat. In "Jackson Ave" she reports the news that her marriage, after ten months, remains unconsummated. She uses cats as a quasi-substitute for children she may never have. Her mother nags her, and presents Lifshin with a Gerber baby-food can and a sledge-hammer, declaring that if she really loved her mother, if she "weren't / like a crazy woman / with those cats," she'd "be getting ready" to need the baby food. In this same poem she fleshes out the truth, as a good poet/reporter would, by confiding in us that when her landlord comes to chop down lilacs she has to stuff her cats in the closet so he won't see she is violating her lease.

Elsewhere, Lifshin recollects herself twenty years earlier when she was fat and man-crazy, seated in a "Caddy," wearing an old-fashioned dress with a plum velvet belt. She chatters on, imagining herself an aged lady sitting on some sand dunes, "in a quilt of gulls," smelling "pines in wind / that's damp as skin," hugging the moon she hugged as a girl. Lifshin's mastery of the intense short-line form, the fertility of her imagination, and her lyric qualities differentiate her from most disquisitional poets who seem to care more for chatting up the reader than for artistry. Like Wakoski and Crusoe, Lifshin transcends the pitfalls of the genre—self-obsession, the prosaic recital of personal facts, and sentimentality.

East Coast Poems

This is a portmanteau designation for the work of poets clustered in or around New York City. New York boasts nearly all of the leading trade publishers in the country, has the best-paying and most visible of all journals publishing poetry (*The New Yorker*), is home to the ultraconservative Academy of American Poets and Poetry Society of America (with its yearly awards banquet), has the Columbia University Writing Program, the powerful *New York Times, Library Journal,* and *New York Review of Books,* contains old cemeteries crammed with the remains of once highly-regarded poets and a Poets Corner in the Cathedral of St. John the Divine, and boasts more poets per square foot than any other spot in America. Boston, Philadelphia, Baltimore, Oronoo, Concord, New Haven, Washington D.C., and spots further south are mere satellites.

New York's power over writers in America is historical, deriving from the eighteenth century when we imitated the British far more slavishly than we do today. America was small and the fount of culture was New York, in itself a shadow of London. Ambitious poets say that one must go to New York, attend publishers' parties, and meet editors, reviewers, and established poets who may respond to your charm or body (both quite distinct from the quality of your writing) in order to succeed. Two poets, I was recently told, declared that since they had reached their forties and their careers were languishing, decided to leave the boonies and plunge into the New York poetry scene. By all reports they are doing well.

No young poet reading this should be dismayed, for literature in America has always been dominated by New York. Poets who believe that if they write their hearts out in places like Otuma, Iowa; Blue Balls, Pennsylvania; Eagle River, Wisconsin; Laredo, Texas; or Citrus, California they will be heard—published, admired, given MacArthur awards and Pulitzer nominations—are misguided.

Ecology Poems

Since ecology poems deal with the destruction of the planet (albeit slowly) via acid rain, smog, and the despoliation of forests, waters, and arable lands by developers, lumber companies, and industrial wastes, they are related to nuclear poems. Gary Snyder is one poet who returns often to these themes; in fact, nearly all he has written either directly or indirectly condemns the wasting of our resources. His "The Call of the Wild" is an example:

> All these Americans up in special cities in the sky
> Dumping poisons and explosives. . . .
> When it's done there'll be
> > no place
> A coyote could hide.

Subtler but no less devastating complaints occur throughout Snyder's *Rip Rap*. In the second poem, he quotes Exodus 34:13 on the despoiling of "groves," then matter-of-factly records the logging off of ancient Chinese forests.

He next lays down a slab of lines making such despoliations contemporary:

> San Francisco 2 × 4s
> > were the woods around Seattle:
> Someone killed and someone built, a house,
> > a forest, wrecked or raised
> All American hung on a hook
> > & burned by men, in their own praise.

In the next poem, also a collage of times and events, he writes from the point of view of a lumberman operating a Caterpillar tractor, ruthlessly and efficiently leveling the firs.

Lawrence Ferlinghetti is no less anguished over the man-created plight of nature and its creatures. In "Rough Song of Animals Dying," from his *Endless Life: Selected Poems* he dreams of "the spinning meat-wheel world" as "a yin-yang yolk of good and evil / about to consume itself." We steal the lives of animals to slake our greed. Steer and seal clubbed to death in stockyards or on the Newfoundland icefields cry out with the same cry. Rare and exotic birds, odd reptiles "& weird woozoos," and rare beasts are captured for zoos "by bearded blackmarketeers / who afterwards ride around Singapore / in German limousines." He dreams of shrinking rainforests, polluted prairies, and contaminated mesas. He hears "all the animals crying out / in their hidden places / in the still silent places left to them. . . ." He dreams of the earth drying "in the famous Greenhouse Effect / under its canopy of carbon dioxide / breathed out by a billion / infernal combustion engines / mixed with the sweet smell of burning flesh." All this destruction, man destroying his own species, Ferlinghetti sees as an "Arrow of Time" flying "both ways / through bent space." There is no escape.

Arthur Lane's "Hooray for Canada," from *Handing Over,* takes the scalpel to those who club seals for money:

> they've finished the slaughter
> of the seals again:
> the right amount of money
> has changed hands into hooks
> hooks into clubs
> clubs into money, what else.
>
> as a recommendation for a species
> as a qualification for any of
> the lower orders of decency,
> the annual festival of
> bludgeoning and skinning—
> often alive, why not—
> a few more hundred thousand
> week-old unweaned . . .
> well, be serious.
>
> behold our man of action
> as he breaks the skull
> of one soft thing after another:
> the crunch of bone, of cartilage,
> of other stuff
> must sound like a cash-register
> ringing, ringing, till he can
> wade in blood like wading
> in gold coins in his paradise.

The motif of a universe despoiled by man is a potent undercurrent throughout Hayden Carruth's *Brothers, I Loved You All.* In his long poem "Vermont," he laments the cutting of white pines (they made the best ship masts in the world) and hungers for "that great classical time before the trees / departed." A more extensive indictment of developers and slaughterers meanders through his twenty-eight-part "Paragraphs." He decries that "the national mean" is taking over. Old covered bridges, dynamited, make way for ugly steel ones that will never float. A litany accretes: the passenger pigeon is gone, the last otter has disappeared from Otter Creek, Indian braves are castrated, their squaws stretched and "bayoneted up their vaginas." In "Paragraph 17" Carruth resorts to a poem "found" in a dictionary. His arrangement understates the enormity of his loathing for these ravagings:

RAVAGE, *v.t.* To lay waste; to subject
to depredations; to work havoc or devastation upon;
to sack; plunder; despoil. *Syn.*—
RAVAGE, DEVASTATE, SACK
agree in the idea of despoiling or laying waste.

"Essay" by its title prepares us for homily—Carruth does not intend to write subtle and sophisticated poetry. The destruction of animals disturbs him. He recalls a handful of poems on dead creatures: "Wilbur's toad, Kinnell's porcupine, Eberhart's squirrel. . . ." The latest such poem he reads is by Edwin Brock, about a dead fox.

Much of Michael McClure's work is ecstatically pro-environment. He writes both in direct complaint of the despoliations and wastings, and indirectly through his mammoth, vastly energized panegyrics to his own mammal feelings, feelings he shares with all living creatures. To display such joy in one's animal self is to assert that animals must be preserved as human frames of reference. Without them we would barely sense what a complete meat-being is.

McClure's "Slicks" and "Xes" are two memorable examples of direct and indirect ecology poems. Both are from *September Blackberries*. "Slicks" envisions a horrible oil spill washing the Bolinas tidal rocks as a huge "leprous vampire elephant." In this mess, cormorants are smeared with bulk oil, and "only their scarlet glittering eyes are clear."

"Xes—A Spontaneous Poem" is a twenty-eight-part threnody of spontaneous sexual joy stimulated by feeling at one with the natural universe. The poem, McClure writes, "is an act of nature." His wondrous zest for all life encompasses a myth of nature as a bonfire of diamonds forming in the earth, the dreams of lambs, the "nectar hungers" in moth brains, and the scratching of all living things on "the nothingness that floats / upon the edge," life that

> . . . Makes facing features, shapes,
> bumps, contrives itself, invents the images
>   it is.

He flashes on transcendent stars cooling, forming galaxies so immense they boggle the mind. In ecstasy, he returns to the finite world of human engineering and creativity and frames this "Social Tract": "THOU HAST KNOWN IT ALL / BEFORE! / NO DOUBT! / Sensory starvation! / STAND UP! / Being-Liberty!!!!!" These possibilities we must preserve, McClure implies. We must value the planet as an extension of ourselves: money and objects are ephemeral and destructive.

Ego Poems

Imagine the U.S. poetry scene as an enormous beehive divided into various regions. Each poet-bee works more or less in isolation, filling his or her cells with poet-nectar distilled into honey. Imagine the individual honey-cell as a poem. Imagine the individual worker bee behaving quite unapiarishly by insisting that he has a clone which is indeed a self, an ego, and which he hopes to reveal to the world in his honey deposits. So too, with these swarms of American poets who scatter "I"s throughout their poems with the abandon of untidy bees expelling their droppings wherever they please.

The "ego" poem, or the "I" poem, is the genre favored by most poets today, and especially by the younger products (yes, poetry in this country is big business) of our ubiquitous writing programs. R. S. Gwynn, in couplets reminiscent of Alexander Pope and Lord Byron (of the vicious satires), writes *The Narcissiad* to lambaste today's self-obsessed "ego" poets. Narcissus, he observes, has displaced Apollo and Dionysius as primary inspirations. At his dressing table, today's "latter-day Narcissus," finds inspiration from adoring his own physiognomy. He soon creates a school of followers:

> Among his postulants, no more requires
> A love of words or duty to the past
> Beyond the headlines of the Tuesday last,
> No binding strictures such as rhyme or meter
> Or any length in excess of his peter,
> The one tool of his trade he thinks so rare
> He keeps it to himself, and will not share.

He reads "gospels of the Self," finding lines therein that urge him to nurture his *angst*. His poems displace "thought" with a catalogue, his cats, grocery lists, favorite t.v. shows, and analysts. He regurgitates

>   page after page of mock-confession,
> Slightly surreal, so private, so obscure
> The critics classify his works as "pure,"
> Because, in digging through the endless chatter,
> They can't discern what is the subject matter,
> And so, instead of saying they don't get it,
> They praise the "structure" they invent to fit it.

Our "Younger Poet," seeking a role-model, imitates Robert Lowell, parading his personal suffering as he enters "therapy, shock-treatments, and divorce." Younger female poets model themselves after Plath and/or Sexton, sing of menstrual cramps at "over-fifty," and arrange "a lovely suicide":

Cookies laid out so that the kids, awaking,
Won't go downstairs to see their mummy baking
And grow up traumatized, unloved, unloving,
Hysterical at something from the oven.

Gwyn sardonically lathers "New York Poets," Helen Vendler, Richard Howard, John Ashbery, James Merrill, Daniel Halpern, and John Hollander. Eventually there's a bloody tryst as "Halpernus" faces "Merrilleus" for dominance of the New York poetry world.

Gwynn's entertaining romp continues for sixteen cantos, and I recommend that you obtain the whole from the publisher, Cedar Rock Press, if it is still in print. If it isn't it should be. "Ego" poets deserve all the notice of this sort that they can get.

A most blatant ego poem was written by Gerald Stern, currently chief honcho of the Iowa Writers Program. "Ice, Ice," (the title itself seems to be a pun on the "I" poem) devotes nearly half of its thirteen lines to first-person trivia before generating sentimental feelings over cave men in a cold cave—once they move back from the fire their tears turn to ice. The "horror" that stimulates these *ur-mensch* empathies is the news that Hubert Humphrey is dead.

In "Fritz," Stern regales us with the news that he's been listening to old recordings of the violinist Fritz Kreisler. Stern, naked, is full of genteel regret about never having known Kreisler. This poem would be much improved by thinning the "I" phrases. Trivia takes over. The last line suffers from "prepositionitis":

Tonight I am partly moody, partly in dread,
there is some pain in my neck, but I am still
possessed a little. I rush into the living room
to listen to either the Elgar or the Mendelssohn.

A recent issue of the now-defunct journal of the Poetry Society of America, *The Poetry Review,* is typical of most journals featuring ego poems. These opening lines, all chosen at random, clearly reveal the malady. I won't identify the authors:

"I don't know the names of things. . . ."
"I am too weak to leave the infirmary. . . ."
"I came to the Petrified Forest. . . ."
"I've not written an Aswan Dam poem."
"Whenever I bring her flowers she cries."
"The year I traced over pictures / in *Paradise Lost*. . . ."
"And so I capture / the sun on that bridge the cows. . . ."

Dan Gerber's book *Departures* is almost a parody of the form. Here is a sampling of Gerber's intensive and numerous first-person verbs: I've wanted . . . I've wasted . . . I've dreamed . . . I'd like . . . I've spent . . . I watch . . . I never learn . . . I've read . . . I know . . . I read . . . I'm rocked . . . I remembered . . . I imagine . . . I begin . . . I travel . . . I grow sad . . . I've acquired . . . I dream . . . I am loving a woman . . . I hold two fingers . . . I think . . . I have no use for . . . I've had a lot of unhappiness . . . I decided . . . I'll buy . . . I suffer . . . I don't know yet . . . I buried . . . I've forgotten . . . I covered . . . I'm back . . . I suspect . . . I'm tired of poems . . . I want . . . I'm not ashamed . . . I'm bored . . . I put on my trousers . . . I came to important things . . . I say goodbye.

Susan Mitchell, a Wesleyan poet, inside a solipsistic cave of small distinction takes refuge from a storm. She finds *Boone* (for Daniel Boone) carved into a rock (which she informs us is "hard"). As she waits, she senses that grass, stretching west, gains speed "like an animal running for the sheer / joy of running." This simile flops on its face—grass running? She zooms ahead and imagines Boone trapping, each of his traps "biting deeper / into the green absence of prairie." (Note the fancy abstraction.) And she conjures some solipsistic life-thoughts: "I lay there thinking," "I listened to the wind," "I prayed / to be unremembered as the dirt."

Michael Goodman's "Little Neck Bay," screams for deletions of ego phrases. I shall quote a few lines and then, much as I might revise a student poem, perform a few excisions. A word of warning: I know that some readers will find my presumption distasteful; to mess with another poet's poem is like altering God's handiwork. Here are Goodman's lines:

> Once, I saw a gull lying on a mound of kelp,
> its neck twisted. When I kneeled
> to stroke it, dogs barked. So I carried it home
> and buried it in the yard below three pine trees,
> spending all afternoon packing and smoothing the grave.
> That night I dreamed of wings, locked underground,
> flapping through dirt. But when I ran outside
> the ground was smooth there,
> covered with a thin frost and needles.
> Overhead, the tops of the pines swayed.
> I felt pulled. Then the kitchen windows lit up.
> Then I was shaking, and walking towards the water.

My revision:

> A gull with a twisted neck
> on a mound of kelp.
> Barking dogs.
> I knelt and stroked the gull,
> carried it home, burying it in the yard
> below three pine trees,
> spending all afternoon packing and smoothing the grave.
> That night wings flapped, locked underground,
> flapping through the soil. Outside,
> the ground was smooth and frost-covered.
> Fir needles.

Pine-tree tops swayed.
The kitchen windows lit up.
Shaking, I walked towards the water.

While I have not eliminated all first-person phrases (I like them when used sparingly), I have tightened the passage. I still don't care much for the trinity of fir trees at the burial site, nor for the image of a Christ-like self walking towards water, a kitsch transcendentalism.

Edward Hirsch's "Omen" which is ostensibly about a close friend, parades the poet's ego and self-pity; it is as sticky as treacle. Hirsch, lying on his side in the grass, drifts sleepily off. A cold October moon rises, staring with a "glassy" one-eye (stale, stale). Clouds gathering are an "omen." Hirsch can't stop thinking about his "closest friend" dying of cancer. "Thinking" directs Hirsch to himself when he was a boy on "immense" summer nights when the "stars were like giant kites, casting loose." Yes, he had his "cruel dreams" during rainstorms and had cough pains just as his friend has his pains, "a mule / Kicking him in the chest."

He presents even more hackneyed nature stuff—the wind "whispers a secret to the trees," hinting at a vague "something," all "stark and unsettling." Trembling and shedding leaves prepare us for a final stab of momentousness. He too will shiver, shudder, and die:

I know that my closest friend is going to die
And I can feel the dark sky tilting on one wing,
Shuddering with rain, coming down around me.

A recent anthology crammed shamelessly with ego poems is *The Morrow Anthology of Younger American Poets,* edited by Dave Smith and David Bottoms. I open the book at random and scrutinize several poems by different authors, seeking that rare entry eschewing the blatant ego. Each single line below is taken from a different poem. If this strikes my readers as tedious, I offer my apologies. I hope to make a point, and since this anthology features poets no older than the editors themselves, this means that we are listening to the voices of writers moving speedily into middle-age. These talents are now teaching the next generation of American poets:

Brad Leithauser: "The pleasures I took from life. . . ."
"Binoculars I'd meant for birds. . . ."

Rika Lesser: "I hold all of a dead / man in my round body."
"I have come here to walk the streets."
"I rush to the newspapers . . . I fly."
". . . in the *Tribune* I happened to read. . . ."

Larry Levis: "I still have a scar. . . ."
"I do not know even why. . . ."
"Once I was in love with a woman. . . ."
"When I was twelve, I used to stare at weeds."
"I think it is all light at the end."
"Sometimes, I go out into this yard at night. . . ."

William Logan:
　　　　　". . . the satin shirt I made you wear. . . ."
　　　　　"I measure the evil dates. . . ."

Susan Ludvigson" "I promised myself at nine. . . ."

In contrast to the negative assessments above, I would like to balance this chapter with some examples of well-written ego poems.

Tess Gallagher's "Painted Steps" (from *Willingly*) is a profound and highly personal poem. A lover is leaving, apparently for good, and Gallagher is anxious to accompany him, but knows she can't. Perhaps her independence has estranged him. Has she been insufficiently subservient? Now, if he would only stay, she declares, she would go submissively, like a farmer following his horse "to keep the rows straight." She invites her reader to see the man as she does:

> Think of me as one who lives things quickly,
> cruelly as a car could live it.
> Think of me as one who stands in the streets,
> speeding past with the stopped wheel
> in my hands, and the radio, its small heart
> flickering along the trees ahead.

In a poem called "Selves," Thom Gunn returns to the room of a former friend (or possibly a lover). One senses that a contretemps two years earlier terminated the friendship. What makes the poem rare, apart from Gunn's technical control, is its point of view: it focuses as much on Gunn himself as on the friend; the two are in exquisite balance. Gunn does not parade his own ego, and talks quietly and lovingly to the absent painter, who is younger than he. He speaks of the changes the latter has gone through—changes Gunn discerns in a self-portrait that required two years to complete and was begun immediately after the rupture. Gunn is nagged by "the new self," the "hard eyes," the rendering of which freed the artist of so much pain. Clearly, he has fashioned himself a new body, one visible in the painting—he's a weightlifter. Gunn now underplays powerful feelings. He misses what the friend was earlier, the "vulnerable and tender man" Gunn has dreamed of "three nights running." The issue between them was apparently dependency—Gunn the older man was revered as a father figure:

> 　　　　　　　I suppose
> it was an imaginary son
> that I held onto during this time
> of mess and understanding.
> But sons grow up,
> imaginary ones as well,
> and perpetual children are tedious.

Another first-rate poem of self is Gunn's "Talbot Road," an elegy on Gunn's straight friend Tony White.

Greg Kuzma's harrowing "The Night of January 12, 1978" (from *Of China and of Greece*) commemorates the death of an only brother in a violent car wreck. In a sense, this poem, like so many of Kuzma's, is "received," beginning as if we were standing in a room listening to him talk. His opening is effortless, and echoes a Wordsworthian truism that takes us into Kuzma's confidence: "Many beautiful things in the world" compete for our attention. There's no indication here of the incredible, almost Sophoclean pain to come.

When beauty overwhelms us, Kuzma writes, we turn inward, fearing that too much beauty will lead us to see the world as a disarming place rather than one which means little good and intends us great harm. Yet when he sees a jay at a feeder, a "necessity like thirst" invites meditation and poetry. Such a necessity guarantees that we shall never be smug or too comfortable. To write poetry worth anyone else's reading, we must be "at odds with life."

Kuzma next takes a sudden turn towards violence, effectively understating the painful triggering event with a parenthesis:

> Our deaths, after all, await us,
> casually in the future
> like so many newspapers left on porches,
> like car accidents, tragic yet
> compulsive (one just destroyed my previously
> invulnerable-seeming brother—twenty-five years
> old, who had fucked maybe only three or four
> women, and not all that well probably,
> who had written not one published poem—
> and who, in dying, has broken not only
> his mother's heart and his father's heart,
> which is somehow inevitable under the
> circumstances—but who has also destroyed
> my life, the one I've known these past 9 years. . . .)

The good poet must be "tested," must know that while rescuings may occur at the very edge of the precipice, they may also never occur. To embellish his point, Kuzma varies the orchestration of this important poem, descending, in the manner of Whitman, from a tragic intensity in a minor key to a reflective interlude, drawing the congenial reader into his private thoughts. These tonal shifts are one of Kuzma's hallmarks, and the often winsome inclusion of the reader/listener as an intimate presence (another hallmark) mitigates against the self-absorbing egotism of more solipsistic poets.

Clayton Eshleman, that speleologist of the self, relating his various visceral, sexual, inner-marrow selves to myths and archetypes, is another poet who often transcends the ego poem. In "Winding Windows," from *Hades in Manganese*, he fuses playful elements with a ghostly prehistoric animal deep within his psyche. The fourth stanza, alas, might better have been edited out:

I am and I am and I am. Like cake
all day long, or crucifusion 24 hours
a night. To pounce from am to am,

to a.m. p.m., to enter the word *enter*
with smoking moss lamp—it seems
that the full ghost presence of the animal

15,000 years ago is the condition
poetry ever since has,
when it is wild with vision, sought

to mate to manganese,
where a tongue mire in I wheel
can't move

winces against the rational
afternoon, the bounce off bounce in,
eye to object, that sterile reminder of

what life would be without
orphan wee wee, the looney hues
that later sight to the chord

climbers of the family vine
romance with which my ear and its honeyed
grotto, layered with dead, is rowed.

Charles Plymell sees his "I" poems as "flashlights" of the self. His odyssey as wanderer, like those of his fellow-Beats Kerouac, Cassady, Ginsberg, and Corso, ranges the breadth and width of America. Each of his locales, whether in the Midwest (he hails from Kansas), in the East and South, or in San Francisco, are all installments in the "news" of his life, his intimate journal. He is both proletarian and a poet of aesthetic purity. His universe is that of underground dopesters, jazz heads, hookers, and protesters. One can imagine Plymell entering William Burroughs's Dr. Benway's Waiting Room of the Doomed Universe, hoping for relief. Once in the Doctor's presence, however, patient–doctor roles are reversed—Plymell is something of a trickster. He will zap Benway and depart the loathsome office self-restored to health. In "Surrealization of Dreams" Plymell sees the world through his own kaleidoscope. Here he expresses a deep personal fear of science:

I'm afraid of science
afraid to point my head north
that the one-sided guinea pig will die.

I'm afraid of the streets at night
that a landslide of barking grease will
chase me past the carbon copy of the blue light.

His defiance of forces in a world gone mad provides an insulating cocoon for those he loves. In "You Fill in the Blanks" (p.47), he overcomes a blue funk by going for a long drive in upstate New York. Back home, in longjohns, he listens to Hank Williams through earphones. The setup almost cries for self-pity, something Plymell avoids by speculating on matters other than himself—a milkweed sleeve, a moon rising as the sun sets:

> And I didn't know
> where the magnetized needle
> would take the full moon
> burning outside my window.
> Maybe a slight reading of biorhythms
> would produce a flight pattern
> into that milkweed sleeve
> the crimson sunset lined aganst the space where I
> could not aim my gliding flocks of memory. . . .

Other fine writers of the ego poem include Charles Bukowski, Leo Connellan, Andrew Glaze, Si Perchik, James Broughton, Allen Ginsberg, Harold Norse, and Paul Vangelisti.

Vangelisti's poetic sensibility is an original and fascinating mix of European tones and styles and his own American craft. He is an authoritative translator and critic of contemporary Italian poetry and has edited a translation of Polish writers. For years he has coedited *Invisible City* and Red Hill Press books. He founded the arts and literary journal *Boxcar.*

Most of his poetry to date has the appearance of being in the ego mode—except for some early collage poems and his recent poem "Villa," a stunning excursion into voices in an epistolary mode: the Emperor Hadrian's secretary G. Suetonius Tranquillus writes a series of letter-poems to various friends, who function as disguises for Vangelisti's circle of poets and artists. I shall quote here from *Air,* first published in 1973, which represents Vangelisti's original tempering of the ego poem, hoping to show how an insufficiently known poet is able to use this mode to create poetic art.

The brief lyric "Style," revealing Vangelisti's highly personal view of poetry, demonstrates his ability to conceal his emotions behind a cool texture of sounds, cadences, and images. The *I* is present by implication. Each line is depersonalized. There are few logical transitions. Yet, in a painterly way, the visual matter is sufficiently precise to prevent the poem's drifting off into whiteness and abstraction. At the same time, "style" is "air," is "free of words," implying an aesthetic purity or distance removed from direct emotion. It's as if Vangelisti wants his poem to breathe so that it numbs or erases the self. What do we see with this cool, detached vision? Street details that fumble and slouch with weight and age: bag-ladies, sandbags, screams. Realism. We feel located . . . but not for long. The ending is mysterious. Someone "enters the glass / and begins to eat." Is the devourer the poet? Is he the reader? I see the eater as a poet who penetrates the "glass" of experience, ravishes it with his knife/words/ego, and proceeds to feast:

    of high heels
    twirl empty streets
    or cloud
    plunge into the air
    free of words
    of suitcases of words
    lift a knife how one
    slices the window
    no shoes but bobby socks
    bundles of old women
    like sandbags
    scream who enters the glass
    and begins to eat

Such writing fuses imagism with surrealism. The blend produces a poem seldom seen in American verse. Most poets elide words for the sake of heightened tensions within their lines; Vangelisti elides tenses, agreement structures, and thereby *constructs* freshly.

Here Vangelisti writes a simple love poem:

Poem for the Wind Poem for Margaret

    bush of hair
    girl's hair
    growing on mother's bone
    breathing
    your shallow navel
    drifts easily as if I
    turned away for a second
    it rises on a low wind
    ripple over you
    bush of a girl's hair
    and disappear

The poem is intimate, lovingly surreal—the movement of the girl's body is a "low wind" rippling, breathing. Vangelisti, aroused, turns for a second from admiring the girl and finds his emotions more delicate even than before. The style is a mix of the strangely depersonalized and the poet's ego. Breath-motion is the primary image. Allusions to bone and wind are quiet, surreal devices.

In a final example, "Deadline," Vangelisti again writes an ego poem, but through his tight lines seen almost as single poems in their own right, and without conventional transitions, oddly neutralizes his private emotions.

Deadline

first the wobbly mattress
Three flights up
into abstraction
heaved here sagging
of voice dog-tired
scissor cough like no cymbal
day in day out to objects
of the personal sit
glue pot and headline
ashes ashes
rumor don't fit
in the schoolyard of what was
windy as China
was promised the gust
of a woman in my arms
simply learning to walk

Epic Poems

Poets grumble among themselves that the epic form is dead, and, yet, if one casts about, numerous modern classics qualify in scope, sweep, and brilliance of technique as epics. Among them are William Carlos Williams's *Paterson*, Ezra Pound's *Cantos*, Hart Crane's *The Bridge*, Louis Zukovsky's *A*, Charles Olson's *Maximus Poems*, Basil Bunting's *Briggflats*, St. John Perse's *Anabase*, David Jones' *In Parenthesis* and *Anathema*, Charles Reznikoff's *Testimonies*, and Sharon Doubiago's *Hard Country*.

Ezra Pound Poems

That giant of modernism, Ezra Pound, has inspired numerous poets to model their styles after his. Among those who have actually written poems to Pound are Robert Lowell, Elizabeth Bishop, Sam Hamill, Charles Wright, and Bill Knott. Bishop's "Visits to St. Elizabeths: 1950," by echoing the structure of the nursery rhyme "This Is the House that Jack Built," ironically condemns the authorities for incarcerating Pound in Washington's St. Elizabeth's mental hospital after World War II. Pound she sees as an "old, brave man," a "cranky man," a "cruel man," a "busy man," a "tedious man," and, finally, a "wretched man."

Like Randall Jarrell and John Berryman, Bishop was taken to St. Elizabeth's to visit Pound by Robert Lowell—who made regular visits. Lowell wrote amusingly irreverent letters to Pound, in one of them (March 30, 1954) telling the old poet that his "Idaho humor" was "hardly the Tuscan of Ovid. . . . sometimes I think you were born in Sioux City instead of Venezia." Lowell's biographer Ian Hamilton prints a "mischievous parody" of Pound, probably included with this letter: "Adolf Hitler von Linz (Siegfried)." Hamilton finds Lowell's poem "too fidgety to make much continuous sense" and "quite clearly *not* a celebration of the Nazi 'dumkopf.'" He quotes the poem, hitherto unpublished.

Charles Wright, author of numerous "academic abroad" poems specializing in Italian settings, begins his "Homage to Ezra Pound" in true academic abroad fashion by reciting the names of Venetian locales as though the names in themselves are magical—as perhaps they are, to American poets abroad. He reaches the street where Pound dwells. Wright neither knocks on the door nor peeps in at the windows, preferring to project his feelings from the street, as the old man lies upstairs, waiting to die: "unspeaking, unturned—he waits, / Sifting the cold affections of the blood." Do, reader, appreciate the classy lit'rary turn, which deprives Wright of his own authentic feelings in favor of contrived, fancy phraseology. Pound appears either to be in a rest home, or a villa so old generations have already died there. Pound, though, is a survivor, and Wright imagines him sitting in his "muffled rooms, / Wondering where it went bad," listening to the splash of a gondola's oar and rustling sea-bird wings. In homage to the old poet, Wright injects cope-and-mitre moments of "prophesy" and an atmosphere "filled with unanswered prayers." He offers Pound "caul and caustic" and what appears to be a shroud—"your garment," before closing off with a pompous cope-and-mitre motif of the resurrection: "Rise and be whole again."

The best of these poems belong to Bill Knott and Sam Hamill. Knott's "Penny Wise" appears in *Becos*. Pound would have loved to hear this imitation of his own voice and would have relished the humor in Knott's closing:

> well alright
> I grant you
> he as a fascist
> ahem antisemitism the
> er war and all
> I'm not defending them
> but at least
> you've got to admit
> at least he
> made the quatrains run on time

Hamill writes succinctly and movingly of Pound's grief, as he reads it in Avedon's photograph of the poet:

> . . . Pound's face was cracked
> with age and grief, the immeasurable pain
> of his learning. Wrong from the start, perhaps
> he remembered Rome Radio, the anti-
> Semitic cracks he snapped in anger,
> what made him believe Mussolini.
>
> Even tears can't wash away those words and wounds.
> Pound wept, and he grieved, and grew silent. What hurt
> hurts still, though he is ten years buried.
> Memory and pain. *What thou lovest well remains.*

Fairy-Tale Poems

Fairy tales have been with us since childhood, and as adults we are still inclined to see much of our world in their terms. When poets adapt old fairy tales or write new ones, the good witch does not always succeed in putting things right. The prince may not awaken Snow White. The frog may remain a frog, no matter how much the princess kisses him.

One of the most fascinating of all nineteenth-century fairy tale poems is Christina Rossetti's "Goblin Market," a unique excursion into lesbianism, far ahead of its time. Rossetti's sisters are seduced in a wood by a group of goblins, dirty little men, who squeeze "juices" from their fruits all over the girls' faces. The sister who manages to withstand their assaults cuddles up with another sister to dissuade her from giving in to these sinister little creeps.

In our own time, Anne Sexton's volume of sharply satirical reworkings and adaptations of fairy tales from Grimm, *Transformations* is notable. And some of Randall Jarrell's best poems were inspired by fairy tales: "A Hunt in the Black Forest," "The One Who Was Different," and "The House in the Wood." Much of James Broughton's early poetry (see *A Long Undressing*) continually echoes the Brothers Grimm in an original, dazzling style. In his "Backyard Elegies," a child addresses a misbehaving apple:

> What are you doing here, little apple?
>   The blossoms are faded,
>   the leaves are no more,
>   the cart's gone to market,
>   the worm's in the core,
>   God's left for the winter,
>   the world's a backdoor.
> Where are you rolling to, little apple?

In "Little Boy's Nasty News," a miserable lad, kin to Strewelpeter, possessed of a pimple, now finds a wart on his fingers, "baubling" them with "tell-tale bumps." He seems to have erred according to adult standards—has played (perhaps sexually) with a "nasty" boy. In "Sweet-Tooth Witch," a not-so-generic witch inverts adult values, to the delight of all recalcitrant children. This creature eats only *good* little girls. If you wish to be spared being eaten, misbehave. What a contrast to the genteel behavior extolled by Robert Louis Stevenson in *A Child's Garden of Verses* where children are encouraged to be proper and mindful of their elders!

Denise Levertov's "Four Embroideries" improvise on fairy tales. The first poem is about Rose Red and Rose White; the second is inspired by a tale from Andrew Lang, "Catherine and her Destiny"; the third, "Red Snow," is about a man who, "crippled with desire," seeks to turn snow red in a denial of his cold white hands and cold spirit; the fourth seeks to reanimate a "lost poem" of "cows and people wending / down mountain slowly / to wooden homesteads." The title poem of the volume, "Relearning the Alphabet," is scattered with allusions to princesses, magical and holy forests, magical moons, seas, ladies, and knights.

To Phyllis Janik ("Red Shoes," in *No Dancing, No Acts of Dancing*) the red shoes of fairy tales and legends are images for color, originality, and sexual power. She sees arguments against wearing red shoes—"the dancer in the movie / jumped in front of the train, wearing them." On the other hand, Dorothy could return from the Emerald City only if she wore her red slippers. Also, she saw other girls made "instantly beautiful" wearing "wine red boots" laced to their knees. She's waited for years without finding the pure red pair for her—those who know color discern touches of blue in hers. She imitates Red Riding Hood, as an easily wrought "image," with a red hood cape hiding her shoes. The hidden shoes now become cosmological, symbolizing those combinations of unlike things constituting magical moments in our lives: "dancer, Dorothy, ruby, satin, blue/red shoes."

While much of Diane Wakoski's work is informed by allusions to real fairy tales, and by others she invents, no book of hers is more skillfully wrought using such materials, often accompanied by madness, violence, and pain, than *Coins and Coffins*. The poems are rife with gold, jewels, and a menagerie of animals—mating black and white foxes, a hawk who picks out a speaker's eyes and then nestles against her "bleeding face," a blue tiger with a marigold in his mouth, spiders weaving webs aglitter in the sun, a magical lion, and a silver-scaled fish. Perhaps the finest poem is "Coins and Coffins Under My Bed." A trio of children, dancing around an orange tree, is addressed by spiders who ask whether they prefer silver coins or silver cups. As the children decide how to respond, the spiders busily expand their webs:

> Three children dancing around an orange tree.
> They are heavy with childhood.
>> We want silver rings to link us together
>> and silver keys to unlock your webs,
>> and we all know our names.
>> they are John.

Quietly, under the orange tree, David, who is dead and buried, settles
    down.
The spiders walk over the earth like tight-rope walkers
playing above the crowd,
and I forget the coffin under my bed.

Marilyn Hacker's sequence "The Snow Queen" (*Assumptions,*), con-
tains impressive improvisations inspired by Hans Christian Andersen's
fairy tale of the same name, with pronounced lesbian overtones. There's
nothing anachronistic or fey here. The witch, the little robber girl, and
Gerda all have their say in wise language.

Victor Contoski also writes fairy-tale poems. One of the most original
is "Dictionary Poem," which borrows the vague temporality of fairy tales
("many many years ago"); the motif of lovers—although here they are
bored; the invention of a monster (the Dictionary); national upheaval
(war is waged over the Dictionary); magical events (the Dictionary flies
like a kite); and resurrection (the Dictionary returns as a vampire from
the dead and must finally be killed with a stake through its heart).

1.

Many many years ago
a man and a woman
both naked
got into bed
and found they had nothing
at all to say to each other.

Still naked they arose
went to their desks
and began writing a dictionary.

2.

It began with a.
By the time it reached
the middle of the alphabet,
it was already jaded.

Yet what could it do but go on?

3.

When Mary Sue used the dictionary
it wanted to close on her breasts.
But she wanted the meaning of *egregious*.

4.

When the state waged war
in its name
it marched in protest
shouting: lies, lies!

But nobody recognized it!

5.

As it grew older the dictionary
envied the distance of the stars.
It grew bitter at its own altruism.

6.

One March day a man tied a string
to each corner of the dictionary.
He took it to an open field,
let out ten feet of string,
and ran as fast as he could.

the dictionary rose in the wind.
It lifted him above the clouds;
it fell on his head and killed him.

7.

The man and the dictionary
were buried together.
From his grave grew a red, red rose
and from its grave a briar.

8.

But the dictionary did not die.

It rose from its grave at the full moon,
entered the library through an open window
and settled in the poetry section.

Each night it lay on a different book
kissing it and sucking its blood
until the librarian found out.

He buried the dictionary in the reference room
with a stake through its heart.

Since fairy tales are fables, "Dictionary Poem" can be read as an intriguing indictment of the ossification (or entombment) of language for political and social power. Establishments fight over the sanctity of their words. The dictionary frees itself and becomes a figure of vengeance, sucking blood from volumes of poetry—which originally sucked words from it.

Father Poems

The wealth of poems on fathers is amazing. Hardly a single journal issue appears without them, and nearly all poets write them. It seems a genre peculiar to our time. Can you think of any father poems by Eliot, Pound, or Yeats? Or by Tennyson, Christina Rosetti? By Browning, Longfellow, Amy Lowell, or Edna Millay?

The phenomenon is related to that of the confessional poem which came into its own after World War II, via Plath, Lowell, and Snodgrass, and was also inspired by W. H. Auden and Dylan Thomas. A poet's personal history became primary subject matter—even poems on other matters were filtered through the spectrum of the author's self. The ego poem, or first-person poem, became faddish, and is still with us, as is obvious when we glance through the spate of recent anthologies featuring work by poets forty-five and younger: Smith and Bottoms's *Younger American Poets,* Myers and Weingarten's *New American Poets of the 80's,* and Heynen's *The Generation of* 2000.

If one believes that personal history is valuable ore for writing, one believes that no matter how humdrum and plain it is it will automatically interest readers. Also, the myth persists (and perhaps it is sentimental) that our parents were themselves mute inglorious Miltons who may have wanted to write but were too preoccupied putting food on the family table, or were ill-educated, or wasted by booze or cancer. A successful poet-son or poet-daughter, by writing up old dad or mom, helps adjust the scales by awarding the parent some recognition, usually posthumous. And it doesn't seem to matter whether dad was an old bastard who beat you or who abandoned the family. Also, it seems true that most of us have unfinished business, as the psychologists say, with our parents, particularly with our fathers, and we perform our personal archeology, turning up relics of hate, disgust, disappointment, and failure. Through our poems, we hope to exorcise these unearthed goodies.

Many father poems allow the male writing them to return to childhood; most of these are recollections of, and often valentines to, dad for having taught us to hunt, to like sex, to fish, and to develop carpentry and other male skills. More men than women seem to write like this; yet, as we shall see, some of the most powerful father poems are by women. Obviously, I have space only to point out a few of these; some succeed and some fail.

Typical of the weaker poems is Kirk Robertson's "My Father." The situation is almost generic—son, grown, realizes that he and pop were never close; in fact, pop split when the kid was "8 or 9 or 10." He would turn up once a year, stay in a L.A. motel near the airport, see the son, and then disappear. When he was in his early twenties Robertson received a letter scrawled on half a sheet of paper in which the dad said: "i guess i haven't been much / of a father / & perhaps i've developed / a jaundiced attitude toward things. . . ." Sure, mom writes that dad *got* jaundice from boozing. No more contact. Robertson was too busy avoiding the draft. One day they found pop sitting in his old clunker of a car, in Santa Ana, "as dead as a battery." To Robertson's credit he avoids sentimentality, except by implication, where the neutral tone seems sufficiently self-conscious and hard-boiled to call up its opposite.

A powerful poem on the theme is Charles Plymell's "In Memory of My Father." His father loved the prairie, settling there and living out his Kansas vision, one that Plymell lacked. To him the Kansas windmills told a "listless joy." If life is not beautiful, all is lost:

> . . . those bison of the clouds
> were pushed from life . . . slaughtered for sport . . . now they are the
> storm clouds watching us from eternity and far beyond.

Plymell does not realize his father has aged—he never thought he would die. The funeral: the "slap, slap, slap of tires on the grey concrete" leading to the cemetery. The death occurred shortly before Plymell and his wife and newborn baby arrived for Christmas:

> Skull of memory, how will your lamp burn now?
> How will the dust, like pages scorch that canopy of bone?
> How will those eyes rest against the dark storm of tears now,
> when ozone rests on sage, calming that stampede of time?

Plymell stands at his grave:

> You were always young and built the fence for your daughter's horse.
> Lifting beams bigger than railroad ties . . . against the doctor's orders.
> Post hole diggers left in the holes of prairie sod never used again.

Another fine father poem appears in Vern Rutsala's *Walking Home from the Icehouse*. The book is a classic memoir of rural small town and farm life fifty years ago. In "The Icecold Freight" (the longest poem in the volume), Rutsala remembers his father's love for country music, the aching meticulousness with which he built the family house, and his illness. Recollected too are the freight train cars packed with meat and vegetables on ice—this was before refrigeration. The train is Death. The father feared the train, was "gunshy" of it, and knew that there are "no second chances."

As Rutsala ages and returns to the site of the old home, remembered sorrows overwhelm him, and in a deep moment he hears the "icecold freight" nearby warming up. The old father is dying in his bed. The son trims the man's nails. The ensuing exclamation is moving and touched with irony: "We built a house together!"

Joel Oppenheimer's father was a railroad man, like those of the Chilean poet Pablo Neruda and the American painter Franz Kline. "The Boys Whose Father" is crammed with vivid boyhood memories:

> . . . my own father
> who rode the commuter/s local
> every day even if business was bad—
> but i remember we, then, were
> hooked bad enough we went down
> to ludlow station, why?, to watch
> the twentieth century—and the
> pacemaker came through, i think
> at 4:17; and, also, from either
> station house high over tracks or
> the railroad bridge a half
> mile down, or even from the
> embankment between, we played
> our games and watched to see
> the trains come through . . .
> and from the same high bridge once
> we pissed on some late afternoon
> locals, boys whose peters hung
> themselves out beyond the bridge/s
> edge and arc-ed the fine streams
> for all we had to offer—but
> never no rocks thrown as now i
> find they do. . . .

He declares to Neruda that while most fathers die "poor dirt farmers," theirs were special, being railroad men, for they had some "piece of themselves to" pass on—"a big gold watch," photographs—from the days when the central ran on time. Such fathers are now few—"trading off for / astronauts, oh / casey jones."

Ed Ochester's "Changing the Name to Ochester" is, Ochester writes, "about forgiving Grandpa—for my not knowing him." His grandfather early on abandoned his family. Now, forty years later, Ochester can forgive:

> Nearly twenty years since your death, father,
> and long ago I've forgiven you, and I think
> you did love me really, and who am I, who was born
> as you said "with everything," to condemn
> your bitterness toward your father who left you
> with nothing?

Edward Field's "Night Song" is a fresh variation on the father theme. As he himself ages, and gets up at night to urinate, he becomes his father, "an old man going to the bathroom, / joyless, miserable, grim— / even my urine smells like him." The transformation is most disturbing: he feels as if his dad has crawled under his skin: "Oh, how I dislike in the night becoming him." When Field turns on the light to write his poem he is himself again:

> But I'm irrevocably awake and tossing till dawn,
> thinking of every stupid thing I've ever done,
> and though I have to desperately, not getting up to pee—
> Oh, how I hate it, hate it, being me.

In "The Meadow," Raymond Carver recalls the undertaker's asking his mother if she wanted to bury his dad in an entire suit, or just the coat. "But, hey," Carver writes, "he went / into the furnace wearing his britches." He examines a photo of the "heavyset guy" in his last year, holding a huge salmon. "My dad. / He's nothing now. Reduced to a cup of ashes / and some tiny bones." Carver's response? He lies down in a late summer field in "sweet grass," closes his eyes, listens, and dreams, glad he's there and not dead. Carver manages a touching mix of vulnerability, toughness, humor, and acceptance. His understatement in treating so bone-close a theme is a model for other poets thinking of writing these personal elegies.

Larry Levis, in a stunning poem called "Winter Stars," attempts to reconcile himself to his long-dead father. He's always assumed that since his dad was a man of few words, what passed between them unsaid was "pure, like starlight." But, since becoming a poet he's come to believe in words "the way a scientist / Believes in carbon, after death." Three-quarters of the poem is addressed to the reader, the last part to his father, a successful strategy. He doesn't busy himself telling his dead father all that he knows (as if he is up somewhere in the stars still sentient), the way lesser poets do, in order to convey information to the reader.

Levis recounts an incident in which his father broke a man's hand by cracking it over the exhaust pipe of a John Deere tractor. The man was going to kill his own father with a fruit knife. The hand broken, the act over, Levis's father ate his lunch, "& then, as always, / Lay alone in the dark," listening to Vivaldi. He never again mentioned the affair. Levis sees his father's slow death as an echo of his silence: "Something / Inside him is slowly taking back / Every word it ever gave him." When Levis talks to his father, the latter seems to be searching for some lost syllable. Nothing gets said.

Now Levis addresses his father directly, informing him that he's in the Midwest, and that it's cold. But it's also cold in that "purple haze of stars," and empty—"Cold enough to reconcile / Even a father, even a son." Another fine father poem by Levis is "To a Wall of Flame in a Steel Mill, Syracuse, New York, 1969."

James Tate's "The Lost Pilot" is a classic father poem. Tate was born in 1943, only five months before his father, aged twenty-two, was reported missing over Germany on his last mission. Tate's simply written, triplet stanzas underplay the enormity of his loss: none of his father's remains were ever found. "Your face did not rot / like the others," Tate informs him. Tate has just seen the copilot, now aging, with a face like "corn-mush," apparently brain-damaged. His wife and daughter, "the poor ignorant people, / stare as if he will compose soon."

Again, Tate takes comfort that his father's face did not rot—"it grew dark, / and hard like ebony." He imagines his father in a "compulsive" orbiting, and if Tate could bring him down he'd "read his face" the way Dallas his gunner would have to, blinded as he was in the war. The confrontation would be totally private. Tate's grief, underplayed, is enormous. His fantasy that the father spinning across the "wilds" of space resembles a "tiny, African god" leaves him feeling "dead." With his head "cocked toward the sky," Tate can't leave the ground, as the father passing once again overhead, "fast, perfect, and unwilling / to tell me what you are doing," seems about to reveal what egregious mistake created the "misfortune" that "placed these worlds in us."

In "The Desk," David Bottoms' anxiety to repossess his father leads him to the high school where the father was a star halfback and sprinter. He breaks into the school, and with a flashlight finds the desk top with his dad's name carved deep into it, allows himself a sentimental moment or two, then runs his finger "across that scar." He wonders about his father's dreams, imagining that while he was etching his name his mind was really out there on the "empty practice field." Then, fortunately, Bottoms deflects what threatens to turn bathetic—he kneels. We assume he'll pray, which would logically follow his earlier sentimental thoughts. But quickly, Bottoms stands his flashlight on end, hammers off the desk top, and takes it home. He still possesses it, an "oak scar" leaning against his basement wall.

In Robert Pack's "Father," a son, abandoned by his father, confronts his lingering hatred. "You left my mother to me like a bride. / To take your place, I shut off all my tears. / And with your death, it was my grief that died". The son dreams that the father, rotting, finds among the worms the son's embryo, which he puts on a hook. The father fishes, using the son's embryo for bait.

Leo Connellan's *The Clear Blue Lobster-Water Country* presents a hero, Bobbledock, a descendant of Irish-Catholic Boston immigrants, who moves from a wretched childhood, through alcoholism and detoxification, to a final period where he goes to San Salvador and dies. Throughout, Boppledock, a stand-in for Connellan, is irrepressably and obsessively dedicated to putting himself right with a brutal father. There is also a younger brother, Billy, always the success Boppledock never was.

The first section, "Coming to Cummington to Take Kelly," in Boppledock's adolescent voice, is written in short stanzas of varying lengths. Boppledock hears his dead father screaming, the father so enraged he chews on a handkerchief, pulling one from his pocket just as he screams "like a man having his arm / cut off without anesthesia." The father's death itself is understated:

You just fell down
in front of a garage, the
cold stained concrete
grease like black blood
was your bed when you
hit that great bald head to death.

Throughout, Connellan employs a poignant refrain: Boppledock speaking to his father says: "We'll meet again. / You can tell me you love me then."

Though women have not felt as compelled as men to write about their fathers, many have. The most famous poem of all, I would guess, is Sylvia Plath's "Daddy," one of the harshest condemnations of a father ever written. Diane Wakoski's absent father appears in many of her poems. In her seminal "George Washington Poems," one poem in particular, "The Father of My Country," is a private and searing confrontation with her own father. The myth of George Washington provides Wakoski with an ironic distance from which to view her own father—shortly, though, the true nature of her psychological pain emerges.

Tess Gallagher has also written movingly about her father. In one of her longest pieces, "Boat Ride," from *Willingly*, she recalls a girlhood early-morning fishing trip for salmon. We see the preparations, the river, the catching of loathsome dogfish rather than salmon, the father's lack of faith in the survivabiliy of either spirit or body, and the lively play of Gallagher's imagination (the boat's chugging motor suggests "pigtails" and "cello"). Her role as a woman is complex: she must see to it that her young friend, a visiting New Yorker, catches fish; she must also humor her father, providing an affectionate gentleness (this proves to be her last fishing trip with him). When he asks for his billfold as if "even his belongings might be pulled into / the vortex of what would come," she anticipates his coming death from cancer. Later, after his death, Gallagher's mother brings out his old silk vest, and cleans it. Women are survivors. They spread the garment on the kitchen table, smooth it, examine it, the mother declaring: " 'that's one thing I never / wanted to be . . . a man.' " Gallagher puts the shiny jacket on and goes into the bathroom to see how she looks:

     Wind chimes
off-key in the alcove. Then her
crying so I stood back in the sink-light
where the porcelain had been staring. Time
to go to her, I thought, with that
other mind, and stood still.

Feminismo Poems

A "feminismo poet" may or may not be a feminist, though she is inclined to see the two sexes in conflict and both drawing vigor from their wars. She may suspect men as lesser but threatening creatures. Like Adrienne Rich, such women can imagine a universe where men are expendable, except as producers of sperm. And if scientists eventually create sperm from oyster tissue, ram gonads, or rooster marrow, there would be no need for males at all. The "feminismo poet," on the other hand, finds her very identity in sexual wars. She is most alive when in conflict with males; or, to be more accurate, since her experience with men is usually dismal and painful, she assumes that the men she attracts will betray her.

Amazingly enough, a woman has written the best poem I have seen on machismo behavior, and it may be useful to present it here, since it is generally inaccessible and will set parameters for my discussion to follow. In Arlene Stone's "Harley" (in *The Double Pipes of Pan,*) the portrait is so thorough one might even suspect Stone herself of having taken a mighty spin on the vehicle.

Harley

"It's only Low Rider, you and the open road"
    (From a Harley Davidson ad)

Masturbating its own length
the open road swells & extends

Safe in your matched leathers
the scarred hide fuming
buckhorn handlebars aimed
lone as a sailor at sea
lashed to the mast between your legs
a stump of custom iron

Junk food stops
Hot & cold blondes
Parades of T-shirts opening
easy as picked locks
dynamite days pulse-pounding as Dolly Parton
& the ocean's blue clitoris
        riding the pink sugar dunes

Toward evening rain
as the wasted sun
finds a cheap motel to party in

Night's chilled beer cans foaming over
Nights that fizz with stars
Night   the long-stemmed babe
in a short mildewed towel
Night   the ice machine that vomits
diamonds   hearts & bad-ass doobies

You party with Night
the black-mustachioed Paladin
Nine wins in a row
"Nine spoke wheels spinning you forward"
You lose your old lady at cards
You lose your partner to some bad speed

Back of the eight-ball   Harley
luck grabbing your balls
every motel a dump
a toothless mother in every driveway
her bones poke through her housedress
like No Vacancy signs

& the rats
the rats as white as sand
rats in your tool kit
rats in your gear
rats that chew through your beer cans
faster than a church key

the miles bumpy now
grip greasy with pork rinds
& behind each job
the pigs in their cages
tuning in to radar
Behind each bend the dog packs
ropes to lassoe your kidneys
or bite your wheels

Beside you the skeleton rides
yelling *Seig Heil*
The sun leaks like Three Mile Island
Wolf jowels rainburst the clouds
You twist full throttle

    Sixty
        Seventy
            Eighty
                Ninety
the sky a greying black mustache
                      One hundred
                    One ten

The roadsides closing in a zippering fly
the bike in its teeth
throbbing

Few poets write as many feminismo poems as Diane Wakoski. Her province is utterly female, seemingly filled with little bushes quivering with vaginas craving penises. Wakoski is the Bodicea of modern poetry; her country behaves according to her rules and obsessions. And that is one of the strengths of her writing, the presence of an original private mythology. She presides over her males—the Motorcycle Betrayer, the King of Spain, and the Receiving Man from Sears—imperiously yet vulnerably. Like the Queen of Swords she smiles, yes, with great charm, and her sword, though in its scabbard, is easily brought to the ready.

In "Ladies, Listen to Me," (*Smudging*), a poem with a Carrie Nation-esque title, Wakoski instructs ladies in the cultivation of *feminismo* (my term) with a vengeance. She begins by splitting herself in an Ovidian (Ovarian?) manner: she *snakes up* on herself as a cottonmouth snake (ho! shades of D. H. Lawrence, that female sensibility). Are we in a Garden of Eden where Diane-Eve invents her own phallus in order to achieve self-awareness?

While the secret she shares with her "ladies" is not exactly clear, and is something that "only a few men have / and all women, if they are not soft and spoiled and foolish / could have," it seems to relate to female strength as a counter to male strength: woman must not be yielding, submissive, "soft." Eve maintained "iron gates against the body," transforming both body and mind into coiling springs.

Wakoski delights in this tough image: Diane, not of the gentle, lambent moon, but of motorcycles and stark sexual conflict, a Leather-Jacket Queen relishing her femininity. Woman, she feels, is "the soft encasing iron" seen, however, by most males as a softness *they* (as iron) enclose. This image is central to her work. Despite the swagger, Wakoski has a vulnerable, ingratiating, and feminine nature.

Beneath many of the poems resides a female persona obsessed with keeping a penis close and, preferably, erect. If Wakoski threatens an attractive male, the struggle, even if it ends disastrously, is worth it. Better this engagement, with its attendant bitterness, rage, and pain, than a cockless life. When men are absent, Wakoski's archetypal woman feels useless.

In a poem from the George Washington series, "Crossing the Delaware," the gender conflict is stark. Wakoski, barefoot, enters a boat with razor blades inserted in the bottom. "George," the lover, has informed her that peace comes only when "we are ready to fight for it." She's ready, she vows, to place her "burning flower" onto his "blazing lake," and declares herself "delighted" with his male "weapons." She thinks no longer in "pacifist terms." She's experienced "too many assaults." As she enters the razor-blade boat, she informs "George" that if he searches her pocket he'll find it lined with something to "compliment" his "steel."

In "Dancing on the Grave of a Son of a Bitch," dedicated to her "motorcycle betrayer," she writes a poem of chant and exorcism, transforming her rage and hurt at being abandoned. Her lover rejects her once too often: she "might as well be a newspaper, / differently discarded each day." His departure leaves her "as miserable / as an earthworm with no / earth." Now, however, she's "crawled out of the ground where he had "stomped" her, and each day stands "taller and taller." Her exorcism/ chant is here at white heat:

> I'm going to dance on your grave
> because you are
> > dead
> > dead
> > dead
> under the earth. . . .

Louise Glück also writes toughly about male–female relationships. Her style is lean, spare, and experiential. In "Mock Orange" a woman rants against sex and men, the latter symbolized by the mock orange, an infertile if fragrant shrub:

> I hate them.
> I hate them as I hate sex,
> the man's mouth
> sealing my mouth, the man's
> paralyzing body—

In "The Mirror," Glück observes a man shaving, proud that she is watching him. He lets her "stare" so that he may turn against himself

> with greater violence,
> needing to show me how you scrape the flesh away
> scornfully and without hesitation
> until I see you correctly,
> as a man bleeding, not
> the reflection I desire.

Lyn Lifshin's version of feminismo is less violent than Gluck's or Wakoski's. Her role is as a tease, always promising more sexual goodies than she will deliver. In one poem, from *Kiss The Skin Off*, she returns to being a teenager, walking the Atlantic City boardwalk, protected by her mom. Dressed sexily, she parades for over six hours, her dress "as tight as / a hooker's stagger," her shoes spiked, her hair frizzy. Sailors

> rub
> their eyes from
> my maybelline cats
> eyes to my
> slick tanned
> legs.

She's safe and knows she'll never need to deviate from this role.

Many of her poems to men commemorate failed or kinky sex, little of it actually realized. One wonders why she attracts sexual losers? Is it because she pretends to be a Venus'-flytrap when she is in fact a night-blooming Cereus? Is attracting such partners a way of preserving her virginity? In one of her fantasies she parades panty-less over a hole in her kitchen floor, just above the lusting gazes of workmen in the cellar. Once again, she is the inaccessible turn-on, distancing herself by means of a play on "crack": the workmen are down there "to fix a crack. . . ." She thinks of *Playboy* and *Penthouse*—there no woman has "a period or hair." Penises throbbing are always nine inches long. Women's "tits point to the / sky." All is fantasy—no law briefs or poems. Blondes rip open men's bulging blue jeans and give great blow jobs. Like the stereotyped completely sex-starved bored suburban housewife, Lifshin's woman lets herself go, fantasizing about women who dive through

> leather with their
> own crotch hairs
> always dripping
> like a porpoise.

In "The Librarian," Lifshin's themes are again the sexually castrating female, the semi-impotent professional male, and upper-middle-class pretensions. She's sardonic—remove the "is" from "penis" and you are left with "pen," a suitable "tool" for a librarian who is also a frustrated poet. Alas, his pen/penis runs out of ink too easily:

> he edits his wife out of
> the house, presses his
> balls up against the dust of
> dark card catalogues, burns to
> draw the world with what's in his head

> He wishes he was bigger, hides
> behind an enormous desk. When
> it comes to women he's
> fast to revise . . .

After trying all of Lifshin's "holes," unable to "get it in," he kicks her out. In "Too Many Readings Too Many Men," she is up front about the teasingly sexual dimensions of her public appearances. "Performing," she writes, "is like / becoming wet after 17 / orgasms in one / afternoon with nearly / half that many men. . . ." Part of her tease act is to absolve herself of any guilt; men alone are responsible for their fantasies. One fan is so excited after seeing her picture in *Rolling Stone* that he fantasizes about her as a centerfold:

Poetry's too easy

he said he was light
but dark on the
inside asked me to read
a sexy poem and would
I mind if he came on
the phone imagining
my he was sorry it wasn't

a taller body.

Here, I would guess, Lifshin has it the way she likes it—the sanitary telephone removes her from the sexual act transpiring on the other end of the line.

"La Loca" (Pamala Karol), in "You Should Only Give Head To Guys You Really Like", employs feminismo to seduce her male. Her potency makes sense only in terms of ancient Egypt, necrophilia, and the Hollywood's siren Pola Negri. A Pharoah's priests summon La Loca to lead her lover through "avenues of afterlife" to Heaven. She strips the corpse of his mummy cloth. His "levitation" (phallic erection) is "improper." Facing his stunning beauty, she stands before him more mind than body, staring like a Sphinx, aware that only by becoming muscle can she enjoy him sexually. First, though, she must become a "woman," which she does by falling into the Nile. The "faint scent of summer orange" drifts from the "airless tomb" where the lover waits.

Her first act is fellatio, imagined in allusions to our atomic age:

Heady with grave robbing
Heady with necromancy
Heady with the mead of sweat on your scrotum
I swipe a saxophone from the atomic age
And with goddess kisses on the reed
Suck you.

His sexy cock is like "a deep vowel." After she has imbibed his semen, he banishes her and returns to his eternal sleep beside the Nile. She returns to a sexually deprived life in the "West."

In Kathleen Spivack's volume *The Beds We Lie In,* sexual struggle is the norm, again with women as tough survivors. Spivack never whines when betrayed, and is most self-reliant during moments of reflection, often when she's alone in bed. In "A Short," a woman triumphs, though locked in a sexual embrace gone sour. Her man seems to demand more than she can give. The book of their lives together must, she decides, close:

You groan and sob above me like a woman;
your black eyes have forgotten
who it is you are screwing.
"erogenous zones."
But the lights go dead.

"The Breakup Variations" focuses relentlessly on a dismal marriage.
In a poem called "he doesn't move," the woman's hunger is a quasi death:

sarcophagi,
they lie together formally,
husband and wife.
she wants
someone to stroke her hair,
a petal breath,
as from the center of flowers,
to be clasped
and called *my honey*
or *my dear*
gently, gently
is this what dying
will be like?

In the final section, "The Mementos-of-Past-Happiness Quilt," Spivack's
image of that most domestic image, the heirloom quilt, evokes the tram-
mels of heterosexual love. A "Rocking-the-Baby" quilt is fashioned by
man and woman together, "until he leaves her." Initially, the quilting
pieces are sun-bright, emitting "clover smells," with a mere scrap (trace)
of something wrong with the marriage signalled in the design. Later, as
the "supper turns to glue / in the pots" and the baby cries, Spivack's
"piecework" threatens to come apart. The male returns angry—his wife
differs from the woman down the road. To pursue his own pleasures, he
stifles his wife by stitching her

down
with the firm needle,
sewing him to her
with sweetest thread.
Put in a scrap of wedding
dress, sheet rags, and one
fuzzy piece of baby
bunting: they are all his.

He loses.

Figurine Poems

The "figurine poem" is by its very nature slight, in the way that a Hummel peasant girl with basket and goose, or an eighteenth-century court shepherdess accompanied by lamb, crook, and swain, are slight. Such artifacts, though not lacking in charm, are to Michelangelo's *Slave* as the figurine poem is to Milton's *Paradise Lost*.

Ezra Pound, in "Apparuit," makes his figurine come alive without ever losing the sense of the artifactual. A girl whose presence is tinged with mystical echoes in the Pre-Raphaelite manner emerges from a "portal" in a "golden rose" house and receives the full flush of the morning sun. She is "carven in subtle stuff, a portent." The morning roses, frosted with dew, bend as the figure moves in the sunlight: "the tissue / golden about thee." Pound is amazed and delighted by the apparition:

> Half the graven shoulder, the throat aflash with strands of light inwoven
> 　　about it, loveliest of all things, frail alabaster, ah me!
> 　　　swift in departing.

Ruth Whitman's "Castoff Skin" can be seen as a figurine poem, with a difference—the old woman in the poem is no pastoral figurine, but a china-delicate being who, when she dies, leaves behind something like "a tiny stretched transparence." The presence of the snake suggests the quick flickering of this ephemeral transition:

> She lay in her girlish sleep at ninety-six,
> small as a twig.
> *Pretty good figure.*
> *for an old lady,* she said to me once.
> Then she crawled away, leaving
> a tiny stretched transparence
>
> behind her. When I kissed her paper cheek
> I thought of the snake,
> of his quick motion.

Maurya Simon in *The Enchanted Room* writes figurine poems, applying much workshop glitter to their surfaces. A "carafe of wind" (if such can be imagined) "empties itself." Does it tip itself over? Does it sprout mystical cicada or angel hands for the occasion? Simon can't be bothered, so avid is she in pursuit of the pretty image. Again she aims for a workshop effect, telling us that true invention constructs fey images out of cheap porcelain and then evoking a human parallel: a "beautiful woman" with "swaying" round hips "enters the dark." Is her new rear carafe-shaped? Is she flatulent, i.e., does she echo the parallel with the carafe full of wind? Shortly, mosquitoes "unzip themselves from the wall." Can you visualize that one? Or this: cicadas "loosen their sprockets /

as if to unwind the heat." Or this: a spider decides to "put up" her knitting needles. Simon has all the stock impulses needed for the figurine poem. She writes prettifying vaguenesses and delicate abstractions ("silence forever," "fades into blue air," etc.). She is an Ella Wheeler Wilcox for the eighties. Her poems are meant for what-not shelves.

Five-Minute Sonnets

These seemingly quickly-written sonnets differ from English or Petrarchan sonnets in that they are so much easier to write. They usually eschew end rhyme and traditional pentameters. Marilyn Hacker, perhaps inspired by Adrienne Rich's "Twenty-One Love Poems," includes a thirteen-poem sequence called "Open Windows" in her collection *Assumptions*. Though Rich's love poems depart from the conventional sonnet length, her tone of intimate address to other women and the free rush of her lines are echoed in Hacker's sonnets. This one is an effective example. The speaker is about to leave a lover to return to her daughter. Her intense loving is not without fire and pain:

> Tonight when I cup my hand beneath your breast
> (fountain and pillow of felicity)
> your womb shudders with possibility
> suctioned from you, and your sigh is pain. Pressed
> even gently against me, you ache; the best
> choice, made, presses us both. How will it be
> held between us, this complicity
> in what we can't repeat? Silken, we nest
> aloft, sleep curled. Reflected from the snow,
> a dawn lamp glints up through your tall window.
> Uptown, my child will wake, ask where's her mother.
> Promised, I inhale you, descend from you, gather
> scattered woolens, gather my wits to go
> from one hard choice, love chosen, to the other.

In her earlier "Three Sonnets For Iva" (in *Taking Notice,*) Hacker uses the five-minute sonnet form in a brutally honest treatment of a troubled mother's harshness toward her infant daughter. In the first poem, the mother is in a rage at being trapped and unable to work. She changes her daughter's diaper, "full of mustardy shit," as rage "blisters" her "wet forehead." The child demands attention, and they go to a park, where she does her best to amuse the girl, pretending she is an "Amazon Queen" and her daughter a "Princess." In the next poem, she has locked the child outside the bathroom. When Iva whines, Marilyn won't open the door, knowing she will slap the child again. She's already hit her six times that morning, thrown her to the rug, and smacked her bottom, face, and hands. Both are "scared," but this time Marilyn refuses to come out:

> I want to stop
> this day. I cringe on the warm pink tiles of
> a strange house. We cry on both sides of the door.

Flotsam-and-Jetsam Poems

Imagine the poet's mind as a sea floating with an assortment of debris, some floating on the surface, some (to be regarded as the more lethal of the two) floating below the surface. Imagine the smashed wooden crates, dead rats, fruit parings, rotting fish, old sneakers and bits of slickers, scraps of fish nets, plastic floats, rented life-preservers, notes for help thrust into bottles—such is the melange of thoughts, images, and bits and pieces of bizarre memories floating and bobbing in the poet's mind. Generally, these surfaces are of two sorts: ones on which very little floats and the waters are calm almost to the point of sterility; and ones with turbulent surfaces where so much flotsam and jetsam jostles and bobs that the waters are scarcely visible.

Now, some of the poets who scoop up these fragments are called "surrealists" and others are called "language poets." Yet, the terms hardly suffice, except as general indications of what poets who appear to write automatically (or semi-automatically) produce. Language poetry shares much with the old-fashioned genre of automatic writing. One thinks of the parlor game in which one writes a line, folds it over, and passes it on to the next guest who contributes a line without having seen the preceding one. Finally, once the paper has made its way round the parlor, someone reads out the results as a poem.

Jed Rasula, in "The Tent of Times," provides the perfect setup. He informs us that as he wades "in & out" of his dream he comes "on bits of broken glass, / floating in silt like bubbles." He also finds transmitters, eggs that glow and "wring the gaze," red ants, "priapic stones," hands resembling "bulls in a pasture," water snakes in a trough, "a little tub where islands fit," etc. Even mystical and mythical objects float about: "a shell of the soul," Athena's shield, "*Amore* splashing," "Mithraic honey," Ananke twisting "her fate device," and "archaic compulsions." Even on land objects conglomerate, "glued to memory's hive / of heat seeped in through an open wound." The very "ground fills up with stones— the inner earth creeps out. / Flakes & shards, concepts, glues, / something grows."

Beneath this lengthy poem runs the motif of language, of words, of meanings. There are allusions to mad King Lear. Rasula sucks "the air out of Lear" and crusts, blears, and gnaws at the "drift" he intuits. And the word "intuit" is a clue. For a poet like Rasula, the psychic jumble rolls with the swell and drifts towards some unifying theme or idea, possibly too arcane for merely rational minds. is the perceiver; Both the poet and his reader must trust Rasula's intuition. No matter how adventitious the connections among the bits of Rasula's flotsam and jetsam, there are "meanings." Fortunately, Rasula's psyche welters with fascinating salvage, and I am willing to examine it without caring whether my feet are on firm sea bottom or not. Lesser poets, though, are apt to irritate when what accrues is merely a collection of broken egg shells, garden pebbles, sparrow bones, and fly wings left over from a spider's dinner—objects of little consequence.

In "The Person," Lyn Hejinian is mildly associative. Each of her stanzas presents ideas which she then proceeds to obfuscate. Some of these ideas are about language and the aesthetic properties of verse. She likes being conceptual, and is often complacent. She says she translates her "thought / into jump-language" as a way of doubling "fate." Jump-start cables seem relevant. Hejinian sets up one idea—here she ends a stanza with "fate"—and then jumps across or sparks over from the next stanza to an anode in the preceding stanza. "Fate" jumps over. Hejinian believes that an altruistic poet who knows "what to want" will be "free."

Most of her flotsam and jetsam consists of shibboleths of a school-marmish sort employed as pontifical beginnings for sections. The result is an embarrassingly dull philosophizing. Here are some examples:

"Each sensation is witness to the congestion of its glance . . ."
"Elation can manifest itself from time to time in finding . . ."
"Music is rational in a thing that affects me . . ."
"Things see their argument go to and fro before my eyes . . ."
"Sound is a sentence of water . . ."

Her yoking of disparately floating elements (copulating frogs follow "the judgment and the matching method," which follows "balls of these intentions," which follows "light and nightmares") seems merely pedantic, despite little whiffs of surprise (the fucking frogs) which emerge and then quickly vanish. My complaint is not that Hejinian rarely completes a thought—certainly our minds naturally billow with partially formed impressions and ideas, most of which we barely notice—but that her thoughts are so trite. While I do admire language poets who seek fresh truncations of images and ideas, I do expect the same substance, originality, and zip I do of more traditional poems.

In the same issue of *Temblor* Susan Howe contributes "Heliopathy," a sequence of word lists and arrangements, and of brief lines slanted in various directions for emphasis. The title, as well as certain mythic references with female overtones, suggests that Howe has been reading her H. D. As I sail through this assortment of flotsam neatly arranged on a poem-museum desk, various words group themselves around faint themes: Eve, happiness, the beloved, form, daughters of the sun, cymbal, mercy, languishment, *The darkness hideth not from thee,* nine herbs, "Inch-pin of civilization," oratory, Iroquois, figure of comedy, "great men of the New World." The themes? Civilization and its female discontents.

There are little exudations of relevancies, so miniscule as to be almost microscopic in the whorl and swirl of words, words, words. At times Howe seems to have had her *Finnegans Wake* beside her; this Joycean scrap occupies an entire big white page:

Ages for long been Oursoul

Fledgling I will go over

Howe and other purists seem to believe that renditions of verbal sound, apart from meaning, have something of the ancient and legendary about them, that the recital of these poems at public readings or in private has a talismanic power. If this interpretation makes sense, we can accept the following passage, by Howe, as runic and possibly talismanic. The informing voice seems to be vaguely Anglo-Saxon in its linguistic origins:

Altogeather togeather
hops fra hoops
Idia sinsly
believe eny belief

My regret is that Howe doesn't write *more* experimentally. Most of this thirteen-page poem induces great yawns. Like Hejinian, Howe seems enamored of herself as a sociologist/philosopher.

Rachel Blau Du Plessis, writing in the feminist journal *HOW(ever)* (May 1984) contributes this illuminating commentary on Susan Howe's work: "whole shadow words, as if visual afterimages, come in her intricate split spell-ings: 'rish sh' (SHDL) or 'life la / nd friend / no lighthouse / marin / ere' (CG). . . ." These lines are simply unreadable. One hungers for a clear idea, simply written. The intellects—aestheticians, philosophers, and poets—have always eschewed darkness visible, darkness inane. What must these *HOW(ever)* folk talk about when they get together on a rainy day and sip herbal teas?

Far more successful than either Hejinian or Howe is Bob Perelman whose linguistic romps are intelligent and brisk. He is sufficiently modest to avoid pomposity. He sorts the flotsam and jetsam, carefully choosing what will give a semblance of sense and will allow him to play freely among puns, syllabic sound-echoes, and word arrangements. Here, he combines humor, some narrative hints, and a fresh comment on aesthetics:

Assertion:
The object can only be created by the senses.
So beat me with your light-saber
make me watch and direct bad movies!
The end is form-fitted space.

To him words are "human persons, / appetitious meanings," the "flesh" he'll sell himself for. He interrupts himself. He appears to struggle for

insight, falling back on a form of declension: "I sing you hear / they. . . ."
His concluding "Coda" displays winsome playfulness blended with a
serious statement on education, poetry, and civilization:

> the education wants the poem, like a sidewalk, waterpipes under
>   the street, wires overhead in every direction, grass
>   and cement under foot, cars, no cars in alterity of
>   sincere disposition
> And my time is gone in the smooth
> code I send before.
> Good night. Good night.

His "Sentimental Mechanics" is a brilliant three-stanza romp that bor-
rows fey moments from Poe ("never") and incorporates child talk with its
cuteness and illogicality ("I need to know, what it was / my mommy said.
The ice cream melted, / I was in my head"). There are references to old
films (Humphrey Bogart) and to Tennyson's "Charge of the Light Bri-
gade" ("Theirs not to reason why, / Theirs but to do or die"). Stanza two
reveals his commitment to finding "another word," a linguist's dream of
discovery, like a geneticist who imagines stumbling at last on whatever
submicroscropic scrap truly constitutes life: "There's got to be another
word. / There's not another world."

Dennis Phillips, also in the language mode, has written a sensitive
lyric called "This plain to the sea fog." He balances an original sense of
language at its best in the concluding stanza which subtly evokes Eliza-
bethan speech, with a narrative more or less clearly seen. A person (I
assume it's a male) who is possibly an Elizabethan soldier separated from
his army, is positioned near the sea, on a foggy, sunless morning. Images
of landscape unify these stanzas:

> the slope in your mind
> a pebble in your thinking
> gradual scoop to continental shelf.
> This pebble on your land-locked street.
> Inhabitant of a coastal zone
>
> ready to ship out, spoils divided, a decade of tilting
> City of the Plain from City of Tents.
> Gravel in your shoulder, gravel in your bedding
>
> Henry Five's easy Illium, Harfleur,
> Whiles yet the cool and temperate wind of grace
> o'er blows the filthy and contagious clouds
> back to the city. Fresh air in your face.

A sensitive poet is Jerry Ratch, who was writing language poetry
before it became fashionable. Some scrutiny of his methods should en-
rich our awareness of how a poet who is interested in pure language
works. His recent collection *Hot Weather* contains generous portions

from his first six books. Ratch's formative years were the sixties, the years of the counterculture revolution, of student uprisings, of mass demonstrations against the Asian wars, of marches on behalf of oppressed blacks and gays. As a young poet, himself scarred by polio, observing and participating in a scarred society about to go up in flames, Ratch took his cues from the Beats, from underground comic books, from the Kool-Aid acid lingo of the times, and from Andy Warhol films. The minimal became a means of protesting a sick culture; to be parsimoniously verbal was to bug the establishment. You were then much less communicative with the enemy, who was unable to reach your conscience and make you vulnerable. Ratch's poetry has connections with this protest culture; and it relates also to the existentialists who were much read and admired then: Albert Camus's heroes, who seem tragic because their minimalist speech entraps them; and Samuel Beckett's abstract figures who stumble around in a wasteland searching for the remotest hint that life has any meaning.

In Ratch's earliest book of poems, *Puppet X*, a doll without a name, operated by strings only partially defined, seems to avoid suicide by emitting his thoughts in half-formed gasps. His speech resembles that inside balloons in comic strips. He talks as if he's made of cardboard, not flesh:

> & now the dead spider
> is running the
> world
>
>   la de da   la de da
>   Let Spider come over
>
> Dead Spider is
> running the world
>
>   "Oh, oh"
>
> Dead Spider
> is running
> the world

(p. 23)

The narrative of *Clown Birth*, Ratch's second book, is presented with utter economy—this clown has little breath to waste, and his songs are a most fastidious interplay of syllable and metrics:

> Your houses
> blessed with bees
> this big, that big
> alcohol every
> what is it
> blue wave

what is it
pieces of crumpled stone
sitting on the steps
the brain a walnut
rattled

In his next two books, *Osiris* and *Helen,* the narrative thread becomes even thinner, and setting shrivels into mere hints of place. Since Osiris evokes ancient Egypt, Ratch has a paradigm for writing even more minimalist poems based on single words and syllables, seemingly chiseled on slabs of stone. Passion is remote, except insofar as language play allows it to enter. In one poem, gouged-out eyes and tomb bats are surprises, suiting an ancient theme of lost kingly power and maimed pride—but only after the grammar of the poem has asserted itself:

what does he feed on
only what he sees
what does he feed on
only what he sees

what does he live on
what he eats
what does he live on
what he eats

who are his attendants
tomb bats
that fly in the night

o who has
gouged out his eye

and who has made him
not to speak

that he might diminish
decrease
& gradually lose power

We read *Helen* as though we were reading breaths translated from an ancient stele. The fragility of these poems evokes a timeless, runic quality, yet they sound totally contemporary in their fascination with minimal language.

Ratch next turns to Chaucer and Pound for a further paring of his verse. If in his first books he was writing half-completed inscriptions on stone, he is now writing "poems" made up of words taken from earlier poets and mixed with words of his own appearing in the margins, a form he calls "marginalia." The poet now seems to urge himself out of language; his presence is merely that of a hand holding a pen, a pointing finger on a piece of film indicating the older language as the necessary artifact. The poem, *"y Cantos,"* inspired by Pound is a blend of the marginalia mode and the stele patterns of *Osiris* and *Helen*. All words are assembled from the older poet.

```
Many
Men
Battle
these days
pallor
slaughtered
poured
unto
Pluto
&
unsheathed
til I should bear
the
unburied
o
peaceful
spirit
Shattered
Facing
the
flood
```

Ratch has this to say: "I first began writing *Marginalia* because I couldn't write at the time & didn't know what else to do. My effective vocabulary after having finished *Osiris* consisted of two words, hand and glove. On a whim, and out of boredom with not writing for a year, I had the good fortune to be reading Chaucer's 'The Miller's Tale,' which I had never really read before. I was working in a paint factory; it was winter, things were slow. Brevity I saw was a necessity, and soon my eye would linger out among the words beside of the body of Chaucer's text, more than I could get myself to stay inside the tale. Soon my eye began to drift down this stringy column of words in the margin; and soon I began to speed through these too. And it began to be interesting; ejecting a few words here and there, misreading now & then, quick takes, like riffs. Then I started writing these experiments down. Soon I was on my way. Within three months I had about six hundred pieces to work with. Then I began to modulate the concept from that base."

This review of flotsam-and-jetsam poetry is much too brief, considering the current importance of the movement. Another writer in the mode is John Taggart (his poems are so minimal that scarcely an item or two floats on the surface of his stilled waters). Charles Bernstein, Clark Coolidge, and Bruce Andrews have so far produced work of mixed quality. Leslie Scalapino, whose work is certainly related to this group and appears in their journals and anthologies, seems not wholly a creature of language poetry—her poems exceed the limitations of the form. One striking aspect of these poets is their fascination with critical theory and aesthetics. They write a great deal of critical prose: essays on one another, on theoretical implications of their work, and on the nature of language.

Found Poems

"Found poems," or what the French call *poésie d'emprunt* (borrowed poetry), according to Louis Dudek, is "the culmination of realism . . . in which significance appears inherent in the object—either as extravagant absurdity or as unexpected worth. It is like driftwood, or pop art, where natural objects and utilitarian objects are seen as the focus of generative form or meanings." This illuminating remark is quoted by John Robert Colombo in his "A Found Introduction" prefacing a generous selection of poetry in *Open: Four Anthologies of Expanded Poems*, edited by Ronald Gross and George Quasha.

Colombo traces some early, important examples of found poetry. When St. Jerome translated the Bible into Latin, and arranged the Psalms and Proverbs as poems in Latin, he was practicing *colometry* or *stichometry*, the arrangement of rhetorical texts into meaningful units, a precursor of found poetry. One of the earliest found poems in French is Blaise Cendrars' "*Dernière Heure*," a verbatim account of an Oklahoma jailbreak taken directly from one line of *Paris-Midi*, which appeared in January 1914. In English, Ezra Pound (in the *Cantos*), James Joyce (in *Ulysses*) and T. S. Eliot (in *The Waste Land*) employed such elements. William Butler Yeats arranged Walter Pater's famous prose commentary on the Mona Lisa as verse and published it as the initial poem in *The Oxford Book of Modern Verse* (1936). The first book of found poetry in English was John S. Barnes's selection and arrangement in 1945 of purple passages from Thomas Wolfe's novels.

A quick scan of the ninety-seven pages selected by Colombo shows the range of the form: Eleanor Antin's arrangement from Sir Kenneth Clark's "The Proportions Which a Perfectly Formed Man's Body Should Possess," Colombo's own arrangement of a passage of Orwellian political significance from David Wise and Thomas B. Ross's *The Invisible Government*, and his dunner for a bill, "Overdue." In obvious ways, for the overall form, Colombo elides words and phrases, and the emphasis on prepositions in end-of-line positions gives the illusion of a tooled lyric.

John Giorno complicates the form in "Leather," a randy piece, by blending different sources: kinky moments from a soft-porn story and passages on insect hormone flow, astronauts in space, and an item on mass murder clipped from a newspaper. Ronald Gross's "Ice Cream Cone," listing as it does the toxic ingredients therein, is enough to dissuade one from bringing one tongue within six inches of one:

. . . Tenox 2
is an antioxidant containing
butylated hydroxyanisole,
propylgallate, citric acid,
propylene glycol.

Another of Gross's poems, a riff on Brillo pads, set in varying types and line lengths, is dedicated to Andy Warhol, and suggests a tie-in with Warhol's use of found objects. Warhol saw a special reality in everyday objects most people overlook, which he called "the heroic of the everyday."

Walter Lowenfels fashions two strong antiwar poems from items in the *New York Times*. Edwin Morgan (as New York City poet, painter, and collagist Carolyn Stoloff has also done) literally clips phrases from magazines and employs rubber stamps to fashion his poems. Richard O'Connell's "Letter from the New World" arranges a description of a shark written by Sir Richard Hawkins in 1593, and shows the possibilities inherent in historical documents. The poem is not unworthy, given some modernizing of the language, of one of Marianne Moore's animal poems. Here are the opening lines:

The Shark

I have seen him some eight or nine foot long.
His head is broad and flat, his mouth beneath
As of the Skate. He cannot bite the bait
Before him, but by making a half turn
On his swift tail, he seizes on his prey.
His skin is rough and russet, splotched with red,
But all his underbelly milky white
He is the most fantastic fish alive. . . .

During the sixties and seventies, George Hitchcock, the indefatigable editor of the Kayak Press and the influential magazine (now defunct) of the same name, did more than any single American poet or editor to encourage the form. Not only did he publish found poems regularly in his magazine, but he also coauthored (with myself) *Pioneers of Modern Poetry*, and edited and published the first anthology of found poetry, *Losers Weepers. Poems Found Practically Everywhere*. The latter includes the work of twenty-five poets, all found "somewhere amidst the vast sub- or non-literature which surrounds us all." In *Pioneers*, we found "poems" in old shorthand manuals, books for farmers on beekeeping and preventing diseases of cattle, Army mental tests dating back to 1920, and a handbook on how one should behave if one meets a Turkish pasha. The intention of the book was to satirize the current fad for projective, Olsonesque verse. The "authors" arranged their poems to look like the fractured free-verse forms loved by the projectivists. Each poem was accompanied by a satiric, yet seemingly straightforward analysis in a thoroughgoing academic manner.

In a recent interview with Hitchcock, Larry Smith asked Hitchcock: "Although you included found poems through most of *Kayak*'s twenty years, there was always some controversy among the readers as to their value. One letter asked who had lost or mislaid them. Since you and Robert Peters did a whole book of them, you obviously had a commitment to the form. Did that commitment have a theoretical or historical basis? By what criteria did you judge found poem submissions?"

Here is Hitchcock's response: "Found poems are constant testimony to the fact that wonder may still be found in places where you least expect it. The sign says ENTRANCE; I am in the habit of reading that as a command. It is as simple as that. The criteria? Where, I think, the language was amazing and the form verged on stichomythia or wrapped itself up in oxymoronic robes of mystery, as in almost any application form or set of review questions to a text on bee-keeping."

A laureate of the found poem is Jonathan Williams, who focuses his antiquarian, risible, sexual, and ebullient selves on these forms, finding them in all manner of places American and British: in cemeteries, in snatches of conversation spoken by earthy folks, in road and street signs, and in newspapers. One of the latter, "The Adhesive Autopsy of Walt Whitman," is a constituted of verbatim quotations from Philadelphia and Camden newspapers:

"Gentlemen, look on this wonder . . .
and wonders within there yet":

"pleurisy of the left side, consumption
of the right lung,

general miliary tuberculosis
and parenchymatous nephritis . . . a fatty

liver, a huge stone
filling the gall,

a cyst in the adrenal, tubercular abscesses
involving the bones,

and pachymeningitis"

"that he was a Kosmos is a piece of news we were
hardly prepared for . . ."

Fruits-and-Flowers-of-Love Poems

One of the hoariest of all poetic traditions is to compare the attributes of a loved one to various fruits and flowers. Rosy cheeks and cherry-red lips are but two of the clichés. Petrarchan love conceits, so brilliantly satirized by William Shakespeare in Sonnet 130, and various erotic inspirations from the Psalms and the Song of Solomon, continue to generate progeny.

A contemporary poet who writes of these matters with elan, skirting (and flirting with) the worst of these clichés, is Joel Oppenheimer. His "The Truck Farmer," in *Just Friends / Friends and Lovers,* is one of the best of his numerous love poems. Reading the poem, one is soon aware that no yokel is speaking—the speaker loves language and erotic love described with simple images of fruits and flowers. He's winsome, his good feelings wafting as various "hoohoos" over his woman. The pair are in bed in the daytime, in full sunlight. He celebrates her flesh using images of plums, peaches, and pears: each time he bites in, "fleshy pieces, the / milk flows richly. /hoohoo stick in my / pull out a / flaw."

The heart, that "goofing rose" whose petals "overlap the emotion" he feels, represents the source of a potential thunderstorm. Perhaps he is not anxious for a complete commitment. Note how Oppenheimer maintains the two themes—the real rose in its pitcher of water, and the metaphoric rose of the heart resisting erotic body flow:

> the goofing rose among
> all the hot flesh
> it sits with one green
> leaf, in the pitcher,
> the water shows the
> pinpoint bubbles of air
> the open petals glitter, and
> the sunlight glitters in
>
> the heart beats constantly.
> all night last night we
> lay next to it hearing
> it beat. how they beat
> as one i still don't know.

The "farmer" (who is no farmer, except insofar as he tends to the lovely orchard of his woman) rejects the heart's conundrum for the loving that continues on all day and into the night. Oppenheimer's lyric skill and tone are, in their playfulness, magical:

> hoo hoo like firmfleshed
> pears, under the apples
> of your shoulders which
> glow in the sun, even

your peachy belly, and,
the plum, stick in my
paw. hoohoo the firm
flesh i sing and here
in the light filtering
in, in the soft light
we are exposed to, and
at night close our
eyes against it's coming
again, or not, but
close our eyes
planting, as always, by
moon or lack thereof, but
not by day, the sun exposes
us, and all our land.

hoo hoo the farmer

Fulbright Poems

These poems are written mainly by poets holding academic appointments who teach undergraduate English literature and world literature courses, with a smattering of art or music history thrown in. The "academic abroad" poem hit the market in epidemic proportions following World War II when veterans returning to academe extolled the fountains of Rome, the baroque churches of Vienna and Bavaria, Stratford-on-Avon, Chartres and Notre Dame, Michelangelo's statuary, and St. Mark's Square in Venice. The poems still persist, though, not in their earlier numbers.

Madeline DeFrees, director of the writing program at the University of Massachusetts, strews her work with facile metaphysical speculations that read like stale travesties of Yeats, Marvell, and Francis Thompson. In Greece, in an orthodox church, she lights the candle "one more time" and finds the attending priest "ensconced in a separate / altitude." Like many of her academic abroad cohorts she loves to make easy cultural and literary allusions: she refers to Henry Miller, Yeats, Marvell, Brueghel, and Thompson. Echoing Thompson's "The Hound of Heaven," DeFrees writes: "Of course I fled: through cobbled porticoes, weed, / brambles, rock, to a dead-end / precipice."

Jorie Graham's "San Sepolcro" and "At Luca Signorelli's Resurrection of the Body" are also academic abroad poems. In the first, Graham enters an Etruscan church in the early morning ("Come, we can go in") and sees a painting by Piero della Francesca of a pregnant girl unbuttoning a blue dress. The conclusion is momentous: the quick-fingered girl is an image for the viewer who senses that "something terribly / nimble-fingered" is "finding all of the stops". In the second poem, Graham meditates on Signorelli's fascination with the body (he had to rob graves for corpses to dissect). This allows Graham to think back to 1500, that year of the imagined apocalypse, to see the symbolical, the beautiful, and the true. Only by climbing into "the open flesh" could Signorelli's mind "mend itself."

Carol Muske, in "Chasers," from *Sky Light,* seems to be near the Ganges in moonlight, observing the whitewashed temples and the "skeletal" boatmen pushing their boats through red mud. Like a good tourist, she visits the ghats where cremations are taking place, and mixes moments that fresh with moments that are stale. She visits an "upstairs room" to see perfumers preparing a woman's body "to float in air"; then she notes street beggars selling "their dreams." At the Hotel Karma all is great—"refrigerated wind," mineral water, a bedside light. She has the American tourist's empathy for the untouchables waiting to sweep out rooms "with their brooms of fire, waiting to open / the heavy dark curtains to pain, obsession, / the malarial insects of the night." This seems too easy, a facile gluing-together of the foreigner's emotional responses to the weakly imagined lives of the unfortunate locals.

Dana Gioia in *Daily Horoscope* doesn't regale us with tourist-thoughts while he's in Italy. "An Emigré in Autumn" gives us the barest of scenery—a general image of the "tops of leaves" played over by "daylight," a "summer palace," and a park. Ennui seems the key. Gioia is thoroughly passive as he repeats the steps (he counts them) he takes around the park. In good existentialist terms, he seems to be going along miles that "span no distances," yet are sunlight journeys "toward the dark." If our energy stirs us a bit, we can follow the advice he proffers in "Instructions for the Afternoon." We should, at the outset, know why we've arrived—a genteel, vague mystery. At any rate, we should quit the museums, "the safe distractions of the masterpiece," and the echoing palaces where no one any longer lives. Go find "dark churches" in obscure towns forgotten by history (this latter idea is just one of the numerous clichés Gioia artfully uses to debilitate his style), and find some "sad hamlets" passed over by "commerce" and profits. Become a statue if you can:

> Wait like the stone
> face of a statue waits, forever frozen
> or poised in the moment before action.

I'm not sure where Gioia's outing leads—and I'm not too sure he knows either, for he turns entirely vaporous at the end, substituting abstract and facile literary turns of phrase for insight and true feeling:

> Strange how all journeys come to this: the sun
> bright on the unfamiliar hills, new vistas
> dazzling the eye, the stubborn heart unchanged.

The issue seems to be, why should academics bother to go abroad? For tax shelter purposes.

Yet, there is one poet who has traveled much abroad and writes of the sights with ingenuity, power, and great stylistic flair. Anyone leafing through the thirty-year feast of George Hitchcock's work, *The Wounded Alphabet,* will find such poems. "Antonin Gaudi" presents marvelous surreal touches, typical of Hitchcock's bejewelled ichneumon's style, to celebrate the Spaniard's great art nouveau cathedral in Barcelona. Gaudi fashioned a primordial "sculpture" of jaws, hips, molars, inverted stone gardens, and the "antlers of newborn deer sprouting / from the earth's asphaltic armor." The architect's depths are elusive:

> sometimes he looks like an empty mandolin
> sometimes he speaks in the voice of the gourd
> sometimes he spreads the peacock tail of dreams
> sometimes he dresses the universe in suffering trousers

"Ultima Thule Hotel" should dissuade any academic intent on going abroad to stay in splendid hotels. This hotel at the end of the world is utterly inhospitable and tacky:

> the armchairs are spavined
> the desk clerk pours corrosive
>
> sublimate in every bathtub
> the awnings rot the corridors reek
>
> of gin and garlic the tenants
> rattle in their cells like dry beans
>
> . . . this is Armageddon
>
> in leatherette the party favors
> have exploded your number is up
>
> your credit card lies dead
> under an egg-stained napkin

Fundamentalist or Academic Revivalist Poems

These are written by editors of the major poetry anthologies who are not dissimilar in their influence and effect from the television evangelists who seek to further old American values among the hordes of the faithful. These collections build on the tastes and canons sanitized by those most successful of all anthologies, the tissue-thin compendia published by W. W. Norton. While I do not complain of the laudable thoroughness with which the Norton tomes represent traditional poetry, I do protest the thinness and conservatism of their representations of contemporary poets.

Among the fundamentalist spinoffs and academic revivalist tubthumpers are these collections: J. Paul Hunter's *The Norton Introduction to Poetry*, "a teaching anthology," aimed for "the indispensable course in which college student and college teacher begin to read poetry seriously together"; A. Poulin, Jr.'s *Contemporary American Poetry*, 4th edition; Robert Wallace's *Writing Poems*, "designed to help a student write poetry—financially unprofitable poetry"; Helen Vendler's *The Harvard Book of Contemporary American Poetry*, which declares that "poets of the second half of the century cannot quite take the work of the great modernists for granted. . . . Replication of the great modernists—in homage, in quarrel—marks the poetry of these later poets"; Robert Pack, Sydney Lea, and Jay Parini's *The Bread Loaf Anthology of Contemporary American Poetry*, which claims to "represent what has happened in the past half decade of American verse"; Dave Smith and David Bottoms' *The Morrow Anthology of Younger American Poets*, a collection for "poets born in 1940 or after" (a cutoff date arranged to include the editors' work); Jack Myers and Roger Weingarten's *New American Poets of the 80's*, which includes poets "between thirty and forty-five years of age"; and William Heyen, *The Generation of 2000: Contemporary American Poets*, slanted against the "quasi-surrealist poem" and "dadaists or faddists or stand-up comics," and "aestheticians tripletalking etheral voices."

Throughout these books one clearly senses the struggle to establish a canon—one that will include work by the editors involved. What seems so sinister for the well-being of American poetry is that these compendia provide the luscious teats from which current generations of fledgling poets and readers suckle. These large anthologies, and the seal of approval stamped by college instructors requiring students to buy them, guarantee that the lambkins will know little more about contemporary verse than what they find in these sanitized assemblages of ewes and gentle, passive rams. Even a once ground-breaking anthology, Donald Allen's *The New American Poetry*, has been emasculated in its latest edition, and is now so useless that it has, I hear, died a sudden death on the market.

We desperately need collections with the liberal scope of Paris Leary and Robert Kelly's long since out-of-print *A Controversy of Poets;* or Edward Field's *A Geography of Poets*, which I gather the publisher is unwilling to keep in print; or Robert Bly's *News of the Universe: Poems of the Twofold Consciousness*, the only anthology I know with any brains.

Funeral Poems

Though actual poems written on funerals are rare, there are enough of them to qualify this as a special genre. One of the very best is Ida Cruzkatz's "Selma: In Memoriam." In lean, subtly broken lines, fraught with strong images, Cruzkatz is lethal in her depiction of an insensitive rabbi at her mother's funeral. (Selma was "just a mother," he avers), and is unsparing of her mother's harsh life. For thirty years she sold franks, fries, and cokes in stadiums saving up tips to buy pizza for the family. She did have lovers (her husband died young), men who "helped break / the stench of a two-room place, / with her sons in bunk beds / and her on the Castro in the parlor." The rabbi directs the family away from the casket to the surviving sons in the first row. This is how the poem ends:

> He buried her there in the parlor,
> covered her, shrouded her,
> completely disguised her
> into the form of her sons.
> Hers is the casket of blue vest and jacket,
> replete with both black tie and cuff-links.
> He will address her as Selma, Deborah, or mother;
> either way,
> it is the front row—
> the blue,
> that must be watched.

In my own poem "Burial" (in *What Dillinger Meant To Me*), a son stands by a grave, observes certain details, and concludes with a note of unexpected violence symbolizing his internal devastation:

> while the grave-digger
> dug his mother's grave
> squirrels romped beneath an oak tree.
>
> The old digger cut quilt-exact
> squares of turf and piled them
> on a tarmac. his shovel
> had a square end and easily cut through
> the sand and roots.
>
> His mother would lie beside his father,
> her concrete box containing her blue
> coffin touching his gray concrete box
> containing his brown coffin.
>
> He had the digger pause while he stroked
> his dad's box: dead twelve years—bones,

shredded clothes, and little black beads
for his eyes. The sand was carrot-red.
would their juices, in the sense of mush,
blend through into some neutral space?

His mother preferred no coffins or cement—
just her corpse arranged feet down, head up,
in the sand. He had touched her hands
and kissed her forehead and knew
how iced-over death is.

spiney carrot tops struck him in the face,
hard across the mouth.

Gab Poems

The "gab poem" is descended from the medieval French fable and the tales of Geoffrey Chaucer. It is full of obscenities and garrulousness, as if the poet had pulled our sleeve, drawing us aside to hear his tale in private, in some noisy tavern. Among the niceties included by Chaucer are these: a husband shoves a hot iron rod up his wife's lover's anus, whilst the lover is taking a crap out the window (they did things that way in ye olden tyme); and a young wife is swived in a tree just out of eyeshot of her geriatric, myopic husband. The mode is so garrulous that it seems nothing has been left out. A variety of "gab" accompanies spittoon sounds and clacking pool balls in some down-and-out-bar. The poet, much in his cups, fills your ear as he leans against you.

The leading practitioner of this type of poetry these days—and he has spawned a huge gaggle of imitators (for which he is not responsible)—is Charles Bukowski. He writes gab poetry both dismal and great, and enough of the latter to qualify as the best poet writing in America today. "Hot" (from *At Terror Street and Agony Way*) is a good example. Bukowski's loquacious speaker, working at the post office, is on a night pickup run in an old mail truck. Miriam, the delicious whore, is at home waiting for him, deadline 8 P.M. The truck stalls. Miriam is waiting. Bukowski arrives late, only to find that Miriam has split, leaving a note addressed to "son of a bitch," the note held in place on his pillow by a purple teddy bear. Bukowski gives the bear a drink, has one for himself, and climbs into a hot bath. The poem moves like narrative prose, cut up more or less like projective verse. It ends as a macho bar poem should: the rejected male refuses to feel betrayed by any woman; in fact, he seems to prefer bath and booze to the whore.

"Burn and burn and burn," from the same volume, is actually set in a bar, and lacks the vision and empathy I value much in Bukowski. He's petulant amidst the vomitings "into plugged toilets / in rented rooms full of roaches and mice." Self-parody? Dreams and ideals are poisons—and since we can't cry, we manage a sinister laugh or two, frosted over with self-pity; life is "a terrible joke." Conclusion?

> well, I suppose the days were made
> to be wasted
> the years and the loves were made
> to be wasted

This is bad Ernest Dowson, the decadent English poet who wrote in the 1890s about flinging life's roses "riotously" with the throng, and who steeped himself in absinthe and died young, before he had enjoyed many of the pleasures he had hitherto anticipated. Instead of Dowson's roses and lilies, vomit and plugged johns adorn Bukowski's days.

One has the feeling that the secret of life may be stuffed deep inside a box of Bukowski Creepy-Crawly-Vomit-Sugar-Coated-Crunch Cereal. Gab-mouths ripped and bleeding. Jesus Christ, Bukowski says, "should have laughed on the cross." How do we know he didn't? There is a theory that since Christ was so utterly mystical he felt no pain and joyously (even laughingly) welcomed his translation from life into Eternity, spikes, thorns, and all. There's a secret here somewhere. Bukowski then equates himself with Christ, a risk for any mere poet-mortal to take.

Many of Bukowski's gab poems work well indeed. From *Burning in Water Drowning in Flame: Selected Poems 1955–1973*, "the tragedy of the leaves," propels us into a rare world: Bukowski has a hangover, is deserted by a woman of the night, and is threatened with eviction by his landlady. His creation of the Loser is to poetry what Chaplin's Tramp is to film. Here instead of self-pity and sniveling, there is a marvelous transmutation of the raunchy through unusual images, a dry, almost saturnine, humor, and an implicit empathy with all losers:

> my woman was gone
> and the empty bottles like bled corpses
> surrounded me with their uselessness . . .

The long vowel sounds are well spaced, dropping in at the right intervals to keep the sound moving. And the interplay of *corpse* and *uselessness* is fine. He avoids self-pity by sensing the positive in the sunlight as it brightens the landlady's note in its "fine and / undemanding yellowness." The occasion, he says, demands "a good comedian, ancient style, a jester/ with jokes upon absurd pain." His wisdom has a telling simplicity: "pain is absurd / because it exists, nothing more." He senses that as a poet he is stagnant, even dead: "that's the tragedy of the dead plants."

Gerald Locklin is generally felt to be the best of the poets influenced by Bukowski. Yet Locklin has his own personal raunchiness and humor, and seems, if anything, to load even more beer into his gut than Bukowski does. In "Self-Portrait," from *Toad's Sabbatical,* Locklin (who sees himself as "Toad" in a number of books), gazes into a mirror:

                    i see two dim eyes, thick
lenses, full but graying har, uneven beard, thin
lips, enlarged pores, and a bulbous irish nose replete with capillary
      damage.

it is either the face of a person old before his time or of one totally

devoid of sensibilities.

the shoulders slope but have a certain power.
central european tits.
a classic beergut.

the legs, like life itself,
are nasty, short, and brutish.

is this the body of a poet?

no, no says the critic,
nor are these the poems of one.

Occasionally, a weird and vague cruelty slips into his work. In "Never Kiss a Fat Girl," from *Scenes From A Second Adolescence*, Locklin loquaciously, and grossly, reports his night with a porker: "the ready-for-slaughtering, / government-inspected variety." He's "grossly" overdone "the old libations," so he invites the girl into his car. She pleads faithfulness to her husband—she's been loyal for six years. "I said that was okay / and went back at the tits." Well, folks, it turns out she has no nipples. This freaks him out; he leaves, and the next morning is wretched. When she pursues him on campus, he tries to be civil—but he knows "that her wrath will not be mollified / until she's left scar tissue / where my own erectile tissue used to be."

Locklin's penchant for humor at his own expense is most ingratiating. His books are filled with such poems. One of the best is "The Nastiest Gland" (*Pronouncing Borges*). He blathers that all his friends have prostrate trouble, and can't figure out why he doesn't. He's obese, has bad posture, sacroiliac problems, drinks excessively, and has "bad attitudes toward sex." Yet, no prostrate trouble. His unluckier friends whisper behind his back: "What's fat-ass's secret? Why doesn't he share it with us?" He declares that he'd like to join their "company of misery." Since he has sex "exclusively in those positions / the doctor book says are apt to be harmful," and since all the rest of his body is a "shambles," except for "that nasty little gland," he pleads with the "guys" to let him alone. He's always been a slow learner. He didn't learn to tie his shoes until he reached the fourth grade.

Rarely does Locklin display any interest in lyricism—he covets the straightforward "gab" tone, the loquacious chatter of the-arm-around-the-soused-friend poem. Yet beneath this manner, a lyric impulse sometimes breaks forth, and intelligence waits there ready to grab you when you aren't looking.

Todd Moore also writes prolifically in the gab manner, and differs from Bukowski in that his vision is far more violent, less immediately devoted to his own past and ongoing personal history, less empathic for the down-and-outers, and less enamored of flirting with sentimentality. He is locked into small-town heartland America, writing in comparative isolation in Belvidere, Illinois, where he teaches high school. It is significant that the one cultural figure who obsesses him is the gangster John Dillinger. Moore is currently writing (and publishing) a highly original fourteen-book epic on Dillinger. To date, most of Moore's writing has appeared in tiny mimeographed chapbooks, some self-published, some apparently set up only to publish Moore. His reputation among small, out of the mainstream, cheaply produced, nonacademic, irreverent journals is considerable, and continues to grow.

His style is lean and hard-boiled. "The night," from his chapbook *D.O.A.,* is typical. Note the rapidity with which he fires off the vignette— it's a vivid bar tale, a sad tragedy of maiming, puking, and sex. He writes about Midwestern boozing, fast cars, guns. Pistols splatter throughout Moore's poems, spewing lead with devastating results:

the night

apache chemical blew
tyler parked his
red pickup in ranchero
tap's lot behind a
crowd gathering next
to cyclone feed &
grain he decided to
use light piling off
a mountain of fire
to show cindy his 45
auto but she was
more interested in
chugging beers than
slapping clips when
she went inside for
another 6 pack he
shot off the first
finger on his left
hand so she would
like him more she
puked when she saw
him dancing in blood

"Great Grandfather's Civil" is a gab boasting poem; the speaker boasts that in the Civil War you could be hanged for spying or desertion, but never for killing a man or being a horse thief. Well, he says, "i've been a little bit / of both since i shot / a man near a torn up / set of railroad tracks" in order to steal his horse. The rifle ball passed through the man's body,

bounced off an iron rail, and hit the horse in the eye so hard that it
collapsed in the dirt:

> & i
> fired another ball thru
> its brains to put it
> out felt worse killing
> the horse than the
> man & yes war is hell
> but walking ain't much
> better

"simon girty the" has the focus of a Western videojournal, and reveals
Moore's skill at adapting the gab poem to historical matters:

> simon girty the
>
> elder tomahawked
>   during whiskey
> imitation of
> a delaware
> indian dance
> falls sideways
> liquor spilling
> from his
> mouth blood
> in the grass
> feet kicking
> as drunken
> indian bends
> down to stick
> fingers into
> the wound then
> smiles &
> spits hitting
> girty in the
> face, girty's
> last words
> no dirt
> in the eyes
> boys, no
> dirt in the
> eyes

Genteel Bucolicism Poems

For manifestations of this genre look no further than David Wagoner's *Landfall: Poems.* Wagoner's sensibility and emotional responses fall within the framework of the entirely possible, noncontroversial, and secure. His meditations on man and nature evolve from this placid center. Although he was merely middle-aged when this book was published in 1981, we find him falling asleep in gardens, standing around in swamps and woods and on lake shores, always evoking a sanitized, calm and pleasant existence. One assumes he is now aging gracefully.

A faithful wife usually hovers nearby or sleeps in her own bed while Wagoner is writing poems. Spiders, moths, and small birds receive his attention. His nights and darknesses contain minimal threats, occasioning only reveries and a gentle metaphysics. His imagination is domestic. He never appears far from home, rarely departing the well-beaten path. One has the sense that survival trips in the wilderness are not for him— he prefers the aging man's (and even poets in their twenties and thirties may sound like aging men) stroll, or the easy day trip, all within a whistle's blow of the boat landing or the lookout tower. His natural fauna and insectivora seem almost noiseless and most patient. We recall that Jonathan Edwards was not far from home either when he observed those spiders drifting to their deaths at sea and started a fad among American writers for recording botanical and biological minutiae.

His "The Poets Agree To Be Quiet By The Swamp" is the epitome of genteel bucolicism. Wagoner's poets seem in awe, holding their hands over their mouths as they stare at a "stretch of water," admiring "strokes of light like herons' legs in the cattails," and frogs below, deep in muck.

As I read his poems, I see them stitch themselves together into an afghan of verse, one that would please Jonathan Winters' Maude Frickert. But, though afghans can be beautiful, they fall short of being true works of art. They are cheery, well-crafted pieces hooked together by fairly easy formulas (patterns)—appropriate pastimes for ladies in rest homes, retirees living on fixed incomes, or poets admired by *The American Poetry Review.*

Not surprisingly, Wendell Berry is an old hand at the geriatric poem. "A Failure" (*Farming: A Handbook,*) is perfect in its genteel regrets over lost lilies that once were, a happenstance that tumbles him into his own aging: "Will they return / next year? Will I?" In "The Grandmother," an old woman craves "gentle dainty things" like a cookie or a hot cup of tea. For she was poor, and had labored over a wood stove throwing off cornbread and dishes of jowl and beans to feed the "hard-handed men" in her life. She eventually became so stooped over (sentimental touch) that they had "to break her / before she would lie down in her coffin."

Berry receives even more impulses from vernal woods than Wagoner. This passage from "The Heron" establishes his general view on man and nature:

The world as men have made it is an ungainly
hardship that comes of forgetting
there is no other life than men have made.

One must "go easy and silent" among warblers, herons, sweet-eyed deer, nighthawks, and sunflowers. You must "drop" your gardens; i.e., drop the seeds to make them grow. Cities, since they have forgotten nature, will eventually "rot at heart." We measure city "time" by noisy motors, not by living creatures. On his Tennessee farm Berry synchronizes time and nature.

The problem, as he sees it in "The Sorrel Filly," is to be more "aware." The "quiet" he loves is threatened continually by the demands of his time, juggling "costs and losses." Be more as leaves are, resting in the air, "perfectly still." Once again, on his placid acres, he looks up to observe a sorrel filly at her grazing. A week earlier, he tried to sell her, but couldn't get the price. He gazes at her, happy that she is there "in the quiet." He's "glad / to have recovered what is lost / in the exchange of something for money."

Gretel Ehrlich is strikingly sensitive to nature. She lives in Shell, Wyoming, where she writes and makes documentary films.

In "A Way of Speaking," she meets a young rancher:

Standing in the stirrups at a dead run,
you showed me how to throw a loop and dally up
without losing fingers.
During the day our legs
touched, moved apart, touched again.
To live with cattle as we did
was to enter the inward blousing of grass
and drift there.

The lovers break off. By the time she heals, he returns. An amazing image of a river slitting its neck occasions a vivid reflection on human separations:

Once we entered that river.
It slit its neck so we
might use its voice.
Even so, I do not know if there is
a way of speaking that ever
takes one person to another,
or forward to what they might become.

"A Sheeprancher Named John" is Ehrlich's seemingly objective, highly detailed portrait of an amazing man. Orange is his color. In "a long overcoat" of bees, by "stings and grace," he crosses the Big Horn Mountains "against an upstream current of sheep." His speech is always "brutally to the point." A diamond ring "orbits" one of his fingers, "glazed by the silkdust of oats." The orange light around him is indirect, slanted, "helplessly elegant, a color of / minor disrepute." His weathered skin shows aging, the "irregular hems," the pulled-out threads:

> His whole body, orange and burnt orange.
> The abalone shell of his back with rich meat
> under it, perfectly plumbed and moving sideways in
> the sign of Cancer.

Sunspots on his arms resemble melted birdseed. His mouth, a "loose tear across" his face, rarely moves when he speaks. His eyes are "steady-state. Burnt all the way brown. / Shy penis, mostly / swirled white."

A poet who sees farm life as anything but genteel is Hayden Carruth. Among the impressive poems in *Brothers, I Loved You All* are three long, Frostian portraits of Vermont locals. One, John Dryden (he's blissfully unaware of his poet namesake), is a seemingly crazy loner who, after a life of incredible labors (among them slugging cows with an ax at a rendering plant) lives in isolation. Johnny Spain, subject of the second portrait, has a farm which might have been one of the best. Now it lies in great decrepitude, surrounded by acres of "accumulated junk" he's salvaged from the town dump. The most straightforward, least romanticized of Carruth's portraits is that of Marshall Washer, a "cowshit farmer":

> . . . Even in dead of winter, even in the
> dark night solid with thirty below, thanks
> to huge bodies breathing heat and grain sacks
> stuffed under doors and in broken windows, warm,
> and heaped with reeking, steaming manure, running
> with urine that reeks even more, the wooden channels
> and flagged aisles saturated with a century's excreta. . . .

Carruth regrets that Marshall's vast efforts, struggles, and pains are soon to disappear. His hilltop farm will disappear, for agribusiness managers prefer the easier cultivations on bottom land farms. Carruth contemplates buying the place so that Marshall will feel that his farm will endure for a few more years.

Bucolic poems are found everywhere in literary journals and anthologies. An educated guess is that 80 percent of the poems written in this country are rustic in some way, either as memories or as direct experiences. One journal (and I could cite several others), *Images,* publishes poems almost exclusively on these rural themes, and photos of silos, leafless trees, old schoolhouses, and Midwestern landscapes. Agriwriters like Berry, Gary Snyder, and William Stafford are immensely popular with hosts of younger writers and readers, especially those who "dropped out" in the sixties and seventies, and chose to withdraw from urban America and live "on the land."

I hasten to add, however, that Snyder, a poet I admire, is never feeble or geriatric or genteelly bucolic. His self-immersion in the isolated mountain landscapes of northern California is the authentic extension of a profoundly spiritual life. When Snyder drinks his manzanita berry tea it's apt to be a revelation; when an imitator does, it's merely an experience.

In "second shaman song," Snyder is deep in a mosquito-filled mountain swamp where he finds karma in feeling that his body joins "the long body of the swamp." As the "still hand moves out alone," it flowers, leafs, and turns to "streaked rock." Numerous poems in Snyder's *Myths and Texts* are about vast fires in the mountains of the Pacific Northwest, fires Snyder helped fight.

Snyder—and William Stafford also—is so unique a poet that he is almost inimitable. Hordes of young poets nevertheless persist in imitating him. In a sense, Stafford, whose work seems far more casual, easily written, and closer to informal speech, is the more dangerous model to follow. And Stafford himself writes poems that seem like an inept acolyte's imitations. Like Berry and Wagoner, Stafford is a gentle man who makes a comfortable living, who has an adoring family, and who seems to prefer the safer aspects of nature to their stark and wilder ones.

There seems to be a hunger in the land among poets lacking roots (or so they feel) who continue to romanticize the American landscape; if they can only find a toe hold, some tiny patch of ground, no matter how rocky or lacking in amenities, their spirits soar. The next best thing is to take imaginary trips into private landscapes of their own imaginings. Sam Hamill is a rare poet who manages to fuse Eastern mysticism with a Thoreauvian attention to nature and avoid pitfalls. His recent *The Nootka Rose* is consistently fine.

The ideal of the quasi-primitive life appeals greatly to American poets who persist in feeling real or imagined ties with Thoreau's bean rows, sunflower heads, squirrels, and cabin. The cabin is *in,* especially if you have built it yourself from begged, borrowed, or stolen materials. Also, like Thoreau who despised such progressive developments as the telegraph and the railroad, current poets romanticize living without telephone and television—but not without a telescope, since it enables them to meditate on the stars.

A funny, and at the same time, serious poem on these themes is Rodney Jones's "Thoreau." Jones is repairing an old Volvo, and is down on his back "among the sockets / wrenches, nuts, and bolts." As "cold grease" drips on his glasses, he thinks of Thoreau on his morning strolls at the pond, "dreaming of self-sufficiency." Jones proceeds with his tinkering:

> I think of the odometer that shows
> eight circuits of the planet.
> I drop the transmission and loosen
> the bolts around the bellhousing.
> I take it in both hands, jerk,
> and it pops like a sliced melon. . . .

He recalls Thoreau's lists, and by the time he reaches the flywheel, his hair is clotted with grease, his knuckles are bleeding, and he is "thinking

of civil disobedience." As he gazes up into "the dark heaven of machinery, /
the constellations of flaking gaskets," he imagines Thoreau's dry cow and
his cornstalks "splintered by twentieth century Europeans."

Gluten Poems

Poets, I feel, worry too much about concocting "palatable" poems—
trimming their recipes to appeal to some common denominator of
taste rather than a highly spiced individualized one. David C. Yates's
"Making Bread" opens blandly before proceeding to a recipe, a variation
on the "information poem." Yates creates an only partially successful
metaphor of poem-making:

> We'll use only
> stoneground unbleached unenriched natural
> flour. We'll sift it much like, to use an
> analogy, we sift words we throw at
> one another to make them lighter and
> fluffier, in short, more palatable.

Fortunately, Yates drops the analogy and returns to his bread making,
reinvigorating it with a fresh analogy, an intimate, personal one:

> Then we heat the milk—scald it, in fact,
> but we don't hit the flour with it, we let
> it cool somewhat and then when it meets flour
> the flour will *feel* its warmth, much
> the way, pardon me, you tingle the back
> of my neck with the *feel* of your fingers
> in my hair which brings us to yeast. . . .

You melt the yeast in lukewarm water, stir, prime, and add salt, the latter
to "absorb" any lingering "bitterness." This is a third analogy: after we
fashion something for sheer pleasure we feel guilt; "salt" erases this.

Yes, Yates is winsome, and his attempt to elevate the "recipe poem"
deserves a minor medal. I keep hungering (if that is the right word) for a
poem devoted entirely to bread making, without coy analogies that only
partially work.

Ruth Whitman's "Act of Bread" delineates the poet's fear of kneading
the life of love and motherhood she craves. She fantasizes a batter that
starts to crawl "up the walls." A "secret passion" overtakes her thumbs:

> into my own
> flour yeast water I plunged my lust
> up the elbows—pounding the white

buttocks of my children, turning
their rosy heels; kneading the
side, loin, groin of him
to whom I long owed this caressing.

Her imagination runs amok. The rising bread flows over "table shelves floor." When she tries to scoop it into a paper bag it bursts the sides and climbs "out the window." If she had succeeded in baking the dough, a single crumb would have been "aphrodisiac," a single slice could "people a continent." In panic, she fills bucket after bucket, carries it all outside, and gives it to "the cold November morning."

Heather McHugh, in a poem called "Recipe," weaves self-dimensions around an image of rising bread-dough. A wind is "indecisive: how high shall the season's / hems be, how much of an out-and-out / tousle the hair of hills and how degraded or adult- / erated or disturbed a green river?" By contrast, bread always "knows from the first" that it will double. McHugh imagines her face as "untroubled dough." She hates her "looks" for lacking the "changeability" of a free-spirited wind. She resembles dough—her life is so predictable: "but sure / old age, and lunch is coming, custom- / ers and husbands to blow / the front door down." She punishes her dough-ego, relegating it to a shelf where she hears it breathe and swell:

I take that gentle, willing
flesh and punch it, hard, with my fist
wherever I see myself. Then leave it,
just like that, fallen on a yell-

ow shelf. But through the afternoon
of scrap and talk I hear it
breathe, I hear it swell. I'll have
to face myself again, what is
never quite done, never outdone,
never done in.

Gossip Poems

Most such poems regale us with chitchat about lives, usually rich and famous ones. James Merrill, that elegant dazzler, is a master of these. In "Lost in Translation," we observe the domestic goings-on of a cultured German home with a bored child and an aging "French Mademoiselle" who are waiting for a special jigsaw puzzle from America. The nosy child regales us with passages from Mademoiselle's scribblings and informs us that the poor old soul is probably not French after all.

John Ashberry's "Self-Portrait in a Convex Mirror" employs gossip poetry as a journey into the mind of his speaker, probably himself. In addition to bits of gossipy news and information about others, we are privy here to an entire floating world of self-impressions, self-assessments, hungers, and fears—and of elegance, wealth, and art. He seems to fear the spinning of life's carousel, which begins easily and then rushes speeding on until all is blurred "in one neutral band" surrounding "me on all sides, everywhere I look."

An even purer example of gossip poetry is Ashberry's "Syringa," which presents intimacies from the lives of Orpheus and Eurydice. Much more plebeian, however, is Rita Dove's "Weathering Out" which provides tidbits of Beulah's life with Thomas, who's been out looking for work. Beulah, in her eighth month of pregnancy, can't see her feet, so she floats "from room to room, houseshoes flapping, / navigating corners in wonder." Thomas is romantic: when he returns from his unsuccessful day, "nearly in tears," he listens to the baby in her belly and thinks he hears it talking. To Beulah "it was more the *pok-pok-pok* / of a fingernail tapping a thick cream lampshade." Dove's gossipy details are poignant; but, alas, she can't leave well enough alone, and must strain after momentousness, as she does at the very end, with a finale that seems made-to-order for a writing workshop—clover in cobblestones hang "stubbornly on, / green as an afterthought. . . ." Too bad.

Haiku

I do not know which to prefer,
The beauty of inflections
Or the beauty of innuendoes,
The blackbird whistling
Or just after
                                —Wallace Stevens

The Japanese haiku, unrhymed renditions of a seemingly slight moment in nature which the poet in seventeen syllables hopes to relate to human nature, is a form often brutalized by American poets. Every fledgling versifier seems to believe that the haiku is where poetry begins, and that even the most minimally talented are capable of executing them. Entire journals are devoted to these coy rather than substantial poems, acrylic finger-painting smudges rather than the stunning ink sketches of a master.

I propose to give a few successful examples of haiku, rather than linger over the failures; for the haiku can be brilliant, even in an American poet's hands. The form depends on the aesthetic principle that less is more, and haiku enthusiasts argue that the beauty of a fine haiku transcends that of the Shakespearean sonnet. Fortunately, we need not choose one over the other. Also, while the Japanese hold to seventeen syllables, an adapter or translator has the freedom to drop or add syllables. What is important, as poet Charles Hood said recently, is "the ability to capture an essence in a dewdrop." He also reported his success at using a favorite haiku, by Issa, in his university classes with students familiar with dry, rock-strewn arroyos. Here is the haiku:

> Dry creek
> glimpsed
> by lightning

He reports being out at night in such an arroyo, without shelter or torch, in the path of a potential flashflood, and thinking of verse: brilliant haiku (like Issa's) conclude "in a snap, as a lightning flash does."

Two masters of this subtle form are Ezra Pound and Kenneth Rexroth. Pound not only translated Japanese and Chinese poetry but fashioned his own. In his superb "Ts'ai Chi'H" a subtle play of color hints at the ochre impression of a delicate poem.

> The petals fall in the fountain
> the orange-coloured rose-leaves,
> Their ochre clings to the stone.

In another haiku, the famous one on faces in a wet crowd as soaked petals, Pound reflects his distaste for the human mass.

> The apparition of these faces in the crowd;
> Petals on a wet, black bough.

Kenneth Rexroth managed better than most American poets to capture the delicate attar of the Oriental poem. Gary Snyder, steeped both in Japanese culture and Americana, adapted the form to an American practicality and wrote of fixing a leaking roof and of a semi rolling through a desert at night "lit like a town."

> After weeks of watching the roof leak
> I fixed it tonigth
> by moving a single board.

> A great freight truck
> lit like a town
> through the dark stony desert

Kenneth Rexroth fixes the magic of dawn striking through a tree filled with birds:

> A dawn in a tree of birds.
> Another.
> And then another.

John Ashbery writes thirty-seven haiku in a poem of that title included in his *Selected Poems*. Some are comments on human behavior: "Too low for nettles but it is exactly the way people think and feel." Others are painterly: "A blue anchor grains of grit in a tall sky sewing." This one has a fey twist: "The wedding was enchanted everyone was glad to be in it." All are frosted o'er with Ashbery charm.

The title section of William Heyen's *Lord Dragonfly* contains thirty-six haiku and haiku-like poems.

While some are successful (particularly one on finding his absent wife's lost earring in a garden furrow), too many are throwaways. Some display the tired pathetic fallacy: the "souls" of goldenrod spike glow softly in a field's drizzling gloom. Others are simply either too coy or too obvious: a mantis "prays" on his scythe (for Heyen not to whack it in half?); the poet leans on "his shovel." His concluding poem is fraught with far more momentousness than the frail bark can transport:

> Cosmos, planet, field,
> and the dead
> aware of everything!

This haiku is by Jonathan Williams: "White cloud in the eye of a white horse." And Ron Androla contributes this gem to *Bogg*.

> Johnny Cash
>
> i love munching on a
> chilled bull-frog between
> 2 slices of burnt toast

Another feature of poems related to haiku is the occasional line that leaps out with such beauty it deserves special attention, almost as if it were a brief isolated verse on its own. One of my favorites occurs in Elizabeth Bishop's "Paris, 7 A.M." She describes the dull "half-tone scale" of a winter day in Paris: "Winter lives under a pigeon's wing, a dead wing with damp feathers." Perhaps some enterprising reader will assemble an anthology of such moments.

An important treatment of haiku can be found in Robert Hass's *Twentieth Century Pleasures*.

Home-Cooked Poems

Home-cooked poems—Robert Frost is responsible for these—commemorate (usually sentimentally) life on the farm when the poet was a boy. (It is curious that men rather than women write them.) The style, as "home-cooked" as the subject matter, is so plain it risks seeming pretentious. The writing itself is often more "verse" than poetry, and is, in fact, a kind of anti-poetry. Here is how William Stafford's satiric "One Home" begins:

> Mine was a Midwest home—you can keep your world.
> Plain black hats rode the thoughts that made our code.
> We sang hymns in the house; the roof was near God.
>
> The light bulb that hung in the pantry made a wan light,
> but we could read by it the names of preserves—
> outside, the buffalo grass, and the wind in the night.

Stafford's celebrated "The Farm on the Great Plains" manages to transcend the limitations of the form. He phones the old farm every year, but no one is there.

> My self will be the plain,
> wise as winter is gray,
> pure as cold posts go
> pacing toward what I know.

David Budbill writes extensively about rural and small-town Vermont, locating some of his homespun narratives and monologues in a fictional place called Judevine. His poetic voice is that of the "down-east Yankee," as delivered from the Green Mountains to coastal Maine, and southward to Long Island Sound, with an overlay, as Hayden Carruth has observed, of "the more guttural, shortened accent of the Champlain Valley." Budbill's work includes *From Down to The Village; The Chain Saw Dance;* and *Pulp Cutter's Nativity: A Christmas Poem in Two Acts,* an adaptation of the medieval miracle play *The Second Shepherd's Play* rendered in terms of local Vermont. Here is a sampling of one of Budbill's homespun monologues:

> Arnie and I harvested Christmas trees three falls together.
> Arnie is emaciated and always dirty.
> He shaves only on Saturday nights
> before he goes to the bottle club.
> His face is more wretched than any I have ever seen.
> All I remember about those falls together
> is how much Arnie knew about the second world war
> and how his nose dripped.
> He'd stand in the snow and shiver like a popple leaf

and his nose would drip.
He never bothered to wipe it
except maybe two or three times a day
he'd sop it gently
with the back of the glove on his right hand.

Readers may also want to consult James Still's collected poems, *The Wolfpen Poems,* drawn from rural Kentucky where he lives.

Merritt Clifton's *Samisdat* is about as homespun and rural a journal as one can read. The look and feel are similar to the old *Farmer's Almanac.* In fact, issues look ephemeral—as soon as the seeds are bought, the sun charts consulted, and the seeds sown, relegate *Samisdat* to the outhouse. The next issues will soon appear to help you through the hot summer, the harvest, and then through winter. *Samisdat* is truly fashioned for "ordinary" consumption—it's to be read right along with your oatmeal, while waiting for the maple syrup to drip, or as your brushpile burns. Nothing about *Samisdat* smacks of poetry lovers in academic clothing sealed off in ivory towers. These are poems for readers who are busy taking in the hay, cooking jam, ice-fishing, or drinking beer and playing baseball.

Homophobic Poems

One homophobic moment occurs in Robert Lowell's "Skunk Hour." A homosexual decorator (Lowell calls him "Our fairy decorator") living on Nautilus Island, a summer resort, after a wretched season

> . . . brightens his shop for fall;
> his fishnets filled with orange cork,
> orange his cobbler's bench and awl;
> there is no money in his work,
> he'd rather marry.

The poem is full of homophobic clichés, including the notion that homosexuals are miserable and want to be straight.

Michael Goodman's "The Testimony" begins this way:

> The elderly fairy at the desk
> was in love with me: mornings, I'd find
> a fresh packet of sugar in my box.
> He had the seedy charm
> and mild, dolorous air
> of the plastic ficus in the lobby.

Not only is Goodman nasty-spirited about this old man, he is even more so about another, a "neighbor" who dislikes him because he was "disrespectful":

> What woman
> would love a man who spat
> in his basin, an emphysemic
> who rolled his own cigarettes. . . .

Diane Wakoski's "Poem For Judy Garland Which Is A Field Guide to Butterflies" develops another gay stereotype, the effeminate youth with "weak hands," a Judy Garland fan, who waits beneath the singer's window.

While it is barely possible to read Michael C. Ford's "The Homosexual" (p. 38) as nonhomophobic, I have my doubts. He imagines that all the gays of San Francisco, "tittering in their / Tinkerbell partydress" will "flit" along "on blurry currents of fey / Air" through the Golden Gate Bridge, and will "swoop" along the coastal range all the way to southern California. There, with glitter-studded ears, "funk-punk" rouged faces, limbs "severely manacled"—another cliché of homosexuals addicted to bondage—with roped and painted tendrils of hair, they will grope all "your [the heterosexuals'?] awful unconscious / Perversions, pushing you into / Silicone paranoid transformations"—pushing you into queerdom for the remainder of your life, in other words.

Robin Morgan's "Annunciation," dedicated to the five men who beat up her "faggot-husband" at dawn on Sunday, February 25, 1968, avoids demeaning clichés while she rages against the heterosexual men who brutalized her husband. As she holds the whimpering, beaten man in her arms, her lap "lavish" with his "uncyclical" (that is, nonmenstrual) blood, she is herself in pain for him. The attackers were of the "white workingclass," a "brotherhood convened to prove each member / capable of beating up a faggot." From the bull-neck of one dangled a silver Our Lady medal, blessing "the effect" of ten powerful fists crushing a skull. Morgan's polemic has the force of blows to the crotch of these "straight patriotic clean Americans."

A brighter turn on the homosexual motif is Jonathan Williams' gently satiric "The Chameleon," spoken by a man who won't accept the fact that he is gay, and changes his spots as the occasion requires:

> at 14 I decided it was avant-garde to dig women
> but, man if I were just the least
> bit queer, boy, you know, man, wow,
>
> and then some; but, like
> I'm not, but
>
> when I write *Dearest* to you in a letter, then
> that's different,
>
> isn't it?

Homosexual Poems

Gay pride as we know it today began in June, 1969, after the Stonewall Riots in Greenwich Village, New York. One result has been a massive outpouring of writing of all kinds, which continues despite the tragedy of AIDS. The two volumes of *Gay Sunshine Interviews* which appeared in 1978 and 1982, edited by Winston Leyland, were landmarks of gay culture. Among the poets interviewed were William Burroughs, Allen Ginsberg, John Giorno, Harold Norse, Peter Orlovsky, James Broughton, Kirby Congdon, Robert Duncan, Kenward Elmslie, Taylor Mead, Edouard Roditi, Ned Rorem, John Wieners, Jonathan Williams, and Thomas Meyer. Anthologies of gay poetry appeared, the first being *The Male Muse* (1973), edited by Ian Young, and published by the pioneering Crossing Press. Winston Leyland soon published *Angels of the Lyre* (1975), and *Orgasms of Light* (1977). The emergence of Paul Mariah's Manroot Press in the 70s gave gays and lesbians a first-quality national press.

Gay poems, or poems by poets who are gay, fall into two general classes: those written for all readers, gay or straight; and those written intentionally for a homosexual audience. Most of Robert Duncan's poetry, for example, though it may have homoerotic moments, is written for the literary world at large, as is the work of Ed Field (his "Giant Pacific Octopus" is a gay classic), Jonathan Williams, and John Wieners. The Pulitzer Prize-winning works of John Ashbery and James Merrill enjoy a large audience. Richard Howard includes a poem called "On Hearing Your Lover Is Going to the Baths Tonight," ostensibly of interest primarily to gays, in *Lining Up*, a book of monologues and "impersonations" directed towards a general audience.

Many older gay poets are still inclined to be circumspect, if not actually devious, about their sexuality. Among the exceptions are Allen Ginsberg, Harold Norse, Thom Gunn, and James Broughton. Ginsberg's immense popularity, almost on a par with a rock star's, is puzzling, given the homophobia in this country. In his latest book (and one of his best) *White Shroud,* he mixes blatantly homoerotic poems with mystico-religious poems and lengthy, powerful elegies to his dead grandmother and mother. Norse's recent *Bastard Angel* is enthusiastically sexual and definitely x-rated; you will not find it on many American coffee tables. Broughton's later work, both in film and writing, is flamboyantly gay and attracts largely homosexual audiences. Paul Mariah's "Persona Non Grata," and most of his other poems, are unabashedly gay. "Persona" is a classic work on the experiences of a gay man in a Midwestern prison.

Thom Gunn manages to bridge both the gay and straight worlds. His prize-winning *The Passages of Joy* is a mix of poems on gay and straight themes. One stunning poem, "Bally Power Play," can be enjoyed both as a turn-on and as a feast of precise observation in which the poet's ego is submerged in his excitement at observing a lad's skill and beauty at the pinball machine. Gunn's "The Miracle" is a straightforward presentation of raunchy gay sex in the john of a McDonald's hamburger shop. The form is a rhyming, five-line stanza. The events are presented as reportage, as if they did not happen to Gunn. His lengthy poem "Talbot Road" recounts the frustrating and sad history of a gay man's love for a straight one, and the gay man's return, fifteen years later (the straight man is now dead) to the street where they lived. Part Three celebrates sex at one of the world's great homosexual gathering places, an area of Hampstead Heath, London, famous for generations.

Younger poets who have matured since *Howl* and the Stonewall days seem much more comfortable with their sexuality, more self-assured than their predecessors. Guilt over loving men is now rarely an issue— nor do these poets dwell, as earlier poets were apt to do, on the tragic elements of their lives. The new tone is positive and celebratory. *The Son of the Male Muse,* edited by Ian Young and published by The Crossing Press (1983), is devoted to work by this younger generation. These poet's don't curry favor with the straight world—times have changed, on the surface at least. Sons of the male muse would just as soon chuck old Socrates under the balls on a bright clear day in Golden Gate or Central Park as ask a stranger for a light.

Some of these poems are throwaways; some aren't. Among the former are poems with lines like these: "He likes to kiss, even french-kissing me, / closing his eyes. . . . muscles / from working in a lumberyard." A crab man loves one poet's "guts and thighs and butt / and soft wiggly plushy toes."

Among the better poets are Steve Abbott, Jack Anderson, bill bissett, Dennis Cooper, Thomas Meyer, Felice Picano, and Rene Ricard.

Of this group, Thomas Meyer is most consistently fine. Always the consummate craftsman, his fusions of ancient Greek homosexual love with modern manifestations appear in four special books, as remarkable for their book-making as for their poetry: *The Bang Book*—discussed in "Billy the Kid Poems," supra; *The Umbrella of Aesculapius*; *Uranian Roses*; and *Sappho's Raft: Le rideau de la Mytileienne.*

In "Uprooted Ganymede," from *The Umbrella of Aesculapius*, a poem very representative of Meyer's themes, tone, and style, the glorious youth is visualized as "a late Hellenic statue, substantial & well turned, suspended." Meyer's aim, he says, is for action at a "stately pace," one suited to "consummation & desire melting into affection." We remember, of course, that Zeus, in love with the handsome mortal, assumes the guise of a swan, makes love to the boy, then wings him off to Heaven to be the mighty god's immortal cup bearer. Meyer's original touch of Ganymede as marble has fascinating contemporary overtones—the youth seems an archetype for all attractive, inaccessible youths who frequent gay bars and other gathering places, lost in their beauty and as hard as marble, daring mere mortals to approach them. The poem appears in its entirety:

Uprooted Ganymede,
spread-eagle,
spins in terror's wing beat whirlwind.

The screaming revenger enters
hard, white,
succulent, marble nates;

god seed animates, heats
cold stone.
Son of Tros,
manhood's joy,

iron talons grip your Hellenic crotch—
the boy's loins caught,
fondles with feathery caresses.

You pour the nectar you take,
your bright cup overflows, spills,
unlocking panic's heart.

The sacred company celebrates your service.
The sight of you
swaying through their numbers
on alabaster legs,
with teasing girdle displaying
slight cheek curves
& hints of secret curls,

sets fires.

Most gay themes parallel those of all love poems: how to find a mate and keep one; unfulfilled longings for real and imagined lovers; the jilted lover; confronting the departure or death of a loved one; first love—gays can be just as giggly and adolescent as their heterosexual counterparts; celebrations of erotic experience, including recitals of praise for all aspects of the loved one's body. Among the themes that seem uniquely gay are these: cruising; promiscuity; the traumas of coming out of the closet; an obsession with being young and desirable, and the newest theme, AIDS, and the horrible deaths of friends and acquaintances. One of the most moving of these latter poems is by Charles Plymell, who is straight, to a friend he lost to AIDS: "San Francisco Ward: for Bill MacNeil, painter, San Francisco," in *Forever Wider*.

What fascinates me is something that seems to occur in the history of all minority literatures: they are begun by repressed, older writers who stress blending in with the culture at large. One thinks of poets like Michael Harper and Gwendolyn Brooks, who seem like Uncle Toms to more militant younger black poets, or of Baraka who as LeRoi Jones, no matter how vituperative, had a considerable white audience, an audience he now seems to care little for. Once a minority gains visibility on its own terms, via social rights, its new writers seem of necessity to turn exclusive, addressing their own group, *raising consciousness*. As the number of gay poets grows, the heterosexual audience seems to diminish. Gay presses and gay bookstores multiply. A minority culture flour-ishes as a large but isolated island in the greater society. The most recent issue of the literary quarterly *The James White Review* is heartening evidence that serious gay writing has come of age, as is the *New Gay & Lesbian Poetry in Our Time: An Anthology*, edited by Carl Moore and Joan Larkin, New York, St. Martin's Press, 1988, despite several glaring omissions of significant writers and the inclusion of too much mediocre work.

Hugo Poems

Graham House Review no. 7, is dedicated to Richard Hugo's mem-ory, a useful clue to the poems the editors favor: all about local types—drunks, bakers, hunchbacks, and family members. Madeline De Frees, in an elegy on Hugo, recalls that he liked "pretending not to read." This pretense, I fear, has been taken as literal truth by hordes of young poets.

Gary Fincke writes about making bread (the baker has his "hands busy inside / The rising, dependent dough") and throws in a dollop of Hugoesque clabber: a drink who "sugar-dreamed his way / Toward morning."

Judson Mitcham's Hugoesque father–son poem contains woefully spavined lines and a tone reminiscent of Hugo's soft, vaporous melancholy:

> Whatever it is
> you have searched for eludes you yet.
> Your own light and the light I read by both guide you.
> A sleepwalker also once, I know those lights,
> how certainty will fade toward certainty. Son,
> come sit with me.

A better writer, Laurie Blauner, presents a daughter–father rela-tionship, possibly an incestuous one. The daughter confesses to the father that she cannot quit "the sound" of his "breath lifting to a scar of light." While she doesn't swamp her lines with literary dreck, dull pre-positional phrases that limp along like snakes with broken backs, her homey tone ties her to Hugo. Here (her mother has been killed in a car wreck) her father visits her bed:

> That night the dogwood catching porchlight in its thin network of life
> was a woman's smooth fingers testing the weight of pearls.
> The architect of the heart is memory. I touched lips and limbs so like my
>   own.

Blauner's blend of nature and passion stimulates wonder, and her closing stanza is potent, subtle, and strange:

> The thin fan of bones in my hands are Mama's.
> They lead like rivulets to the heart she wanted to offer
> to an acceptable beau. Honeysuckle roses eclipse my breasts.
> I cannot grow away from you. This night's moonlight lies against my bones
> to listen, to hold the shape of my body in its light.
> You call me your ghost. A still wind rests in my hands.

Also in this issue of *Graham House Review* are poems filled with Hugo-inspired flora and fauna, accounts of the seasons, and slack first-person opening lines. Robert Gibb starts "March" this way:

> If I were good enough,
> Patient enough, and attentive,
> I would be able to tell you
> Everything I've seen today—
>
> . . .
>
> The loving minutiae of a world
> Turning into spring.

Later, after remarking on "the face of your startling presence," Gibb throws in snow nudging "its bank"; a turtle "clacking over stones"; and geese, skunk cabbage, crocus sprouts, and some "tiny berries" he can't name.

A featured poet, Cleopatra Mathis, wrenches John Donne's famous compass image; God's creation of Adam leads to speculation about his leg:

> God means that leg as tree
> rooted to one place, as the other will want
> always to carry him away
> on feet which are the boniest of fish.

In the Hugo tradition, standing in snow, she faces up to "the pearls" of her inadequacy. While she can't see much in the blizzard, she keeps icicles from her mind by meditating on earth and life. She's very sentimental, one of Hugo's failings: a babe's breath has "tiny white flowers," a cat's yawn is a "pink-tongued sigh." Here I can't tell whether her fists, or the chest she's pressing, are ovate:

> I hold my two fists
> against the middle of your chest,
> the size of my own heart, the shape of an egg.
> And in the egg, the filled cell
> dividing, the pull and release.

Madeline De Frees contributes a cloying elegy on Hugo, and succumbs to a trap many elegiasts can't avoid: the fiction that since the departed one doesn't know what's happened since his death, the survivor must report the news. If Hugo dead can hear a living De Frees, why isn't he capable of seeing her on her Fulbright tour of Greece? Souls have ears but, apparently, no eyes. At the close of her poem, De Frees reaches a nadir of chatter rather than felt emotion. She imagines Hugo as a coat wrapped about her in "grey weather." His voice, she promises him, will continue "strong" in her ear, "falling like those coastal rains / to fill the reservoir or float the Big Sky / home, riding your favorite thermals." I'm glad *thermals* refers to clouds, not to underwear.

Images in Poems

No literary term is more elusive than *image,* nor can I hope here to do more than delimit some kinds of images and provide a few examples for each, emphasizing the practical rather than the theoretical.

Some images, like Robert Frost's pasture spring or Elizabeth Bishop's old fish are immediately clear. Others, like Denise Levertov's Jacob's ladder or Archibald MacLeish's poem dumb "as old medallions to the thumb" (he also saw other poems as "palpable and mute as a ripe fruit") are far more problematic. Some images appear almost in passing; others appear singly with sufficient force to dominate an entire poem. Those of this latter sort are sometimes called *deep images,* a term associated (wrongly, I think) with Robert Bly's poems in which an image acquires a special tactility of the sort he prizes in his seminal anthology *News of the Universe: Poems of Twofold Consciousness.*

Poets employ images for their readers' senses: touch (the old medallion), smell (Richard Eberhart's groundhog), taste (William Carlos Williams's cold plums in the icebox), sight (William Stafford's dead doe), color (T. S. Eliot's yellow cat rubbing its back "upon the window-panes"). Occasionally, a poet will accrete or cluster images for all of the senses, as Richard Wilbur does in "Potato." Cut open the "common brown" potato; feel it; catch its "cool clean stench / Mineral acid seeping from pores . . . / the taste of first stones, the hands of dead slaves."

The poem itself may be an image, as Ezra Pound, H. D., and Amy Lowell fashioned them. Lowell's "Patterns," an unjustly neglected poem, is one example.

Images appear also to fall into several primary sorts: hard or soft, deep or shallow. Gary Snyder's rip-rap, those chips of stone and rock piled along switchbacks to secure footing while one is hiking a mountain and to control soil erosion and flooding, are hard images, and must be imagined as resistant surfaces emitting rays that the sensitive poet may "read." Robert Bly's ant motel, that chunk of wood excavated into little crevices, which he takes home and later interprets in a poem, is another hard-surface image. Robert Frost's pasture spring is a soft image—it can be directly entered and explored. Other such images are Elizabeth Bishop's fish, Robert Duncan's meadow, and James Merrill's octopus.

In Denise Levertov's "The Jacob Ladder" a single image dominates an entire poem, an image imported from the concrete world to render something visionary palpable. The Jacob's ladder is exact and ascendable, a stairway "solidly built" of "rosy stone," with "sharp angles," something quite other than the legendary "thing of gleaming strands / a radiant evanescence." Angels now must do more than "glance in their thread" without touching stone; they must "spring / down from one step to the next, giving a little / lift of the wings." A man ascending must grip with his hands and expect to scrape his knees. Difficulty has its rewards: the "cut stone / consoles his groping feet. Wings brush past him." Another poet might have stopped here. We now find that what Levertov has been writing about all along is the ascending poem. The image sustained so beautifully throughout is now a symbol and achieves a unity larger than the sum of its parts. We *see* the poem as that ladder. We *feel* the appropriateness of the image, and are delighted at its fresh representation of the art we care for.

William Stafford in "Traveling Through the Dark" writes out of a literal experience which he describes in gently fashioned quatrains, allowing the material event itself to unfold without the assistance of imported mystical trappings. Driving along a narrow mountain road he's stopped by a dead doe lying in his way. He gets out, leaving the headlights on, the car idling, and examines the deer in the reddish tail-light. She is already stiff. He drags her off the road, and soon notices that her side is warm. She is pregnant, and the fawn inside is still alive, lying there "waiting . . . still, never to be born." Stafford's dilemma is brief—what can he do? Without considering the possibilities, or at least sharing them with us, he pushes the animal "over the edge into the river."

The incident is thoroughly particular. Of the thousands of does in those Oregon mountains, this one is unique. The spot in the road is specific—Stafford could drive back there today if he chose. What is masterful are Stafford's reverberations, always within the framework of the literal. Yes, the dead doe is an image. The night itself, the mountains and the road, the dying fawn, and Stafford himself are also images. Not one adds up to a single red stone ladder—but they all contribute to converting the incident itself into an image. The finding of a dead deer is an image assembled out of various lesser images which works towards one end. The larger image emits meanings: birth and death are inextricably interwoven, and survivors may be utterly helpless to assist in either parturition or death. Also, what is commonplace for one person may be revelatory for another: most drivers would probably have driven around the deer and kept on going. By stopping, Stafford performs a quietly intense and moving ritual for the dead, totally in keeping with that spirit of nature which seems to say that no death (or birth) should go unattended and unwitnessed. Stafford's lovely trope works within the context of the real and definable.

An instance of a hard image that does not work appears in Gregory Orr's "Concerning the Stone," where the permutations, costumes, and guises a stone is put through seem far too contrived. Orr's stone goes out in male dress to a party where it dances. "Late at night," that facile witching hour, apparently drunk or miserable at having been rejected by someone, our stone presses its mouth to "damp earth." Where on a stone exactly, except in cartoon stones, will you find a mouth? It's brave, for it does not weep, until later, when "the gray bowls of its hands would fill with tears." Its hands are useful also for grabbing a stick and beating away the clouds, and for carrying a mirror "to remind itself." Kitsch Moments of Importance! A stone metaphysics! The poem is both contrived and trivial.

Joel Oppenheimer, in "The Fourth Ark Royal" from *Just Friends / Friends and Lovers,* creates a magic image for time. An "old lady," sister to the three Fates, perpetually weaves our lives:

> . . . she is an
> old lady concerned with
> the pattern she is
> weaving, only every
> stitch is true, and
> might even have saved
> nine

In a local bar, the poet regales a friend with his talk ("talk . . . what / else were we constructed / for even?"), and thinks he triumphs over the old creature as she giggles away at her knitting, thinking she "has us there." Via friends and lovers we shape our lives (Oppenheimer's image is of bowling) with "a grace directed at / the limited world a game is." Finally, as the poet confesses, all the talk, grace, and fine intentions have little power to save us:

> i offer you a drink, my
> bare soul, and a half
> memory of when we last met.
>
> and i remember best that
> time is an old lady, like
> madame defarge, somehow
> weaving us all in, humming
> old tunes we might not
> remember, at the door.

Information Poems

These poems appeal to the American reader who believes that imaginative literature, since it deals with illusion and not reality, is a waste of time. If you provide this reader with new information, he or she may continue reading your poem. We Americans love to feel that we are not wasting time, particularly while reading poetry.

The first lines of William Matthews' "Nurse Sharks" resemble prose from a child's encyclopedia. Because "most sharks" lack "flotation bladders" they must keep on swimming or they'll sink. When they sleep they do so in underwater caves, wedging themselves "between reef-ledges," or in shallow water where their dorsals "cut up from the surf." Anita Endrezze-Danielson's "Helix Aspersa" is almost a parody of the information poem. She treats us to information on snails, reassuring us that the creature "has no insight":

> Observe its two front tentacles
> which scent leaf-mold and lance leaf.
> Its two longer tentacles are feeble eyes,
> sensing only the light
> which fogs its lusterless shell,
> and the shadows that are boneless and flourishing.

John Updike's "To Crystallization" is an information poem with complex appeals. The poet uses basic scientific facts about the formation of crystals, and thus appeals both to scientifically aware readers and to others who may like gaining practical knowledge. The poem glitters with allusions: the atom is figured as a sort of crystal, creating a "most pleasing" planarity of "salt and tourmaline." Updike interweaves the theme of "a Grand Artificer" responsible for this beauty. He moves to the "graceful layered frost-ferns the midnight elves / left on the Shillington windowpanes" for his "astonishment." Supernovas exploding, elements annealed "to the atomic number of 94," valence electrons, malleability, conductivity, molecules "mounting . . . one upon the other," all connote "that inner freezing whereby inchoate / innocence compresses a phrase of art." Music, yes, chilling our veins "with snowflakes of blood." Updike provides a potpourri of information, plus just enough of the esthetical.

A poem by Clayton Eshleman (who loves giving esoteric facts as he paddles through bays of "archetypes") begins this way:

> Trégastel has pink & black speckled rock,
> in French: "granit rose," dolmen-contoured in soft lifting heaps, or
>   saucers—
> their ridges, furrows, lobes or lobbies invite the early Dali of imagination,
> forms arrested melting, kidneys that excite my intestines to want to fish
> interiorily,
>
>   the bay of archetypes is at hand—

While we may not know exactly where Trégastel is, we nevertheless feel well informed on the nature of its rock, which substance occasions Eshleman's speculations on anatomical forms. Rock "kidneys" excite Eshleman's "intestines to / want to fish. . . .": try to imagine reeling those in on the line! The earth becomes an "imaginative act," a "bay of archetypes" arrived at by playing poet-geologist.

A variation on the information poem, the "recipe poem," is supplied by Daniel Halpern. You yourself are "the best company you'll ever have," so it's well to celebrate that self-loving fact by cooking yourself a good meal and serving it in style. You'll need a red linen tablecloth, a white place-setting, a salad bowl, and good silver. Prepare a leg of lamb—a three pounder will do, well rubbed with pepper, cumin, salt, and garlic cloves. Cut up some fresh vegetables and herbs and "the crudest olive oil / you can find." Be sure you create the salad dressing out of fresh dill, mustard, and juice from "hard lemons." (The lemons might serve also as images for how life tastes.) While a bottle of "good late harvest zinfandel" is breathing on your table, open some cold chardonnay and read for awhile. Relish the smell of the lamb and vegetables cooking, "the best part of the evening." Later, when the timer goes off, toss the salad and set the veggies and the lamb on the table. Light candles, pour the red wine. Now, before you start, raise your glass and toast yourself. You deserve this honor: "The company is the best you'll ever have."

Insomnia Poems

(*See also* Self-Pity Poems and Sleeping Spouse or Lover Poems)

While one of the archetypal insomniacs of literature is Macbeth, poets who can't sleep seldom proceed to slaughter sleeping guests. If they manage to transcend their frustrations, they may while the night away scribbling poems.

James McMichael in *Four Good Things* writes at length on insomnia. It's 2 or 3 A.M., and he feels pressured to fall asleep within an hour. He chats himself up: "Even if I / don't go back to sleep, I shouldn't worry that I haven't / slept enough, that I'll feel it in my eyes." He listens to his wife sleeping beside him, and times his breath to hers thinking it will help. It doesn't, so, feeling calm, he tries to get up. He's "too tired," and decides he'll "give up here." His mind rambles, flotsam and jetsam bits drift past, possibly yielding something to fix on and allow him to sleep:

> And even the
> giving up is trying, a counterfeit that takes me into
> harmless things, a seagull, my socks, into the drowse of
> someone giving up who meets that first improbable

ellipsis, slips beyond it to a second and a third and,
losing count, goes off between the scatter, sleeps,
is someone who's asleep, not me at all, who's only
almost there and pleased to be this close, too pleased,
now coming to my hold again with all the shifts
intact and unrelieved. I've lost my chance.
Having been so close and missed, I can't start over.
Nor can I trust that even now I've given up.
I'm left remembering the times I've gone to sleep,
and what I've done each time is to forget.
It's happened before. I've slept. I was asleep an
hour ago when nothing woke me, when I was simply
awake.

An unfelt poem on someone else's insomnia is Stanley Plumly's
"Cows." There are no clues as to who "you" is, and it doesn't matter, for
Plumly is caught up in cuteness—when "you" can't sleep "it off" the
speaker goes outside and regales the cows with singing. The cows return
the favor, singing *"moon, moon,"* a not-particularly-fresh variation of
normal cow-talk. Should we assume there's a full moon, and that Plumly
bangs out reverberations of the sort Yeats managed in "Byzantium"? Yes,
indeed, the moon was up, and the cows were mooing; in fact, years later,
the moon is still ascendant, as Plumly, penning this poem stays "awake
with you."

Iowa Workshop Poems

I am not afraid
That my head
Will not hold
The little I know.
—Janet Piper, "Vista"

Is there an "Iowa Workshop poem"? I recall once getting a letter by an
exorcised Donald Justice complaining that there was no such animal
and that it was unfair to say there was. Yet, it is true that the
reputation for spawning inferior, predictable poems Iowa has earned
implies that there may just be such a creature as the Workshop Poem.

A special issue of the *Iowa Review* (vol. 16, no. 1), the Iowa Work-
shop house organ, gathers up what the editor opines is some of the best
work written by workshop alumni (both teachers and students) over the
past fifty years. Featured are thirty-eight poems by twenty-three well-
known poets. The oldest poet is Paul Engle who taught in the Workshop
for twenty-four years. Doth he know what he hath wrought? Reading

through this collection convinces me of what I have all along suspected—yes, Virginia, there is an Iowa Workshop poem. My analysis reveals eleven features of these poems:

1. *An avoidance of anything cerebral or profound beyond an occasional platitudinous transcendental emotion.* Minds indeed produce little for these writers' heads to know. Here's Robert Mezey: "Remember the fullness of the moon / And the mountains drinking in that sea of milk." Laurie Sheck, writing of Giotto's "Annunciation," waxes sentimental over a "worldless loss by which we come to see / the opening of these lilies. . . ." She treats the virgin in sanctimonious tones; the virginity is enough to make a sensible person's skin creep. Janet Piper lies on her patio chair, gazes into "the deep gulf of space," and thinks of Gerard Manley Hopkins' Oxford. She prefers her sky ("this is Heaven itself") to Hopkins's university. There, recumbent on her patio, she sees that no walls close in on her universe, "no graceless growth" of cities, or "base or sour noise." No bull farts in a nearby pasture. No Greyhound bus with bad piston rings exudes smog along her country roads.

Buildings in early morning after rain come "forward from darkness," offer "their windows for light," and provide William Stafford with a visionary experience. Stafford recalls farm evenings when personified sunsets "donated farms / that yearned so far to the west that the world / centered there and bowed down." Stafford seems to have done better than those painters and poets who imagined farm animals on their knees at Christmas—Stafford's buildings and sunsets do the most reverential things.

2. *A preponderance of ego poems: first person singular and plural disquisitions on trivial, commonplace figures and events.* Thirty-one of these thirty-eight poems fall into this category. One of the most pretentious is by Michael Dennis Browne, who, writing of the Nazi exterminator Mengele, reduces the enormity of those murders to an easy solipsism: "I tell you, the bones are alive and well," so "don't tell me about the bones of Mengele."

3. *The "you poem."* There are a baker's dozen of these. Here the poet addresses a real or an imagined "you" (usually dead), providing him or her with information about the person's own life, information he or she probably already knew. The only workable poem of this type is Tess Gallagher's "Accordingly."

4. *"Childhood remembered" poems.* I count fifteen of these written by both men and women. None is memorable except Andrew Hudgins's "From Commerce to the Capitol: Montgomery, Alabama," James Crenner's "Young Hormones Madrigal," and Michael Van Walleghen's Detroit poems. Crenner's skillful ballad celebrates a young lad's rampant horniness and perpetual beating of his meat. All he has to do is read "Blondie," James Joyce, or James T. Farrell and he comes "a barrell." A meandering walk through downtown Montgomery, along the Freedom Marchers' route, on a scalding day, reminds Hudgins of his childhood in the 1960s. Small details relate: three black girls toe loose tar in Court Square where blacks were sold as slaves. A bus rumbles past Dexter Baptist Church where the Kings preached. Hudgins recalls his mother's

disapproval when as a child he accepted an egg a black man cooked on the hot hood of a Dodge Dart. The walk continues, past the spot where Jeff Davis took his oath as president of the Confederacy and where the crippled George Wallace was wheeled into the capitol. Times have changed. Wallace

> shrank into his chair,
> so wizened with paralysis he looked
> incurable, face white as schoolroom paste,
> hair black as just-paved road. He's fatter now.
> He courts black votes, and life is calmer than
> when Muslims shot whites on this street, and calmer
> than when the Klan blew up Judge Johnson's house,
> or Martin Luther King's. It could be worse.
> It could be Birmingham. It could be Selma.
> It could be Philadelphia, Mississippi.

5. *Dying relatives or acquaintances poems*. Donald Justice commemorates a composer he knew, whose papers he has inherited. He sorts through these scores, lingering over a piece called "Elegy," seeming to see the notes flying "above the staff like flags of mourning." Robin Behn, faced by a grieving father who asks her what they should do with her mother's ashes, meditates briefly on the woman's "soul," deciding it may be "the space / of air she once displaced," and then, though it's up to dad to decide, wants to brush the ashes all over her father's body, as he stands in the rain: "he'd look like he's standing in the rain that rains / just after the end of the world." Mary Swander gives us news of a small-town doctor who eventually dies; she wheels his remains over to a Catholic grotto for prayer and redemption. She spoils the poem (it's by far the longest in the magazine) by entering the saintly doctor's psyche after he's had his stroke. All is forced and sentimental.

6. *Family stuff*. James McKean's barely literate dad has difficulty writing a letter. Michael Van Walleghen's Hamtramck pa drank a lot, bought offal from a slaughterhouse and kept it rotting in the car while he was drinking. Well boozed, the dad would buy up "brains, testicles, tripe / all that precious offal / grocery stores disdained—/ whole hog heads for headcheese / fresh duck blood, fresh feet / kidneys, giblets, pancreas . . ." In "The Age of Reason," the drunken dad engages a drunken friend with a Piper Cub to take Van Walleghen flying, as a seventh birthday present. His dad weighs somewhere between 250 and 275 pounds. He brings along a case of beer, and forgets to take parachutes. Miraculously the plane lifts off: "What a birthday!"

7. *Plain folks poems*. There are many mute inglorious Miltons and Mrs. Miltons here. Mary Swander gives us a procession of them: Edith Hill with her lockjaw, Gloomy Heinz's swollen prostate, Putt-Putt McNut and his harelip, Shorty Long's lumbago, Billy Kunkle's lost leg. Also see Michael Van Walleghen's father's slaughterhouse cohorts, Jane Cooper's shrimp fisherman's daughter doing handstands, and George Starbuck's redneck "practical shooter": "They've took my Mach-10 Special."

8. *Nature, nature, nature.* These poems abound, though rarely are they about Nature red in tooth and claw. William Stafford sets the genteel tone: pastoral, calm, and with the implied, easy sentiment that things were better when rural life flourished. Cute deer leap amid empty Midwestern landscapes. Norman Rockwell *Saturday Evening Post* covers.

9. *Rural poems: farm stuff.* Poets seem to boast perpetually of farm origins, and some even save up from workshop teaching sinecures to return to old family farms. Implicit always is that farm folks were noble—another variation, I assume, on the idealized toughness and grit of frontier Americans. In Robert Dana's "Victor," the old abandoned farmhouse stands in high grass, clapboard, "wind-scoured bone." The doorway is "a mouth." One of the windows is "battered shut." Stories gibber in and out of its "empty head."

10. *"Cultural veneer" poems.* By supplying cultural orts, these seem intended to enrich a generally flat, plebeian style. Jane Cooper likes Rousseau's "Sleeping Gypsy"; Robert Mezey remembers Empedocles; Laurie Sheck rhapsodizes over a pair of Giottos; and Linda Gregerson is inspired by an anonymous engraving of a whale washed ashore in Holland.

11. *Use of a journalistic or epistolary tone.* An opening line by Donald Justice reads like a news item: "The Bestor papers have come down to me." Robert Dana begins: "So, you walk along nowhere." Michael Van Walleghen launches forth: "It was early Saturday." The dullest epistolary start belongs to Janet Piper: "I lie on the patio / In my long chair."

With the exception of poems by Michael Van Walleghen, Tess Gallagher, George Barlow, Stephen Dobyns, and Andrew Hudgins, I'm left feeling as trivial as Marvin Bell ("Classified") says he does: "I am no more stupid now than I ever was; I am the same." A good poetry journal should do more. And a famous workshop, after fifty years, should have generated better work. Recently, Donald Hall, in his *Poetry and Ambition: Essays, Nineteen Eighty-Two to Eighty-Eight,* devastatingly scrutinizes the Tour Workshop product.

Itinerary Poems

The "itinerary poem" recounts journeys of the body and the spirit, either imagined or real, which are experienced by the poet or by some historical or mythological personage whose exploits the poet recites. The history of this form is old, going back to the *Bible* and the *Odyssey.* The most ambitious of these poems are based on the journals and letters of such explorers as Lewis and Clark and Wesley Powell, who traveled throughout the American West; the explorers of the Poles, Elisha Kent Kane and Robert Falcon Scott; artists like Vincent Van Gogh and Benjamin Robert Haydon; and politicians and leaders like Napoleon,

Abraham Lincoln, John Brown, and Andrew Jackson. Lesser poems report the peregrinations of poets on their travels either abroad or at home, and various childhood and adolescent rites of passage recalled in narrative detail. Byron's "Childe Harold" and "Don Juan," Allen Ginsberg's "Mugging" and "Howl," Paul Blackburn's *Journals,* and James McMichael's *Four Good Things* are among the better examples of this second order.

A most impressive use of an historical figure's journals is Charles Hood's *Red Sky, Red Water: Powell on the Colorado.* It joins a sequence of impressive works on the American West, a genre all its own. Among these are George Keithley's *The Donner Party,* Richard Shelton's *Hohokam,* Gary H. Holthaus's *Circling Back,* and Bernard Pomerance's poem about General Custer, *We Need To Dream All This Again.*

Hood's narrative poem, of some seventy-five pages, strives for historical accuracy in treating John Wesley Powell (1834–1902) and his explorations in 1869 along the Green and Colorado Rivers. Powell was a self-taught geologist, ethnologist, politician, and conservationist. He had fought in the Civil War, during which he lost his right arm at Shiloh. He made some thirty trips to the West, and wrote a landmark book on the nature of the region, arguing for homestead law reform and clear watershed areas.

One of Hood's challenges (and he literally spent a summer retracing Powell's journey) is that none of the various journals and diaries kept by Powell and his men agree completely on either dates or incidents. Powell's journals, published in 1875, blended details from two trips—the 1869 one, and a second trip down the Colorado in 1871. Hood depends for his poems on Powell's journals, and has been precise in noting his sources.

The "Prologue" displays Hood's lean writing. He senses right off that his own style must not differ drastically from Powell's own:

It is the 19th century
and everything
is possible.
Even so, the man with one arm
worries about money,
and whether the boats will hold up,
and about the crew, who dot
the platform like mounds of rare soil,
sleeping away the rain
and delays. In 5 a.m. humidity
the mosquitoes drone
like distant trains, trains
on their way
carrying wooden boats,
boxes of fruit,
black cassocks of smoke.

Hood evokes both nature and the passing of days via a spare style reminiscent of Gary Snyder's *Rip-Rap:*

> May 26, 1869
>
>   Sky dun
> as lint,
> trickling rain
>   into the scrub willow.
>
> A phoebe plucks gnats
> off the tarpaulin
> river.
>
> Some days just itch
> like a new wool shirt.

In this poem, Powell and his men, ferrying a rapids, are in great trouble:

> June 9, 1869
>
>   "The bones, draped in white, at the door."
>
>   An unfiltered climate
> White, with some tan or gray fittings,
> iron blue in the bindings of shadows.
> It creases the eye,
> reaction reduced to a hinge: squint
> or full-shut.
> Seneca Howland weeps.
> Powell, on the shore, waves
> but cannot block it.
> The *No-Name* & co. miss the signal.
> The surge sucks them in.
>
> The rapid howls
> full of hurricaning limestone
> and standing waves.
> The boat rolls over
> as smartly as a dog.
>
> Goodman and the Howlands swim;
> *No-Name* eddies briefly,
> they reboard,
> flooded but afloat,
> racing through the millrace.
>
> The expedition follows,
> breasting scree and pool.

No-Name broadsides
then halves
and sinks.

Below the holes
is the lost face of the deep:
silence and darkness,
a current soft
as air, cold as fish.
Goodman's face
plows bedrock five times.

From a midstream rock
he vomits
all the chapters of the river.

The Howlands have raised an island.
They rescue him there.

The others line the *Emma Dean* through the worst of the rapids.
Sumner ferries across.
Straining; near-loss; success.
"We are as glad to shake hands with them
as though they had been on a voyage around the world
and wrecked on a distant coast."

But
lost: barometers (all), food, guns, clothing, the new map, one quarter of the
    navy.
And already,
    so soon,
            "the fucking night spreading
            itself like a pee-cock."

I have also dredged journals for three recent books: *Hawker, Haydon,* and *Kane*. Robert Stephen Hawker was an eccentric, almost saintly, visionary, nineteenth-century Cornish vicar and poet who drew drowned sailors from the sea and buried them in his churchyard, played mermaid for his parishioners, loved having animals attend his services, and wrote many poems, among them the Cornish national anthem. Benjamin Robert Haydon was the early nineteenth-century British painter of vast history pictures no one wanted to see or buy, at odds with the Royal Academy, the father of a large (and usually starving) family, denizen of a debtor's prison on several occasions, who decided finally that the way to see to his family's needs was to kill himself—the public outcry would suffice to elicit a public subscription of monies to support his family. This indeed happened.

Elisha Kent Kane was an American explorer who tried to reach the Arctic Circle in 1865 and whose brig froze fast in the ice off eastern

Greenland and never thawed free. My *Kane* recounts his harrowing winter on the ice and eventual return to civilization, via dogsled, down the coast of Greenland. Kane was not only captain, but also ship's doctor and surgeon, meteorologist, biologist, and journal keeper. On his return (he was to live for only two years more, a victim of rheumatic fever) he published his account of this voyage in two huge volumes illustrated with engravings made from his own on-the-spot drawings. His journals provided much crucial information on flora, fauna, the nature of ice, and the nature of survival in this hostile desert of ice. He was the first of the major explorers, American or European, to realize that for survival he would have to live as the natives did.

Paul Christensen's *Weights and Measures: Selected Poems* contains a long section which forms an intinerary dream poem set in Africa, called "East Africa, 1952: A Dream Sequence." The theme is the Conradian/Rousselian one of a questing spirit traversing rivers, lakes, and jungles in search of visionary experiences. Everywhere there is evidence of Western civilization in decay—wasted men and rusting machinery.

Among the dispossessed and displaced souls Christensen meets are a half-Hamite gardener who recalls the bitter day of his marriage oath, an English colonel who lies dying in a stifling room at Djibouti, and a drifter who goes to Toten ("Death") Island, populated only by rats. "Lake Nyasa," the longest poem, runs to well over 500 lines, and is a fascinating narrative written in supple blank verse in which an old Nyasa sea captain stabs a rival and is doomed to wander Africa as a ghost.

Other fine itinerary poems appear in James McMichael's *Four Good Things,* a most unusual long itinerary poem, arranged around personal geographical displacements, tragedy, and isolation. The iambic blank verse lines recall those of the Victorian master Arthur Hugh Clough—which is not to say that McMichael is old-fashioned. *Four Good Things* has an entirely contemporary ring. The point of view is that of a child growing up in Pasadena, California, whose mother dies of cancer. The cancer flower, the poet believes, began to grow at the time of his conception, and he feels guilty. In the following passage (note the superb line beginning "When I'm afraid") he sorts out his ravaged feelings:

> With my conception, I was virtually
> coincident with cancer in my mother's body.
> To exist is to be *placed outside,* where there are
> things to fear. My body. Me. The visible
> pulse at my right ankle, thick blue vein, the skin,
> sunlight on my ankle in a cold house, now.
> When I'm afraid, I try to think of everything.
> I try to change the possible by thinking some one
> part of it and giving it a place—gratuitous
> murder, accident, a flood, the separate and bizarre
> pathologies that could be mine and final.
> . . . . .
> Each thing I worry is secure,
> familiar, almost home. Its difference is

mine and not the world's. The house wren, when it sings, says
"Here I am." It looks around and says it.
My worrying and fear are notices that I don't
have a place outside and don't know how to
find or make one.

The boy is further shattered when his father remarries and gener-
ates a new family, leaving young James feeling superfluous:

No one would hear me.
Or back outside the attic, from the eave,
I'd use the beam-end as a hoist and pull myself
over the rafter to the highest roof. It had
good footing, a broad low pitch and several vents.
I don't know why I'd go there—maybe for the sublime
assurance that I could. Being there was almost to be
doing something. The sky went on at that level,
intervened below the trees and rooflines and withdrew.
There was more to see than I could choose from. . . .

For perspective, he interweaves sections on his English forebears with
ongoing personal intineraries, seeming to discover that while his own
immediate family is out of joint, his connection with a longer sweep of
history is not. He continues his journeys, through marriage and divorce,
and through remarriage.

For a far less ambitious itinerary poem, see Elizabeth Bishop's *Ques-
tions of Travel* the first part of which consists of separate lyrics written at
different moments on a tour she made of Brazil. The most ambitious
traveler among recent poets, however, seems to be Laurence Lieberman,
who proceeds from country to country—including some most exotic
ones—leaving fresh books all along the way.

Jazz Poems

(*See* Celebrity Poems: Musicians)

Journal Poems

These poems are either based on personal journals or daybooks,
giving the appearance of casual matter quickly jotted down. The
journal poem flourished during the 1970s as an outgrowth of
women's consciousness-raising workshops.

The journal poem dominates the verse in a recent issue of *Helicon
Nine: The Journal of Women's Arts and Letters,* and most of it is not good.

Judy Ray's two contributions show the weaknesses of the form. "Ten Stations of the Sweet Briar Lake" reads like ten moments lifted from journal jottings. Here Ray turns cute:

> Slither of salamander on the bank had shone with iridescent
> green and blue. A pink lady peered and said, "The creature
> must be fashion-conscious: those are this year's colours."

Does the English spelling of "colours" intensify the lady's pinkness? One can almost imagine Ray sitting at the lake, notebook in hand, jotting. There is a moment though where she drops her book and proceeds to swim out to a dam, a venture not without its "special satisfaction." The poem concludes on a note of genteel camaraderie:

> Not one of us ventures alone. Afraid of cramp
> and faltering breath? Of monsters from the deep?
> No, only of missing the slow camaraderie
> found thus in swimming alone.

Ray's "Writing in Virginia" goes absolutely wild in its parallels between nature and scribbling. The "concrete-floored study," chirruping cricket, cobwebbed bookshelf, and headache remind one of swift jottings in a journal rather than a well-made poem. She tells us how she moves the bookshelf hoping to silence the cricket. She's defeated. She resumes her "pen" and listens to wind as it brushes "gold" (viz., autumn) leaves. Remorse enters. What if, folks, she's squashed the little crittur by moving the bookcase? Oh, dear! But, no, she's relieved now to hear his "tiny chirp" starting up again. In phony relief, as Jimminy "gathers voice," so does her pen.

Doris Radin employs the journal technique to create a monologue spoken by a Yiddish wife with five children who runs a shop and hungers to be classier than she is. "I" phrases, rampant throughout, provide the illusion that the speaker is writing her wishes down between cooking kettles of borscht: "I'd love to live in Kiev," "I want to know / music," "I want to be smart," "I want to have evenings / people visiting," "I've never been to Kiev."

Laura Jensen, in "Sleep in the Heat," can't sleep, so she switches on the light. Crickets "tick" and the hands of a clock "grow together." She assembles a gaggle of boring notes designed, I gather, to cure her insomnia—alas, they don't cure ours. Jensen loves pompous abstractions: a sheep "is a shapeless chance," another is "disobedience" and another is "regard." The sheep are "in" her, "grazing in the pastures" of her tongue. Since she brushes them out in the morning, I gather that her tongue is very coated indeed.

Men also write journal poems. Most embarrassing is Gerald Stern's "Fritz." Here is the chattery start, sans clothes, sans imagery, sans vitality:

> This is too good for words. I lie here naked
> listening to Kreisler play. It is the touch
> I love, that sweetness, that ease. I saw him once
> at the end of the 40s, in Pittsburgh. . . .

Stern meanders as he reaches the final movement of the Kreisler. Stern's "journey" began in 1947. Then, he confesses:

> I wrote
> four hours a day, I read five books a week.
> I had to read five books.

Seeing Kreisler was a magical opening for a decade or two, and stood Stern "in good stead." And now he turns coy, as if he's been flipping over pages of an old daybook from the period. These also stood him in good stead: "Marlowe's / tears, and Coleridge's soft flight, and Dostoevski's / rack. . . ." Academic sleaze!

Richard Shelton includes "Notes Toward an Autobiography" in his *Selected Poems: 1969–1981,* and regales us with a mix of self-obsessive remarks and easy philosophisizing. He boasts about his marriage; loves his old poems returned as "strangers"; finds that desert-dwelling teaches him "to go inside" himself "for shade"; likes giving gifts if he isn't asked for them—when asked for a match he blushes and fumbles; his life flaps over the ground as the "shadow of a dark wing / with no bird to guide it"; self-indulgence is like guilt; a "well-directed life" ends in death, as does a "misdirected life."

Galway Kinnell, in "December Day in Honolulu," transcends the limitations of the journal poem by moving from a list of the mail he receives one day to the wailing of a cat, possibly in heat. As the crying intensifies, Kinnell wonders if "propagation itself must haul its / voice all the way up from the beginning." He concludes that perhaps the noise is that of an old cat dying, "making its last appearance on the / clanking magic circle of its trashcan lid" and "turning totally faithful forever" to "life's first, irreplaceable lover," death. "This one or that one dies but never the singer."

No poet approaches Allen Ginsberg in the imaginative use of the extended journal poem for a smorgasbord of themes, moods, and obsessions, both political, international, and private. Of his many such poems, "Journal Night Thoughts" (*Planet News*) is generic. Time: September 28, 1964 (although he is looking back to the events of January 1961). Place: New York City. He's stoned. He's with Harry Smith, a small press editor and publisher. He remembers Kerouac hallucinating. He rushes to Boston, where he peers through Robert Lowell's window. He walks "unsteadily" in Manhattan near the spot where Poe wrote "The Raven." Nuclear blast burning babies, "sending them back to the Sun." Believe it or not lore: A man with genitals all over his body. Images of Khrushchev going crazy. He lingers over a flower "slowly awakening its petals," as he finds himself again, alone on Broadway. An image of his father, an old retired schoolteacher, holding sheafs of poems he's written in "singsong." Body trivia: examining his wiggling toes, belly, dumb lips and loins. Life

Consciousness Poems—these he leaves behind written on stones in Oklahoma near an Indian mound. Death Consciousness: an ancient hieroglyph of a serpent writhing through its folds "like a scaly / swastika—a green dragon / with ancient fangs." A memory of his mother so freshly buried her skull has not yet turned white. Terrified of a snake, he orders it to GO BACK! The release of all memories, fears, desires in a raunchy homosexual ending written in the style of the erotic Songs of Solomon.

Language Poems

A term with as many shadings as the colors in Joseph's coat, fully treated earlier. (*See* **Flotsam-and-Jetsam Poems.**)

Latino Poems

Nicolás Kanellos, writing in *Contact II* (Winter–Spring 1984–85), an issue featuring Chicano art and literature, reviews the responses of mainstream American academics to minority literature, including Hispanic, or Latino, writers. The academics attack such literature for "its orality and dependence on performance," attributes they see as departing from literary traditions. The minority audience is limited, they feel, and the cultural base is also limited, foreign, regional, and ethnic in dialect. Bilingualism hampers accessibility to the literature. Other academics exalt and romanticize "primeval roots—the chant and dance-drama, and even . . . the literature's 'marginality,' its *communitas* or soul—all the while talking about 'man' living in the most technologically advanced civilization where poets have mastered the refinements of computer music, mass marketing and distribution, quadrophonic sound, and the blessing of the American people in the form of the dollar."

Oral quality has exalted the "noble savage," the "child of nature," mystically avoiding, writes Kanellos, "the real question of politics and economics and its relationship to the aesthetic of orality and performance." For Kanellos the "orality" of much Latino literature is a "major" contribution to American culture as a whole, and is "part of a model for survival of literature and art in modern technological societies." Moreover, the "real popularity" of Latino literature among the working classes proves that the "lumpen" can not only produce such art, they can consume it. Latino efforts, then, are central, not marginal to literature in America, and are capable of repossessing audiences ursurped by the broadcast media.

Kanellos proceeds to consider the work of four contemporary Latino writers, one a street-corner bard, another a poet with university connections, another a bilingual poet, and a fiction writer. The street poet is Jorge Brandon, nearing eighty, who lives in New York City, and who for years performed his work in the public plazas of Puerto Rico, Central and South America, and Mexico. He is a pure performer, one with a large following, who does not allow his work to be printed. His gimmick for attracting attention on street corners is an empty coconut with a painted face, holding a microphone.

Tato Lalviera, Brandon's apprentice, differs in that he publishes his poetry and plays, and writes commercially recorded songs. He, like Brandon, believes that poetry is "irrevocably an oral art," and must be shared with "a community." He has memorized all of his works and Brandon's as well. He writes in what he calls "Spanglish," a blending of the two tongues. Like Alurista (who is well known in American academic circles: see his *Spik in Glyph*) and Evangelina Vigil, he employs the mix of English and Spanish used by Latinos in their everyday lives, creating aesthetic possibilities by "contrasting and mixing sound and sense in both languages, even to the extent of stretching both linguistic systems and virtually creating a new one."

Another poet, playwright, and prose writer, is Miguel Algarin, a professor of English at Rutgers and one who connects avant-garde American writing with grass-roots folklore. Despite his sophistication (he travels to many world poetry festivals), he remains an oral poet.

The question to be asked is what sort of poetry do the more visible Latino poets write? How carefully have they listened to those poets who are writing and performing in the oral tradition?

Two very visible Latino poets are Albert Ríos, born in Arizona, with an M.F.A. from its state university, who now teaches in Tempe; and Gary Soto, whose M.F.A. is from the University of California at Irvine, and who is now Professor of Chicano Studies and English at the University of California at Berkeley.

Ríos's "I Would Visit Him in the Corner" sounds like a workshop poem with a calculated primitive touch. The story is about an old uncle who when young felt a spider crawl inside his ear. Though he crushed the insect, he was winsomely stupid (aren't postcard primitives this way?) and believed the spider remained inside his skull. As a result, being loco kept him out of the war, and as he kept hitting the ear all his life, the ear kept growing.

In another contrived poem based on a looney native, "In the Woman Arms of the Ground," a man who has eaten dirt all his life grows up stunted. Ríos describes his simple breakfast coyly:

His secret was that the apples
from the orchards grew
from trees, and trees grew in dirt.
with each apple he swallowed
his insides chased each other . . .
without plan . . .

Gary Soto's poems defy pigeonholing. While many deal with his Fresno childhood and adolescence, he seems uninterested in writing for a pure Latino audience, as the poets praised by Kanellos do. And he is a vastly better writer than Ríos. Work from his recent *Black Hair* his fourth book, appeared initially in most conservative journals. The matters Soto writes about are intensely personal, sometimes rife with humor at his own expense. He loves women, and many of his poems are about their attractions for him (see "Shopping For A Woman"; and the "The New Movies," which closes, after sex, with an image of pants zippers that yawn lying on the floor but that "grit their teeth / When they close to say good-bye.") He writes affectionate poems to his daughter. He also writes about trees, words, an Estonian coming to dinner, a yard sale, and schoolboy days. He is unpretentious, inviting, and always in control.

Another much-published poet (whose work, however, appears in more obscure presses) is Alma Villanueva. Three of her poems are in *Alcatraz* no. 3. One gives voice to "planet earth," a "lady of longing" who aches for men in prison, and an "ignorant old woman" who suffers in the Beirut massacre of September, 1982. All of these poems strive for a quasi-primitive tone and are riddled with clichés and slack writing. Planet Earth speaks in frayed wisdom-nuggets: she glues humans to her with "love," humans "swim toward" her every night crying; I, she says, "am / entirely obvious," hence you must not regard her as a secret. She dances "through the fabric" of human dreams, etc. Villanueva is best in the second section, where she lists natural objects: from butterfly wings to the eagle's back to "all scrotums," baby feet, and tomatoes—at least she has come down from the stale heights of the earlier abstractions.

A recent issue of *Contact II* featured Latino writing. Max Benavidez contributes a mood piece on Los Angeles; Cherrie C. Moraga has a fey poem on cutting out desserts; Sandra Cisneros celebrates young love—she's "an odd geometry / of elbows and skin"; Lucky Cienfuegos reports on Santo Domingo in Spanglish, but tepidly so. I can't find a single poem among some two dozen that treats Latino culture freshly or profoundly.

What I miss as I read collections of Latino work is a sense of true "community." I see none of the rage, vigor, linguistic experimentation, or originality I discern in so much black, gay, lesbian, and prison writing. Latino work, by contrast, seems passive and derivative of mainstream American writing. Have I read the wrong poets?

Lesbian Poems

(*See also* Homosexual Poems, Love Poems, Marriage Poems, and Prison Poems)

Lesbian poems seem to differ from gay poems primarily in that the sexuality is far less explicit and more tender. Lest I be accused of being sexist here I hasten to add that the reasons for these differences are probably political. Homophobia in America has focused primarily on males. Females living together have always been accepted, even in reactionary communities. The tale of the town librarian living with the town nurse, both unmarried, is generic. In my home town the couple was made up of the town nurse, a mannish, gruff soul who later directed the County Welfare Department and became a vigorous member of the town council, and her partner, a delicate lady who worked for the local newspaper. The town "queer," though, was another matter. The son of one of the minor officials of the local bank, he was pelted with garbage as he dressed in shorts (which no men then wore) and walked his dalmatian on a leash down the local main street during the summer tourist season. He was forced out of town and went to live anonymously in Chicago, braving the locals on his rare trips home to see his ailing and much-loved mother. If he had chosen to stay in our small town, and live with a friend, both would most likely have been beaten or even killed.

A double standard for males and females persists: no lesbians that I know of were beaten by the police during the Stonewall riots in New York City during those nights in June, 1969. Lesbians have never been obliged to take the same flamboyant, public stance that gay men have had to, flaunting their power in the streets, hurling back the loathing and rage perpetrated against them. An overtly sexual gay literature in which no intimacy, no matter how gross or violent, is omitted, is intended to disturb and defy the straight world. The creation of such literature (see John Rechy's controversial, courageous, and disturbing works) is a challenge, a gauntlet if you will—an attitude lesbians have not had to adopt. "Let's beat up a queer tonight" is not so easy now to execute as it once was. Yet, with the advent of AIDS, "fag-bashing" is once again on the rise.

Marilyn Hacker, one of our best lesbian poets, in "Taking Notice," puts the issue well:

> If a man sleeps with men, and women,
> he's *queer: vide* Wilde, Goodman, Gide, Verlaine.
> A woman who does can be "passionately
> heterosexual" (said Norman Pearson of H. D.).
> Anyone's love with women doesn't count.

Adrienne Rich's "Twenty-One Love Poems," from *The Dream of A Common Language,* have become models for dozens of lesbian poems by other writers. In addition to the hatred of men for which she is famous, Rich presents something of a manifesto for women loving women. Though bearing the scars society has awarded them, women

> want to live like trees,
> sycamores blazing through the sulfuric air,
> dappled with scars, still exuberantly budding,
> our animal passion rooted in the city.

She also shows how to be both vulnerable and tough in loneliness, especially in a world brutally controlled by men. She is "crying helplessly, / and they still control the world, and you are not in my arms." In a marvelously delicate poem about her lover's hands, Rich demonstrates that seeming fragility can in fact correct much violence and rage. The implicit sexuality is underplayed.

The inheritance of woman historically is exploitation and suffering. Though Rich is proud of this scar tissue she, with her lover, will move on, "fighting the temptation to make a career of pain." These are "woman outside the law," singing those old songs with their own "new words." These new women who dare to live intimately with other women are "out in country that has no langage / no laws." All that they now do together "is pure invention," for "the maps they gave us were out of date."

A writer very much in Rich's pattern is Marilyn Hacker. "Why We Are Going Back To Paradise Island," in *Taking Notice,* envisions a violent male as "the hurt idealist, poet" who reads the same books his wife does—shares the same life. His life is marked by violence: he skewers a rat with a broomstick, shoots a milk doe (a nursing mother) "sloppily and badly," purposely lets a friend's kitten starve to death, shoots a small brother by mistake. His newborn son lives twelve hours and dies, his father dies under an oxygen tent, the shot brother hauntingly revisits him, his "fat smart / baby daughter" steps in front of a truck and is killed. What does he do? He buys an identical truck, kidnaps a girl of eight, drives her to the woods near a motel, and bashes her. But does he really? Hacker is inside his imagination, weltering as if in a maniacal rage. He hates his wife—he beats her with a two-by-four. He fantasizes that he hires a black with a huge penis to sodomize her. His notions of sexuality are most abnormal:

> Would a sheep's hole feel the same, or the cold
> tight gap of a beached dog-shark, last gasps
> coming together, before limp flesh?

Enlightened women withdraw from the violence of the actual and dream about the worlds of men, insofar as they can. The sad women are those who through indifference or fatigue can't or won't change, locked as they are into conventional roles: see Hacker's "Ordinary Women." Hacker commemorates these enlightened women (many of them are lesbians) in the twenty-five-part "Taking Notice," which opens with these lines from Rich's "Twenty-One Love Poems": "two women together is a work / nothing in civilization has made simple." Hacker's sonnet sequence is also in homage to Rich. In number seventeen, Hacker writes a love poem—intimate with just a hint of crudity, fraught with the daily incidents and small objects of life, evoked through delicate images of the partner sensed and deeply loved.

Eloise Klein Healy's "Wood, A Love Poem" delicate and sexual, celebrates her love for a friend in a cold house. A skillful image of logs and wood symbolizes love. The women have piled their lives together "like rough lumber":

> The night chill has made our nipples
> pull in on themselves,
> dark knots in split pine
> or the puckering surface
> of a frozen pond.
>
> You push logs through quick doors
> opening in the fire,
> igniting a volley
> of small-bore ice pistols.
>
> Our skin flows again
> like resin,
> lies down like a warm lake.

"There Are No Words for the Sexual Acts of Lesbians" celebrates sexual intimacy by understating it:

> just vowels
> passing from mouth to mouth to mouth
> like fish in their unbroken element,
> turning so, breathing, no bottom.
>
> There are no words for such acts
> so simply flesh
> canyons stippled with pink,
> no words for such landscapes
> of the color her eyes go
> from brown to dark so suddenly
> she catches the blood root
> in my body and counts and changes
> my pulse.
>
> She's the vowel in my mouth
> in a language of water,
> the longest note in the eddies
> we sift out
> upon a sandbar, wet stones
> wet gems.

In "What It Was Like the Night Cary Grant Died," Healy blends themes of an almost invisible lesbian love with the public nature of the actor's dying. She imagines a geriatric Marlene Dietrich (by legend a lesbian, though her public face has always been heterosexual) dancing with an aging Grant. If only Marlene had declared her love for women. But she's "no more talkative alive / than dead, that one."

In a love poem to Judy Baca, the painter and muralist, Healy commemorates Baca's obsession with "the facts underneath history." This driving force behind her art, Healy implies, is also the driving force behind her lesbianism:

> You like the facts underneath history
>
> set straight
> so you draw
> looking into the leg
> and you draw bones inside a foot
> with the same outward presence
> as a braid down a woman's back
> or railroad tracks plunging miles into a continent.
> You make bodies spring from walls
> because history is a flat lie
>
> . . . .
>
> And all of this changes you
> like that thicker muscle
> at the base of your thumb
> as it strengthens and grows each mural
> up your arm, makes your back broad.
>
> . . . .
>
> Paint in your hands is a wonderful danger
> like life is
> or history with all the colors back in it
> as large as people's true courage
> in everyday steps, in stroke after stroke. . . .

Michelle Clinton's "Tween a Mammay & a Stud," from *High Blood Pressure,* is written in the voice of a tough black lesbian who has a "rabbit" for a lover, one of those college "white girls with limp hair in barrettes / & thin arms in cashmere sweaters." Whenever they cry, all "the men & nigguh / women" want to comfort them. Rabbits are marvelously submissive sex partners:

> They give up the grind too & afterwards stare at you
> with wonder filled eyes, like you were Superman,
> a wild King Kong tamed or sumthin'.

She delights in toughly rebuffing white men anxious for her lady:

> Back off home. This here's mine.
> My bitch. She wants me more than you
> & I ain't even got no penis.

These white rabbits love black girls to keep their hair short—they like theirs long so they can fling it about in the morning. They never call them "pretty / or soft," and don't want their girlfriends wearing earrings or bras. When a black man enters the room they twitch, and they always, in bed, manage to be on the bottom. Black women, both gay and straight, despise black brothers with a rabbit on his arm, brothers who've "bought the shit about Cinderella / & Snow White." A "fragile princess" makes him feel "power."

Her possessiveness takes over in a bar where a beer-bellied white boy eyes her rabbit. She wonders, affected as she is by the bar light playing through her lover's red hair, why she wants to bust the white boy licking his lips and staring:

> I wonder just what you want, just exactly
> how strong you think I am, & just how deep
> & funkey all this shit is
> that I'm playing into.

Lesbian Poetry: An Anthology, edited by Elly Bulkin and Joan Larkin (Watertown, Massachusetts: Persephone Press, 1981), features sixty-four American lesbian poets plus a seminal essay by Bulkin on teaching lesbian poetry in the classroom. Among the recurring themes are these: the crippling evils of male domination; facing up to one's sexual and sisterly feelings for other women; rearing children alone; the personal traumas of living a lesbian life in a straight world; being black, brown, or red and lesbian; and the necessity of accepting one's lesbian self with pride. Not all of these poems escape the limitations of prosy journal entries, or sentimentality.

Well-known poets whose work appears here include Audre Lorde (she takes on the difficult issues of motherhood, poverty, and the need for black women to triumph over "black maled streets"); Adrienne Rich; Lynn Strongin (she writes of a stunning woman professor who dresses down, wearing olive-drab so as to decoy the men in her department who have the power); Joan Larkin (she recalls the conventional "inheritance" she received as daughter, adolescent, and young woman, and feistily observed that society allows men to write freely about their penises but women can't write about their vaginas); Paula Gunn Allen (she relates her lesbianism to her native American roots, and her anger is thus intensified because of her cultural status on two counts); Judy Grahn (she is best with her non-serial, non-incantatory poems, such as three stunning portraits: the tough waitress, the "electric" woman at her own carpentry, and the "common woman" Vera); Irena Klepfisz ("death camp" and "contexts" are fine; the longish poem in the voice of a female zoo monkey has to be read to be believed—the creature speaks in such literary language you just know she's read her Virginia Woolf and Jane Austen); Marilyn Hacker (many poems); Susan Griffin (she's a powerful, sexual, but repetitious writer); Fran Winant (a memorable poem is "Yesterday," about Gertrude Stein and Alice B. Toklas); Pat Parker (she has written a recitative on the history of the "Black woman"); Honor Moore; Karen Brodine; Jan Clausen (who writes about Sylvia Plath, who is as much a martyr figure for lesbian poets as she is for other women poets);

and Donna Allegra (she turns the tables with "A Rape Poem for Men").

No other minority movement seems at once so mature and so cohesive.

Love Poems

Though contemporary love poems may be romantic and old-fashioned, lovers are never idealized in the way that Petrarch's Laura, Dante's Beatrice, or Dante Rossetti's Pre-Raphaelite women were. Psychiatry, encounter groups, consciousness-raising sessions, and feminism have guaranteed that today's lovers sweat, grunt, steam, grind, quarrel, engage in fisticuffs, and grossness. By comparison, even the poems e. e. cummings (possibly the best American love poet of the twentieth century) wrote to French whores seem like valentines.

Since so many poets write love poems, I shall name none of them. Instead I present a list indicative of current approaches to love, all derived from randomly chosen poems in *The Morrow Anthology of Younger American Poets.*

1. I love you so much it hurts me.
2. Where were you last night? Can't I hold you here?
3. You may be a pilot but you're grounded with me.
4. You don't owe me nothin', so let's roll in the hay.
5. I don't owe you nothin', so let's roll in the hay.
6. I sink into the bathwater, brush my bush, and think of you.
7. I'm hard. Slide down me if you dare.
8. This good Catholic boy loves you so, your face reminds him of St. Francis of Assisi.
9. How women in love differ from men in love: In the jokes men fuck sheep, turned on by "their puckery assholes." When a woman dreams of sheep, she thinks of a stiff, heavy, thick penis running along the sheep's underside, "steamy in the cold."
10. Waiting for you to take me to the prom, I was so happy my glass sizzled with stars.
11. I love your abalone shell back, your birdseed/sunspot arms, your rarely-moving mouth, your steady eyes, your tan, your "shy penis, mostly / swirled white."
12. Mom disgusted with pa is drunk and is frying fish for his dinner.
13. If I was "a catfish swimming / In the deep blue sea / I'd start all you women / Jumping in after me."
14. I don't want your "ripe behind," thighs, breast, or eyes, just give me your mouth, that "tasty labia."
15. I want a man passionate enough "to burn his love out / in me, nightly, daily, the white-hot / tongs of love."

16. When you face me after you've poked the fire a "blue movie" burns in my brain, you animal!

17. Man, as you admire your beauty in a mirror, I hate you, and love you: I want to see you "as a man bleeding, not / the reflection I desire."

18. I like thinking about you as you sleep beside me. Are you really *you* coming into existence?

19. A woman disguised as a wife tells me lie after lie.

MacDonald–Eddy Nature Poems

As a rule, male poets have seen far more sermons in stones, and intimations of immortality in tarns, tors, yurts, and teepees, and have had their passion aroused more often by Alpine storms and exploding volcanoes than women poets have. That men have had this corner on nature puzzles me.

None of the great nineteenth-century nature poets were women. Men alone removed nature's clothing (was not nature "the living Garment of God" as Thomas Carlyle said?) and the removals were not necessarily erotically tinged. When Wordsworth in his skiff was frightened by the louring presence of Mt. Skiddaw he was responding to incredible forces he imagined beyond himself, forces he read as a universal consciousness innately responsible to and caring for him, even when its moods were hostile. Following Wordsworth and Carlyle, Emerson and Thoreau set the pattern for generations of Yankee males who gathered transcendental buckwheat in the wilds. Despite her nosiness, the American Transcendentalist Margaret Fuller was pretty much left out of it, albeit she did own one of the more cantankerous heifers at Brook Farm. Transcendentalism was a male province.

Nature's diaphanously clothed nymphs and seraphs continue to lure male poets, who have continued to yank, snap, pull, and tear, revealing hints of warm nature-flesh: Gary Snyder peregrinates up, into, over and through the Sierras and the Cascades, feasting (metaphorically) on centipedes, lizards, and manzanita berries; Howard McCord returns romantically to the navel of the universe, that primitive omphalos located somewhere in Iceland; William Stafford, Robert Morgan, and Wendell Berry arrange domesticated landscapes.

What strikes me is an arrogance in these poets (and others who take their cue from nature): they assume that Nature cares! A useful term for the phenomenon, perhaps, is the MacDonald–Eddy Nature-Poetry Syndrome. It's an old but not very well understood malady. Let me explain. There's an unforgettable scene in the movie *Rose Marie* in which handsome Canadian mountie Nelson Eddy seats himself on a Rocky Mountain peak at night beneath a scintillating moon. He begins to sing. Opposite, across a sizeable valley, sits Jeanette MacDonald comfortably positioned on her mountain peak. She's wearing one of those marvelous hats and a gauzy frock, suitable wear, certainly, for roughing it in the Rockies. The pair sing to one another, and like gypsy moths who send sex signals back and forth in a similar (though silent-to-human-ears) fashion, they bathe the Rockies in delicious chocolate-covered sound. Nature herself is immersed in human love trills, lilts, and vocables. The bears forego rending stumps for ants and honey, deer perk up their ears and interrupt the flow of fecal droppings, martens allow the freshly caught partridge to flop free. . . . The singers *inspire* nature; nature *inspires* the singers.

There's something sentimental here, of course; and the treacle is male induced. (Wasn't Jeanette an Indian maid?) The question persists— why is it the male artist who calls these tunes? Is it because women were generally back at the main camp, brewing coffee, whipping up biscuits, or taking saunas with their kids? Here are some other explanations: since nature is female (Mother Nature), women may be repelled by the thought of getting it on with her. Lesbianism? Also, traditionally, American men have had a rough time displaying emotions; women have not. Women are supposed to be sensitive and emotive—if only as a display for their males. Nature for repressed men, however, serves as a kind of safety valve; emotions receive a sanitized sanction. Exhausted burly linemen guzzle down their Coors, look up at the wilderness and are stunned. The mountainside trembles, momentarily chilling these hunky males.

Let us take a brief look at one of these male nature poets, Howard McCord, who is termed by Thomas McGrath "a kind of ecologist of the spirit" questing after "the numinous element in landscape." My assessment of McCord—is that his desire to merge with the numinous outdistances his perceptions; he's a latter-day Wordsworthian receptive to great spiritual earth-throbbings but lacking Wordsworth's focus. The whole world becomes a Lake District, as the poet meanders through the lost and forgotten depths of Nature. He has Whitmanesque conductors stuck all over him—charged B-batteries of the spirit set to receive Mother Nature's good news.

Such a poet remains a type of White Rock Maiden, kneeling beside a limpid forest, gossamer wings twitching: sexless and fairly bloodless. The White Rock Maiden is a creature of culture; she'd dissolve into a mist if Whitman's "greasy" Eskimo got out of his kayak. What I'm saying is that much contemporary myth-writing by males is sanitized, deriving from literature rather than life.

Here McCord elevates the trivial:

At Salt Lake, rock climbing in the Wasatch,
Sanskrit, Matthew Arnold, and I turned
Catholic and stopped getting falling-down
drunk. Bought a .44 Magnum and a .303 Enfield
but I haven't been able to kill anything
since I was seventeen, before I bought the boots.

The allusions to hip reading, pacifism, religion, and alcoholism are dull. The compressed writing is insufficient to make the details pulse and

glow. And a line like the following one (verifiable no doubt) is charac-
teristic of the chatty nature of the book (*Selected Poems*): "I had never
met anyone I had not invented / until Dora." Even the name suggests
Wordsworth.

In another poem, "All Hallow's Eve," McCord supplies more personal
details. He helps dig a basement, gives "a beggar man" a jacket, studies
Anglo-Saxon, Old Spanish, and Chaucer, and answers his son's questions
about sunsets and dashlights. After three pages of surface matter, he
adapts a not particularly good passage from Dylan Thomas: "and so Dora
and I hum a bit, on our / sweet and swinging way to death."

When he waxes religious and momentous, he spins out bald clichés.
These appear in "A Letter of Saint Andrew the Dancer":

> The Risen Christ . . . the dualities / in great sanity . . . the divine
> madness that is the power . . . a stately, measureless blur of light . . .
> the immense dance purified by light . . .

When McCord tries to move within an American Indian psyche, he
adopts a voice more interesting than his own. But even here he falls into a
cultural trap. His primitives regard mountains, life, and art and see their
relevance through the lens of a culture that does not belong to them. In
"Walking to the Far Sea: A Suite for Bear," there is a metamorphosis as
McCord transforms himself into a bear. The suite moves between two
consciousnesses, the bear's and the human's, the latter laved over with
phrases borrowed from *litrachur*. Bear even becomes something of a
literate, contemplative Christian, speaking lines from the English Ro-
mantic poets.

But Bear or Massassoit or Urff the Paleolithic Man regarding a tree
or the distant horizon would not speak introspective lines out of Romantic
poets; and so the integrity of the primitive voice seems to me violated.
What we receive from McCord are Nelson Eddy postcard views of life,
poems that are the equivalents of all the beaded bags and jewelry hawked
at "authentic" native stands throughout the United States.

By contrast, how refreshing Judith McCombs' *Against Nature* is. At
last, an American poet has put the thumbscrews to nature, and a woman
has done it. No filmy-gowned, floppy-hatted Jeanette she. McCombs has
earned her right to be "against nature"—the title of her book. These
poems should be required reading in all writing programs throughout the
country, and should be framed and hung in all Sierra Club shelters and
recited in the main lodges of the U.S. Forest Service as parties of back-
packers take off into the wilds. "Against," in her lexicon, has at least two
meanings: the one I've already implied, that she opposes Romantic no-
tions of nature; and another, more personal one. She reveals herself as a
minutely observant wanderer of the wilds, and projects herself "against"
the immense backdrops of trees and mountains. This second meaning is
the dominant one.

In one poem she nags a male companion who finds glaciers "messy."
In the face of great glacial shifts, human warmth is slight and fleeting:

Why can't you take Nature as offered?
Shut up & be grateful, you can't afford
your private dynamite, so don't interrupt

Out on the ice it's our one chance to listen
to whatever the glacier is muttering, to see
how this great swollen hunk & its Neanderthal drains
are ploughing the bedrock   Here we can notice
how accidentally the glacier creates
soil & water, valley & life

Look, we are mammals, tramping the surface
The warmth we have
                      is small & not lasting

She is satiric about the equipment hikers think they need for wilderness survival—a mark of their vulnerability and their exclusion, finally, from the nature they idealize:

What are you proving, importing yourself
& your gear to the wilds? Your daily calories
exceed the environment   What you can gather
is sour, or breaks, & besides you are questy
about killing
        You stop on a ridge & the safe water gurgles
out of your plastic container into your mouth
In your left breast pocket the keys to the car
are jingling
        You can always go back
You can always go back

Earlier in the same poem, McCombs exposes the common Romantic fallacy that we can talk to stones and babble with brooks, upheld by most male nature writers. She neatly dumps several manure-loads of American poems, clearing out this particular Augean stable:

The hawks don't want you out here, they're too ignorant
to beg for garbage   The bears & the clever
mammals avoid you   The trees are just trees,
they all look alike   The stones have no numbers
no shapes you remember (but they seem to multiply)
Did you come all this way to gibber with stones?

The main trope for most nature poets is the Garden of Eden. If God had been giving Pulitzers for poetry back then, chances are that Adam's efforts would resemble Wordsworth's or Snyder's. Eve, if she wrote at all, would treat the small disasters of rose petals, flies trapped in spider webs, the deaths of raspberries. Here is McCombs on the matter of Paradise:

Nature is not like you & me, dear,
whatever its virtues it doesn't have hands
& it isn't our garden   If the inhabitants
squeak to each other, if the stones understand
what hooks them to earth, that does us no good
The clever things hide when they hear us, & the rest
move so godawful slow, we can't notice, or follow
A strange kind of time is elapsing, outside
our watches   We can't make the mountains conform
to the lines on our maps   They slide in the night
& when we're not looking   Between boulder & boulder,
forests and scree, summit & summit,
There aren't any numbers   There is only the earth
. . .

There's a pefect night view of the mountains behind us,
a real panorama, just like the brochures
but it's bigger & colder & harder than us
Let's talk about something more human: my hands
in your pockets, you're ticklish, & who left the grease
in the stewpot again, & why is the bedrock
on my side of the tent   My watch says it's 8
& here comes the moon with her merciless light
so where is the flash

No matter how far in we go, how long
we are what we are

                    unnatural, human

Elsewhere she attempts to retrieve an old table in order to make her camp more hospitable. When she rights the table, it collapses into the lake. Her conclusion:

                    Aristotle was right
(& my shins are leaning): a thing is its usage:
& a table that is through with being a table
is not a table at all

How refreshing! We are, finally, small figures on planet Earth. Our lovings are best when intensified by an unblinking realism. McCombs's metaphor for transcendental insight is the striking of a match in the dark—a paradoxical act, since her brief flame (her life) prevents her from seeing what might possibly surround her in the dark primeval forest:

                    In the blackness a lapping
of water or muzzle; the air says something,
gibberish or warning, & quits when I move,
matches in hand, to strike open the fire
that stops me from seeing.

Mantric Poems

Mantric poetry, or chant poetry, is transported from alien cultures to our own. Some poems are derived from American Indian sources—examples can be found in the work of Maurice Kenny and Jerome Rothenberg; other poems have their roots in the Far East and particularly in Zen Buddhism, as do certain pieces by Allen Ginsberg, Phillip Whalen, and Gary Snyder.

One of the purest of all mantric poets is Michael McClure, whose poems have been better understood by the lions at the San Francisco Zoo at feeding time than by American poetry-lovers. McClure allows sheer sound to exist as his mantra, without any trappings from the Far East, from Jeremiah and other ranting prophets, or from lost or imagined American Indian seers and shamans.

McClure's writing is, like action painting, spontaneous. He wants the reader to reexperience the excitement he felt while writing the poems. The energy screaming (at times) or streaming (at others) is as important as any direct poetic statement the reader might receive of a traditional sort. McClure fractures the expected and the preconditioned with excitement, fear, a sexual connection, a discharge. The act of the poem for McClure is mantric: chanting, caressing, shouting, or simply breathing. Communication is the conveying of nonverbal ideas spread like warm honey on the slabsurfaces of the mind, giving them from my mind over to yours, from McClure's mind over to ours.

As a "mammalian" communicator, McClure ennobles man, who through the poems re-achieves or recognizes the mantric force of language. The lamb's *baa* responds lovingly to the *graaah* of the lion and meshes with it. Jean Harlow responds with lascivious purrs to Billy the Kid's growlings and chest-beatings. Declaiming the delicious sound *graaah* freshens our spiritual nodes: we vibrate with recharged life.

In his *Ghost Tantras* McClure's beast (mammal/mantric) language is *love:* we are to form strange creature sounds with abandon and pleasure, with love-explosives, love-verbal-fun-ejaculations.

Marilyn Monroe Poems

(*See* **Celebrity Poems: Film Stars**)

Marriage Poems

Marriage poems run the gamut from utter bliss to utter despair. Since most American poets today dredge their personal lives for poems, and since most poets are heterosexual (gay and lesbian poets have marriage problems too), marriage poems are as numerous as fleas on the family Schnauzer. Unfortunately, not many of these poems are worth writing to your mother-in-law about.

Exceptions, of course, are certain poems about failed marriages by W. D. Snodgrass, Diane Wakoski, and Robert Lowell. The latter's "Man and Wife" ("Tamed by *Miltown,* we lie on Mother's bed") as well as some of the poems scattered through *For Lizzie and Harriet* are particularly harrowing.

David Ray, the former editor of *New Letters,* writes marriage poems, and has published several by other poets. In the Winter 1984 issue, Peter Everwine contrasts a wife and her two husbands, hinting that he may have been the first. Husband number one responded to the spouse's efforts to dominate him with off-the-wall remarks. When she banged a kitchen pot and said "The cracked dish," he jibed: "The princess is dancing in the ballroom." Husband number two, far less independent, agrees with everything. When she says "cracked dish" to him, he says, "Just as I've always thought." This second marriage, though secure, is boring: "The man died looking out the window. The woman died with her eyes tightly closed. Their children gave them a grand funeral and took a different name."

Roger Pfingston develops an effective conceit for his intense love for his "dear one":

> I'm going to love your bones,
> I mean love your bones so they will know
> that they've been loved . . .

Marya Mannes almost slurps past the good taste and reticence expected of most *New Letters* poets. Her formal sonnet celebrating the "sexual thrall" of a good lay, despite its inherent loneliness, is as germane to married as to unmarried sex:

> Rocking and rolling locked on tumbled bed,
> priapic penis plunged in vaginal deep,
> withdrawn and plunged again as exultant head
> looms over face of woman whose fingers keep
> pressing on urgent buttocks or sweating nape,
> here is the playful, lustful, prideful male
> in favorite exercise and fittest shape,
> wanting no more from woman than her tail.

John Morgan, in "The Bone-Duster," writes frankly of one aspect of love few men confront—loving a woman so much sexually that marriage spoils one's craving for her. Lee Upton's "The Wives" (*Connecticut Poetry Review,* confronts a rare domestic problem. A new wife lives in an apartment above her husband's former wife. At the start, she's unaware of the truth until a boy appears to say he is her husband's son and asks that his train be fixed. The new wife says: "I loved them both, / your wife and son, wanted them near me more than I think / you did." When the women meet, exchanging smiles, the old wife and the boy convey "a form of tenderness."

Linda Gregg's "Marriage and Midsummer's Night" is a self-consciously relaxed and underplayed rendition of what must have been a painful experience: through a window a wife watches her husband in an adjacent apartment make love to a rival:

> . . . She was like a vase
> lit the way milky glass is lighted.
> He looked more beautiful there
> than I remember him the times
> he entered my bed with the light behind.

Three years have passed and the pain lingers, a pain Gregg evokes through the subtle images of *legs, edge,* and *knife,* since she sat

> at the open window, my legs over the edge
> and the knife close like a discarded idea.

Menses Poems

Phyllis Koestenbaum writes a thoroughgoing menses poem. "Blood Journey" equates her menstrual blood with her "poetry":

> The odor of blood on napkins,
> the odor of the ground, if you put your nose to it as dogs do,
> scratching and sniffing.
> The fire from ripe bodies is a stench.
> Books also burn.

Koestenbaum recalls her first bleedings, where, behind a closed kitchen door, her mother calms her. There's a poignant mix of feelings—childhood, womanhood, distaste, and celebration:

> I bleed.
> Rags, pads, underpants,
> jeans, sheets, pyjamas, nightgowns,
> slacks, shorts,

bathing suits,
a green checked playsuit with a matching skirt.
I am a young girl, I am a young woman,
I go to sleep tired and wake refreshed,
I start again
and again,
I have been everywhere.
I run and bleed a cup of blood.
I shout hello and the blood jumps out as a great breath.
I cannot stop.

My pad drops down from between my legs on the way home for lunch.
When I go back to school,
the pad is gone.

Later, when she does not bleed, she is dismayed, seeing the absence of blood as a failure: "The truth is / my not bleeding is an unnatural / halting." She aches for evidence of her period from that "clay pot / with ridges like doll carriage tires." She runs to a public bathroom, wipes herself on cheap paper, and prays "to see red. . . . praying not to be pregnant."

Terry Kennedy, in *Heart, Organ, Part of the Body,* recollects the onset of menstruation in the unusual setting of a hut where men are fishing through the ice. Her anguish is checked by the fish image, which echoes the men's insensitive comments on "the fish smell of their wives":

Ice Fishing on Lake Champlain

I am menstruating inside the ice
hut where the husbands, my father's buddies,
are baiting their hooks and making fun
of the fish smell of their wives. My mother
is happy that I am safe, with my father
and far away from my Saturday girlfriends
who listen to Elvis and shave their legs.
I am aching, watching the faces
of these married icers, the blue
lights of their eyes as dull as the wedding
crystal locked up in my mother's closet. Dizzy,
I reel in my first catch of the day.
The scales flickering like rainbows.
The blood swimming over the lids.
Fire splitting me open
from fin to fin.

Sharon Olds, in "Monarchs," from *Satan Says,* links the image of butterflies to the bleeding associated with a first sexual experience. From the seventh story of a building, she observes hosts of monarch butterflies flying south, their wings recalling the "dark red" of a "butcher's hands," the veins in the insects' wings like a man's "scars." The recollected delicacy of the lover's touches reminds her of the "scrape" of an insect across her breast. She is naive and doesn't know enough to open her legs. She feels his thighs, "feathered with red-gold hairs, / opening" between her legs like a "pair of wings." Afterwards, she notices a "hinged" blood print she's left on his thighs, "a winged creature pinned there." She recalls his numerous departures from her, and stunningly reinvokes the monarchs,

> . . . floating
> south to their transformation, crossing over
> borders in the night, the diffuse blood-red
> cloud of them, my body under yours,
> the beauty and silence of the great migrations.

Anne Sexton, in "Menstruation at Forty" (*Live or Die*), on the occasion of her fortieth birthday, observes her bleeding as continuing evidence of the son or daughter she will never have. With this she interweaves a craving for suicide, as she feels "the November / of the body as well as of the calendar," and longs for death, something present in her womb "all along."

Ann Fox Chandonnet's "In Velvet" (*Auras, Tendrils*), is about an Athapaskan girl, in a wintery Alaskan village before 1800, shut up on the occasion of her first menstruation. Such confinements might last anywhere from four months to several years, until the tribe found the girl a husband. She was allowed no heat, neither hot nor fresh food, and was forced to wear gloves or mittens (she was not allowed to touch her "contaminated" body). She drank from a special tube fashioned from a hollowed swan's bone, ate from her own cup and bowl, and wore a menstrual hood and special hair ornaments. Throughout her life, during her menses, she would cover her head and take separate trails (to protect the others of her tribe).

The girl hears the tribal preparations underway for her "woman's feast," and imagines the new bear, raven, and spirit-teeth masks created for the occasion: "No one speaks of me / but the rattles speak." She observes a bee painted on matting,

> to remind me
> of the spring,
> when honeybees migrate,
> and the old queen takes half the colony in a swarm
> to a birch.
> Scouts fly from the birch seeking a new camp,
> one that will keep them warm and dry
> during the dark time.
> When a camp is chosen, the swarm goes there.

And here they have carved a bee,
yellow cedar from the south,
with ivory wings
and baleen eyes,
and hung it by a length of sinew
from the rafters.
And this is to remind me when I am a woman
I will never rest.
And to be thankful for this seclusion.
For the bee never rests,
but is always seeking wildflowers as we seek marten-skins.

She considers her lucky charms: red and blue porcupine quills and a
swan's leg bone. She fears the pleasure and pain true of her lot as woman.
All she's known of pleasure is "the swansdown on the strap / of my grease
bag." To still her hunger she smears her lips with grease. In her isolation
she considers her plight as a woman:

I am twelve winters, a despised female,
my grandmother and aunts whisper when
they bring my dry fish;
they whisper I am lucky
that my nose was not stopped with moss
and I left to die at birth in the forest.
It was a good summer for oolachan
so they kept me, a despised female,
and the oil ran down my fat chin.

That her small brother is petted and preferred because he is male does
not offend her—she accepts her lot. She refuses to cry, and avers that she
will marry whatever husband is chosen for her:

My breasts flourish like these chevrons of beads,
red and pointed,
soft as cottonwood down, as eider bellies.
(I shall please my husband,
and he shall bring home fine skins to sew.)

The gush of her bleeding mingles with her memory of being thrust into
her "closet";

Ice formed on my hair when they washed it,
and then quickly, quickly, quickly,
they cast me inside this closet,
mother only whispering a few words:
that I must no longer be seen until married,
that I am no longer a child because of this redness.
they pulled this new hood (my velvet) on me;
the ice beneath melted down my back.

I must stay, grandmother says,
until the end of next salmon season,
through the time of darkness,
and the time of birds' eggs, the time of Fireweed greens,
the time of lighted nights.
Auntie says to be thankful I am not a princess,
for then I would stay here longer.

When the red runs, I dream of slippery fish,
slipping down my thighs to our nets.
I dream of the crooked salmon,
fish, fish, fish.

Minimalist Poems

(*See* **ABC Poems**)

Mock Heroic Poems

Poets who write mock heroic poems in the tradition of old Breton lays, Chaucer's beast fables and scatological tales, Byron's *Childe Harold,* and Tennyson's *The Princess* are scarce. One poet who does is Brooks Haxton. His "Breakfast Ex Animo" is the one bright spot in an otherwise dull issue of *Poetry* (March–May 1982). The poem describes Haxton working up the courage to run to the henhouse to see what's disturbing his hens. The poem, a dozen pages long, is thoroughly anachronistic. Haxton eventually finds his nerve and discovers that a harmless egg snake has swallowed one of those porcelain eggs placed in a hen's nest to get her to set. The snake in panic can't crush or digest the "egg," and finds himself stuck trying to exit through his crawl-hole. When our hero returns to his breakfast (the serpent is dead), an obnoxious fly samples some greasy breakfast eggs, an armadillo sleeps under a wood-pile, and "Venus will have slipped into the blue folds of translucent sky, / And I will find myself at breakfast, / And begin."

In an even more ambitious work, *The Lay of Eleanor and Irene,* Haxton seems to hold the mirror up to Tennyson's Arthurian poems. The poet meets Irene in a supermarket, and is so turned on he abandons his monogamist wife Eleanor and accompanies Irene to her apartment. After much frustration, indecision, foreplay, and eventual copulation, the hero discovers that his Eleanor and Irene are lesbian lovers. In a passage full of self-irony, the epic touches of bay and ocean and the Tennysonian/

Miltonic phrasings contribute to the humor. Irene's charms drive Haxton crazy:

> At this, my blood,
> More radical than the Atlantic
> At the Bay of Fundy,
> Poured its tide in homage
> Into a member shrunk
> With fear.
>
> The fear struck deeper
> While my erection doubled,
> Snagged by the glans penis
> On the crotch seam, wherefrom
> It sprang broadside, stopped
> With audible, immodest
> Whack by the cool flank
> Of the inner thigh.

Contemporary astronomical motifs enhance Haxton's epic strain:

> A little moonlight, bulblight,
> Emanations from the planets,
> From red dwarves, from quasars,
> Pulsars, from black holes.

A freshly turned Homeric simile evokes his stunned response to Irene's lesbianism:

> The membrane
> Of the waterbed shook
> As the rippling hide on the flat
> Breadth of a horse's neck
> Does when horseflies light; then
> Waves into which I sank;
> And under them one heard
> The joist-groan and the jamb-creak,
> And I pictured my swift
> Entree into the downstairs
> *Salon* through the ceiling
> With a metric ton
> Of water and a hard-on.

Momentosity Poems

"**M**omentosity" occurs when a poet yanks a poem towards an easy metaphysics, into *significance*. Such a poet feels obligated, especially if he is well known, to say Big Things—he becomes a sort of Shelleyan sky pilot for mankind. Big Statements, if ill-felt, are illusory; and when a poet like James Dickey (in "The Strength of Fields," which he read at President Carter's inauguration and later published in the book of the same name.) attempts to net the big statement, he goes slack, reminding us of Matthew Arnold, who stopped writing poetry in favor of essays—he could no longer, apparently, sustain his melancholy without puffing up abstractions he didn't feel. In one poem, "A Summer Night," Arnold concludes an otherwise nicely detailed and felt poem with this hollow ejaculation: "Plainness and clearness without shadow of stain! / Clearness divine! / Ye heavens. . . ." Instead of blowing our socks off and addling our brains, Arnold is soporific. His metaphysics is shallow stuff.

Walt Whitman was not above straining after the momentous. One of his efforts, a blatant failure, appears in the midst of some of the best poems he ever wrote, in *Drum-Taps*. After the superb "Vigil Strange" and "A March in the Ranks Hard-Prest" comes "A Sight in Camp in the Daybreak Gray and Dim." The opening lines read like uninspired notes from a journal:

> Three forms I see on stretchers lying, brought out there untended lying,
> Over each the blanket spread, ample brownish woolen blanket,
> Gray and heavy blanket, folding, covering all.

He gently lifts a blanket and finds there a gaunt, grim elderly man. Is Whitman moved? Not much, and he lingers just long enough to ask him his name, before moving on to a more attractive male, a young "darling," a "sweet boy with cheeks yet blooming." Even here, the emotion seems false. But there's a third stop, before a "divine" young man whose face is "nor child nor old, very calm, as of beautiful yellow-white ivory." "Divine" is the gin which clamps itself over Whitman's foot, for the concept allows him to see "the face of the Christ himself" in the soldier's face—"Dead and divine and brother of all, and here again he lies." The yanking forth of his totally uninspired narrative and the awarding of stale religious connotations are sad.

To return to James Dickey's inaugural poem: Language is a problem. The first line informs us that a small town "always" has a "moth-force," once we are "given the night." I'm confused. Does a moth's force drive the moth to fling itself suicidally into light? I thought that earth-anchored small towns were incapable of leaving their earth-moorings and wafting toward glimmering bulbs. Perhaps, though, if one is a lonely man walking in the fields outside town, the streetlamps seen from across the fields are like moths—but doesn't a firefly rather than a moth cast a winking light? "Moth-force" is a phrase that sounds important but means little.

Dickey separates these lines with white space, indenting freely, forcing us to assemble his lines as a meditational act of sorts—we linger over "moth-force"; we linger over "night" (a frayed image); we linger over "field-forms"; and we linger over a "solar system" floating on above this walking/thinking man as "town moths." Stars as moths? Stars as fireflies? I'm lost.

Dickey's attempt to develop an "idea" also seems enervated. Men appear around his striding figure, including dead men; yet, he obfuscates, they are "not where he is exactly now." A kind of cosmic significance labors to be born, as this *Ur-mensch* (symbolizing Dickey?) in his night meanderings, quests after the metaphysical.

Dickey's conundrum, posed on behalf of his walker (and us), is this: what should we do with our lives? A good riddle for a laureate. He prays to "Dear Lord of all the fields" for an answer. In another inflated, sentimental turn, he hopes his good ambulator will find his "secret blooming" by taking help from the dead who lie under the pastures. How did these dead get there? I thought even in small towns people were buried in cemeteries. And who says the dead have nothing better to do than worry about our individual destinies, taking time out to prod and guide us? Does Dickey have in mind a general image of rot, as Walt Whitman did in "Earth's Compost?"

Dickey next imagines the ocean as an answer-giver (thanks again to Whitman). Hundreds of miles away, the sea fumbles in its "deep-structured roar," a roar like that of nations in struggle with a "profound, unstoppable craving . . . for their wish." Well, what is that wish? Some variety of manifest destiny? And aren't *profound* and *unstoppable* hollow attempts to jerk the poems toward meanings only vaguely and ineptly felt by the poet? "Hunger, time and the moon"—another trio of frayed abstractions, indented way over to the right—don't provide answers. The repetitions of the three prepositional phrases beginning with *on* are like running a dull bit of film over again, hoping that to recreate the scene may ignite the fuel-tanks and blast the poetry-ship into space. It doesn't happen, alas, and Dickey's observation that "it" has to begin "with the simplest things" recalls some of Robert Frost's shibboleths (see, for instance, "Directive"), but lacks Frost's sense of the specific and the graphic. The poem concludes with Dickey's wanderer aware—as if there were any other choice—that his life belongs to the world. Knowing this now, he promises "to do what he can."

Much less ambitious, but equally a failure, is Wendell Berry's "The Snake," in which the speaker finds a chilled snake in the October woods, one who has just "thickened" himself with a mouse or a bird. Since the weather is cold, the creature is "stuporous," hardly troubling to "flicker his tongue." Momentosity occurs when the speaker takes up the snake, cradles it, and thinks Big Thoughts:

> I held him a long time, thinking
> of the perfection of the dark
> marking on his back, the death
> that swelled him, his living cold.

Even the unsubtle line break which keeps the lengthy adjectival unit removed from its noun "marking," points up a fake and exaggerated heavy-duty thought: "the perfection of the dark." Let's hear it for Mr. Existentialism! I for one feel greatly deflated when I find that Berry was merely describing a snake. At the end he is simply windy: he thinks of the creature lying under the frost, "big with a death to nourish him / during a long sleep." The final paradox of death as nourishing is facile.

Sherod Santos, in "The Evening Light Along The Sound," strains after Significant Abstractions and ends up merely platitudinous. His verse sentences meander along, attached to much verse brummagem— pompous conditional elements ("As if the sky could no longer hold its color"); slack relative clauses more at home in prose than poems; vague tags ("it all seems / so impersonal"; "something difficult / is reappearing in our lives"; "in that quiet hour / you forget yourself awhile"). The wind- off is pretentious: "The truth," he tells us, is "the light is sinking into itself, as we, in an absence / of light, will sink back into ourselves . . ." We offer ourselves "to the dark" as "the dark closes down around us." Only "momentarily," light glitters—it's only in our minds, "like a cluster of stars on the Sound."

Peter Cooley's "Orchard Bordered by Cypresses," from *The Van Gogh Notebook,* a meandering and bland series of poems occasioned by nearly all of the painter's best-known works, strains for profundity. Van Gogh's fairly simple painting is frosted o'er with mystical strivings. The rhetoric is pretentious, containing phrases like "until the pear tree is reinvented by the sky . . ."; "until the ground be divided by your sight . . ."; and "who will bear it [a ladder] upwards towards the cypresses?" One senses Cooley groaning under the weight of the poem-ladder he invents for himself, trying to thrust it up toward Heaven.

The mishap Cooley falls into—and it is one that many poets writing on painters do—is imagining that the creative act is fraught with mo- mentous insights as the painter visualizes his canvas. The truth is that a professional artist would not be thinking of "earth . . . calling heaven," or waiting for a foreground ladder "to be lifted toward the clouds." He'd be sketching and painting, an almost mindless act compared with the mys- tico-ecstatic riff Cooley imagines. Cooley's straining betrays his own failure to generate his own passion for or need to write this poem. Here in the concluding stanza, the ladder motif generates blatant rhetoric:

> Who will bear it upward toward the cypresses?
> Their procession holds up the firmament with flames.
> Who will keep you marching through the dark green fire,
> who keep you singing beyond the canvas
> as you ascend, who won't look back?

The American Poetry Review perpetuates this manner with a ven- geance. Robert Pinsky's "Fairyland," complete with photograph of the Yuppie poet in white, his shirt open at the throat, hand in pocket, loins tipped slightly forward, smiling and casual. His poem, though, lacks a similar charm. There's too much "fur and absurd finery" in "Fairyland."

Pinsky's tired ear settles for facile sounds: "our most ancient decayed hope / Is gross infantile greed." More stones weight Apollo's celestial jockstrap. The fairy of poetry didn't stroke Pinsky quite enough with his/ her magical wand. One hoped for more.

In Mark Strand's "Keeping Things Whole" deadened words fall off the page as fast as his insights, which are on a level with the pronounce- ments of some bright student in Philosophy 101 who sees glimmers of the vast scheme of things. Strand imagines himself in a "field"—force field? farmer's field? Edward Field? He is "the absence / of field." Has he no aura? At any rate, his condition seems perpetual: "This is / always the case"; wherever he is he's always "what is missing." Walking, he resem- bles a paper airplane (my parallel) or a shambling shadow (wasn't this one of Plato's more facile ideas?) who is fascinated by the fact that, as he parts the air, air always moves in to "fill the spaces" where his body has been. That's nice, isn't it? Who or what is the shadow? Who or what is the reality? Strand moves "to keep things whole."

Charles Wright's "The New Poem" is rife with pretentiousness and a fatigued ear. Its serial design, tedious in the extreme, is merely a clever workshop idea. His "Northanger Ridge," more ambitious (i.e., longer), is a pastiche of tired ideas and vapidly hollow phrases. As "something" drops from leaves, a "drugged moon" is an insomniac, a black widow spider "reknits her dream," "Salvation again declines." Too bad, for in the first stanza there's a patch of vivid writing:

> One cloud, like a trunk, stays shut
> Above the horizon; off to the left, dream-wires,
> Hill-snout like a crocodile's.

(Vendler, pp. 328–329)

Jorie Graham displays an ear as delicate as an electrified wire of fairly low voltage strung around a cow pasture. Just listen to the first stanza of "San Sepolcro" where the individual cadences resemble pallid AC/DC surges:

> In this blue light
>   I can take you there,
> snow having made me
>   a world of bone
> seen through to.   This
>   is my house. . .

Examples of momentosity are, alas, seemingly endless, and will always be with us as long as poets feel obliged to see themselves as "legislators for mankind." There seems to be a ratio, as I have already implied, between pomposity and the degree of a poet's renown. The better known the poet, the greater is his or her urge to serve as a wisdom- platitude figure. I could fill this entire book with examples of such writing.

One poet at ease with transcendental ideas is Robert Duncan. The range of his learning is incredible, from the Oz books to Madam Blavatsky. Take a look at "The Law" (*Roots and Branches*). The ramifications of his various frames of reference are complex—Duncan calls the poem "a series in variation." Platonic ideas of order, Blakean snake coils, Shelleyan anarchy, Heraclitean ideas of flux, the conflict of old vs. new ("new needs are new commands"), seeing and plain speaking, song/poetry as fate, the Oedipal act of ripping out one's eyes, Shakespeare's murdered Duncan, the coils of natural events, evil, poets as lawgivers, Justinian repressiveness, Satan's nets in the guise of law, the human will as inventor of law, Blake's despising of law(s), the crucifixion, Robin Hood as the out-law, the pronouns of writing—particularly "I"—all winding off with a superb attack on "the deceitful coils" of all institutions, which stifle the freedom required of the artist. Like Blake, one must rebel, and "*What is* / hisses a serpent / and writhes / to shed its skin." I fear that by assembling the above list I may dissuade readers from turning to this amazing poem. Duncan is never for a moment swamped by the dense material he uses. He makes it entirely his own. The alembic of his stunning mind in consort with his feelings allows him to swing old-fashioned censers of ideas that would seem flatulent and heavy in the hands of lesser poets.

Mother Poems

Though most "mother poems"—and they are legion—droppeth as gentle ewes from heaven, occasionally they explode with the force of driving, cutting hail. Unforgettable examples of the latter type are S. S. Gardons's (W. D. Snodgrass spelled more or less backwards) "The Mother" and "To A Child." The mother is content only when she is certain that her "martyrdom" has paid off, that her children hate her. The "labyrinth" she weaves is "of waste, wreckage / Of hocus-pocus." One by one, areas of her brain "switch off" as she fills them with hate and evil: "If evil did not exist, she would create it."

In "To A Child," the poet and his small daughter (he's enjoying visiting rights) walk a dog in a field. The spot they reach is exactly the one where twenty years earlier S. S. "lay" with his first girl and was forced by fear to flee. He reviews other locales he's visited with his daughter: a cemetery, a creek where they caught a live turtle, a children's zoo. He reminds her of the long letters he's written and mailed, enclosing "maple wings that fly, / Linden gliders and torqued ailanthus seeds, / The crisp pine flyers that flutter / Like soft moths down the sky." "They" (we assume he means the divorced mother) threw the father's letters away, saying that "he had probably forgotten" to write. And worst of all, he has shown the daughter her grandmother:

That old sow in her stye
Who would devour her farrow;
We have seen my sister in her narrow
Grave. Without love we die;
With love we kill each other.

A view of mother, with a power akin to that of Sylvia Plath's "Daddy,"
is Kate Braverman's "Milk Run," in *Lullaby For Sinners*. Mother wanted
her daughter to be a "rag doll" propped on the stoops of houses where her
cuteness would be admired: "You even ironed the ribbons / on my baby
smocks." Mom chain-smoked and baked pies, and often woke her at 3
A.M. to give her hot chocolate. At ten, the daughter is puffy, wears
"second-hand party dresses," fails in math, needs eyeglasses, is friend-
less, and waits for her mother's love, which rarely comes. Mother is often
in her bedroom crying "over conspiracies." Father dies of cancer. Mother
sees her daughter grow up with her nightmares intact and with wretched
posture. The daughter knows she can never be as pretty as her mother,
even when mom is crying, hurling herself against her locked door. To
escape, at nineteen, the daughter marries "the fat one," saving both
herself and her mother; but the marriage fails. A second marriage also
fails: "He had a sick smell / of dark rooms and smoke / enameled to his
skin." Now she has lovers, who take "nothing," since there's "nothing left
to take." Life has become for her, by choice, "a milk run."

Movingly intimate poems by Tess Gallagher treat mothers and chil-
dren. In "Black Silk," from *Willingly*, women are survivors with complex
issues between them. Gallagher's mother was always cleaning—"there is
always that to do"; and on this particular day she brings an old silk vest
from the closet. It is Gallagher's dead father's vest. The mother unrolls it
"carefully / like something live / might fall out." With Gallagher's help,
she smooths the wrinkles, and forces the cloth down into its proper
shape, until "the little tips / that would have pointed to his pockets / lay
flat." No buttons are missing. The mother slips the vest on over Gal-
lagher's held-out arms, observing that she never "wanted to be a man."
When Gallagher goes to the bathroom to see how she looks wearing the
vest, "in its sheen and sadness," she hears her mother weeping and
chooses not to return immediately, seeming thereby to assert her own
self-reliance, her need as a woman to act on her own terms.

In "Each Bird Walking," a son must bathe his invalid mother—
something each of us fears we may be called upon to do. Simply seeing a
parent naked, in any circumstances, often constitutes a Biblical taboo, as
in the story of the drunken, nude Noah revealing himself to his sons. I
would assume that for a son to bathe a nude mother is more difficult than
cleansing a father. Gallagher deals acutely with a basic, almost totemic
fear. She heightens the drama through enjambment, and by alternating
pentameter and tetrameter lines. A series of present participles thread
through the poem, softening the stark beat. The son is Gallagher's lover.
The ill mother helps her son

> moving
> the little she could, lifting so he could
> wipe under her arms, a dipping motion
> in the hollow. Then working up from
> the feet, around the ankles, over the
> knees. And this last, opening
> her thighs and running the rag firmly
> and with the cleaning through
> up through her crotch, between the lips,
> over the V of thin hairs—

A lesser poet would wind off here, but Gallagher does not. The poem takes an amazing turn—the new theme is the "end of our loving," a declaration which prompts Gallagher to look "to see what was left of us / with our sex taken away." The style changes; lengthy adverbial phrases, in the manner of Whitman, are the primary sound clusters, with single, interrupting words dropped in between to hasten the stanzaic flow:

> On our lips that morning, the tart juice
> of the mother, so strong in remembrance, no
> asking, no giving, and what you said, this
> being the end of our loving, so as not to hurt
> the closer one to you, made me look
> to see what was left of us
> with our sex taken away. "Tell me," I said,
> "something I can't forget." Then the story of
> your mother, and when you finished
> I said, "that's good, that's enough."

(pp. 77–78)

The simplified delivery of a momentous resolution, the absence of self-pity, the implicit personal strength—all limn Gallagher's image of herself as a woman.

The stunning title poem of Allen Ginsberg's *White Shroud* is as powerful and intense as any he has ever written, and is a mystical journey poem through Hades (Manhattan). Ginsberg borrows one of the hoariest conventions in all literature, the Homeric and Virgilian journey to the Kingdom of the Dead, an obligatory rite for all epic heroes. This City of the Dead is the ravished Bronx of Ginsberg's childhood:

> under old theater roofs, masses of poor women shopping
> in black shawls past candy store news stands, children skipped beside
> grandfathers bent tottering on their canes.

The first Homeric shade lies in a chamber open to the street. His old grandmother is on a bed, sighing, eating "a little Chicken / soup or borscht, potato latkes, crumbs on her blankets, talking / Yiddish, complaining solitude abandoned in Old Folks House." He greets her, then wanders on, hoping to find his own "hot-water furnished flat" nearby, so that he can easily visit his anile grandmother. By nightfall he's found a niche, and continues wandering around Manhattan. It is the day before Christmas.

He passes heated subway gratings where bag-people and derelicts sleep, and finds an old lady living in a side alley on a mattress:

> I was horrified a little, who'd take care of such a woman,
> familiar, half-neglected on her street except she'd weathered
> many snows stubborn alone in her motheaten rabbit-fur hat.

This is incredible writing, deeply felt, compassionate, lingering just long enough to create a full sense of character, full of imaginative touches (the "horseshoe of / incisors" and "cranky hair"), and some of the subtlest long-line free verse cadences of Ginsberg's career.

Now comes the great surprise: the bag-lady is his mother, the dead Naomi Ginsberg! The recognition is totally without self-pity, even quasi-humorous, and entirely within character—she's an old Jewish mother greatly disappointed in her son and her relatives for having abandoned her: "I'm living alone," she declares when Ginsberg asks her what she is doing. "You all abandoned me, I'm a great woman, I came here / by myself, I wanted to live, now I'm too old to take care / of myself, I don't care, what are you doing here?"

He examines her "cave" and finds a place to live where he can attend to her, compensating for his absences when she was alive and dying. He'll cook and write books for money, paying for her medicine, food, and false teeth. "Best of all," he tells Naomi, he's just seen her "old enemy Grandma, living a couple of blocks away." Ginsberg is overjoyed.

When Ginsberg's dream-descent concludes, he awakens in Boulder, in his current home, returned from "the Land of the Dead to living Poesy." He immediately writes his "tale of long lost joy" in having seen his mother again. When the poem is finished at sunrise (his notation concluding the poem is "October 5, 1983, 6:35 a.m."), he descends the stairs to find his lover Peter Orlovsky watching television. He kisses Orlovsky and weeps.

Few women poets appear to write poems to or about their grown daughters. The most poignant I have found is Arlene Stone's "Helpless," in *The Double Pipes of Pan*. Here a mother visits an overwhelmed daughter who has either committed suicide, or is contemplating it. Effective, indeed, is Stone's matter of fact tone; there's not a shred of sentimentality:

Helpless

> Knee-deep in soiled wash
> you are drowning
> the dishes unscraped
> & the dust thick enough to talk to
> Outdoors the hills cave in

Indoors is a pressure cooker
the mirrors cracked
with the creases in old skin

You are not old
a woman in the daisy knot of
samplered life
the room so cold it could
be full of falling snow
your name written clearly
in English or Hebrew
a prophecy some moving finger left
on a frosted New England window

This room could be ice
& you the sculpture of a dying swan
or I five hundred miles away
or five million
for all the difference it makes

yet say I were here
in this room
we know I would not lift
a pricked finger to help you
as you wound about your neck
your father's sleeve
the father I chose for you

I lick the thread
I steady the needle
I put up water to boil
so not to hear you gurgle

Why did I bring you
O hook
into the eye of my world

Myth Poems

So many contemporary poems reflect the influences of myths that to count them would be as impossible as counting pebbles on a beach. The literature on the subject is vast: see, for example, the list appended to the brief discussion of "Myth" in the *Princeton Encyclopedia of Poetry and Poetics*. Pagan myths, prehistoric myths, Christian myths, Hindu and Eastern myths, African myths, Gnostic myths, Jungian myths, Freudian myths, Reichian myths, pop culture myths, Western U.S. myths, private myths (of the sort Blake and Yeats created). . . the list goes on and on, and poets have written about them all.

Among the great modern poets who recreated received myths in their own image were Eliot, Pound, Rilke, Yeats, and Lawrence. In our own time, Charles Olson, Robert Duncan, Gary Snyder, John Thomas, Clayton Eshleman, Thomas Meyer, and Robert Kelly have all made use of myths, often passing them through the prisms of such thinkers as Freud, Jung, and Reich.

I have chosen two poets to represent all other poets currently laboring in these austere and refined realms. *Cochise* is the book; Peter Wild is the poet. Wild's Cochise is a place in Arizona, a name derived from the primitive Americans whose legacy of flattened stones and a complete absence of weapons showed them to have been an unusually pacific group. In later ages, they apparently developed from a seed-growing people into a tribe of hunters.

What makes Wild's blend of myths special is that he is non-anti-quarian. He doesn't posture or stuff his work with intellectualizations so as to impress and overwhelm us with his erudition. His ancient Indian culture is maimed, tortured, and diseased because of white culture. His Indians, Mexicans, Spanish-Americans, and Americans are all somewhat passive, immobilized in the present, except in their fantasies.

"Cochise" is a myth. Wild's surrealism keeps the reader unsure of the exact details. The speaker is visited by a woman, possibly a descendant of Cochise primitives: a mystical "mud woman rearing from the landscape / dissolving in her own salt lake." The speaker does not welcome her: "You are the last person in the world I want to see today," he declares. This earthy Persephone makes herself comfortable in Wild's leather chair. He puts his arm around her, lights her cigar, and fetches liquor and canapes from his refrigerator. She is a visionary figure who touches the speaker's misty perception of his own "troubles, with family, friends and church." She would be at home with Carlos Castenada.

The visitor tells Wild about a one-legged lover who has nothing but love to give her and asks the speaker how he stays sane. "Being experienced," he says cryptically, "I know what to say." This seems to give her courage, and as he settles back in a dentist's chair, she becomes erotically aroused:

> . . . while your breasts slump beneath the sweater,
> the nipples looking around my room like baby birds
> expecting food. they start to eye me. they want
> to bite me on the face.

He escapes her lust via fantasy, and tracks Cochise, "our stronghold," stalking a lion, "taking strength from the beast." He becomes Cochise—a figure symbolic of the vanquished ancient tribe, laboring up the mountain, his own hands "veins climbing over the labyrinth." Cochise shows him how to "win." He participates in the ancient apprenticeship of novice to master, receiving wisdom while in the barren mountains.

The tracking of the lion becomes in a curious way the tracking of the woman, who is so far out on remote mudflats that she dissolves into a salt lake. Across the sky, an Apollonian boy ("the person we fear most") drives a flock of sheep: "they stumble, sparks fly from their hooves, their curly heads." Stars "dive down" to eat the woman's hair. The speaker's lips are coated with "powdered gold." The boy, smiling, opens his magical pouch, takes the speaker's arm and they begin to dance, rejecting the woman. But the speaker has a pact with the woman—there have been promises and an exchange, and he must wait for her. Yet, dancing, he says: "We swear never to go back." The poem is more cryptic at the end than at the beginning. It provides the mythic substructure for the entire volume, the whole of which reads like a single poem built up out of many complex, rich elements.

Myth informs "Cochise" in almost every line: the odd old cigar-smoking Indian/Mexican woman seems to symbolize the ancient past brought forward to the age of refrigerators and dental chairs. She is also physical: earth and sex. The speaker (a persona for Wild) escapes, fantasizing that he performs the Jessie–Weston act of stalking the ancient primitive hero stalking the golden lion stalking himself.

Tranformations of the literal into the interpretable happen easily in Wild's poems. It is a simple matter, therefore, to see the Cochise figure of the lion-stalker transformed into the Apollonian boy following his sheep across the sky. Also, the dance they perform is ritualized, ancient. The decision never to return to the mudflats and the woman (the past?) asserts the reality of the present—one can't retreat from it. The woman must come from her place in dream/reality to the speaker's house, sit in his leather chair, eat from his refrigerator. The dilemma is obvious: the fantasy life when we become most man/woman is never wholly real: our heroic acts (stalking beasts, enjoying primal sex, inhabiting the skies) occur only in our minds, prompted by our acquaintance with myths, some of them read from books, others residual in our blood, dating from our primitive ancestry, totemistic:

> you scream as the stars dive down
> to eat your hair, powdered gold coats my lips.
> and he smiling opens his pouch,
> takes my arm. we begin to dance,
> and though I wait for you
> he knows about the promises, the exchange—
> we swear never to go back.

The facts of the poem are equally real for the modern brown man with Cochise blood and the modern white man who, like Wild, compassionately pursues Indian/Mexican/Spanish lives. Few writers convey such empathy so convincingly.

Another intriguing, thoroughly original poem, oscillating between various myths, is Wild's "Sins of the Tongue." The poet is assertive and poignant: "The tongue is bit between the teeth." The whole body follows the tongue, and is, in a sense, its straining, guided horse. When the tongue speaks the mist shoots droplets, rainbows, clouds. A burning pillar (the ubiquitous myth-touch) beckons you to keep talking and moving. The pillar itself is transformed, "a phantasmagoria with legs and fingers" looming before your face. Like the tongue, the skies sprinkle rain. You may choose to keep the tongue's rain within your mouth, the tongue folded within, "a snake swirling in a barrel, / a snake finding a place among leaves."

Then Wild brings off a characteristic feat—he introduces an image so extravagant it shouldn't work. The tongue, a frustrated swirling snake, trying to speak, locked inside its mouth, its jaws "curled around it," is a bulldozer with its rudder jammed. During the daylight, trying to extricate itself, the bulldozer/tongue/snake overheats. At night, quiet, it enjoys auras of calm. The strain and tension contrasting with the peaceful cause the tongue to grow brittle

> until it shoots from the head
> > all muscle,
> until like the swelling Phoenix
> you stand skin clothed in flame and words,
> eyes empty.

This ending is swift and kaleidoscopic. The striving tongue locked inside the mouth explodes with an orgasmic force. Like the phoenix reincarnated from its own ashes, the man/tongue stands clothed heroically in flame and words. His eyes are "empty," i.e., he has become his own vision and, hence, has no need for vision. This resolution is a rare and inventive mythologizing of sexual/religious ecstasy. The quest for the burning pillar, present in men's physical minds from the beginning, leads to intense physical clamor. One must rape his own landscape (bulldoze it, even if the rudder is jammed) in order to achieve an ecstatic vision.

The theme of suppressed or redirected lust as a means to vision is common in *Cochise*. I read it as Wild's acknowledgment of the heavy Roman Catholic imposition of sexual guilt over the once-primitive natives, a guilt shared by all whites, especially those living near or involved with these multiracial peoples.

Name-Dropping Poems

Name-dropping is like spreading stale peanut butter over a half-mile-long delicatessen roll—a waste of good bread. Ann Waldman's "Pressure," from *Fast-Speaking Woman*, is a rare instance of this malady. Here are a few of her names:

> Joan Sutherland's astounding voice
> the cocktail party [yes, T. S. Eliot's]

the starry night [Van Gogh's]
Mozart's legacy / and Satie's
The Great Chain of Being [this from a course in the History of Ideas at
    Hunter College]
talking about Kerouac
Louis Ferdinand Celine [all three names]
Bach
Beethoven
Buddy Holly
Jelly Roll Morton.

Her "Light and Shadow," also from *Fast-Speaking Woman,* contains the
following orts culled from books: "the long shadow of Jesus," "Locke's
reasoning light," "Homer's voyaging light & shadow," "Aristotle, dark &
consuming," "Goethe's elective affinities," "Newton's arrogant light,"
"Calvin's stoic light," "poor Abelard," "Socrates' wise forehead," "Ein-
stein's brain the speed of light," "Aquinas, Plato, Pasteur all light-bulbs in
the brown study. . . ."

Frank O'Hara did a fair amount of name-dropping too; very often the
names are those of friends and acquaintances, contributing to his image
as a most lovable Joe. These figures appear in "The Day Lady Died":
Bastille Day, Ghana, *New World Writing,* Linda Stilwagon, Patsy, Bon-
nard, Hesiod, Richard Lattimore, Brendan Behan, Genet, Verlaine,
Mike, Strega Wine, Ziegfeld Theatre, Gauloises, *New York Post,* and
Mal Waldron.

Ditto for John Ashbery. Count up the many references in
"Self-Portrait in a Convex Mirror," a veritable index of his tastes
and enthusiasms.

Naropa Poems

These constitute a hive of revved-up cultist poets led by Allen
Ginsberg and Ann Waldman, all clustered around guru Trungpa
Rimpoche (who has himself been known to scribble poems) at the
Jack Kerouac School of Disembodied Poetics in Boulder, Colorado. The
focus is heavily on the old Beat poetry, blessed by Ginsberg. Worker-bees
who have frequently taught at these cloistered retreats include Gregory
Corso, William S. Burroughs, Edward Dorn, Michael McClure, and Gary
Snyder. As current aging mentors reach their dotage it will be fascinating
to see what younger blood will do to perpetuate this strange mix of fairy-
dust, OM-ism and verse.

Native American Poems

"**U**gh poetry," a subcategory of native American poetry, is written both by native Americans and by white Americans trying to sound primitive. James Fenimore Cooper in "The Leatherstocking Tales" originated Indian talk: the grand abstract clichés for Sky, Water, White Men, Coyote, etc.

One of the most glaring examples of ugh poetry is Robert Penn Warren's *Chief Joseph of the Nez Perce,* a poem on the tragic history of the great Chief and his people, and their slaughter at the hands of the U.S. Grant administration. Warren's treatment is ill-felt, ill-thought, and ill-executed. Yet, he is on the right side; he ennobles, if feebly, Chief Joseph.

At the same time, superficialities abound. The Indian mind is cluttered with clichés: forked tongues, Great White Fathers, and commonplace flora and fauna. When Warren seeks to encompass the red mind (he zings from one Indian paintbrush to another, like a bee taking sips before buzzing off), he imagines the most obvious preoccupations of those minds—much as comic book figures would think them. The very last section of the book is a disaster, in which the poet pretends to have a "vision" of Chief Joseph, and reports the event in ugh talk: "I see lips move, but / No sound hear." The abstractions are a pustulence: "I saw," he writes, "Vastness of plains lifting in twilight for / Winter's cold kiss, its absoluteness." His Indians speak in a mixture of verse styles reminiscent of Longfellow and Tennyson (with an occasional Transcendental sentiment tossed in from Emerson and Thoreau). Some examples: "We touch not the locks of the honored dead"; "There, southward, a steel pipe, / With marker screwed on, defines the spot / Of the tepee of Joseph." Here is ugh talk at its purest: "I slow-squeezed trigger." "For a true chief no self has." "Men have fallen from saddle before echo came." "For the kill, to make *coup* / To dab cheek with the blood of a brother." These lines alternate with a great deal of pompousness: "the unperturbed gray purity of sky," "the friendship of mountains," hearts "swollen with rage . . . and gratefulness." Also: "When the slug plugged her bosom, unfooting her / To the current's swirl and last darkness." What about this line for a typing exercise: "The unhived lead hums happily honeyward."

Marianne Moore, in "Enough," included in "Naming the Land," a pretentious feature edited by Henri Cole for *Harper's* (August 1984), is also insensitive to Indians. She writes with all the insight of a child's primer: "Poor Powhatan" and flowering Pocahontas are celebrated in near-doggerel:

> John Rolfe fell in love
> with her and she—in rank above
>
> what she became—renounced her name
> yet found her status not too tame.

Can you believe this? Moore, a major American poet? Read your Kenneth Rexroth on this score.

William Oandasan, a Yuki/Filipino, seldom transcends ugh language. "The Presence" is stereotypical. A wise man gathers his "children" round, and declares:

"I have something old
to voice.

It was spoken

by my Father, his Father, the Fathers before. . . .
so you might listen
and tell your children.

Oandasan's "I have something old / to voice" strikes me as neither good Indian nor good Anglo speech. The chief continues, his declarations couched in the slowest delivery imaginable—Oandasan strings the obvious words over the page as though they were momentous truths for all time.

By contrast, in writing of Native Americans, George Hitchcock eschews phony language (ugh talk) and condescension. In "Retribution," from *The Wounded Alphabet: Poems Collected & New 1953–1983,* he chillingly extols the patience of a surviving people as they wait for the appropriate time for fashioning the "magic arrowhead" to right the tragic wrongs perpetrated by whites. The poem follows:

the stolen campfires of Indians
are hidden in our cities
they illumine the rivers
of quarreling shoes they
are reflected in the vanishing
bumpers of Chevrolets their
sparks float upward
in the darkened windows
of orthopedists

on summer nights rawhide
flags and reed trumpets stain
the retreating horizon
drums are heard
deep under the roots of houses

already in some back street
a manhole cover breaks open
disgorging painted bowmen
with their lean expectant dogs
and wild pigs

while in the gloom of cider
smelling cellars bronze women
sit crosslegged
sifting our used ashes for the lost
magic arrowhead

A similarly sympathetic reading appears in Gary Holthaus's *Circling Back,* an epic of the American West during the days of Custer, Lewis and Clark, and Sitting Bull. There isn't a discernible false note in Holthaus's extensive account of the Blackfeet and Cheyenne, of their tribal mores and battle successes and failures with the white man. When Sitting Bull is interviewed by the *New York Herald* ("Sitting Bull Talks To the New York Herald, November 17, 1877") he speaks simply, but without any of the stupid clichés and elisions Robert Penn Warren thinks Indians used.

Holthaus's work should be a model for other poets exploring historical materials. He creates *Circling Back* out of intensive research, which he respects without being enslaved by it. Some of his sources he merely rearranges (The Joe Meek stories from Frances Fuller Victor's *The River of the West*), others he edits by introducing new line breaks (passages from actual U.S. Government official reports), still others he compresses (numerous original journals and recollections of the time). Throughout, he says, he has sought to use "the original words or phrases, trying to retain as much of their flavor, individuality and perspective as possible." He feels that it is unwise "to try to put oneself into an Indian psyche, or use material that is more properly the terrain of Indians themselves." What a refreshing point of view! He relies, therefore, on both Indian and contemporary non-Indian accounts, and on stories translated by the Indians for whites.

Ray A. Young Bear, in "Nothing Could Take Away the Bear-King's Image," is free of ugh talk as he movingly juxtaposes his Indian culture with white culture. Both white and Indian see the stars their own way— the white astronomer looks in the skies for Greek gods and goddesses, while Young Bear and his friends (two Hispanics, and a Zuni, sloshed on booze, outside the Griffith Park observatory in Los Angeles) see the heavens as charts for familial origins.

The astronomer does his best to explain Orion, the Greek hunter, to them:

"I think that's me, Grandfather,"
responded my Zuni companion,
"but I will believe you more
if you sell us your scotch whiskey—
and consider the magnitude of my belief
if I told you the bubbles of my Creator's
saliva made the stars, Grandson."

The astronomer is not amused—the Zuni and the Hispanics bump him "with their expanded chests," and his bagpipes are broken. He weeps. Young Bear and friends flee to the Greek amphitheater. More ironies—

the Zuni "national anthem" is played under the stars. Police turn up with nightsticks. The poem closes with a panegyric to the permanence of Indian gods:

> Nothing can take away
> the Bear-King's own image
> who is human and walks.
> There remains a bottle of champagne
> beside the charred concrete block;
> the half-smoked cigarette
> of corn husk and Prince Albert tobacco. . . .

An Indian boy (Young Bear as a child?) is painted black and illuminated with blue spots. Young Bear and friends follow him into a mound of earth, where an Indian Orion (a small man wearing a red headband) sets an arrow "in the bowstring / of his left hand." His message: honor the birds the bison dreams of, the sharp flint shaft, and the wolfskin draped over the hunter. Young Bear's defiance works because his tale is subtle, mixed in as it is with what the white world prizes—the world of sky populated by sterile Greek gods.

Duane Niatum's *Songs for the Harvester of Dreams* evokes the animism and spirit of his forebears without resorting to ugh talk. "Bald Eagle" is consummate in its merging of creature, human, dream, and power:

> In a long cloud-patch fall
> toward the river, his wingtip
> gathers the force of sun, wind,
> and rain from sea to valley;
> cascades down your spine;
> spirals through your mind watching
> its talons curve into the wave
> rising and dropping like salmon.
>
> Seasons later you swear to friends
> this grandfather perched on the black ledge,
> underneath your retina that fed
> the fear with the greatest hunger,
> showed you its precarious shift
> from the sky's rolling-over prism
> to the shaggy tilt of the morning star.
>
> Then as the earth slides away
> from the river to a dream,
> this white-headed drifter of green air
> travels back up your spine
> with the story of how you must live
> and die with the animals you destroy,
> if his shriek is to address your bones.

Niatum has just published the best anthology of native American poetry to date, *Harper's Anthology of 20th Century Native American Poetry*, New York, Harper & Row, 1988.

Among other fine Indian poets are Leslie Silko, Peter Bluecloud, Joy Harjo, Simon Ortiz, and Jim Barnes. Few of these poets, I would guess, are full-blooded, which does raise a question: which voice within a mixed-breed poet dominates? Is it a matter of pushing one button rather than another? I like Jim Barnes's answers.

In an interview in *Paintbrush* (Barnes is one-eighth Choctaw—his other ancestors were Welsh and English), Barnes says he is as proud of his white blood as of his red. His reverence for the land, the sky, and nature is indigenous in him, and not, he says, simply a result of his modest Choctaw inheritance. I admire his honesty, for many "Indian" poets are "Indian" with a vengeance, lacking Barnes' sense of balance.

When Barnes does incorporate the Indian part of his identity (see *A Season of Loss*), he avoids simple-minded renditions. Apart from a few literary phrases, these poems work well. One, "In Memory of a Day Nobody Remembers: September 26, 1874," bitingly commemorates the slaughter of Kiowas and Comanches by Union troops. On September 26 the braves were slaughtered, and on September 27 the cavalry killed over a thousand horses. Barnes's couplets powerfully understate the horrors of this event.

"Reading Santa Fe" has an effective double thrust: Barnes "reads" the town as a tourist trap where Hopis sit selling belts, beads, and trinkets. As he observes Indian sellers fallen from their ancient past, he imagines sad ghostly horses tossing their manes into "the twilight of someone's ancient gods." These powerful intimations do nothing to instruct, clarify, or edify the poet:

> You are here to read your work to faces
> lined by wind and red earth. You do not know
> the angles of this land nor what the wind
> hides from the hands that have summoned you.

National Treasures Poems

Alfred Starr Hamilton and Wilma Elizabeth McDaniel are two of our unacknowledged poetic treasures. You will never find their poems in anthologies edited by Daniel Halpern, Al Poulin, Jr., Dave Smith, Roger Weingarten, William Heyen, or Helen Vendler, or discussed by Marjorie Perloff, Peter Stitt, Harold Bloom, or David Perkins.

Hamilton was born in Montclair, New Jersey, in 1914, was graduated from high school, and from 1932 to 1940 was a catch-as-catch-can laborer. He was drafted into the Army, went AWOL, and was dishonorably discharged. (He sometimes signs his poems D. D.) *The Poems of Alfred*

Starr Hamilton is still in print from Jargon Press. In the 1960s, when David Ray was editing *Epoch* at Cornell University, Hamilton sent cardboard cartons full of his writings to Ray, who believed in their amazing qualities, published samplings in *Epoch,* and persuaded Jonathan Williams to read the poems. As Williams says on his jacket blurb: "We are living in the Badlands. Dorothy's ruby slippers would get you across the Deadly Desert. So will these poems." A smaller edition of some later poems, *The Big Parade,* was published by Greg Kuzma in his Best Cellar series, in 1982.

When the Jargon book appeared, Hamilton, unemployed, was living in a rented room on a thousand dollars a year, cooking frugal meals on a hotplate, and writing poems. Williams wrote a guest essay for the *New York Times Book Review* on Hamilton's plight. The result was a flurry of interest in Hamilton's poetry (which shortly abated) and in his welfare.

Trying to characterize Hamilton's verse is like trying to report the color of a chameleon before he changes hues. Whatever one says about Hamilton seems *almost* true: he is an American primitive, a Grandpa Moses of American poetry. Or, if you prefer a more sophisticated parallel, he is the Charles Ives of American poetry. He doesn't use many literary allusions (among the rare ones are Alice in Wonderland and Thoreau), thus avoiding the trap of literary sleaze.

In "Sheets" he improvises on a mundane act, as a primitive poet might, without references to literary models. The simple task of ironing becomes a metaphor for refashioning the moon. He invites us to share on his own terms, which resemble animated cartoons: there are quick dissolves of forms into other forms and a resultant hilarity, a tonic disruption of our sense of what ought to be:

How wonderfully the moon was to have been ironed last night
And carefully kept the moon in its place
And last night I ironed the moon
And lifted the daffodil back on top of the daisy
And folded the daffodil back on top of the moon
And carefully carried the moon upstairs
And kept the moon in the daffodil closet
Last time I ironed the moon.

One of his several poems on angels (he seems to live with them as easily as old Emanuel Swedenborg did) is a good example of his irreverent attitude toward normal syntax. The poem remains open-ended; the angel will understand:

If you're an angel
that has been sent to the cleaners

More often than
a farmer has been sent to gather the harvests

but if you're an angel
that has been to the city to gather its dust

Well, if Hamilton is not a Grandpa Moses, perhaps he's a Munchkin prince dropped to earth from Munchkinland where he's been regaling Billie Burke with his verses. An informed Munchkin might indeed have written certain of these childlike arcane riddles, delightful non sequiturs requiring an agile fantasy to be deciphered. There is a splendid play of language, including puns, juxtaposed objects radically evoking one another, sudden Rocky Horror Show jabs. A golden sun evokes a housewife's golden dishwashing suds. Manpower is "M.P.H. faster than manure-power." "Thank your iron stars, bub" becomes "an iron sea bubbles." In "Chinaware," broken dishes become broken angels and our own broken Humpty-Dumpty lives:

> But they are the fallen angels
> That fell downstairs
> I picked some of them up
>   I left the pieces behind
> Others were whole
> But others were more like ourselves
> I wanted these most of all
> Some of the broken parts of our lives that are never
> To be put back together again.

His "June Silver," like many of his verses, owes something to pop music. But how lyrical and original he is! Here images of black and blue silver, and images of motion, result in a childlike spontaneity, with hints of black and blue hurts:

> I wanted you to know of
> The black June bug
> That buzzed silver
>
> But I wanted you to know of
> June silver, of blue silver
> During the month of June
>
> I wanted you to know
> I rocked in a rocking chair
> And all along the silvery vines
>
> I wanted you to know I knew
> Of a boy who rocked on top of a rocking horse
> And up and down the wiry plains
>
> I wanted you to know of
> Blue silver, of black silver
> During the month of June silver.

The riddle form is one of Hamilton's hallmarks. The answers to his often fey questions are open-ended, depending upon the freedom of your own imagination, and your willingness to risk. Here he evokes the spirit of Thoreau:

Walden House

Are you a fierce nomad?
Are you a friend of sword and disaster?
Do you know of the only star in heaven?
Do you know of only the sun's daily sword
that pushed the scorched wagon wheels forward?
Are you a goldhunter?
Are you a Scythian mountebank?
Are you a plainsman who fled the plains?
Will you recross the deserted desert airways?
Or are you a Walden traveler?
Do you have your meals at the Walden House?
Do you read your wanton heels to your shoemaker?
Are you a city traveler?

I referred earlier to Charles Ives. Ives's cacophonies resemble Hamilton's cacophonies of syntax, grammar, and imagery. And the latter's use of puns and blatantly frayed folk and nursery rhyme materials would have appealed to Ives, who in sophisticated ways took the prosaic and the mundane from small-town American life and made them his own—the brass bands, the popular tunes, the patriotic songs. Also, like Hamilton, Ives was always his own man, quite indifferent to the world of conservative and popular classical composers, who ignored him as well.

One more parallel may help fix our elusive Hamilton, a parallel with Christopher Smart (1722–1771), the English poet who wrote incredible poems from a madhouse. His "Jubilate Agno," with its famous apostrophe to his cat Jeoffry, has a marvelous fey inventiveness. His cat becomes a cherub: "For he is of the tribe of Tiger. / For the Cherub Cat is a term of the Angel Tiger." Hamilton's angels have affinities with Smart's. Nothing is either too bizarre or illogical for either poet. As we pursue them along the conch-like trammelings of their free minds, if we fail to reach a Munchkin castle or cat heaven, it's our fault. Elsewhere (see "War Poems") I have written on Hamilton's bitter anti-militarist verse.

When I first opened Wilma Elizabeth McDaniel's *Sister Vayda's Song* I was sure McDaniel was a reincarnation of that homespun figure of turn-of-the-century American verse Julia Moore, the Sweet Singer of Michigan. Moore makes me think of that dear little woman in *Huckleberry Finn* who was always in demand for her obituary poetry. Moore was a flesh and blood poet who attracted a coterie of followers addicted to her no-nonsense journalistic poems. She wrote without adornment, without subtleties. This poem of mine imitates hers:

On June the 16th, 1882
Little Ruben Thew, aged 22,
Fell up past his neck in a slimy slough.
We drug him out
But did too late.
There was nothing we could do
To abate
What happened to
Poor Ruben Thew.

You will be relieved to know that Wilma Elizabeth McDaniel, known as "the Okie Laureate" (she emigrated with her family from Stroud, Oklahoma to Tulare, California during the 1936 dustbowl disaster), is far more literate than her predecessor. She has written poems all her life, a novel, and books of stories. Like Moore, though, she is never egocentric; she is always the observer and recorder and never the songbird obsessed with her own voice. If she appears in a poem, she is there as the voice of her subject, as she is in "Laundry":

Riley Burns' favorite
Hawaiian print shirt
that still fades orange

is drying on a string
stretched across the
bathroom

beside his black trousers
inherited
from a Saturday night
tragedy

Elsewhere, a son scrounges for a pot of shabby mums at Alpha Beta, marked down to fifty cents. He buys them for "his old mother's resthome eyes." She'll be as thrilled with them as if they were fresh. Welfare recipients drift through McDaniel's poems, as do other figures dying in hospitals and nursing homes. She also is partial to idiots and other bent figures. At eleven years of age, Melvin, as big as a man, insists on hunting Easter eggs with the smaller kids. He "hogs a fistful in one / coat pocket / a fistful in the other." To show off, he cracks a red egg on his head and eats it in a couple of bites. Another retarded man, Jyrus, is exploited by a neighbor for whom he labors all day pulling stakes. He gets a little tin cricket instead of pay, and is thrilled:

Comical thing
with big bugeyes
dressed like a man
in morning clothes.

McDaniel's responses to death are always understated. Bonnie returns home after her Dub's funeral, puts the Memory Book (now signed by the mourners) on top of her TV, and starts churning ice cream. When she finishes, still wearing her heels, she beats eggs for a cake, so skillfully she doesn't ever spatter her black funeral dress. Flossie Hicks, hearing that her husband is dead in a car crash, keeps on making the big lemon pie she had started for him before the news arrived. She piles a "cloud of meringue on top that reached / the thunderheads / she and Coy used to watch from a window / with four broken panes." Yes, it's her heart, all four chambers, that is broken now. But, thank God, McDaniel doesn't say so out loud.

People return to old family sites, long after their houses are decrepit. Dewey Martin visits the home of his Depression years. He finds a woefully sagging farmhouse, a tumbled barn, and an outhouse choked with dust:

> his thoughts got caught up
> with his dead parents
> and went round with them
> in the rusting windmill.

Old-time religion also figures in her poems, the simple spiritual suste-nance proffered by mindless evangelists. In one poem, "Tent Evangelist," Sister Vayda Walker, a big woman in heels, wearing a bright red dress with gold sequins, her hair in "a biblical bun," rouses her followers from a makeshift pulpit. She plays the guitar and sings "Will the circle be unbroken," shrewdly measuring the dimes and quarters rolling in. She's gifted, sounding like "Mother Maybelle / Carter / on the thick hot night / bye and bye / bye and bye."

Here in seven simple lines McDaniel undercuts years of painful arthritis:

> Lumbago
>
> The four o'clock dark
> sky
> has churned up clouds
> so full of pain, they call
> Manuela to the window
>
> where they add their anguish
> to her back.

"Forgiveness" turns on folk humor and the poignant motif of men's casual comings and goings, a freedom denied however to women:

> Cousin Darla Hayes fried
> three rabbits and made

us kinfolks a big dinner
when her daddy

showed up from Alabama
independent

as a hog on ice
after deserting the family
thirty years ago

Hanging Loose and *Wormwood Review* are almost the only magazines
regularly publishing McDaniel, and I am grateful to them. The Spring
1985 issue of *Hanging Loose* includes new work of hers, vintage
McDaniel, as this poem shows:

Fronie Has Lost the War

    In light skirmishes
    or heavy battle
jewelry has always been your
                    Waterloo
    dear dumb-bell Fronie
    emeralds certified
    genuine soda bottle glass

your ruby earrings
are red gumballs
fluke from a Kiwanis Club
            machine

    when you dropped your
    last two quarters in
        and turned the handle
            twice

But war is always with us
        and you gird up
and move on to other arenas
            fake diamond strikes
            bonanzas of pure gold
that will turn green tomorrow.

Navel Poems

(*See also* Dazzle Poems)

Navel words are those inserted into poems by poets who hope to startle readers with their originality, words that send one scurrying to the O.E.D. The ideal word is one that can't be found in any but a thoroughly arcane reference work. I call these "navel words" since it's as though they've been neatly stored inside a poet's navel until such time as the poet decides to pluck them out and display them. Gerard Manley Hopkins's navel was well-stocked, including "buckle," "cleofa," "shiv," "burling," "duvet," "barrowy," and "churlsgrace." Thomas Hardy resuscitated "thrid" for his "Convergence of the Twain." W. B. Yeats' repetition of "gyres" has restored it to our literary consciousness. John Crow Ransom pulled one forth for his "Here Lies a Lady": "Sweet ladies, long may ye bloom, and toughly I hope ye may thole." Wallace Stevens opted for "concupiscent" and a string of words of the same ilk: "Thrum with a proud douceur / His grand pronunciamento and devise." John Ashbery scatters navel words like dragon's teeth, adding yet another formidable difficulty for the reader to overcome. In "Daffy Duck in Hollywood," a thorny poem, brilliant in its dazzle, which appears to be about the persistence of violence in fantasy, from *Amadis of Gaul* to "Daffy Duck" cartoons, we find these navel words: "Vegetal jacqueries," "a *carte du Tendre*," "pecky acajou harpoons," and "puckered garance satin."

New York Poems

Of all the great cities of America, more poems have been written about New York than any other. San Francisco would rank second, I think, followed by Los Angeles, Boston, and Chicago. Whitman and Lorca, of course, made massive contributions to the genre, and there is no sign that suggests the tide will turn. True, *The New Yorker* encourages and often features such scribblings.

Paul Blackburn particularly loved the New York vignette. One of his poems, "The Slogan," incorporates lines arranged to mirror the grids of Stuyvesant St., which form a right triangle with Ninth, a triangle intersected by a "wellknit blond in a blue knit dress & / the hair piled high" who "crosses on the hypotenuse." "The Once-Over" occurs on a subway. Another blonde, though there are empty seats, stands and is ogled by half the car: "1 teen-age hood, / 1 lesbian / 1 envious housewife / 4 men over fifty / (& myself). . . ." Her high breasts are bra-less, and her legs, neck, and waist are long. Her shirt "cuts in under a very handsome / set of cheeks." The riders have her, and she "has us" all the way to Brooklyn.

Few poets write as extensively about New York life as Robert Hershon. His *The Public Hug* is a feast of such poems, observant, witty, and compassionate. "A Boy Who Smells Like Cocoa" is a fine example:

A boy who smells like cocoa
sits beside me on the train.
            It is too pat
that a boy the shade of cocoa
should smell like that, but sweet,
in the cold subway, the fat Brooklyn redheads
begrudging him his seat.
            He nods to sleep,
leaning against me, shuddering upright,
leaning again. His mother,
across the aisle, stiffens, afraid
            I will push him away.
Wall Street. Bowling Green. Under the river.
Two women in hats compare their shopping trips.
Under the river. When you talk on the subway
            you talk to everyone.
I got off at Borough Hall. The boy slept.
I never saw his eyes.
            A very old messenger
took my seat.

John Ashbery writes of sitting in a tall New York City building, bored as he faces up to writing an "instruction manual on the uses of a new metal." Implicit is an equation of the American city with boredom; he escapes by looking out the window and fantasizing that he's in Guadalajara ("The Instruction Manual,"). In Thom Gunn's "Outside the Diner," bums feed off garbage, sleep in abandoned cars, and visit the Detox Clinic. Gunn commemorates his fascination with the girders of New York bridge and ferry ("Iron Landscapes," *Contact II*, Summer 1982).

Ezra Pound wrote with a mix of love and distaste for the city. In "N. Y." (*Selected Poems*, London: 1928, p. 75), New York is a white, slender, soulless beloved into whom Pound promises to "breathe . . . a soul," if "she" will listen as he pipes his poet's reed. Her response?

Now do I know that I am mad,
For here are a million people surly with traffic;
This is no maid.
Neither could I play upon any reed if I had one.

Disillusioned, Pound declares her a breastless "maid," silver-reed slender. If she would only "attend," he could make her immortal.

The centerpiece of Andrew Glaze's *The Trash Dragon of Shensei* is "Fantasy Street," a poem in which a boy bikes through the city, fleeing confinement to enjoy "freedom." The poem actually grew out of a "parallelism," Glaze wrote me, "which existed in my own head with L'Allegro and Il Penseroso. Of course, I'm incapable of doing such a thing without tongue in cheek." The earlier companion poem, "Reality Street," published in the *Atlantic Monthly* in 1974, begins with a youth readying his bicycle, observed by his Puerto Rican neighbors. This is his street, Reality Street:

> . . . littered
> with dog shit and broken auto parts, full of holes
> and broken glass to protect a full block
> of private cars of policemen in no-parking spots.

He skids to a stop at Seventh, enters a "crazy poster" store, buys a paper, and continues his journey downtown:

> I sail past the back garden and the trees
> of the Modern Art Museum, avoid the driver-training car
> of the Rhodes School, look up the skirts
> of the girls with their books and their backs to the wall,
> neatly slip past the back corner of a growling truck,
> and up to the curb at the service drive.

"Fantasy Street" is speedier and more intense. The lad races along, feeling he will "explode" out of his skin as the city transforms itself into stripes of life:

> Now I am gathering speed; everything begins to hurry into a blur,
> the people in red, purple, yellow-green, violet
> sew themselves along the quilt-strip of the sidewalk like checks.
> My time of day! Excitement and events
> bob in and out of windows like winking eyes!

He speeds past artists, "a furious cockpit of battling cacophonous" street music, a bagpiper on some church steps "squawling," earning money. "There's talk he lives on East 76th Street with a Neapolitan mother." Screeching, swarming yellow trucks. Chassidic hymns. Shy little Jewish men "with burning eyes . . . showering down on us with / flashing religious courage." A steel band, hammering "wildly, dexterously, mellifluously." Horas "diced in the knives of the pipe chanters." Taxis. A single violinist scratching away. A beggars' arcade at a church. The Museum of Modern Art. "Marilyn Monroe's enormous lips poise to eat / a nameless art student looking somewhere else in a timid beret." An old beggar resembles Khrushchev. Up Sixth Avenue. The sky fills with clouds "weighing hundreds of millions of tons." The old CBS building. A doorman sneers to prove his manhood. An old black man standing beside Roseland. Eighth Avenue. 6:15. The traffic:

> Stupid, enormous, brutal,
> meaningless—you can almost see the empty-headed marshal
> whacking the brass guns with the furious butt of his sword.

He feels pursued, almost panics, as he wheels now through the darkening streets. A "red banner" of sirens and patrol cars. "Is the Last Judgment arriving?" He gets off his bike, passes "where there are sounds of everything burning up." The traffic resembles "vast rivers of candles . . . turning north." He is now almost overwhelmed:

> I catapult my imagination
> to the front of the Bodega Garcia,
> where twenty-five of my neighbors wait quietly
> standing on the sidewalk with beer cans.
> It's cocktail hour.
> Frantically I urge them, Look up at the windows of my house!
> Find out what's happening!
> Is everyone there broken on the floor?
> Is my kitchen crammed with policemen
> looking at cut throats? Or are they—Is everyone gone?
> Snatched away to Little Neck or Patchogue?
> "Wait! Wait! Christ, don't go, even if you are dying,
> wait for me! I'm coming, I want to go, too!"
>
> My heart crowded with catastrophes, I vault across,
> half running, half riding,
> thick with foreboding and excitement,
> pick up my bicycle and stumble up the stairs,
> face full of tears.

George Oppen's forty-part title poem for *Of Being Numerous* is a series of reflections on living in New York, on that "absolute singular" self Oppen so prized. Cities result, he feels, from our shipwrecked "singular" selves; to resolve our "obsessed, bewitched" natures we choose "being numerous" in cities. As our individuality dims (Oppen does not reject the city, rather, he loves "the streets / And the square slabs of pavement"), our language falters, and we lose "the roots of words," living on with "a ferocious mumbling," in a "public / Of rootless speech." His longest section considers the poet estranged from any "metaphysical sense / Of the future," who feels himself "the end of a chain / Of lives, single lives."

Elizabeth Bishop's "The Man-Moth" is inspired by a newspaper misprint for "mammoth." She views New Yorkers from the height of a skyscraper and writes humorously of "man-moths":

> He emerges
> from an opening under the edge of one of the sidewalks
> and nervously begins to scale the faces of the buildings.
> He thinks the moon is a small hole at the top of the sky. . . .

After his office day ends, he descends the skyscraper to the subway and returns home.

Nathan Whiting's perspective is that of the indefatigable runner. He has jogged the entire city, by night and by day, in all seasons. His rare *Running* is his verse panegyric to the experience. True, the running is hard on his ankles. He's sprained them, takes a week off to recuperate, and is shortly back on the streets. He writes of being in pain, running to Eighty-Sixth Street, then to Canarsie, Far Rockaway, Coney Island, Staten Island, and Forest Hills. Here he reaches Bell Park Gardens with its rich two-story homes:

> Today I have crossed 4 expressways 7 times
> and there are more.
> When will people learn to live without cars?
> This could be Los Angeles
> where they arrest runners.
> What do they do to dogs?
> Electchester houses, incomplete city.
> The urinal is more detailed than a newspaper.
> The german shepperds (sic) can't decide who's king.
> Why do the humans think they have destroyed nature?
> On the hill they put slabs.
> They turn off the fountains
> to keep us from water.
> The dominant life form are their strollers.
> I'm too dirty for babies, a dog.
> I cross 2 more expressways.
> I pant up to Forest Hills
> where someone could afford to plant lilacs.
> Here I search the garbage.
> There is always one more thing to look for.

Nuclear Poems

(*See also* Ecology Poems, Political Poems, and War Poems)

As the threat of nuclear destruction grows, so do the numbers of poems on nuclear themes. This is not to say that many of these transcend the limitations of overtly political or hortatory designs. Poems of outrage are seldom subtle. Here are a few of the better ones.

Allen Ginsberg's "Plutonian Ode," the frontispiece and title poem for his *Plutonian Ode and Other Poems: 1977–1980*, commemorates (with a photo of Ginsberg and others sitting on the tracks of Rocky Flats, Colorado) the halting of a train carrying waste fission matter, on July 14, 1978. The poem is a mantra or chant, in the pattern of dozens Ginsberg has written, designed to rob plutonium itself of power.

Ginsberg was already exclaiming in verse against the threat of nuclear disaster as early as the fifties. One poem, "Television Was A Baby

Crawling Toward That Deathchamber," sees television as a negative force exacerbating international arguments and leading more quickly to nuclear death. Lucien Stryk writes quietly of nuclear destruction. "In Our Time" assumes that a poet survives. When asked by other survivors to help, he requests nails, starting the rebuilding—there is no time for song:

> No bittersweet,
> no roses now. He knelt
> in silence in the wasted
> town—a stain under the
> fallout noon. Nails, line
> by line, his only song.

Steven F. White, who has traveled extensively in various Latin American countries and has edited *Poets of Nicaragua, 1916–1979* and *Poets of Chile, 1965–1984,* both for Unicorn Press, has also written two volumes of his own verse, *Burning the Old Year* and *For the Unborn,* also from Unicorn. "Poem to a Foreign Country" recites the usual complaints against national leaders and investors: they think they are in control, "even though everything smells / like money. What they bought is rising / over the White House: a wheel spinning / in a wheel, and an eagle with the hands / of a man under its wings." This force is nuclear, and like sunflowers following "the explosions at the center of the sun," we too follow the blazing light of our bombs:

> Perhaps those who are in power believe
> that they can watch their sculptures of fire
> destroy the planet from a safe place
>
> without dying like the rest of us.
> Perhaps they think the cataract of ash
> will not touch the ones who are important.
> I hear the sun call the next day
> like an orphan lost on the streets of some nightmare.
> Maybe those who would trade our eyes
> for more precious stones love us so much
> that they will extinguish our future by kissing it.

The title poem of White's second volume, "For the Unborn," is longer and subtler. He addresses those who will never see this planet because that "cloudburst of light blossoming over cities" will have destroyed it: "death shall have no dominion / because death will have swallowed itself whole." His vision is one of floods after the holocaust, and, finally, of a planet turned to ice.

Old Object Poems

This genre evokes images of Norman Rockwell paintings and sentimental objects from the past (churns, coffee grinders, jukeboxes, slot machines, etc.) restored with loving care by current-day collectors. It also evokes past issues of the now-defunct *Kayak Magazine,* which displayed as page ornaments wonderful found objects from old medical, botanical, and other scientific books, and from old catalogues.

The Winter/Spring, 1984, issue of *New Letters* has numerous nostalgia poems, frequently deriving from a poet's youth. David Perkins considers a 1946 nickel, envying all the fingers that have oiled it, "all the change you have / made right, / all the cool black purses you have / dropped into . . ." The most elaborate of these poems is by Pati Hill who actually photocopies close-ups of portions of the old garments she writes about, such as riding pants from 1940 or 1950. E. L. Mayo returns in memory to "a beautiful room" filled with bright rugs and gleaming furniture, a boyhood home, we assume. Etheridge Knight observes a dog urinating on a tombstone that reads "Hoosier Poet." So much for James Whitcomb Riley. J. J. Maloney's poem has painful sociological overtones—the scene is a Parole Board meeting. The old door he enters is both artifact and nightmare. As he departs the room, unsure of his parole, he turns for "a final look" and sees his "fate" propped in an empty wooden chair.

For David Ray, in *The Touched Life,* snapshots reconstitute objects from the past:

> all the generations are on the table
> corpse piled upon corpse
> tender face we knew
> spilled out of a valentine box
> and new generations   faces
> between us and them
> those we loved
> calling for attention. . . .

In another poem, "Poe's Anvil," a blacksmith at a swap-meet is trying to sell his past, represented by a black anvil with his name, "Poe," written on it. Over the years tractors replaced mules, cars replaced wagons:

> He tired of horse-shoes,
> wagonwheels and plows, of hitches, barrows,
> and lugs, of axles, crankcases and flywheels,
> and he sat somewhat amused (and dying, his wife
> told us), presiding over the sale of his own
> monument, which he wanted someone to go on
> hammering on, and in the midday city sun
> the theatre's white screen was blank
> like a faded quilt or Moby Dick's stretched skin.

The authenticity of Ray's feeling is tarnished by his sentimentality and by the easy nostalgia induced by the old objects he names. The concluding image of the faded quilt works, but Moby Dick's stretched hide does not. For me, Ray is much too intent on his literary allusions—he relishes too much that the farmer's name was Poe; the ending with its allusion to Melville is facile.

Marvin Bell, not known for energetic poems of large scope, in "Trinket" meditates on the crack of an old fern pot, oozing water. His triplets do nothing to energize the trivial nature of the event or Bell's facile ruminations on it, those "ideas of becoming":

> I love watching the water
> ooze through the crack in the fern pot,
> it's a small thing

Like other poets, he confesses, he has looked at the ocean and found "too many / presences" for easy absorption. "This other," though, with its "little water, used, appearing / slowly around the sounds / of oxygen and small frictions," these "tiny embodiments" provide the "self" with "the notion of the self" that is always being lost.

In Simon Perchik's *Who Can Touch These Knots* swift turns flagged by colons are rife with objects recollected. One poem sets the tone: every junk yard, Perchik writes, "has one leaf / one tire and a couch." He remembers a dead twin sister, and his father's car: "rotting, the leaf: junk / shaded from cotton." It appears that the father is dead—the bed is empty, and in a homey concluding image, a couch symbolizes the lost past, a subtle elegy to the sister taken away by her father, to death:

> Each couch begins with the numeral F
> ends: the room cleared for company coming
> ends where he's taking my sister.

Another poem describes objects from the past, as a grown man returns to close up a family attic and finds his old clothes, including what appears to have been his World War II uniform. The box image evokes interment:

> —I don't remember my tie :corpse
> knotted between two rows :buttons
> drawn by wings :wheels
> turning through slow banks—I flew
>
> two holes :my eyes
> my pants fastened on this dark :a pocket
> ripped, a uniform, by itself
> entering this wooden box.

A final poem by Perchik, "This penny has the name," shows a tender and moving use of the old object theme. A penny his father long ago gave him, probably in his childhood, was part of an old Sunday ritual. Memory is dust, the father is dust, the penny itself remains hard and vital, making possible the taking of the father's hand into the poet's own, after a vast interval of years.

In "A Clock," Jane Shore displays her genius for "reading" a found object—a huge old planter's clock. Like Elizabeth Bishop, Shore enjoys an uncanny "negative capability" that allows her to enter an experience and create poetry from the inside out. On the large face of the clock a farmer (near the "wrought iron bars of III") "squints at his wife beyond the IX / tending her even rows of greens." The steady hands of the clock keep moving, "rising and falling between them." Images of sun and moon also run their cycles, and a cornucopia spills forth stars and planets—"a tomato Mars, a turnip Saturn, and four / greenbean comets whipping their tails." A single ear of corn, as huge as the silo "floats light-years over the barn." Like the lovers on Keats' urn, this farmer and wife may never touch. She'll never "slip inside / her pretty trapezoid of home" to cook him a hot meal. Light from an onion falls over the couple's "awestruck faces morning, noon, and night," and sheds no tears. The wife seems to cast her vision "higher even" than the moving mechanical "parts of heaven." Shore speculates on her thoughts: do identical farms like hers exist in other galaxies? She seems to cup her ear, in order to catch the sounds of "heartbeats coming from so far away. . . ."

This poem works so well, despite Shore's moving inside the farm woman's thoughts, because Shore herself is self-effacing—the object observed and read breathes on its own and becomes almost tactile, allowing us to generate our own life-thoughts without being subjected to those of an ill-read and ill-formed poet showing off, as most ego poets do.

Dave Smith's "Under the Scrub Oak, a Red Shoe" is an only partially convincing meditation on a red woman's shoe that "simply . . . appears" while he walks through an arroyo. The opening owes something to Robert Frost's "Directive." Like Frost, Smith reports vast universals, concepts of recovery, arrival, and forgiveness. Both poets guide us to spots in nature where time no longer obtains, and where some sort of realization, personal and/or spiritual, might occur. Frost's excursion results in an act of communion (drinking from the broken cup) via which he (and we) are made "whole" again.

Smith's red shoe, it seems, heel-less and wrapped in an old brown nylon stocking of the sort worn by "our grandmothers," belonged to a scarlet woman (they all wore red shoes, right?), who, not as drunk as she pretended to be, undresses in the arroyo. Certain flagged, sentimental notions, typical of the sort of writing encouraged in workshops, rear their heads: the "twisting" arroyo is as "empty as memory"; you proceed through as if "you were looking for a lost child"; and on seeing the shoe, Smith, reverent, kneels to pick up the object. This triad of mixed observations and acts seem like mystical window dressing. Seeking the lost child seems not to fit at all. And Smith loses me when he confuses his senses: "hearing also / the nylon flake like pieces of skin against my skin." Though we "tell ourselves to walk away from such moments," we do hang in there, hoping, I gather, for "absence," but finding none. Nothing momentous or transcendental occurs. There is no flaming bush, no tutelary angel, and we are left with the physical object, the old shoe, waiting (as do most "absent" objects—or is it the former owners who are the absent ones?) to claim our attention "as best it can":

>   as if forgiveness
> were what it meant, and love, as if any weather
> that red shining endured was the bruise
> you might have kissed and might not yet refuse.

The master of the old object poem is, of course, Robert Bly. He writes the proverbial rings around most other poets who try these themes. "Finding an Old Ant Mansion," from *The Man in the Black Coat Turns*, beautifully reveals Bly's skill at moving from the concrete to the universal, and avoiding such sentimental and ill-felt gestures as those in Dave Smith's poem.

Bly, asleep on a cabin floor, dreams that a rattler is biting him. He rises, dresses, and goes to a nearby pasture. He senses the ground beneath his tennis shoes, their rubbery texture allowing him to *feel* in a way leather would not. He marvels at the elasticity, the "rolls and humps." The earth "never lies flat," and it must accommodate a varied debris both falling down upon it (trees) and emerging from its depths (stones). He passes through a strip of hardwood to another pasture and finds a chunk of wood on the ground, eaten into some sixteen layers by ants. He carries the piece home and props it on his desk.

The cavities in the wood create doors into "cave-dark" places— Persephone redivivus. Leaps evoke memories: the shadows recall the "heavy brown of barn stalls" he knew as a boy, and other dark insights. The ant-artifact is a universe all its own, a paradigm for our psyches, in their obsessions so antlike and male. We scurry to execute our father's hopes and wishes for us: "infant ants waken to old father-worked halls, uncle-loved boards, walls that hold the sighs of the pasture, the moos of confused cows . . . some motor cars from the road, held in the same wood, given shape by Osiris' love." According to designs taught us by our great benefactor and primal father, himself son of Net and Geb, the legendary Osiris who provided our ancestors with civilization and taught them agriculture, we shape our achievements.

The ant-riddled wood suggests primeval forces (it recalls, perhaps, in its unchewed state, the erect father) and provides residences, "apartments," for spirits. The ants, thus, have wrought "a place for our destiny," that sweep of time within which "we too labor, and no one sees our labor." Uncannily, and with a delicate compassion, Bly retrieves the specific from the universal, returning the motif to himself. He recalls his own father whose labors he has symbolically discovered in this chunk of wood. What ensues? Who will discover Bly's labors when he dies? *His* wood will lie somewhere in a pasture "not yet found by a walker."

This poem moves me: the gentle voice, so mature and exploring, is from a man large in both physique and spirit. Bly's leap into that final image of our lives as wood pieces waiting for discovery resolves the poem profoundly in areas of the psyche hitherto untapped. To most observers, that ant-eaten, riddled hunk of dead fibers would deserve, if noticed at all, to be thrust aside by a boot.

Seamus Heaney writes of one of the oldest objects of all, a mummified woman dug up in a peat bog in Britain, the rope she was hung with still intact around her neck. When Heaney confines himself to describing the old creature, and imagining her death, he writes well. When, however, he assumes her feelings ("I can feel the tug / of the halter at the nape / of her neck, the wind / on her naked front") the poem sounds forced, even pretentious. When the woman (Heaney assumes she was an adulteress) is first unearthed, she appears to be merely another "barked sapling." Visible then are "her shaved head / like a stubble of black corn, / her blindfold a soiled bandage, / her noose a ring. . . . ," her "tar-black face," and the hanging rope. Heaney assumes guilt—if he had been present at the time, despite her blonde beauty, he would have remained silent, flung in his own "stones of silence," sharing the tribe's "civilized outrage" over her crime, understanding "the exact / and tribal, intimate revenge."

Olfactory or Scratch 'N Sniff Poems

Cold-drill, a journal published by students at Boise State University under the tutelage of Tom Trusky, has initiated this new form of verse, and to date, so far as I know, has as yet to stimulate followers forming a school. The journal features a "Scratch 'n Sniff Sestina" which invites you to scratch a colored rendition of a pizza slice, releasing a credibly pungent pizza aroma. For the scratch 'n sniff sonnet on old Grandpa Bill's clothes, scratch an image of western boots, and, yes, an odor of old leather rises. Other scratchables: chocolate-dip cone, gas can, watermelon, money, pine woods, apples, flowers, and gumball machines. Other variations come to mind. Rather than actually print an image of some redolent object, simply patch a noun with the appropriate aroma. Can you imagine a more offensively redolent poem than Robert Lowell's "Skunks," or anything lovelier than Whitman's "When Lilacs Last in the Dooryard Bloom'd?" And how useful the device would be for protest poetry: scratch 'n sniff images of bodies rotting in Ethiopia and El Salvador, poison gas, laser-bomb smoke, Congressional Fruit-of-the-Looms after a night spent in the chambers, the unwashed groins of the homeless.

I envision entire new journals devoted to the olfactory poem.

Opening Lines of Poems

"But was the language alive?"—Robert Friend

Examining only the first lines of poems is possibly a superficial activity. It's akin to a doctor taking your pulse but not your temperature, or thumping your chest but not proceeding to your nether parts where the trouble is; or, like a vet's dropping flea powder behind a poodle's ear when the whole creature is infested; or, finally, it's like a bright student who supplies the opening sentence of an essay and asks you to intuit what he or she knows from that sentence.

So, I am aware that what I am about to do is risky. I shall try to be fearless though, in the interests of serving poetry and the fledgling writers of verse who may see this essay. For my purposes, I have taken Edward Field's anthology *A Geography of Poets,* since it is an ambitious presentation of poets known and unknown from all over the country. Moreover, since everybody in the book was alive when the book appeared in 1979, we had a guarantee of sorts that the poems reflected a pretty good spectrum of contemporary writing.

Until I started copying first lines and classifying them, much as old Charles Darwin classified beetles and finches, I had no idea that they would group themselves as neatly as they do. I suspect that much of the monotony of contemporary poetry is due to the monotony of lines generating poems. In general, there is a ubiquitous declarative, plain-language, detrital opening. Eschewed is the old-fashioned rhetorical start, the overtly alliterative line, and the highly inspired opening moment we associate with the ancient ode or epic start—"Arms and the man I sing," "Lost midway this path of life in a dark wood," "Of man's first disobedience . . ." Modern launchings often read as if lifted from newspapers, or from letters back to dear old granny on the farm, or from tacky autobiographical details. I hope that my examples (I mean to be entirely scientific) will startle poets into testing out first lines before they freeze them in print. If they sound stupid and self-indulgent they probably are.

I realize that I will be accused of being unfair for not presenting entire opening verse sentences rather than first lines. I hereby throw down a scented glove. My challenge runs this way: Since most contemporary poets using the fashionable free-verse modes swear by their linebreaks as necessary, pregnant, and even beautiful, they should gladly submit to such scrutiny. Obviously, sentences cut off in mid-air, as most of my examples are, do often sound ridiculous without their lower parts, legs, feet, and slippers. Some unintentional double-entendres occur: one poet offers her man some "head." Some sound far more self-important and pompous than they should. Others do manage to intrigue us over what is to come. My apologies to any poet (and many are my friends) who may be offended by finding his or her line parading around sans fig leaf. Like all good satirists, I can only hope that my bolus will effect cures, and that future poems by some of these poets will have less questionable beginnings. And, as you will see for yourself, the more prestigious the poet, the sappier some of these lines are. There are moments, too, where they wonderfully evoke one another, making comments and completions never intended by the poets, their critics, the gods, or anyone else.

To be entirely fair, I should encourage another critic to return to an earlier anthology—say to one by Selden Rodman, Oscar Williams, or Louis Untermeyer, and make a similar study. We may find that all along opening lines, in general, have been lousy. At the same time, we may find some stunning empirical evidence for evaluating the merits of poetry then and now. The more data and related instruments of measurement we can develop the better. Since poets as a *gens* are pretty self-obsessed, we need to remove their work from the scramblings of the critical marketplace, and freeze, dissect, classify, and analyze—much as the Darwinians examined their flora, fauna, and insectivora. I caution though against using any sort of laser beam or related technology—the state of our poet-science is not ready. Rudimentary steps first, please! We are in our infancy. I turn now to the major classes of opening lines, with examples and interpretative commentaries.

Reportage

Reportage is one of the more frequently used devices. Two of the assumptions here are that poetry is for plain folks (so throw out anything that might smack of the literary or traditional) and that we limit our subject matter pretty much to our families and friends, and to the often humdrum events of our lives. This confusion of poetry with journalism is endemic in much current writing. Whether this mode will ever disappear remains to be seen. I doubt that it will. American poetry will continue to sound like a vehicle of thousands of gears and parts, all indistinguishable as to function—although colors, sizes, and manufacturers may vary.

There are two main types (subclasses) of reportage. In the first, the poet tells you about people other than himself. In the second, he tells you about himself. Here are some examples of Type A. Notice how beautifully Simpson's line squints at Soto's grandmother and Oritz's sister. Hitchcock lets us know that Kinnell's bear is doing more than defecating or eating blackberries. Finally, Dickey delivers Gildner's bitch. I have grouped the lines that tie in with one another:

"My oldest sister wears thick glasses" (Simon J. Ortiz)
"Grandma lit the stove" (Gary Soto)
"Her face turned sour" (Louis Simpson)

"A black bear sits alone" (Galway Kinnell)
"He sits in a deckchair reading Colette" (George Hitchcock)

"The boxer bitch is pregnant" (Gary Gildner)
"Next door they've finally brought home the new baby." (William Dickey)

Type B, personal reportage, falls neatly into five sorts, all of them possibly suspect unless they predict some devastating irony or drama to be worked out in the poem as a whole. It is almost impossible to detect much lyrical beauty in any of these lines—although some of them scan pretty regularly. Here are the five kinds:

a. *What I Look Like:* Here we have a choice of physiognomies. For evocativeness, I prefer Le Sueur's:

"I have a wide, friendly face" (Paul Zimmer)
"I am a crazy woman with a painted face" (Meridel Le Sueur)

b. *What I'm Doing:* This one allows for a delicious poetic license—unless you can imagine the poet composing his poem as he bends over a stump or stares out at the trees:

"I bend over an old hollow cottonwood stump. . . ." (Robert Bly)
"I am looking at trees" (W. S. Merwin)

c. *What I'm Really Like:* These starts don't always help us. King, Ortiz, and Stafford are pretty straightforward, except that one might want to see Stafford's love for flat country as a paradigm for some of his poetry. Browne's "green books" aren't very helpful though—Graham Greene's novels? Books Browne hasn't read and which, therefore, remain green? Or, has he literally painted all his books green as part of a decorating scheme? I like the ambiguity.

"I like a man around" (Linda King)
"I happen to be a veteran" (Simon J. Ortiz)
"In scenery I like flat country." (William Stafford)
"In my house I keep green books" (Michael Dennis Browne)

d. *My Guilts and Traumas:* This subclass does overlap somewhat with a larger class I shall call "problems." I include them here because they seem to deal frankly and overtly with some basic autobiographical fact the poet requires us to know at the outset. I assume that Haines never became a cauliflower—which may be a metaphor for his having left Alaskan snow and ice (cauliflowers are either white or polar-bear-piss yellow). Norse deals with his frustratingly potent gay feelings for an elusive Mr. Right of the Golden Calves. Meltzer supplies a religious turn: centuries of Jewish religious life confront him, and we are anxious to know what he has done wrong. Kunitz's speaker makes us wonder on whose side he is, and how heavy the guilt trips are.

"I wanted to be a cauliflower" (John Haines)
"A pair of muscular calves" (Harold Norse)
"The Rabbi is before me." (David Meltzer)
"My mother never forgave my father" (Stanley Kunitz)

e. *Irrefutable Facts About Me:* These might be placed under sub-group c, but they do seem better set off. Whittemore's event, entirely factual, is so casual that we assume it means little more than what it says. Or was he setting himself up to write poems in French forms? May Swenson's bit of news about herself is indeed shocking—and refreshing. Mei-Mei Bersenbrugge's first line begins nicely with first things—honkings? Alta's confession, unfrosted with guilt, seems almost metaphysical and, as such, anticipates McClure's scream of joy, a scream all poetry and art worthy of the name moves toward—the intense, personal apotheosis:

"At breakfast I had french toast." (Reed Whittemore)
"I took my cat apart" (May Swenson)
"I was born the year of the loon" (Mei-Mei Bersenbrugge)
"I'm frigid when i wear see thru negligees" (alta)
"I HAVE INHERITED THE UNIVERSE!" (Michael McClure)

Placings

A few poets try to energize their starts by placing themselves in unexpected locales. I admire such poems because they begin as if they were more than journalistic drivel. The rarest and most freewheeling is Nathan's appearance in the Indian Ocean. Barker and Lawson write while borne aloft. Huff is ethnic and earth-located. Brinnin's panegyric to suburban life (actually a threnody on Dachau) turns more melancholy in Levine's line and achieves violence in Barker's, although the violence is that of movie illusion. In all these cases, we refreshingly share the poet's locale, where he was when the poem was conceived:

"I come sailing through the Indian Ocean" (Leonard Nathan)
"Here in the open cockpit" (David Barker)
"We're up in a balloon" (Paul Lawson)

"Sitting down near him in the shade" (Robert Huff)
"Such a merry suburb!" (John Malcolm Brinnin)
"In a coffee house at 3 am" (Philip Levine)
"On these sunny steps / they stabbed Sal Mineo" (David Barker)

Flamboyancies

Flamboyant openings are intended to draw us into the poem via sheer style, or by saying something outrageous to arouse (or offend) our grosser instincts or our sociopolitical sense. Of the three subgroups here, the first is the most traditional: Wagoner and Jong love alliteration. I do wish though that the sibilants had rolled less trippingly from their lips. Duncan is much less serpentine—his joy is cathartic; naming is a celebration, and the dance of syllables provides a special pleasure. Ashbery employs sibilants to evoke memories of delicious breakfasts past:

"On sloping, shattered granite, the snake man" (David Wagoner)
"Stiff as the icicles in their beards, the Ice Kings" (David Wagoner)
"A man so sick that the sexual soup" (Erica Jong)

"Most beautiful! the red-flowering eucalyptus" (Robert Duncan)
"A pleasant smell of frying sausages" (John Ashbery)

Here is a pair of much less daring examples of alliteration:

"The planet that we plant upon" (Knute Skinner)
"There was a brightness in the branches" (Ron Loewinsohn)

The second subgroup includes beginnings meant to jar us by presenting human universals in semitragic or gross conditions—scroti, abortions, etc:

"They [genitals] droop like sad fuchsias from our bodies" (Henry Carlile)
"Cell by cell the baby made herself . . . (George Oppen)
"My sweet-faced, tattle-tale brother was born blind" (Mona Van Duyn)
"After she finished her first abortion" (Judy Grahn)

In subgroup three fall those lines boasting a funky, folksy, or intimate touch, singly and in combination. Their colloquial tone frequently suggests the anti-poetic. Genital and breast orientations provide zippy beginnings for Ochester, Stetler, Barker, and Koch. Sometimes these starts are surreal (Edson) and funny (Broughton):

"Ordinarily I call it 'my cock,' but" (Ed Ochester)
"Karl, my friend, caught the crabs" (Charles Stetler)
"I know those tits. They are" (David Barker)
"Happy the man who has two breasts to crush against his bosom"
    (Kenneth Koch)
"He had hitched a chicken to a cart" (Russell Edson)
"In Zen you can't yen for anything" (James Broughton)

Imperatives

Since poets are so inclined to be assertive, even bossy, I was surprised to find so few poems opening with imperatives. This may, of course, reflect the wisdom of the editor who eschewed command poems in favor of those of a more congenial sort. But there are a few. Wagoner tells us to "stand still," Meinke says "stop," and alta, with a little help from Contoski, informs us how to behave once we have followed Meinke's command. Field is about to show us what to do when those drums appear at the door. Bronk hates turn-on stuff and waxes nicely metaphysical.

"Stand still. The trees ahead and bushes beside you" (David Wagoner)
"STOP: if you're racing at night" (Peter Meinke)
"hunger for me hunger hunger for me" (alta)
"Kiss the one you love." (Victor Contoski)
"When the drums come to your door" (Edward Field)
"Yes, look at me; I am the mask it wears" (William Bronk)

Ejaculations and Apostrophes

The ejaculation as a starter is also rare in this anthology, demonstrating, I suppose, how far behind we have left the English Romantics and the writers of neoclassical odes. I find only these three instances of the orotund apostrophe. Kuzma's line would seem to have sexual overtones; his sex life seems no longer to move as it once did. Rakosi is nicely ambiguous—a circle of friends? a circle of early poets presided over by *rare* Ben Jonson? a fairy-circle of mushrooms on a lawn." Rukeyser's line may be read as a refreshing comment on my entire study.

"Oh to be moving as we once were" (Greg Kuzma)
"O rare circle" (Carl Rakosi)
"O for God's sake" (Muriel Rukeyser)

You Do This, You Do That

One of the most pretentious of all openings is the "you do this, you do that" opening. This method has not only afflicted starts but entire poems. I am happy to report only a scattering of these in *A Geography of Poets*— evidence, I hope, that this once immensely popular form (nourished by workshops) is on the wane. The device was useful particularly for evoking dead people—such as dead fathers and grandmothers once hated by the poet. Sometimes historical figures are addressed. What sounds so phony most of the time is that the persons are told about what they once knew they did—and if they are stone dead and unresurrected, the effect is of talking to a tombstone. Here are the examples:

"When you walked down the stairs / to touch my root" (Steve Orlen)
"You drive down MAIN STREET" (Jim Heynen)
"As you are walking / down the street" (William J. Harris)
"You remember the name was Jensen. She seemed old." (Richard Hugo)
"You raise the ax" (Ai)
"You follow, dress held high above / the fresh manure" (Lucien Stryk)
"you know" (Charles Bukowski)

Direct Address

A related form, and one of the most common, is the direct address opening. Here the poet zeroes in on a listener, with dramatic effect. It is often used for getting even with a parent or lover who has caused torment, or to commemorate a lost or departed person, showing thereby the poet's enviable sympathies. There seem to be three subspecies here. The first treats sexual matters. Interestingly, the examples together create a brief short story of sexual favors and vengeances:

"Do you love me? I asked," (Gerald Locklin)
"darling here's my head" (Judith Johnson Sherwin)
"Haunt him, Mona! Haunt him, demon sister!" (Larry Rubin)

The second subclass addresses parents and siblings. Kumin remembers her mother's girlhood. Scott reassures his parent that her life-teaching was not in vain. De Frees establishes a meaningful relationship with a son who may have good reason to doubt her affection. Ai arraigns her man for abandoning her in a truck. Huff, enamored of passing years, addresses an old ventriloquist, an image perhaps of the seamy life of the poet himself. Dickey says goodbye to his teeth, items even more intimate and necessary than parents in one's life. Shelton brings a dear departed up to date. Aubert, almost divining Dickey's problem, blames Jean for the loss of incisors and bicuspids. Did Jean, Dickey's mom, feed him too much refined sugar?

"Mother my good girl / I remember this old story" (Maxine Kumin)
"Mother Dear, I am being careful." (Herbert Scott)
"It's right to call you son. That cursing alcoholic" (Madeline De Frees)
"You keep me waiting in a truck" (Ai)
"Four years ago, dear old ventriloquist" (Robert Huff)
"Now you are going, what can I do but wish you" (William Dickey)
"Five years since you died and I am" (Richard Shelton)
"you should have, jean, stopped them" (Alvin Aubert)

The third subclass (the reader may wish to flesh this one out with examples from other anthologies) flashes certain political apostrophes (Knight), lines directed to people in general (Corso), and apostrophes to devils and supernatural entities (Clifton):

"And, yeah, brothers" (Etheridge Knight)
"Folks, sex has never been" (Gregory Corso)
"Demon, Demon, you have dumped me" (Lucille Clifton)

The Pregnant Problem or Question

We arrive finally at lines preoccupied with stating a problem the poet is obliged to work out. Since poems traditionally deal with strivings and spiritual struggles, we would expect to see numerous examples here. For, as philosophers and linguists keep pointing out, the age-old problems vex us and put snow-white hairs upon our heads. Nor are the responses helpful in one generation helpful in a later one. If time is but the stream we go a-fishing in, as Thoreau said, we keep dropping different baits, hoping to lure the bass of ultimate wisdom into our nets. What the starts and castings from *A Geography of Poets* show is our dismal failure to resolve these preoccupations. These lines work from the metaphysical concern down to the most mundane of difficulties.

Finkel and Di Prima, by asserting the *whoeverness* of self, represent the first subclass. Ammons supplies a more responsible grip on the issue by declaring his intention to pursue both unity and difference. By simply not seeing the point, Alan Dugan actually absolves himself from questing. Miller Williams shows more courage, framing his conclusions around an image of banging. Watson, at least, is in motion as he moves through "invisible glass"—a nicely Wonderlandian metaphor. Gregor, again, is in a dilemma over which role to choose in the face of the existential abyss. Shapiro merely responds by assuming there is a "dawn"—question-begging, I think, since the case may be, however tragically, that we are rather in an eternal dusk, and one which no amount of poetic querying or haggling will resolve:

"Whoever I am. . . ." (Donald Finkel)
"who is the we, who is" (Diana Di Prima)
"I want to know the unity in all things and the difference" (A. R. Ammons)
"I never saw any point" (Alan Dugan)
"No one knows what the banging is all about" (Miller Williams)
"Was I moving through the invisible glass" (Robert Watson)
"If I could choose a role" (Arthur Gregor)
"What dawn is it?" (Karl Shapiro)

A second class of opening lines develops the problem of lost cultures and societies in trouble—problems of a different order than the strictly metaphysical. Bloch worries specifically about lost tribes. Schulman evokes the Cassandra-wail, with some consciously stilted writing in the manner of a nineteenth-century translation of the *Oresteia*. This is the only instance I find of an overt imitation of a dead style in Field's anthology. From Heyen's line we can't be sure of the folk needing to be saved—the implication seems to be that since we can't save ourselves why should we try to save others? Tate seems to provide a telling epitaph for our own age, seen from the scary perspective of a forthcoming era, one uncannily anticipated by Josephine Miles's line: "Shall I pull the curtains. . . ."

"What happened to the ten lost tribes" (Chana Bloch)
"What happened to Cassandra? She who cried" (Grace Schulman)
"I do not think we can save them" (William Heyen)
"They didn't have much trouble" (James Tate)
"Shall I pull the curtains against the coming night?" (Josephine Miles)

The most frequent problem line (and these make up the third subclass) is personal rather than grandiose. Extremely solipsistic at their worst, and generally anemic in imagination, these lines work best when they transcend self-pity, contain surprises, or are humorous. A series of these, again, counterpoint one another. Poverty is the theme for Howard Moss, who is awakened by his refrigerator to the issue of having and not having. James Wright comes on with a whistle in the wind. Corman dips back into his personal history, as does Rutsala, to find contrastingly poignant material situations—an encapsulation perhaps of growing up in America during the late twenties and early thirties. Nathan's question, as refreshingly literal as it is, is confusing—we can't tell whether he himself is impoverished, or whether he's well-off. Does he merely hope to experience poverty by simply wearing a poor dude's shirt?

"The argument of the refrigerator wakes me." (Howard Moss)
"I still have some money" (James Wright)
"I had so little" (Cid Corman)
"We had more than / we could use" (Vern Rutsala)
"What is it like to have just one shirt" (Leonard Nathan)

Other lines in this general group treat pregnancy, alcohol, and pseudonyms:

"I have this bulging belly because" (Ann Darr)
"If I needed brandy alone / there would be no problem" (Keith Wilson)
"I was content with the pseudonym" (Vassar Miller)

Coda

As I pull the curtains on this perhaps needlessly arcane but scientific excursion into the very core of poetry, I can only hope that poets will think more about their opening lines. Do your first lines sound silly taken all by themselves? Do line-breaks really matter so much that you are willing to risk writing nonsense if one reads individual free-verse lines as if they were single-line poems? Are you too much enamored of the ephemeral and the tackily solipsistic? Have you done well to abandon a style merely because it sounds like one of your grandfather's? If you are writing journalism (which much poetry seems to be) why should you expect your scribblings to endure longer than the daily newspaper? Other questions will come to mind, I am sure. Obviously, there are other kinds of beginnings not evident in *Geography*: the nonsense line, for example, or the language-syllable line which makes no sense as ordinary syntax, or the overtly scatological line, or the badly parodic line. Please, reader, contribute your own kinds to the list.

I hope I have performed a basic and useful chore by examining this host of poem-beginnings. I can foresee similar studies of second, third, and fourth lines. The consummation of all such studies would be, of course, a monumental *Arithmetic of Poetry,* or a *Muse's Math,* which would indeed take the teeth out of Jonathan Williams's first-line command: "Stop all the literary shit"—or provide a stunningly affirmative answer to Robert Friend's opening query: "But was the language alive?"

Pathetic Fallacy Poems

This device originated in ancient Greece where the elegists Moscus, Theocritus, and Bion, lamenting the death of a fellow poet cut off in his prime, endowed rivers, mountains, plants, and creatures with human grief, as a way of expressing their own sorrow. Later, Samuel Johnson complained about Milton's "Lycidas," the elegy to Edward King:

Milton's mourning Nature was "easy, vulgar and therefore disgusting."
Johnson was right. The device was tacky and insincere then and it
remains so. Its presence is almost always evidence of ill-felt, uninspired
verse. Three contemporary examples will suffice to show that the pa-
thetic fallacy remains popular with poets.

Charles Wright is a contributor of seasonal poems to *The New Yorker*
(an analysis I made of the issues of the magazine published during the
spring of 1982 revealed that of the dozen poems published then, only one
was not about spring). Wright wrote the Easter Poem, "The Other Side of
the River," which appeared in the April 5 issue. It is lengthy, written in
flocked and flickering lines:

> Easter again, and a small rain falls
> On the mockingbird and the housefly,
> On the Chevrolet
> In its purple joy
> And the TV antennas huddled across the hillside.

Well, a Chevrolet possessing a "purple joy" is a new wrinkle: manufac-
tured items now feel (and express) human emotions. The poem aches for
a cover artist. And I love this rendition of the pathetic fallacy: Easter's
"little mouths" are all "open into the rain." Wright-riffs follow: recollec-
tions of boyhood days hunting with "Princess and Buddy working the
millet stands / And the vine-lipped face of the pinewoods." Spring seems
to ease Wright's melancholy, as gulls whimper over the boathouse, mon-
arch butterflies cruise flower beds, and "the soft hairs of spring" thrust up
"through the wind."

In the May 24, 1982 issue of *The New Yorker*, Donna Joy contributes
"Finches, moths, herons." The latter are the weepiest of the lot: "angels /
of a common and amazing sadness."

Michael Waters, in "Frogs," from *Not Just Any Death*, finds that
frogs, those "green / almost shapeless, bits of rotten mushroom," have
minds. In their "tiny brains" they "can forgive anything." This is on the
order of cows on their knees praying to God, or of minks forgiving the
killers who are taking their furs to make coats.

Political Poems

Serious poets, suspicious of all verse that seeks a popular audience,
have always denigrated political poems. Poems like the one by
Emma Lazarus inscribed on the Statue of Liberty; most national
anthems and college songs; "O Beautiful for Spacious Skies"; and man-
ifesto poems of whatever persuasion, are bad poetry. The lyrics are
clichéd, the metrics unsubtle, and the thinking tabloid.

Rare, indeed, are antiwar poems with the aesthetic qualities of e. e.

cummings's "i sing of olaf" and his other satiric poems on World War I. Here is a list of some other fine achievements: Robert Bly's "The Teeth Mother Naked at Last" and "Counting Small-Boned Bodies"; Denise Levertov's "From a Notebook: October '68–May '69" and "Staying Alive"; Lawrence Ferlinghetti's "Moscow in the Wilderness, Segovia in the Snow"; Allen Ginsberg's "Plutonian Ode" and "Birdbrain"; Carolyn Forché's "In Salvador"; numerous poems by Daniel Berrigan; and the Vietnam poems of John Balaban, and W. D. Ehrhart.

To say that political poems are intended to arouse their readers is a truism. As the incendiary nature of the cause intensifies and the numbers of involved people grow, the more the quality of the poetry devoted to the cause decreases. Poetry becomes a form of propaganda in which subtlety and aesthetic values have little place. This is not to say that some fine poets who have devoted their talents to such causes have been ineffective. Consider the seminal role that Bly, Levertov, Kinnell, Ferlinghetti, George Hitchcock, the Berrigans, and Ginsberg, among others, played in focusing attention on the Vietnam War. Kinnell not only participated in the dangerous Freedom Rides in the South during the fifties, but wrote poems about his experience.

Today many of these same voices, plus a vast influx of newer ones, are exclaiming in public and in print against the insane nuclear race and against American involvements in Central America. Allen Ginsberg's *Plutonium Odes* contains a picture of Ginsberg with Peter Orlovsky and other courageous friends meditating on the railroad tracks outside the Rockwell Corporation's plutonium bomb trigger factory in Colorado, succeeding however briefly in halting a trainload of nuclear waste. Indefatigable poet, translator, novelist, and publisher Teo Savory, though very ill, accompanies her husband Alan Brilliant on nuclear protest marches, she moving along in her wheelchair. Their Unicorn Press, specializes in quality writing focused on current turmoil in Central and Latin America. Two recent titles are Pablo Antonio Cuadra's *The Birth of the Sun,* translated by Steven F. White, and Belkis Cuza Malé's *Woman on the Front Lines,* translated by Pamela Carmell.

The Berrigans keep placing themselves in sensitive protest spots where they will be arrested. Carolyn Forché's *The Country Between Us* has had a profound influence on poets in crystallizing views against American intervention in San Salvador. Lawrence Ferlinghetti has written a "Populist Manifesto," chiding poets for hiding in closets to escape the reality of a world falling down: "The trees are still falling / and we'll to the woods no more." There's not time for any artist "to hide / above, beyond, behind the scenes, / indifferent, paring his fingernails, / refining himself out of existence." Poets must be engaged. Ferlinghetti extols "a new wide-open poetry" of political and social commitment where poets "descend / to the streets of the world once more."

Stephen Kessler's annual *Alcatraz* shows that poems with strong political and social themes may be beautiful. The third volume runs to almost 350 pages and features work by Vicente Aleixandre, Leonel Rugama, Julio Cortazar, Francisco X. Alarcón, Ernesto Cardenal, Juan Felipe Herrera, and Saul Ibargoyen. David Fisher writes about mental hospitals, Nichola Manning on the H-Bomb, Sam Abrams on "the Plague Planet," Charles Bukowski on terrorism, Gary Gach on nuclear war, Vilhelm Ekelund on destitution and disease, Alma Villanueva on Beirut, James Scully on poverty and nonviolence, and Giaconda Belli on the Sandanistas. I know of no other comparable journal so dedicated to issues of the day. In the issue of *Alcatraz* described above, Paul Metcalf reviews Alicia Ostriker's *Writing Like A Woman*, a fashionable revisionist look at feminist letters. He quotes Ostriker quoting Emily Dickinson, that most indirect of poets: "Tell all the truth but tell it slant." Ostriker on her soapbox stresses that today's female writer aims "to tell all the truth and tell it straight." Dickinson, she says, was being evasive. Metcalf observes that while Ostriker never says so directly, such "unshackled" contemporary writers as Plath, Sexton, May Swenson, and Rich are "far better poets than Emily Dickinson, simply by virtue of having thrown off the shackles." Ostriker, he notes, excludes hosts of fine women writers apparently because they do not appear in "the forefront of *any* movement" and are not "overtly political." He recollects Ostriker thrusting a signed copy of her book into his hand, remarking (if his ears "heard aright") that her book would "continue" his "education." Metcalf concludes his review with a devastating paragraph: "*Writing like a Woman.* One could see this as the first in a new Time-Life series, to be followed soon by *Writing Like a Black, Writing Like a Lesbian, Writing Like an Eskimo*, etc. I'm not trying to be absurd. Such contentious partisanship provides its own black humor."

Certainly Metcalf puts his finger on a problem indigenous to all poets with causes: the arrogance with which they presume to judge others not sharing their enthusiasms. The bullying implicit in Ostriker's gift of her book is often characteristic of militant poets of very minor creative gifts. Large-spirited writers like Ginsberg, Bly, Levertov, Kinnell, Ferlinghetti, and Metcalf, have far more tolerance and class.

Postcard and Old Letter Poems

Ted Kooser writes of the home-crafted Midwestern rural life in poems as lovingly and skillfully turned as a fresh piece of harness. There are no false notes, no genteel bucolicisms. For making transitions between sections of *A Local Habitation and A Name*, Kooser employs early twentieth-century postcards written by rural people. The first, dated April 1, 1913, is, like the others, arranged as a found poem:

All kinds of
water here the
creeks are run-
ning bankfull

almost imposs-
ible to get a-
round. Your card
at hand last night.

This one is postmarked August 27, 1919:

This picture is of
the hoghouse here.
We have been having
a rain this morning
and fore-noon but
I guess it is about
over now and dinner
will soon be ready.
Yesterday there
was a man supposed to be
a patient here found dead
in the hog-yard.
Had hung himself
with a wire about Thurs.
I got my hair cut this forenoon
and day after tomorrow
is shave-day but I
won't get shaved until
next Thurs. Once in two
weeks is all I get.

This one is dated March 29, 1917:

The crows are
getting my turkey
eggs so bad I don't
believe I will have
any to sell. I hope
you find some.

Between the cards, Kooser places short, sophisticated poems on rural
themes: spring plowing, making rhubarb wine (he actually provides an
old recipe), Kansas wildflowers, field studies, an abandoned farmhouse, a
gas station, country-western music, wild pigs, nursing homes.

Kooser's latest chapbook, superbly produced by the Bieler Press in
Minneapolis, *The Blizzard Voices,* turns to folk material of a different
order, writing from firsthand accounts of an overwhelming blizzard that
hit Nebraska on January 12, 1888. His strategy is to alternate rural voices
in short poems evoking the horror of the event. Kooser gains much
through the stark simplicity of his voices. This woman, with devastating
understatement, recounts a birth amidst the horror:

Father was ill with the mumps,
and Mother none too strong
and only nineteen. She brought
our milk-cow, Betty, right into
the dugout with us, and there,
on the following morning,
Betty gave birth to a calf
we named Rufus. But our oxen,
out in the straw shed, perished.
As the snow drifted in, it seems
they kept tramping it down
until their backs were up against
the rafters. After the storm,
nearby, we also found
the body of an antelope.

A man finds his young cousin frozen to death, still standing upright, with only a pitchfork handle and his cap visible above the drifts. A neighbor becomes tangled in barbed wire just yards from his barn and dies. Two brothers, returning home from school, are lost, and dig down into a drift to wait:

      Billy
died in the night. I thought he
was only asleep. At dawn,
I dug out, finding that we
were in sight of the home place.
They had to cut my feet off.

Gary Gildner has written a moving series called "Letters from Vicksburg" (*Blue Like the Heavens: New & Selected Poems,*), based on the letters a Union soldier, John Blood, wrote to his wife Cecelia in Iowa. Most of these are fourteen-liners and could be called, I suppose, free-verse sonnets. While Gildner did not use "all of the original material and departed from it whenever it seemed necessary or fruitful," he maintains the original spellings, lack of punctuation, and misread words. These few lines from the first letter indicate their flavor:

Dear woman I am well and hope you ar
the same   to tell you wher we ar will be
a mater prety hard for I dont hartly
now my self   but now the River is not far
we hav to stop and fix the leavy ther
at Carthage wher we aim the enemy
is fortifying fifteen hundret men. . . .

In the next to last letter Blood complains of fever, yet is optimistic that he may be able to get a "furlow" if he continues ill. The final letter is from one of his superior officers to Cecelia Blood:

. . . As time went on no further word
from John until a week ago we heard
that he had died aboard the "R. C. Wood"
of Typhoid fever August 4. I have sent
his final statements and his military
history on to Washington D.C. Truly
I assure you, Madam, I was hurt,
for John was hardy, in the best of health—
but O alas! in life we are in death.

Poultry Poems

Chickens are not among the subjects poets find very appealing. Though farm families have indeed made faithful pets of poultry, for most of the world the chicken evokes laughter and satire. As a boy on a Wisconsin farm one of my pets was a white leghorn rooster who lost all of his toes during a particularly cold spell. He stood by, propping himself against his spurs—we called him "Crip."

The chicken lacks all bird-grace, and, in this regard, is kin to the rhea and ostrich, although the latter two are known for their speed on the ground, something hens lack. Stripped of its feathers and butchered, a chicken's limp form is also risible, and the unkindest cut of all is to see those rubber chickens used in slapstick routines by comedians.

Poets have never extolled the chicken, as they have nightingales, hawks, owls, sparrows, wrens, thrushes, and skylarks. Could any poet, in good conscience, "hail" a Buff Orpington or a Rhode Island Red as "a blithe spirit?" The occasional tabloid *Poultry: A Magazine of Verse* is devoted entirely to parodies, about chickens and other topics. A magnificent treatment of the fowl is Chaucer's tale of Chanticleer and Pertolete. Belying the famed stupidity of roosters, Chanticleer has brains. An authority on dreams, he is aware of much arcane medieval scholarship. And yet, though Chaucer does not belittle or denigrate the bird, he does use him to create a sort of mock epic.

A recent poultry poem is William Dickey's outrageous "Chickens in San Francisco." If he were to keep chickens, Dickey writes, this is how he would do it:

Deduct the cat and the dog, which are imaginary,
and you have two chickens, a male chicken and a female chicken
(chicken sexing is high paid work, but you have to travel).
They are walking around the deck. They are Plymouth Rocks.
The male chicken wears a buckled hat and carries a shotgun
and the female chicken has the New England ABC:
A is for Abstinence, B is for Boils, C is for Colonel Sanders.

The chickens look terribly sparse on the windy deck,
as if born plucked. They look at each other,
conscious of a hidden camera. They approach a cabbage
and under it they discover Shirley Temple.
They register the salvation of the race.
Shirley clucks a little, she is well into
what they call the skin of the part. . . .

Hayden Carruth is that rare poet who sees chickens as something more than an occasion for satire and ridicule. In "Missing the Bo in the Henhouse" (*Brothers, I Loved You All*), he blends regret for his lost boyhood with some exquisite lyric writing in which the hens who peck at his feet (he's caught in a storm and takes refuge in the henhouse) are "ladies." The clue for Carruth's tone perhaps resides in the phrase "a higgeldy-piggeldy / planet," evocative of the old nursery rhyme "Higgledy-Piggledy, my black hen." As Carruth ages, he finds that the great desires he's had in the past have now diminished:

Keep close and keep warm. Bless me if you are able,
commend me to the storm. Goodnight, good night.

"A Blue Ribbon at Amesbury" shows Robert Frost in a most playful guise. Listen to the rock-a-baby rhythms of this stanza (the prize-winning hen has just returned to the henyard):

Here common with the flock again,
At home in her abiding pen,
She lingers feeding at the trough,
The last to let night drive her off.

These homespun devices call up something of the mock epic feel, in the manner of Pope or Chaucer. The latter, though, would have invented some raunchy fable or dream tale for the occasion.

I once began an epic called *The Heniad* and wrote a dozen or so "cantos" before deciding that not even chickens should be so abused. My idea was to write a parody for each of as many living and dead poets as I could on the motif of a rooster's mounting a hen. Some of these actually appeared in *The Brand-X Anthology of Poetry: A Parody Anthology*, edited by William Zaranka.

Pregnancy Poems

Chana Bloch, in "Magnificat," writes of her wonder at the life forming its little gills, fingers, and other parts secretly inside her. Female readers will feel most at home here. I find her device of talking to the fetus corny and tiresome; I wish she had used more original imagery. Her conclusion that the embroyo "safe in salt waters" is heading "for dry land" is predictable. And seeing herself as "an ark," the belly of a ship with animals aboard, is almost laughable—as is her defiant exclamation that she will carry her "belly to Timbuctoo" where she will "bare it to the moon . . . wear it forever," and "hold it up every morning" in her "ten fingers," "crowing / to wake the world." Gender zooms off track: roosters crow. Roosters are male. It's hard to see a pregnant woman crowing at dawn, complete with feathered shanks, wattles, and red comb.

Sharon Olds turns militant in "The Language of the Brag" (*Satan Says*). She craves "some epic use" for her "excellent body," and finds it via pregnancy. She feels cowardly, and various physical manifestations cause pain:

> my stool black with iron pills,
> my huge breasts oozing mucus,
> my legs swelling, my hands swelling,
> my face swelling and darkening, my hair
> falling out, my inner sex
> stabbed again and again with terrible pain like a knife.

At delivery time, she sweats, shakes, and passes blood, feces, and urine, lying in "the center of a circle" of attendant medical faces. It's over, and she gloats, perhaps with a smug smear of homophobia directed primarily at Walt Whitman and Allen Ginsberg.

While giving birth is the province of women, the occasional male poet appears who fantasizes he is also capable of generating young. Whitman, as Olds implies, was there first, and among various poems of empathy for women in *Leaves of Grass* these two stand out: "A Woman Waits For Me" and "Twenty-eight young men bathe by the shore." In our time, however, Robert Phillips' "The Pregnant Man" turns the idea of male birthing into a clever joke, barely a cut above light verse. It's all metaphor, written in undistinguished lines, borrowing totally conventional trappings: first pains, breaking of the waters, cleaning up the sheets, phoning the doctor, etc. The rhythms are as "regular as Lawrence Welk." At 8 A.M., while clutching the bedpost, screaming: "a duck squeezing out / a Macy's Thanksgiving Day / parade balloon," he gives birth to an eight-pound, blue-eyed, bouncing baby poem! Birth trauma past, the pregnant father spanks the little crittur into "life," lies back, and has a drink. Well, things go foul—two hours later the baby/poem dies . . . There's just time for a final cozy joke:

> . . . You know
> how it is with poems.
> (My last one had two
> heads and no heart.)

Prepositionitis Poems

Among the diseases of verse, prepositionitis is a minor malady. Yet, no affliction better reveals the sterility of an author's imagination, or a dearth of feeling. Michael Harper, in *The Pushcart Prize*, Vol. 7, writes chummily of giving a reading in New York City during a blizzard, of being introduced by Galway Kinnell and riding a horse around Central Park. He also does a bit of in-house thinking about James Wright and Philip Levine. Harper's tongue is coated with a bad case of prepositionitis. The italics are mine:

> *In* the year *of* the blizzard
> *In* the month *of* February
> I have traipsed *up* the middle
> *of* Lexington Avenue, a spectacular
> middle passage *in* the snow
> *to* my own poetry reading. . . .

Jonathan Galassi, in "If Anger Were Power," piles up prepositional phrases in the very first stanza, revealing how ill-felt his poem is:

> I want to hold on to the hand of the man
> who is stronger than I am, feed on his energy.
> I can't look him in the eye; when I do I see
> blue crystal, dangerous sand.

Mekeel McBride opens "The Will to Live" with three dull prepositional phrases:

> On the green lawn of a city park
> a sentence of dark insects completes itself . . .

In "Good People," a sentimental piece, Maura Stanton is buying flowers "*for* my mother, who lies / *In* the hosptial with a blood clot *in* her vein" [Italics mine]. She's aware of all "these" other people jostling one another in the streets, going in "a dozen directions." Her mixed feelings of estrangement and union occasion a series of debilitating prepositional phrases, all fatal to the vitality of a real style:

I stare in wonder down the crowded street.
I could be part of one of these strangers
Breathing hard in the cold, Kentucky air,
That tall man with gnarled, shaky hands
Or that heavy woman, or part of someone dead
Who thought that life was choice, not accident.

Towny Towle's "Works on Paper," a ten-pager featured in the March 1975 issue of *Poetry,* is a tedious, preposition-ridden dramatic monologue delivered by a post-Brunelleschi architect who really can't get his life together. He is a dim reflection of Robert Browning's Andrea del Sarto, but without Sarto's energy, gusto, or intelligence. Towle lavishes clichés shamelessly, as though the Renaissance world were partial to them: "Sweeping reforms," "strong beliefs," "the tools of their trades." He is also most momentous: we are treated to phrases like "in their realities," "the impressive accoutrements of office," and "in my contemplated youth." Towle is also addicted to phrases beginning with the preposition *in*. I count six of these on a single page. What draws my eye (ear) to them is their recurring deadness. When I hit one of those clusters a little bell goes off, and I see that either Towle's strategy betrays him, or he simply writes badly. He fails to do more than raise a little bump on the biscuit.

John Yau seems consciously to deaden poems with prepositional phrases, obtaining an effect like rhythms beaten on metal garbage can lids at regular intervals. "All This Changing Trouble Luck and Suddenness" sounds this way:

I lengthened the comfort of moving on
Someone to stand with for a distance
Instead of listening to the noise of a clock falling
A string of fish. . . .

Prison Poems

A searing subculture of writers has emerged over the past twenty years or so who are either in American prisons or have been there, often more than once. Their voices have been nourished by dedicated writers (some of them former inmates, some not) who regularly give writing workshops within those grim walls. Among these selfless teachers are Joseph Bruchac, Charles Plymell, Michael Hogan, Sam Hamill, Richard Shelton, Bill Witherup, Galway Kinnell, John Cheever, and Carolyn Forché. Funding has come largely from state and federal government funding. Carol Bruchac directs the COSMEP Prison Project, which collects and distributes literary magazines and small press books free to people in prisons. And Joe Bruchac, assisted by Michael Hogan, Richard Shelton, and John Paul Minarik, in 1984 published *The Light From Another Country: Poetry From American Prisons.*

There is a tradition, of course, of major writers having written masterpieces while in prison: Malory's *Morte d'Arthur,* Villon's *Grand Testament,* John Bunyan's *Pilgrim's Progress,* Cervantes' *Don Quixote,* Oscar Wilde's "Ballad of Reading Gaol" and "De Profunidis," and Dostoyevski's *Notes from Underground* were all written behind bars.

Of the sixty poets presented in *The Light From Another Country,* all are worth reading, many are amazingly fine, and all write out of lives seemingly ruined and so anonymous they exist only as numbers. John Paul Minarik extols the value of the writing programs:

basic writing 702

take 25 basic convict students
collide them with
standard american english
throw in
a dash of
michael hogan
and
joseph bruchac
and out come
15 new writers.

5 lost to the
games of prison
1 transferred
1 paroled
1 withdrawal
1 fell in love with a sissy
and 1 never showed once.

since numbers
are important in prison
15 over 25
might seem like a nice fraction
but somewhere between
commas and semicolons
metaphors and images
10 men were lost.

like a prison within a prison
10 men were locked into
ignorance of their potential to grow.

"forget about the ones who can't make it."

but here at the last conjunction
those 10 men are the 1's
who will sell dope to your children

rape your daughters
and that's why
my red pen is crying
my grade book is ashamed
and my soul is
a sentence fragment

As one might expect, there are many recurrent themes: the claustrophobia and dehumanization of being incarcerated; the bonds of love with families on the outside and lovers on the inside—both so difficult to maintain; the struggle for a sense of self-worth, particularly moving when a poet hopes to assure his (or her) children that their dad is not as evil as he may appear; fantasies about life after prison; poems written by men and women who have done their time and look back on the experience. What these poets do not do is snivel. Their braggadocio saves them. These writers are survivors, realists. They know they may (as other talented men and women have) go under, either outside the prison or within its walls.

Among the better-known poets represented here are Etheridge Knight, whose *Born of a Woman: New and Selected Poems,* appeared in 1980; Paul Mariah, founder of *Manroot Magazine* and Manroot Press, and author of a small classic of the prison experience, *Personae Non Gratae* (1971); Michael Hogan, who while serving twelve and a half years in maximum-security prisons for robbery and forgery of Supreme Court documents, earned a law degree, won a National Endowment for the Arts fellowship, and has since published four books of poetry. He works now as a director for the Colorado prison literature program, and is a consultant for similar programs elsewhere.

A fine poet not included here, but one who should have been, is William Wantling, who began to write poems before there were government programs. Wantling was forty-one when he died on May 2, 1974 of a heart attack brought on by codeine and wine. He was introduced to heavy dope, he said, through the military, when he was hospitalized in Korea and given morphine. "It was beautiful," he said. "Five years later I was in San Quentin on narcotics."

Thanks are due to Len Fulton for publishing Wantling's first book, *The Source,* as a Dust Book in 1966; to Marvin Malone who published Wantling in *Wormwood Review;* to A. D. Winans of Second coming, who published Wantling's last book, *7 on Style;* and to Peter Finch, of *second aeon,* Cardiff, Wales, who published *San Quentin's Stranger.* We still have no collected volume of Wantling's work.

"Poetry," from *San Quentin's Stranger,* presents a conflict between allegiance, on the one hand, to "good word music and rhyme" and, on the other, to the guts of prison life. Wantling writes in non-rhyming couplets, giving a sense of a self-imposed structure. But though he appears formal, his voice resists the form; or, rather, he allows his slack, Midwestern voice to have its way:

I've got to be honest, I can
make good word music and rhyme

at the right times and fit words
together to give people pleasure

and even sometimes take their
breath away—but it always

somehow turns out kind of phoney.
consonance and assonance and inner

rhyme won't make up for the fact
that I can't figure out how to get

down on paper the real or the true
which we call life.   Like the other

day. The other day I was walking
in the lower exercise yard here

at San Quentin and this cat called
Turk came up to a friend of mine

and said Ernie, I hear you're
shooting on my kid. And Ernie

told him So what, Punk? And Turk
pulled out his stuff and shanked

Ernie in the gut only Ernie had a
metal tray in his shirt. Turk's

shank bounced off Ernie and
Ernie pulled his stuff out and of

course Turk didn't have a tray and
he caught it dead in the chest, a bad

one, and the blood that came to his
lips was a bright pink, lung blood,

and he just laid down in the grass
and said Shit. Fuck it. Sheeit.

Fuck it. And he laughed a soft long
laugh, 5 minutes, then died. Now

what could consonance or assonance or
even rhyme do with something like that?

The prison poems ring true because a considerable human being emerges from the pain. Wantling was gifted with kind of braggadocio. Perhaps calling this quality a crazy gusto might be more accurate. Wantling sensed somehow that his best chance of maintaining balance, confronted by shock treatments and other prison brutalities, was through an ironic detachment. This he expresses superbly in "Who's Bitter?":

when Judge Lynch
denied probation
& crammed that 1–14
up my ass
for a first offence
I giggled

when Dr God
stuck 7 shocktreatments
to me
for giving my chick in Camarillo
2 joints
I laughed aloud

now when the State of Illness
caught me bending over
2 jugs of Codeine
cough medicine
& charged me w / Possession
and Conspiracy
I shrieked
in idiot joy

a bit worried
they all inquired
—What are you Wantling?
—A goddamn Masochist?
I, between hilarious gasps
O howled—No,
—I'm a Poet!
—Fuck me again!

Patrick Mackinnon's "outdoor mall, boulder colorado," in *Walking Behind My Breath,* also deserves inclusion in Bruchac's anthology. Here a brutalized prison inmate gazes down on the society brutalizing him. Mackinnon's empathy is amazing, an indictment of a smug culture which transforms men into beasts:

the brick sidewalk prison
where hoodoo victor brown's
currently doing his time
rabid on cheap angel dust

he buys & sells same as
anybody takes a breath
then breathes it out &
only thing he loves
more than dressing up
heavy rasta is ramming
the barrel of his
cock rifle eyes
up vacationing retinas
like maybe you've watched
snakes stare down mice
& this is just like it
only shot thru with hate
an empty driverless train
raging across the tumbleweed
heart bowels of hell
then he smiles up two
razor sharp fangs
tipped with blood &
whispers a howl
that sounds just enough
like *hi*

Projective Verse Poems

(*See also* West Coast Poems)

Projective verse is a mode of writing inspired and fostered by that Paul Bunyan of mid-twentieth-century poetry Charles Olson, who elaborated at great length on its properties in a famous talk at Berkeley in 1950. The gist of his remarks appeared in the appendix for Donald M. Allen's *The New American Poetry: 1945–1960*, and followed precepts of Ezra Pound and William Carlos Williams. Olson totally rejected all qualities typical of academic verse; and as mentor of an unusually gifted circle of young writers at Black Mountain College in the early fifties, watched his ideas and theories take hold. Two magazines of the period, *Origin* and *Black Mountain Review*, featured work by Olson and his followers. Among them were Robert Duncan, Robert Creeley, Edward Dorn, Joel Oppenheimer, and Jonathan Williams. Other poets influenced by Black Mountain theories but having no connection with the school were Denise Levertov, Paul Blackburn, Paul Carroll, and Larry Eigner.

Donald Allen sees the emergence of what was called the "San Francisco Renaissance" in the late forties as a direct result of Olson's teaching and writing. Duncan, the key figure in the Bay Area, was associated with William Everson, Robin Blaser, Jack Spicer, Philip Whalen, James

Broughton, Madeline Gleason, Helen Adam, Lawrence Ferlinghetti, Bruce Boyd, Kirby Doyle, Richard Duerden, Philip Lamantia, Ebbe Borregaard, and Lew Welch.

In 1956, the Beat Generation arrived in San Francisco: Allen Ginsberg, Gregory Corso, Philip Whalen, Gary Snyder, Michael McClure, and Charles Plymell. The mix was rich, and boundaries were erased.

Today, the issue of which poets write projective verse and which do not seems confused. A poet like Clayton Eshleman who appears to write in the Olson manner is uneasy, I gather, about the label. Perhaps the term has been so dispersed that it is now almost meaningless, unless applied to Olson's own poetry.

Proletarian Poems

A thoroughgoing proletarian poem is Antler's *Factory*, published by City Lights in 1980. With clarity, honesty, and humor, employing Allen Ginsberg's long line, Antler recounts his labors in a factory punching aluminum can lids and bottoms:

> Here are the 24 presses chewing can lids
>   from hand-fed sheet of aluminum.
> Here are the 10 monsters chomping poptops
>   nonstop into lids scooped into their jaws.
> Machines large as locomotives,
>   louder than loudest rockgroup explosions,
> Screeching so loud you go deaf without earplugs,
>   where the only way to speak is to gesture,
> Or bending to your ear as if I were telling a secret
>   the yell from my cupped hands less than a whisper.

The dehumanizing power of such a place and of such labor seems to challenge Antler—can he survive? How will he occupy his mind as the work increases in deadly monotony? "O Reveille my Reveries to Revelry again!" he shouts, almost joyously. He thinks, while he slaves away, of rich boys fulfilling his "wildest desires." He thinks of Beethoven, so anxious not to leave his composing that he had a chamber pot affixed to his piano stool. How long, he asks, would it take him to listen to everything Beethoven ever composed if he listened for eight hours a day—the same workday he puts in at the factory? He memorizes poems and daydreams, wishing there were a log cabin erected in the "most deafening part of the factory" where he could "hermitage" and listen to wind howling down the chimney, and, as he scribbled away, look out to see other workers slaving. A wonderfully jubilant word play, a glaring sanity, guarantees he will neither go mad nor lose his humanity:

O HUMAN CANNONBALLS OF EPIPHANY

Can cans-ever be canned? Can the can-can ever be canned?
Can cantos of cannonfodder ever be canonized
    or the Canticle of Canticles of Cannabis
    never be cantabiled?
Can canasta in Canada canyons or going to the can
    never be cantata'd
or can't it be canted
        because of cannibal cancer's uncanny candor
      making even cantaloupes cantankerous?
Hum-drum! Hum-drum! Hum-drum!

Finally, "The Miracle of Factory passes" from his life, the experience now remains no larger than a remote kite on a string. He refuses to release the string until all dehumanizing factories become "playgrounds in moonlight," all applicants for factory jobs must memorize his poem, and he is hired "to dress like a grasshopper and fiddle / 'O the world owes me a livin' / to the nation of ants. . . .'"

Lew Welch, who is inspired by the Greek poet Anacreon, was a cab driver. "After Anacreon" is structured serially around the adverbial phrase "When I drive cab." It has both elevated and randy moments. Here is one of the latter: "I bring the sailor home from the sea. In the back of / my car he fingers the pelt of his maiden." Welch is humorous, cool, and detached: "I watch for stragglers in the urban order of things." He closes on a cozy symbolic note:

When I drive cab
    I end the only lit and waitful thing in miles of
darkened houses.

Thom Gunn's "Night Taxi" is like a companion poem to Welch's. It too is spoken by a cabbie who loves his job. He's always proud, on his toes, "obliging but not subservient." He boasts of his skill in taking short cuts, savint time. His fares "are like affairs," he says, sexual. He's capable of the intriguing speculative question: "Do I pass through the city / or does it pass through me?" As he zips down Masonic Avenue, San Francisco, he woos with his cab. He is both "bridegroom and conqueror."

Doren Robbins, in *Sympathetic Manifesto*, writes of a broilerman's life in a busy, exploitative restaurant. These poems are written in a rambling, free-verse mode, tightened by Robbins's skill for alternating punching short lines with longer ones, and for hard internal rhythms. Robbins's point of view shifts from being the worker-poet objectively describing other workers on the job, to himself as he confronts the human cost of such demeaning employment. "The Ensuing Voyage," an elaborate portrait of Rossetti, the chef, is the most joyous of the four pieces. The protagonist, a night dishwasher, scrutinizes Rossetti as he cleans seemingly endless pots and pans:

butchering and broiling,
eating standing up, working
continuously—with no sense of harassment, or giving
the illusion of that sense—chopping, sauteing,
smoking cigarettes—testing the mousse,
tasting every sauce—quieting
the alarmed maitre de, coaxing
the produce-man on the phone
to deliver to him first. . .

Daryl E. Jones' "The Hotstrip" is another steel-mill poem of scarring and endurance. A youth is induced into his labors by an old foreman who's been horribly disfigured. His most conspicuous wound is a hole in his cheek, "perfectly circular," just below his cheekbone where his teeth show through. The kid feels impossibly green, imagining how gangly he looks "in the hardhat and oversize gloves, / in the heavy steel-toed boots" he can barely walk in. He finds it hard not to stare at the "mauve O just below" the old man's cheekbone, where his teeth show:

. . . he must have been caught with his mouth wide open,
perhaps while he was laughing, or shouting instructions,
or perhaps, near the end of a long day, yawning;
as he sweated into his beard and glasses,
stained with the fragrance of lamb shanks
and rosemary—whimsical,
solemn, anointed
by what he worked with—not talking
not wasting a branch,
a slice,
a spoonful—
Rossetti worked continuously, symphonically,
peremptorily—the veins
thick along his forearms,
sweeping the fallen wrappers from his path.

The man's skills so intrigue Robbins, who learns from him how to mix herbs, use a cleaver, and chop garlic, that he pretends he likes his menial job, a dissimulation, he knows, for when he stands outside his apartment he's chilled by the June night.

The final poem in the set, "Collecting My Self," is a potent complaint by the minimal-wage broilerman who has 25 percent of his pay taken out for taxes, disgusted that his money goes to support United States "causes" like Pol Pot, Pinochet, and Somoza. The agents of his victimization are the "pallorous, almost freakish clerks" in unemployment offices who determine his legal eligibility (or lack thereof) for benefits. He's driven to be "non-productive" by a "pernicious government," to work jobs without declaring the income.

The reader comparing Antler's account of demeaning labor with Robbins's will, I think, find that Robbins has more empathy, is more sympathetic to fellow workers. Antler is more egocentric.

in any case, the angle of trajectory
through his cheek and open mouth a perfect paradox
of randomness and surgical precision;
and in any case, the parting and closing of flesh
instantaneous, probably not even felt, not then.

The image lingers, a poignant premonition of what brutality awaits this lad just starting his job, a lifetime, possibly, of glintings "off grilles and mirrors, a world of flying slivers."

A most impressive first book, Jim Daniels's *Places/Everyone,* is unabashedly proletarian. Studs Terkel must be overjoyed. And what is more, it won a prize given by the University of Wisconsin Press poetry series, not an organization one would suspect of having the slightest liberal tendency. Yet, Wisconsin is a strange state—after all, the Lafollettes came from there. Also, the Press had the foresight to appoint an iconoclastic poet as judge—C. K. Williams. *Places/Everyone* reads like a photo album, the title itself suggesting that the poet is arranging snapshots. Sure, there's plenty of grit, grime, poverty, disease, crippling, and violence. As the son of a factory worker, Daniels obviously knows this life well, and presents it with eyelids peeled—there's no condescension or romanticization. His hero Digger comes complete with a fat wife, failure, and a fondness for beer and television. We see him driving to work, hunting, having Thanksgiving, shoveling snow, dreaming, watering his lawn, suffering from insomnia, going on vacation, and being laid off. "Digger Laid Off" is superbly understated—the hero, now without a job, turns victim. Violence waits just below his skin:

Tonight you beat up four little kids

to get a baseball at Tiger Stadium.
After the game you sit in a bar
watching fat naked women
rub mud over their bodies.
You throw your ball in the mud pit
and a dancer picks it up
rubs it over her muddy crotch
and throws it back to you.
In the parking lot
you throw the ball against a windshield
but it will not crack.

"1000 Apply for 100 Jobs" hurts, and one reason is Daniels's form; recurring end-rhymes built around *door/poor/wore* evoke the villanelle and a singing pattern that belies the grimness of his subject matter. This poem is a tour de force:

I stood in line, drunk with the cold
shuffling toward the factory door.
Hundreds danced slowly in front of me,

hundreds behind. Some of us I knew were poor
with pink skin sticking out
of what we wore.
When the man said *go home, that's it,*
some kicked the ground and swore.
Others moved on quickly
having been here before.
At least I have another job—minimum wage—
washing windows, sweeping floors,
so I felt a bit of joy inside that big sadness,
like Happy Hour at the Goodwill Store.

In Gary Metras's "The Mechanic as Metaphysician," from *Destiny's Calendar,* a "mechanic" father repairs the family car. Only his "grease-stained / ass and legs" show from beneath. To the child watching, the car seems to be "slowly swallowing" his father "like the ruby-throated lizard / that takes two hours to eat a frog, and then crawls to some shade and waits there with the legs still dangling from its mouth." The father is vexed, cursing. His workman's hands have "knuckles / scraped / on grimed iron, / the torn flesh lost like a tadpole / in the hugeness of a black swamp."

Once home, his wife, dismayed by these hands, will never understand the male fascination with machines—"for what is hidden metal / sliding smooth, as fish, / against metal / bathed in oils." As the mechanic cleans up, if he finds blood on his hands or on the valve cover or carburetor throat, he'll turn his rag until he finds the last clean spot and, before cleaning the blood from his own skin, will wipe the "stained metal" clean, with strokes gentler "than any woman could conceive." Unlike the woman, metal never rebukes his caresses:

he is
hard, leaning against
the fender, ready
for sex, ready to strike, if he must,
the stubborn parts
with screwdriver or wrench
until it purrs
under the gentle
weight of his hands,
his blows.
        He is slave to this;
he feeds himself to it, and it feeds him
a self.

Leo Connellan's "Amelia, Mrs. Brooks Of My Old Childhood" is a starkly moving rendition of personal guilt and a portrait of a woman who worked most of her life in a sardine factory supporting herself and her children. As a youth inducted into the army, Connellan, yearning to "say goodbye to a mother," sought her out: "where sardines stuck / to your hands, I came and said / goodbye in the fish smell." Over the years, Connellan failed to keep in touch, until he hears from the woman's sister-in-law that she is in a nursing home and has never understood Connellan's neglect of her.

Proletariat poems exist that reveal distaste for the laboring and middle classes. Ezra Pound wrote several. One, "Salutation," is a self-ironic, almost contemptuous piece in which barbs prevent his reader from feeling superior and smug. Two vast generations of humankind exist—that of "the thoroughly smug" and of "the thoroughly uncomfortable." Pound has seen the "untidy families" of fishermen at their picnics, has heard their "ungainly laughter," and witnessed "their smiles full of teeth." Pound then declares himself "happier than you [his reader] are," and "they [workmen] were happier than I am." A veritable round of happiness, concluding on an image of fish swimming in a lake—none of them "even own clothing."

A final note: proletariat poems are not much in favor, although the poets who write them do so with impressive skill. In the thirties many such poems were published. Maxwell Bodenheim wrote some good ones. Proletariat poems seem to increase with unemployment and bread lines. Perhaps if unemployment continues to grow, we'll see more of these poems.

Puppy Love Poems

These poems need little definition, for, as one would expect, they deal with teen-age love. Most of these are poems about early sex. Three pieces of this kind appear in *The Bellingham Review* (Spring 1984). Robert E. Lawson, writing what he calls a "self-journal," luxuriates in his dumbness on a date. He sits with the girl in his car, "immobile, impotent with uncertainty." Maurice Scully writes this apostrophe: "Margaret Dunne. / I name you for the magic of it, / Your marvellous school uniform / Still on." Fabian Worsheim makes love in her "little-girl bed" with all its lavender and lace pillow shams and ruffles.

Dave Smith, (in *Poetry*, February, 1986) recollects a nubile sweetie (though both are nineteen, they seem so inexperienced they are still in a puppy-love stage) in a "skin-tight and moon-sluiced" swim suit. He thinks she may be "barely pregnant." As the waters go "webby with cradled starlight," and "dawn" *lays* "the [sand] bar bare," the happy couple trek into the water. As he dawdles, bends "for the blue / of a clam's dome" (an obvious, schoolboyish vaginal image), she evanesces, excusing Smith from having to evoke more sexual odor that might offend a staid reader. He's left, as we are, feeling that the world (and his poem) is "empty."

James Hejna writes of the transition from puppy-love to the next stage, crisply rendered in terms of monarch butterflies, hibiscus, and wasps:

A Baffle of Appearance

    for H. W. Bates

The viceroy affects the monarch's bad taste—
unlike the girl who dresses like a popular girl
and succeeds in looking delicious to the red-and-gold
suited team lunching in the commons
where popular girls appear Saturday wearing
red-and-gold skirts, white blouses,
and black ribbon bowties before the game and the
post-game dance, after which the players
dribble back to the dorms, one-on-one
or alone. Some orchids mimic female wasps.

A male wasp, mistaken twice, engenders orchids—
unlike the starting forward who asks the lilac-scented
girl with a crimson hibiscus in her hair
out because he thinks she's kind of nice, worth taking
to a restaurant or a disaster movie occasionally,
or a concert, though he doesn't want to impress her
because a repeated focus of her eyes on infinity
betrays in her a character getting ready to get
depressed, as if just living were a manic high to come
down off of, a honeymoon that ends in silence.
She nods. The flower falls from her hair.
Anyone entering now would take the lilac-scented girl,
bent down to rescue a hibiscus, for a popular girl,
until she straightens to hear her starting forward
ask another girl, rose-scented with a yellow braid,
up to his room to review Greek Art:
    she straightens, half-smiling, half-reaffirmed.
Monarchs never mistake viceroys for monarchs. Courtship
discriminates dislikes, yet going out with the forward
does not waste time—there are pleasures . . .

Reptile Poems

The reptile poem is, of course, *Paradise Lost*. All later works seem like moulted skins, emptied of venom and blood. Other forebears are Emily Dickinson's "A Narrow Fellow in the Grass" and D. H. Lawrence's "Snake." (From whatever afterworld he is in Lawrence probably still regrets his urge to kill that creature.)

Anthony Hecht, in "Lizards and Snakes," reports that he and a friend Joe hid snakes in Aunt Martha's knitting box. Joe said they were simply broadening the woman's life. One day a "big wind" swung through, the trees creaking "like rockingchairs," and put an end to their fun. Aunt Martha, frightened, had a vision of Satan: "He can crack us like lice with his fingernail," she exclaimed. "Look how he grins / And swings the scaly horror of his folded tail."

David Bottoms, in "The Copperhead," fishing for bass, casts a lure near some stumps and a large dead oak fallen into the water. Stretched across the oak, as a "dwarfed limb / or a fist-thick vine," is a large copperhead, "dark and patterned / large on years of frogs and rats." Bottoms works the lure around some stumps, watching the snake's "spade head shift on the dry bark." When no bass strike, he watches as shadows envelop the reptile, feeling an urge to "drift into the shaded water," to become a snake, pulling himself down a fallen branch toward the tree's trunk, where the snake waits "quiet and dangerous and unafraid, / all spine and nerve." The ending is cryptic: does Bottoms relish putting himself at risk? Does he wish somehow to assume the snake's qualities? I admire Bottoms's lean writing. He unpretentiously illuminates a mystery—our fascinated responses to reptiles, a mix of fear, awe, and envy.

Denise Levertov's "To the Snake," in *Poems Nineteen Sixty to Nineteen Sixty-Seven,* apparently in Eve's voice, reworks the famed seduction in the Garden. Eve loves the phallic creature, verbally caressing him, praising his "cold, pulsing throat," "glinting / arrowy scales," his weight on her shoulders and the "whispering silver" of his dryness. To her "companions" she swears he is harmless. But she is not certain; the joy of holding him is so intense, she opts for "a long wake of pleasure" as the serpent fades into grass and shadows. She returns "smiling and haunted, to a dark morning."

Patiann Rogers produces a homily on a horned lizard's ugliness, "Justification of the Horned Lizard." Her accumulation of reasons why such a creature should live is condescending—I can see her writing another such poem about a deformed person. She loves the pathetic fallacy. Among the good things the lizard "will never know": lush things, moss floating in a river current, a glossy white belly like a bullfrog's. "No touch to its body, even from its own kind, / Could ever be delicate or caressing." Yet Rogers provides a sentimental out: the fact of the lizard's willingness to fight for itself, to rise up, apparently confers dignity on the creature, as if the act of defiance itself were worthy.

In James Reiss's "The Snake Man" (*The Brothers*), a girl is horrified by a monstrous figure pursuing her. The chase begins in a park. The girl, hit in the back with a baseball, does not cry. Next, "he" flies at her along a wall of trees, and hits her again with the ball, this time in the chest. She still does not cry—perhaps she is too terrified by the "bad teeth and black skin." If only she can make it past the trees to the hot dog stand. The assailant now trades the ball for a rock, and is about to grab a broken bottle, when, finally, she bursts into tears. As she stands there, covering her eyes with her hand, she recalls a nightmare of a girl running through an apartment, pursued by a toothless Snake Man, whose face is her father's.

Reiss's transformation of snake to human embodies some of the worst human fears regarding reptiles—if Satan in Eden could assume the serpent's body and speak through him with such disastrous results for man, doesn't it follow that the creature could inhabit a human and threaten a girl? I like Reiss's use of the reptile motif. With the fascinating complex of meanings, totemistic, Jungian, and otherwise, assigned to snakes, it is perhaps surprising that more poets don't write these poems.

Rilke Poems

American poets almost obsessively revere Rainer Maria Rilke. One of the best-known poems he inspired is James Wright's "Lying in a Hammock at William Duffy's Farm in Pine Island, Minnesota," in *Collected Poems*, which concludes with a direct adaptation of the famous conclusion to Rilke's "On A Classic Torso of Apollo": "You must change your life." I doubt whether Wright would have written his poem if Rilke's admonition weren't spinning around in his head. Here is Wright's close:

> A chicken hawk floats over, looking for home.
> I have wasted my life.

Wright's son, the poet Franz Wright (see "Self-Pity Poems") seems to be making a fetish of such Rilkean closures.

Translating Rilke has become something of an industry, the most recent of his translators being Stephen Mitchell. *The American Poetry Review* (January 1982) showcased eight of Mitchell's efforts. They are OK. But do we need any more of them? Rilke should look down from Heaven, and, after a certain number—say fifty-two—derivatives of his poems have appeared within a single year, either in full-scale translations or in passages baldly derived from them, should shout "Halt!" and jab out the eyes of the poet or translator busy on the fifty-third perpetration. I urge him to jab out the person's eyes with rose thorns. After all, translating dead poets is a form of necrophilia.

Robert Frost Poems

On the one hand, Frost and Stevens; on the other Williams and Pound—these are the two poles which have influenced most American poetry written over the last thirty years. In sheer weight (how many milligrams do 100,000 heavily inked letters of the alphabet weigh?), poems inspired by Robert Frost must certainly far outweigh those inspired by the other three poets. Curious, if indeed this is true; for not until Randall Jarrell's essays in the forties turned academic tastes positively toward Frost—he had been seen as a tacky rustic relative of the city slicker T. S. Eliot, a facile bucolicist of verse—did Frost's reputation soar. And his influence persists, stronger than ever. Take up nearly any journal or magazine containing poetry, and chances are that the Robert Frost poem will dominate. *The Northwest Review, Images, Ironwood, The Pikestaff Forum, The Black Warrior Review, Prairie Schooner* . . . the list seems endless. William Stafford, David Wagoner, and Wendell Berry are but three contemporary poets who trek down often to clear that pasture spring. (The poems referred to are all in *The Poetry of Robert Frost,* 1969.

What follows is a breakdown of those of Frost's recurrent themes that seem most to inspire today's poets:

1. *Wonder over small natural forms:* The tuft of flowers left behind by a busy mower in "The Tuft of Flowers"; the coralroot you pluck "as a trophy of the hour" ("On Going Unnoticed"); the "pent-up buds," "flowery waters," and "water flowers" near spring pools; the engaging "small bird" of "The Wood-Pile."

2. *A stubborn optimism as one meditates on nature:* "The Silken Tent," though seemingly slight, is a fancy call to gazing "heavenward" in a security "of the soul" owing "naught to any single cord, / But strictly held by none"—rather by "countless silken ties of love and thought. . . ."

3. *The commonplace object rife with inducements for meditation:* The decaying rick of maple ("The Wood-Pile") all cut "four by four by eight," neatly piled, and forgotten by the farmer piling it there. Conclusion? Whoever piled it there was someone who could easily go on to the future, "turning to fresh tasks," enabling him easily to "forget" the "handiwork on which / He spent himself."

4. *The slight and unexpectedly restorative natural event:* "The Dust of Snow."

5. *The easy homily passing as folk or frontier wisdom:* "Good fences make good neighbors" (in the ironic mode); and this (straightforward) from "Reluctance":

Ah, when to the heart of man
 Was it ever less than a treason
To go with the drift of things,
 To yield with a grace of reason,
And bow and accept the end
 Of a love or a season?

6. *Assisting nature in granting quasi-mystical views:* Clearing off the surface of the pasture spring, so as to enjoy reflections in the clear water below, a humble and gentle act, allows one a better view of nature's wealth hidden below surfaces. One might also find treasures by brushing away deposits of fallen leaves to find spring flowers blossoming there.

7. *The casual tone:* Indigenous to all of Frost's poems, including the dramatic monologues and tales. Frost's "Death of the Hired Man" and other poems owe much to Wordsworth's "Michael," which in its day set the norm for writing about rustics.

8. *The profundities of nature lie just steps away from one's house:* Wagoner and Stafford know this well—Wordsworth over Byron, the gentle Lake District scenery over the rugged Alps, the New Hampshire lake rather than Crater Lake; the thrush over the bald eagle.

9. *The ennobling of the rustic:* Rustics, as in "The Death of the Hired Man" are capable of high tragedy. Yes, Eugene O'Neill knew this too.

10. *Understatement, the gentle ironies:* The true rustic is never loquacious, and is a doer rather than a thinker. His thoughts, when they occur, are flashes of insight rather than sustained reflections. In tragedy, as in "Home Burial," the father wastes no words over his grief, and approaches the loquacious only when his wife is about to leave him. The image Frost creates is that the deeper a rustic's suffering, the less necessary are words.

11. *The best fatigue occurs from energy spent doing chores:* After the exhaustion of apple-picking, the sleep and dreams you earn are rife with satisfactions and insights. There is much joy in any well-done chore. Frost celebrates the workman/farmer who takes pride in piling his wood, stone walls, or hay ricks with careful symmetries.

12. *To confront your deepest self does not require travel:* "I have it in me so much nearer home / To scare myself with my own desert places" ("Desert Places").

13. *A cozy, quiet, self-reliant self-assurance:* The life-road you take, since it is the one "least-travelled by," the most individualistic and independent, is the one that matters.

14. *Gentle humor, winsome ironies:* See "The Cow in Apple Time" and on conversing with hornets, "The White-Tailed Hornet."

15. *Nature's subtlest patterns, once seen, are paradigms of human behavior:* the white heal-all, the "snow-drop spider," the white moth "like a white piece of rigid satin cloth," form a visual *insectary* (as distinct from *bestiary*) of fate and design.

16. *The homemade parable:* The ostensibly wise hornet of "The White-Tailed Hornet" is as fallible as any presumptuously wise human who mistakes illusion for reality. The hornet mistakes a nailhead twice for a fly he hopes to feed on, then zooms towards and strikes "a little huckleberry/ the way a player curls around a football." He's missed again. The homily?

Won't this whole instinct matter bear revision?
Won't almost any theory bear revision?
To err is human, not to, animal.

17. *The boy is father to the man:* Pure Wordsworthian sentiments occasioning spates of boyhood recollections, a genre much admired and written by American male poets who see in lost boyhood implicit wisdoms they seek to recapture as adults. Frost's most influential poem here is probably "Birches."

18. *The seemingly effortless, cozy metrics, telling end rhymes, and general proud craftsmanship:* A good farmer wouldn't parade his complex skills at erecting fences, barns, outhouses, or sheep-cotes. Why should a poet close to the soil do otherwise? At times Frost's homespun qualities are almost laughable: see "A Blue Ribbon at Amesbury." At other times, he's playful, as he is in this couplet from "Departmental," in which a busy ant crosses over a dead moth:

But he no doubt reports to any
With whom he crosses antennae.

19. *Easy trappings conducive to imagined profundities:* Frost's perpetual references to darkness, night, stars, open spaces. See "Acquainted with the Night."

20. *Women and men:* See "Home Burial" and "West-running Brook." Women and men seem always in polarity, in conflict, sometimes with tragic consequences. The roles and psyches of the sexes are very dissimilar.

21. *Communion/communing ritual:* More formal poets would receive their communion wine from a wrought gold or silver chalice. Frost, however (in "Directive"), prefers drinking his from a broken piece of china found near a sunken well-hole where a house once stood, a piece he kept by him secreted "in the instep arch" of an "old cedar." His drink helps to get him "saved," in St. Mark's sense: "Here are your waters and your watering place. / Drink and be whole again beyond confusion."

22. *Scary nature:* When Frost is alone in the woods, occasional stirrings abroad chill him. In "Directive," for example, he speaks of the "serial ordeal" of "being watched from forty cellar holes / As if by eye pairs out of forty firkins." Such events are never life-threatening, as they would be if a grizzly were to lope through the hemlocks, or a wild man of the woods burst forth yelling, knife in hand.

A quick scrutiny of Wendell Berry's *Farming: A Hand Book* reveals these motifs: a hill pasture; birds singing at nightfall; wells and spring water; birds in "nest crotch"; beans lifting "their heads up in the row"; the good weariness of breaking up stones in a field; earth-loving: thrusting one's hand into the ground while seeding is an act that remains with one for life; and a man and a woman as Frostian contraries.

Few poets have Hayden Carruth's perspicacity on Robert Frost. Himself a poet who has mastered the Frostian mode—see the rural characters and histories filling the last half of his *Brothers, I Loved You All,* he sees Frost as

> a frightful burden
> on all younger Vermont poets, who have spent years
> fighting him off. . . .

He wonders whether he's been "too hard" on old Frost, who did, after all, fashion from "his own bad temper / and this forsaken and forsaking land, / a large part of our context." All poets living in Vermont must "come to terms" with Frost or find themselves "cut off completely." Frost's great virtue was his "curiosity." He "got around," knew Vermonters as well as their land. At his best, "he saw, he apprehended, he perceived"—"and by God that's / seven-eights of the battle and five-eights further / than most of us ever get"—"Vermont."

Thomas McGrath, a poet of far more complexity and variety than Berry, grew up on a North Dakota farm, and though in a sense kin to Frost, has a deeper and less comfortable sense of the harrowing aspects of life. His style is far more vigorous, pared, and intense. McGrath wastes little time with coy effects, which are the golden apples decoying Frost and poets writing like him. Here is a sampling from McGrath's motifs: hiking north, the "colorless silence, unraveled by the flies, / Stitched again by the locusts . . . / Swamp-smell, dead coulee water"; visions of "immaculate mutinous bodies" or "the brutal / Inhuman faces of angels, among tree leaves; barley leaf and clover"; small soft things: the cotton-tail, the wild dove "nesting among thorns"; butterflies and catbirds. Here is a sampling from McGrath's *Passages Toward The Dark:*

> So—full awake I rise from the fur of my sleep to the cold,
> And go to the front of the sled to stand at my father's back.
> On the seat beside him is the man we stopped to pick up
> When my dream broke in half . . .
> The chime and rhyme of the horseshoes ring on a roof of ice—
> We have come to the dark of the river trees, no farther.
>   The moon
> Etches their coarse lightning of shadow across the snow,
> Where a wooden cannon of cold explodes in the heart of an oak
> Its wintry thunder.
>   The river is frozen brink to bed
> Almost, and the fish will be rising and rafting up where the springs
> Open an icy window and the deer come down to drink
> Through the fox-lighted brush where the coyote sings . . .
>   faithful . . .
> —How faithful these confederates hold to their single lives!

Science Poems

Few poets write thoroughgoing science poems, despite Walt Whitman's pioneering use of the mode in *Leaves of Grass*. One can imagine how his reference to electrical conductors must have compounded conservative tastes already dismayed by his overt celebration of hirsute sexuality:

> Mine is no callous shell,
> I have instant conductors all over me whether I pass or stop,
> They seize every object and lead it harmlessly through me.
>
> I merely stir, press, feel with my fingers, and am happy,
> To touch my person to some one else's is about as much as I can stand.

Robinson Jeffers sees the issue clearly in "Science." He marvels at man, that "introverted" creature, who since the nineteenth century has "begot giants" through experimentation and study. His flaw? Man is a "maniac" fraught "with self-love and inward conflicts" so huge he is unable to manage his "hybrids." Comfortable with his dealings over "endless dreams," he breeds "knives on nature" and "turns them also inward," hastening his own destruction:

> A little knowledge, a pebble from the shingle,
> A drop from the oceans: who would have dreamed this infinitely little too
>   much?

While you will find occasional references to meteorology, bursting novas, DNA, Einstein's theory of relativity, formula cloning, and archeology in contemporary poems, rare indeed is the poet who focuses on such motifs. The rarity of such poems has fascinating implications, for it bespeaks a gulf between poetry and science. It also underscores the timorousness of poets who hesitate to use diction that a reader might not know, and reflects the paucity of the vocabularies of American poets. Three poets who do write science poems are Michael McClure, James Hejna, and Anselm Parlatore.

McClure's "Shiva Speaking" (*September Blackberries*) employs metaphors of extinct or dying animals to condemn our despoliation of the universe. We draw all life into "BLANK HOLES" of our creating, hastening thereby our own "Pleistocene" age. Shiva, McClure's mouthpiece, names some of the creatures who have suffered: sixty million buffalo, billions of passenger pigeons, giant ground sloths, the moa, the giant condor, the woolly rhinoceros, the Irish elk . . . all are "eaten" by time, "killed" because of man's death wish—the drive to pull all into BLANK HOLES "faintly scented" with musk:

> A mountain of wild mustangs turned to dogshit
> is studied by ghosts of eagles from the gables
> of forests turned to houses and disposable
> diapers. Invisible wolves changed to spaces.
> Empty cartridge clips and flint chips
> buried under concrete
> aggregate from ex-river bottoms.

"Gray Fox At Solstice" shows McClure's sense of creational time. Space (the galaxies), animal biology, maturation (squid embryos), diurnal progressions (the solstice), and detailed plant forms are among his themes.

Most of *September Blackberries* shimmers with McClure's passion for science. Not only does he read voraciously in these disciplines, he enjoys serious field trips with specialists, studying flora and fauna. A central sequence, "Xes—A Spontaneous Poem," incorporates many of these interests, ranging from the intergalactic to the minutely physical to the mystical. McClure's joy, contagious, results from his feeling thoroughly *mammal*, "UNTRAMMELED BY THE NAME OF *MAN*," intimate with rock, crystal, and entire mountains: a mountain is a "vibratory aura-statue / of WARM FLESH." He craves to be "free to know (BE) / a Quasar, cyclone, foot of forest floor, ring / of Saturn, flatworm, philosopher, free atoms / drawn to solid heavy space again." He is a "FEELING-BEING," drawing in all past memory, one who feels *ex-cessively*, as the title asserts.

James Merrill's "Syrinx," in *From The First Nine*, is a stunning turn on a mathematical formula: the square root of x over y to the nth power becomes an approach to a poet's aging, possible fatal illness. Merrill's Syrinx is a panpipe formed from reeds, an image of summer, of green and pagan sound. Who fixes his mouth to the Syrinx "draws out the scale of love and dread." The scale, simplistic, fails to "ramify"—to branch out, and fails, in contrast to foxglove, the years, clouds, hornets, and diseases, to proliferate by "metatastasis," [sic] still keeping root as "total" in the stream of life. Flower-children have probably forgotten the ancient formula for dealing with "the great god Pain"—a play on "the great god Pan." Yet, Syrinx and "you" (the "y" of the formula) persist, struggling with this painful aging, their tones sounding until "Pain" slides the flute back into its "scarred case," and sounds cease: the "silvery breath-tarnished tones" that hitherto riveted "bone and star in place" persist.

Anselm Parlatore has degrees in medicine and psychiatry, and was the editor of the Dartmouth literary magazine *Granite*, notorious because Governor Meldrim Thompson was offended by a poem published there and withdrew state support (a most modest amount, I might add). Parlatore's ongoing work, "The Mexox Poems," celebrates a huge, marshy wildlife refuge near his home.

Reading Parlatore is not easy—his poems depend on scientific language. His readers require a dictionary, and this fact (since most readers and editors are lazy) has kept him nearly invisible. A collection of his work is long overdue. In Parlatore's "Seduction at Mecox" the following words appear. While it is true that most of these terms would be known to the scientist, and are not at all exotic, I shall supply definitions for non-scientific readers:

radial perturbations: Variation in a designated orbit, as of an electron or planet, resulting from the influence of one or more external bodies.

laminated turbinates: A spiral form decreasing sharply in diameter from base to apex, as of sea shells, here made of thin covering sheets (laminae).

protoplasts: The living material of a cell, as distinguished from inert portions.

stomatal openings: Small apertures in the surface of a membrane.

biogenic carbonates: Salts or esters of carbonic acid from living organisms generating other organisms.

Here is the poem:

Radial perturbations in Uranus's rings
rakishly tilted magnetic fields
conglomerations of coalesced comets & dingy moons
a retinue of new moonlets braided
in strands, clumped in dense condensations

the shreds of darkness, winter's bare hieroglyphic
vines, shadows through the ilexes by the quay
an interlude of winter light

these moons' orbs sobbing, stars eating their seeds
her stockings lying crumpled on the floor
the breakers crashing on the empty point

the orb's rondure, the grand ensemble
unrecorded, ephemeral data at tide-line
the littered margin that beckons you

my laboratory notebook strewn on the floor
her hair gathered up & spread out, uniform gone
shadow of growth in the hollows under her arms
arms raised, her laminated turbinates
glisten like splicing precursors, dark globes
filamentous proteins in their nucleic envelopes

the hollow sobbing now in the ravines of Mecox
the viaducts & catacombs of memory
a ditch teeming in the furrowing night
a bog filled with her brocaded spirals
her bare footprint in the marsh mud
wanderings in the bog of stupidities

the moon's path upon the surface of the sea
guiding me upward to the light, Heaven
past the stomatal openings, protoplasts,
the vortex of swelling cells, the lure of deep water
& suction of her swirl, of the ion uptake.

It's the dance of the strands, the draperies
her DNA threads in their choreography
the bare nape of her neck, lowered eyelids, the epaulets
primordial latencies, the harmonic, glyphs.

Out beyond the seaward-facing escarpments
trawlers reaping halibut
the seaward flanks of Mecox
under the scarp crumbled underthrust
of the converging oceanic plate, woman of sand

her sandy debris apron spreads, green waves
the sediment full of ancient biogenic carbonates
tribal blood mixed since the Conquest, species, eggs

the long wail of grief from the veranda
calling to me, heraldic birds she releases
their song, her song, nexus to my lonely migration

solitude since she dropped all the charges.

The "woman"—Hertha, lover, and cosmic female power—has "dropped all the charges," a phrase with both serious and playful overtones. What has the poet done? Has he presumed to know too much? Or are the "dropped charges" depth-explosives, vast TNT metaphors for the uterine life of the Mecox, one of the most fertile spawning areas in the Western Hemisphere?

Another poem from the as yet unpublished series is "Mecox Paradox." Here is the poem followed by a gloss of unusual words:

Somnambulations culling the biota
sea foam & sluice her arm's hoax
swatches, leitmotifs of DNA
at ptyx the silence, her nails
phalanx of acqueous channels
in the fermenting marsh. Azure

giant arcs of luminous filaments
cosmic strings in the void, defects
of melancholy's fabric, the anchor
old & deep moves in the sand
the sea's archipelago a rotunda
for mutations' cannibalism

the helices spanning the membrane
the proteins criss-crossing in bewilderment
stochastic coiling, geoid anomalies
of forlorn bivalves & gastropods
their lonely biochemical strategies
our wild & vacant dreams

the arc's filaments, threads of the universe's
commotion, strings in coalescence, splitting
at the core of the spiral wave
an autumnal path, the detour shawled in mist
as she was, wafted to me
to us, from the crux, to death.

The words:

biota: The animal and plant life of a particular region.

ptyx: The original title of a sonnet by Mallarmé (written in 1868 but not published until 1887, and then titled "La Nuit" and republished later without any title). "Ptyx," for Mallarmé, writes Parlatore, was "about the making of a poem, the search for meaning, the creation of an 'island' of language." Jarry has his "Isle of Ptyx," which "prefigured Dada collages & randomness." For himself, Parlatore writes, "Ptyx was a deliverance from denotative meaning into possibility; through it one could enter a world of randomness & chance. Because it meant nothing it meant everything & became meaningful. Forms of discourse in a culture may be disjunctive but the culture matured & evolved anyway . . . Mallarmé located a disjunction & called it Ptyx . . . between Phoenix & Styx . . . resurrection and Hades." Parlatore concludes (in his letter to me of March 24, 1987): "In MECOX I like to use a lot of X ending words . . . And you are totally correct . . . it relates to the silence."

stochastic: Random.

geoid anomalies: Situations where the hypothetical surfaces of the earth do not coincide everywhere, as they ought, with mean sea level.

Parlatore has concocted yet another soup of Mecoxian life, centered on the image of a fertile creationist, the woman of the earlier poem. Her "nails" are evoked by sluices of water running from the sea through the marsh. She orchestrates germinal leitmotifs quietly, in her "fermenting marsh." Life as she fashions it spins forth from "luminous filaments, cosmic strings." To conjecture about these subtle, delicate, aesthetically pleasing forces dispels melancholy. While the sea as it meets the sand seems an old anchor, the dotted marsh islands of the sea are rife with "mutation's cannibalism." Here in these salt/fresh marshlands, as stanza three shows, newly born life evolves into more complex forms—bivalves and gastropods become primogenitally human, possessing the emotions of bewilderment, wildness, and loneliness.

In a Whitmanic close, Parlatore orchestrates his own music, receiving a sonata from the sea, a life-sonata rife with chords of death. Walt would have approved.

No poet employs the argot of science as devotedly as Parlatore. To make his work more accessible, he might consider assisting his readers by appending a glossary for the difficult words. The typeface could be unobtrusive, and would not have to interfere with first readings. But should he meet his readers on easier turf? Is the burden ours?

Lorine Niedecker (*Harpsichord & Salt Fish,*), in brief projective verse quatrains, employs spare language to evoke Charles Darwin's adventures and ideas. The diffidence of the great scientist, his fatigues and cravings for privacy, are all here, as he emits almost journal-like observations on the species and recalls his investigatory travels, craving for home:

'Dear Susan . . .
    I am ravenous
        for the sound
of the pianoforte'
                (this was written from the Andes)

When Niedecker writes of the Galapagos Islands she suggests the bizarre life Darwin found there:

A thousand turtle monsters
    drive together to the water
        Blood-fright crabs hunt ticks
  on lizards' backs

Flightless cormorants
    Cold-sea creatures—
        penguins, seals
  here in tropical waters

Hell for Fitzroy
    but for Darwin Paradise Puzzle
        with the jig-saw gists
  beginning to fit

At home, the tedium of writing sickens Darwin: "I am ill, he said / and books are slow work." He recalls his amazement at discovering the drosera, a plant that traps insects, secreting "an acid acutely akin / to the digestive fluid / of an animal." His conclusions? Man is "in the same predicament / with other animals"; the universe was "designed by laws," not "built by brute force." Let each man, Darwin wrote, "believe / what he can."

James Hejna manages to incorporate the vocabulary of science so easily that the flow of his poems is unimpeded, and in fact enriched. "In Memory of Jeffrey Lee Gaylord," hitherto unpublished, is an ambitious disquisition on the nature of evolution and the mind of a vibrant fellow scientist who died of cancer;

All collected, from a column of powdered bone:
fractions—eluted leaves, an orchard picnic, soft brown
apples deep in coarse grass, leaves floating on wine,
surface of Lethe. A man resting lightly, prone
on a blanket patterned with nautical designs—
sextants, sailing ships, gulls, and knotted lines—
follows a fruitfly's evasive course with a frown.

Instinct, merely? originality? Its wings
realize the notion of escape; the air
spilling by his flat hand lofts the swerving fly
upward, and it follows its imaginings
out a way, veering and diving, eventually
circling back to sample a wine-soaked gull. Memory:
both instinct and learning identical, the structure

of nerve endings, the patterns of synaptic recall,
subtle currents guiding a fly to a pleasing smell,
programs which instruct a bee to dance or a man
to couple a *tour jeté* with a memorable *cabriole*—
growth factors; plasticity; a change in certain
membrane potentials with a concomitant, sudden
emergence of a new spot on an O'Farrell gel,

a protein modified in relation to a thought's usage
and maintenance. How might aging, or grief, induce
a cellular change which would bring a gardener to let
cosmos overgrow a path, blocking his passage
out a back gate to an orchard? Deciduous
capitulation: cold, sunny weather; detritus
settling under fruit trees; there, too, a dark blanket,

region of heat, laden with hand-sized winesaps,
bread, dormant on its paper bag, salami, knife,
knapsack, white jacket associated with a man
pondering the intelligence of flies. Does a lapse
in third instar knowledge which occurs during pupation
coincide with a rearrangement, or acquisition,
of neural traces? One might purify a life,

thus, by unlearning, as in sleep, irrelevant dates,
streetnames, hats, integrals, in order to stare
intently at a room preserved as the mind found
it to be: a lab, a sandy-haired man hunched over agar plates,
counting plaques. In his research he observed a profound
asymmetry in the recombination of phages—just before his unsound
body, set upon by toxins intended to deter

fast-growing cells, such as a malignant tumor,
weakened him . . . A student of his returned at Christmastime,
as if the shock were saved all fall for her, and cried,
and cried. How much does the mind control? To remember
him, is there a self-fulfilling joy that comes allied
with the joining of his face to his voice, itensified
by repetition—his vexed look, like a rhyme

with his expression, "Are you absolutely serious?"
The man mapping crumbs on a picnic blanket recalls
a final game of tennis: his partner's muscular
right arm hit well-placed shots; the other, superfluous,
carried along like an arm in a sling, his irregular
left side steadfastly overlooked as though a cellular
accident in development altered the protocols

for nerve function, and he forgave the mistake. Why,
though, can't a man teach his arm to move? Where
would he start? With the uncoiling of heterochromatin?
A change in histones? How could one identify
a tissue-specific set of genes, or a surface antigen?
How do the various cells link tears with a loving grin
and an appealing shrug as one tells one's wife she must prepare

for one's death? In the remaining time she recognized
the spreading completions transpiring in his mind, the process
of the self revealing itself in hindsight—one concludes
a happy marriage with a wedding party stabilized
in a forest clearing by the imprinting of the senses: multitudes,
it seems, circling, settling into attitudes
compatible with champagne and cake enjoyed to excess;

wool blankets; the smell of a roasted lamb blending
with pink smoke; laughter and music; summer air;
children running through weeds, flapping their arms like birds
flitting between blankets moored to the ground; the extended
reception lasting into evening; the murmured words
of the new couple softening, as a man drifting into an orchard's
darkening current recedes, as if to vanish there.

Seance Poems

The term "seance poetry" was invented by Michael McClure. In a special subgroup are James Merrill's renowned Ouija board poems, contained in *The Changing Light at Sandover*. Assisted by Donald Jackson, Merrill "receives" elaborate conversations from W. H. Auden and others who bring news of Gertrude Stein, Chester Kallman, et. al., and their cavortings through Heaven.

Self-Pity Poems

The self-pity, or sensitive plant, poem requires no definition. The degree of self-pity may vary, from blubbering hopelessness to a soporific, passive acedia. Such poems either present the poet's personal misery and distress, or those of some character presented in a portrait or monologue. Poets may take their cue from various passages in Shelley's poems, particularly lines from "Ode to the West Wind," which when taken out of context, appear far more self-pitying and miserable than they really are:

> Oh, lift me as a wave, a leaf, a cloud!
> I fall upon the thorns of life! I bleed!
>
> A heavy weight of hours has chained and bowed
> One too like thee: tameless, and swift, and proud.

Paul Goodman wrote many self-pity poems. One of the best is "Long Lines," in which he finds himself blocked in the Alps in winter, and blames his own "bad choices" for it. He invites us to read the falling snow, ice, and glacier as a sign of his own self-pitying life:

> Yes, I know
> I cannot move these mountains, but how did I stray
> by cunningly bad choices up among these snows?
> Are most of men as miserable but only some
> enough communicative to declare how much?
> Balked! balked! the dreary snowflakes do not cease
> drifting past my window in the demi-dark.

Delmore Schwartz, no stranger to paranoia, falls asleep and pretends Baudelaire (or someone like Baudelaire) is talking to him, a voice, he says, that has "no relation" to his "affairs." Yet, his plaint is too magical and intense not to be autobiographical:

I am sick of this life of furnished rooms.
I am sick of having colds and headaches:
You know my strange life. Every day brings
Its quota of wrath.

The laurel for self-pity poems written by a living poet goes to Charles Wright. In *The Iowa Review*, in a New Year's Eve poem, he wallows in the solipsism we have come to expect from him:

Will Charles look on happiness in this life?
Will the past be the present ever again?
Will the dead abandon their burdens and walk to the river bank?

He saves himself by identifying with some hermit crabs on the beach, brainy little crustaceans all:

What matters to them is what comes up from below,
    and from out here
In the deep water,
    and where the deep water comes from.

A gathering of nouns and adverbs from "Lonesome Pine Special" reveals the claustrophobic and depressing narcissism of many of Wright's poems: *windowless, doorless, desolation, cold, isolate misery, loneliness, emptiness, shivering,* and *downhill.* Still middle-aged, Wright seems to have given up, observing: "There is so little to say, and so much time to say it in." Memory itself (the matter of this lengthy poem, made up as it is of various Southern locales from Wright's younger days) brings us to our knees, begging for something better as he invokes those last days and those "bitter edges of things" that slide away as "tissue and memory." Wright would like most of all to be in Henderson County, North Carolina, on an old wagon trail meandering through blackberry and raspberry brambles and poison ivy, a trail so disused that trees now grow between the old ruts. The trail is a perfect image for his wearying, facile solipsism. The poem ends, as Wright slips along the "downhill" trail toward an effortless death and reflects an opiate numbness similar to that Keats expressed in the "Ode to a Nightingale": "Now more than ever seems it rich to die, / To cease upon the midnight with no pain." Keats's vision was induced by tuberculosis. Wright's stance (it's hardly a vision) merely arises from genteel self-pity.
    Certainly, since all poets are sensitive (why else would they be poets?), one could easily create an entire anthology of sensitized passages of pain. The trick is to find those that transcend the snivel. As a gesture of good will toward poets anxious to write sensitive plant poems, I reproduce poem 32 from Whitman's "Song of Myself":

I think I could turn and live with animals, they are so placid and self-
    contain'd,
I stand and look at them long.

They do not sweat and whine about their condition,
They do not lie awake in the dark and weep for their sins,
They do not make me sick discussing their duty to God,
Not one is dissatisfied, not one is demented with the mania of owning
    things,
Not one kneels to another, nor to his kind that lived thousands of years
    ago,
Not one is respectable or unhappy over the whole earth . . .

I would require all poets who write more than half a dozen self-pity poems each year to read one of the truly archetypal pity poems in English, and read it at least twice a week, aloud and slowly. "Elegy, Written With His Own Hand in the Tower Before His Execution" was composed in 1586 by Chidiock Tichborne, eighteen years old, on the night before his execution in the Tower of London. He'd been found guilty of taking part in a Roman Catholic plot against Queen Elizabeth I, and was hanged, drawn, and quartered:

My prime of youth is but a frost of cares,
    My feast of joy is but a dish of pain,
My crop of corn is but a field of tares,
    And all my good is but vain hope of gain:
The day is past, and yet I saw no sun,
And now I live, and now my life is done.

My tale was heard, and yet it was not told,
    My fruit is fall'n, and yet my leaves are green,
My youth is spent, and yet I am not old,
    I saw the world, and yet I was not seen:
My thread is cut, and yet it is not spun,
And now I live, and now my life is done.

I sought my death, and found it in my womb,
    I looked for life, and saw it was a shade,
I trod the earth, and knew it was my tomb,
    And now I die, and now I was but made:
My glass is full, and now my glass is run,
And now I live, and now my life is done.

Semantic Hang-Up Poems

These poems are written by Language Poets who waltz with words, switching them swiftly from one partner to the next, hoping that at every switch some new meaning will scintillate forth. In "The Rothko Chapel Poem" John Taggart slips easily along, improvising on the idea of a doorless doorway, which assumes a hint of the mystical since it is "almost the last doorway." Hold on. Here comes the first red-slipper, semantic twirl: "one at a time" go inside. "I am the one the I me one." Narcissism does a square dance, assisted by a hapless predicate nominative. Taggart makes sure we know he's gavotting with language: "a sentence is a choice." What he's going to choose we don't know, although he does hint at a straightforward theme—he is "the child of pain," a "primitive I" who is "inside / inside the turbulence / almost the last time / inside the black rooms." We assume that he is within the doorless room. (Note the little two-step Taggart does with "inside.") "Inside there are black rooms." "Almost the last time" reverberates, going all the way back to the second line "almost the last doorway."

In the same issue of *Temblor*, Charles Bernstein in "Surface Reflectance," a title fraught with semantic sleight of hand, has a joyous romp over many pages, many puns, and many ideas, some of which are these: "An irrepressible torque / meets an unsaturable torpor"; "early warning sighs"; "afraid of meaning, afraid / of the words, / which are its body"; "poetics makes stained bedfellows;" "the hermeneutic ovoid crashes in/ on the Pesto Principle; or, he's hooked up / with a poststructuralist woman who's changed / his pew"; "emergence of mush." Enough said.

Sleeping Spouse or Lover Poems

Poets predictably write sleeping spouse poems when they are in marital difficulties. They either remain in bed beside their partner, or they stand or sit elsewhere in the room thinking hateful or, less frequently, loving thoughts. One of the best-known poems of this type is Robert Creeley's "The Whip." Creeley spends the night "turning in bed" while his "love" sleeps beside him as easily as a feather, "a flat / sleeping thing," white and quiet. The apparent cause of his restlessness is a fantasy woman on the roof, one he also loves. She's inaccessible, and he's lonely. He gives a yell, which wakens his wife, who emits an unromantic "ugh" and places her hand on his back. She represents reality, it seems, the women he actually *has*. He is grateful for her presence and feels apologetic for having lusted elsewhere: "for which act," he concludes, "I think to say this / wrongly."

In "Sing Song," a wife escapes a marriage by sleeping all the time. She's "married to sleep," Creeley says. In a lovely play on words, reminiscent of e. e. cummings, we see that nothing keeps this woman awake once she insists on sleeping:

yet
[she] never cannot go to sleep if there is
good reason not to go to sleep.

She "sleeps to sleep" and "has no other purpose in mind."

Robert Hass, ("In Weather") regards his wife beside him. He's depressed after hearing a friend read poems of rage against women. Hass understands "why men cut women up." The

> heavy cock wields,
> rises, spits seed
> at random and the man
> shrieks, homeless
> and perfect in the empty dark.

Hass now almost hates his wife's genitals:

> the sweet place where I rooted,
> to imagine the satisfied disgust
> of cutting her apart,
> bloody and exultant
> in the bad lighting and scratchy track
> of butcher shops
> in short experimental films.

The "cunt" is a "spider," a "raw devourer." But when Hass hears owls at their mating calls, "ecstatic / in the winter trees," his wife stirs, overcoming him with loving joy.

William Logan has written a sleeping spouse poem, "Deborah Sleeping." While making a ferry-crossing during a downpour, Deborah sleeps in a plastic chair. "Pre-Raphaelite curls" wreathe her head, and are "immune to rain," Logan says, "unlike the satin shirt I made you wear / in Paris, that did not outlast the storm." She was not pleased, and as she huddled for warmth, "whispered phrasebook curses" in his ear. He meditates on sleep, "our disease, the heart's adagio," ready to conclude that sleep provides "the only ease bodies so close can know." As he watches her though, drugged with Dramamine, sleeping in "hard daylight," he feels some "distant fear," as the boat lands in fog.

That affectionate laureate of earthy women, Charles Bukowski, enjoys a sardonic moment as he considers a "lump" sleeping beside him. He senses "the great empty mountain / of her head." Yes, she's alive, yawns, scratches her nose, and pulls up the covers. Shortly, they'll kiss and say goodnight, and in his dreams, off in Scotland, gophers will run under the ground. He hears "engines in the night" while a "white / hand whirls" through the sky: "good night, dear, goodnight."

"Sleeping Woman," from *The Days Run away Like Wild Horses Over The Hills,* turns on essentially the same theme as Creeley's "The Whip." Bukowski sits up listening to his woman snore. He gazes at her back,

> sick white and stained with
> children's freckles
> as the lamp divests the unsolvable / sorrow of the world . . .

He guesses that her feet, which he cannot see, are "charming." To whom does she belong? Is she "real?" Since we are each "selected to be / something, the spider, the cook, the elephant," she can't help being a woman. He imagines himself and her and each of us as paintings on a gallery wall. At that point she turns over:

—and now the painting turns
upon its back, and over a curving elbow
I can see ½ a mouth, one eye and
almost a nose.
the rest of you is hidden
out of sight
but I know that you are a
contemporary, a modern living
work
perhaps not immortal
but we have
loved.

please continue to
snore.

Michael Sheridan, in "Shooting the Loop" uses the occasion of lying beside his wife to meditate on various thoughts about life and death occasioned by the noise of boys in souped-up cars in the street, boys who toss their beer cans "till the sun comes out, / Then spit on the sidewalks and idle." He walks through their "echoes" and examines "their skid marks." He teaches them at school and lives in their neighborhood. His aging seems to induce thoughts of graves being dug, clinking shovels, a casket falling into crematorium fires ("the combustion of evening"), and his soundly sleeping wife. An odd juxtaposition, to be sure.

Brad Leithauser's "The Ghost of a Ghost" trivializes the experience. His chatter is commonplace, and he has one of the deadest ears for cadence I've encountered in a long time. Leithauser is not writing about himself, but about a character who died in an accident and returns as a breath of wind to frighten his family. His life is far more challenging now that he's a ghost. He was a simple husband and father who liked playing catch with his sons, teasing his daughter ("Princess Pea"), and watching television curled up on the floor. Best of all was the "delight" he had waking at one or two A.M. to find his wife "huffing" (soft, not quite a snore) next to him, "a comforting sound." Sure they had their problems. Things got out of hand, and once she threw a juice glass at him. Yet, "love ran / through every word we spoke." Sentimental, sentimental. The conclusion? Our ghost describes his current life as "a shadow of his former self." Early in his ghost days, he longed to taste the life he'd left, "the downy scrape of a peach skin, the smell of the sea, / the pull of something resinous." But grown "other-wise," he now drifts and drowses towards "a clarity / of broadened linkages," in "a state wholly too gratified / and patient to be called eagerness / that I submit to a course which homes / outward, and misses nothing at all."

The ninth and concluding section of Joel Oppenheimer's "A Long Testament" (*Just Friends/Friends and Lovers*) has a voyeuristic, urban flair. The poet and his sleeping wife, lying in bed, are visible through their window to boys in a typing class at a neighboring school. Oppenheimer reminds himself to hang a shade or cover the window with bamboo, sure that they'll be seen,

> your
> body naked next to mine
> it being warm, her cover
> had been cast aside, partially
> revealing

He conjectures as to what the boys in the typing class will do: tell their priest? tell their Irish cop fathers who will rush in to arrest them?

> and they
> will destroy this bed like
> the maypole at merrymount,
> and for much the same evil.

The lads will tell neither priest nor father, only other boys who will be caught "beating it," letting "the cat out of the bag."

David St. John devotes the concluding section of "The Orange Piano" to the image of a sleeping woman:

> Her arms hooped perfectly above her head
> As if she were a girl at her morning class
> About to go on pointe before

> The mirror. . . .

Orange is the color of the "eccentric" soul rather than the ordinary soul. The old Bechstein St. John once played in a spa hotel recurs, intertwined with memories of his father inspiring him to pursue classical music. Nature motifs: sparrows and a silver birch. The father appears in heaven, playing concerts for "God the father." And his wife, lying in graceful sleep, induces yet another memory, of stroking her shoulders and seeing her as orange and unworldly.

Edward Hirsch, "Sleepwatch," from *Wild Gratitude,* coyly yawns toward an out-of-body experience, as he lies beside his sleeping wife "in the middle of the middle of the night." He's a sort of Emperor Jones who hears "dull" tom-toms thudding in his chest and "keening" voices off in the dark, giving him insomnia. Throughout, Hirsch uses the tacky device of addressing "you," a tattered domino for poets hoping to decoy the reader into thinking they aren't talking about themselves.

He imagines his wife's dreams. Whatever originality resides in the passage disappears with the "white egg" image—if it's a fertilized ovum it's up too high in her body. If it's a breast, it wouldn't be growing, would it? And how do you explain the "skin of water" somehow "pulled over her watery lungs?"

Next comes a flashback to Hirsch's walk on a cold, snowy beach the night before. As he walks, Hirsch's legs are there with him while his hands are home "fastened" to his "wife's body." Sort that one out, reader.

The wind-up, alas, is unfelt; in the bedroom all of his bones "make music" (as in this poem?) and, in an unexciting reference to a pallid moment in stanza one, "in the middle / of the middle of the night" he listens to his heart's "steady drumroll," so "ghostly" with his "losses," his "tribal chant."

Turn about is fair play; for, yes, women also write poems about sleeping spouses. Heather McHugh, in "Against a Dark Field," in *Dangers*, hates the male beside her. Her head is "light with hate," which "rides its particulars, styled / after fireflies, after envy." Hating his "heavy-handed body" next to hers, she withdraws, turning, under the covers, into "pure fuel"; "you blacken with sleep. I green with burn." Judith Minty, in "Prowling the Ridge," feels excluded from her husband's dreams. His legs are "running / from or after some / thing." He's prowling moon-drenched ridges with the pack. As a wolf, he rests his paws on the wild fur of his victims, baring his teeth to "raw meat." Minty, excluded, is fraught with an urge to "tame" the husband by brushing her hand over his body. Perceptively and honestly, she realizes she truly envies his dream—"Wolf, leave tracks now. Quick. / Let me follow your scent."

Sharon Doubiago writes poems while her man sleeps. In "Letter to Luke Breit in Point Arena" (*Hard Country*, 1982), she spends an entire night composing—a pioneering act. A woman is caught in the "middle of this doomed and damned continent," in a world of "sullen men." Anxious for self-identity, swollen with much to say, she feels unable to say it:

> I've always felt
> as Billy Budd, my life at stake on words
> that won't come, mute before the obvious.

All through the fruitless night she works, using pen rather than typewriter so as not to disturb her husband and the kids. Her ambition is enormous; she tries to pull into herself

> . . . like sperm to the egg:
> the American soul, hard, isolate, stoic, and as Lawrence said:
> a killer.

In "Insomnia: Somewhere the Four Corners of the Sioux," Doubiago proudly displays her vulnerability as she lies with her sleeping man on the floor of a small stucco house. She is greatly distressed; he plans to leave her the following day. She travels west searching for her "blazing man," and on her journey seeks surcease by imagining that they are again in bed. She is now the Amazon, a legendary female warrior, a necessary posture for a woman to assume in a world of hostile males who see themselves as larger than life, certainly always larger than woman. She is the mythic huntress, an American Diana,

> the mythic California woman
> who removes her breast
> to more precisely
> aim the bow.

Small Creature Poems

Poems on small creatures have a blessed and hoary tradition, and the best I can do here is to suggest some of the possibilities. I think of Chaucer's Chanticleer and Pertolete, the anonymous Middle English "Cuckoo Song", the folk ballad "The Three Ravens," Shakespeare's song "Where the Bee Sucks, There Suck I," John Donne's "The Flea," Richard Lovelace's "The Grasshopper," John Clare's "Badger" and "Mouse's Nest," Christopher Smart's "Jubilate Agno" (My Cat Jeoffry), Robert Burns' "To A Mouse," Percy Shelley's "To A Sky-Lark," John Keats' "Ode to a Nightingale," Emily Dickinson's "I heard a Fly Buzz—When I Died," Thomas Hardy's "The Darkling Thrush," Gerald Manley Hopkins' "The Windhover," and W. B. Yeats's "Long-Legged Fly."

Nearer our own time are Wallace Stevens' "Thirteen Ways of Looking at a Blackbird," Richard Eberhart's "The Groundhog," James Dickey's "The Owl King", Robert Lowell's "Skunk Hour," Denise Levertov's "To the Snake," Theodore Roethke's "The Bat" and "The Meadow Mouse," May Swenson's "The Secret in the Cat," Galway Kinnell's "The Porcupine," and Robert Duncan's, "An Owl Is an Only Bird of Poetry" and "My Mother Would Be A Falconress."

With so impressive an array of models, it is not surprising that the genre remains in exuberant health. The sampling I give below is merely that—the reader will want to add his or her favorites to the list.

Kenneth Rosen's "The White Egret" displays its beautiful bird in lines written in a pallid telegram style. Rosen asks us to imagine the bird's "bitter lips" as it whunks into the lake to catch "a little fish." Do egrets have lips? The beak is so potent that it hyperbolically "breaks the lake / into a glitter." As the bird flies away to some pines, its escalation seems assisted, according to Rosen, by "a breast of air." He concludes with a childish apostrophe to both bird and fish, predator and victim: "O little white bird, / little fish," and informs these creatures that "in every beginning" there's a "sliver of silver" (the minnow) and "a death and a hunger" (the minnow and the egret). How the minnow is to see his death as a beginning baffles me. Perhaps as the egret's gastric juices dissolve the creature, the fish will begin a new life as scraps of DNA in the bird's gizzard.

Robert Lowell loosed numerous small creatures, almost as if they were images for living forms busy gnawing away inside the poet's brain, excavating, moving capillaries of madness to the fore. In "Waking Early Sunday Morning," a searing masterpiece on the disappearance of joy and the advent of madness, this segment appears:

> listen, the creatures of the night
> obsessive, casual, sure of foot,
> go on grinding, while the sun's
> daily remorseful blackout dawns.

In "Running the River Lines," David Baker recalls as a boy using a crawdad for bait, and catching a loon instead of a catfish. There's a lean excitement in Baker's lines:

> It shrieks and splashes as we draw close,
> straining against the willow pole
>
> until it finally rips itself loose, beats its way
> low over the water,
> lifting at last, disappearing
> into the depth of the river evening,
>
> its cry still strung between us like a fine line.

Lucien Stryk, influenced by Oriental art and poetry, masterfully scatters numerous creatures throughout his *Collected Poems*. "Bream" is one of the best. Here Stryk observes a "big-eyed" fish swimming in a florist's window tank, between dahlias, chrysanthemums, hydrangea leaves, and tulips. He empathizes with the lovely creature—"Keep talking to your self," he advises. Since it does not know what transpires after death, the fish enjoys a tranquillity humans lack. Stryk concludes with this oriental-seeming sketch:

> Brushed by trumpet lilies, roses
> The dream opens / shuts his mouth

There are other poems on a crow, a cormorant, a squirrel, a jackal, a rat, a sparrow, a goose, a duck, and a snail.

Sydney Lea's "Coon Hunt, Sixth Month (1955)" makes a potent, understated social comment. Lea, his two brothers, and three young blacks set out to hunt raccoons in Georgia. They can't use their dogs, for the cottonmouths and rattlers are out. When black Purdy sees a coon, he laughs because the whites are so blind, and shoots it. Nights later, on another hunt, hearing hounds bawling and seeing a police cruiser approach with its spotlight trained on them, they are amazed when a "fat cop" pulls a gun and bellows: " 'What / the fuck you niggers doin' here?' " When he sees the three brothers, "as pale as possum kits," he realizes his mistake. One brother speaks up saying they were "just out hunting coons." " 'Hot damn,' " laughs the cop, " 'So are we.' "

Galway Kinnell's "Duck-Chasing" is a fantasy, almost childlike, of pursuing an agile duck through a sea, imitating all of its paddlings and divings. When the speaker reaches the bird, "from the side, like a dead-man," and yells, the bird flies off, skimming the sea, soaring into the sun-drenched sky:

Brown wings burning and flashing
In the sun as the sea it rose over
Burned and flashed underneath it.

Maxine Kumin is one of our finest writers of small creature poems. In "The Hermit Has a Visitor," a mosquito bites a man:

And then she sings. She raises the juice.
She is a needle, he the cloth.
She is an A string, he the rosewood.
She is the thin whine at concert pitch.

Another poem, "Creatures," displays Kumin's careful scrutiny of nature's smallest forms. A pond is alive: there's a diving beetle "split / flat on the underside like a peachpit"; dragonflies are "frail biplanes" touching "head to tail"; water measurers "on jury-rigged" legs and whirligigs dent the pond surface, the latter insects spinning "clock-wise and counter . . . locked / in circus circles and backswimmers all / trim as college racing shells / now trailing their four eyes upside down." There are mayflies seeking sites beneath stones for squirting their eggs "in rows as straight as corn" before they clamber out to die. The pond's quiet is "nippled as if / by rain," "pocked with life."

Kumin's "Woodchucks" takes an unexpected turn toward violence. To protect her farm, she must gas the pests. She tries the humane way: instant death via knockout bombs. Failure. The next morning they appear to be no worse off than we are after inhaling cigarette smoke and drinking "state-store Scotch." Meanwhile, the animals fell her marigolds and start on her vegetables, "beheading the carrots" and "nipping the broccoli shoots." She decides to use a .22-caliber rifle, seeing herself as "a lapsed pacifist fallen from grace / puffed with Darwinian pieties for killing." She kills one animal, which falls among some everbearing roses. She next drops the mother, who dies with her "needle teeth / still hooked in a leaf of early Swiss chard." Eventually, one "old wily fellow" remains. He eludes her, obsessing even her dreams, in which she finds herself sighting along the gun barrel. Kumin closes with a wish: "If only they'd all consented to die unseen / gassed underground the quiet Nazi way."

Elizabeth Bishop's "Florida" is a fine companion to her more famous poem "The Fish." Despite a Disney-like observation of herons taking flight (their screams rushing "up the scale / every time in a tantrum"), the poem succeeds, with its groups of "helpless and mild" turtles dying on the beaches, leaving behind their barnacled shells and "their large white skulls with round eye-sockets / twice the size of a man's"; the names of sea shells (Job's Tear, Chinese Alphabet, the rare Junonia, pectins, and Ladies' Ears); thirty buzzards; wood-fire smoke filtering "fine blue solvents"; mosquitoes "hunting to the tune of their ferocious obbligatos"; fireflies; the "coarse-meshed" moonlight; and, finally, the alligator with his five calls—"friendliness, love, mating, war, and a warning."

Carolyn Kizer's "The Worms" in *(Midnight Was My Cry)* borrows from Christopher Smart, the eighteenth-century poet and denizen of madhouses. Smart wrote: "Let Dodo rejoice with the purple worm in the rain. . . ." This passage becomes the epigraph for Kizer's meditation on childhood. Kizer's child is keenly sensitive to life, and after it rains tries not "to wound" a single worm. To perpetrate "any kind of death," even for an elementary form of life, is to "maim the self." Childhood is a time for carefully stepping over cracks:

> Move among the worms,
> Pearly and purple,
> Curling and opal,
> Tickled by the sidewalk,
> Heaped over the lines
> Of childhood's first map. . . .

Life's small forms, hop-toads, lobelia, worms, the "recently born," overwhelm us as children. Maturing, we move "close to the ground" with "eyes in our toes." Kizer's final lines are cryptic: "When the torrents end, / God gloats at the world." One meaning is that her rain of worms and our caring movements among them remind us of both origins and earth-connections. When the torrents cease, we lose such wisdom, and God, not the kindest of spirits, gloats.

Jane Shore dedicates her brilliantly orchestrated "A Luna Moth" to Elizabeth Bishop. For nearly a week this "prize specimen" of a creature pins herself to a sliding screen door. When a gust of wind blows her off, she affixes herself again. When the rain ends, she returns: "to meditate and sun herself." As Shore observes her closely, this is what she sees:

> A kimono just wider than my hand,
> her two pairs of flattened wings were pale
> gray-green panels of the sheerest crepe de Chine.
> Embroidered on each sleeve, a drowsing eye
> appeared to watch the pair of eyes
> on the wings below quite wide awake.
> But they're *all* fake.
> Nature's trompe l'oeil give the luna
> eyes of a creature twice her size.

Her pride ("she ruled the grid of her domain") suggests something of an artist's pride—self-assured, removed from the "dull-witted cousins" surrounding her, those "homely" brown moths "madly fanning their paper wings" or "bashing their brains out on the bulb." When, finally, Shore draws the glass door shut, she provides the luna with an image of itself, "hatched from an illusion—like something out of Grimm," her "long-lost twin." Then, a sunbathing "weekend guest" thinks the wind has blown a five dollar bill against the screen, so grabs the moth, gasps, and throws her to the ground. Shore's gentle and intense experience with this special creature ends as the moth disappears

Similar qualities mark Hayden Carruth's "August First" (*Brothers, I Love You All*) in which a closely observed moth batters a screen on a hot, completely dark summer night, triggering the poet's memory of his marriage and a poem he wrote then. His wife is dead, but what remains is an old, huge geranium—the moth "wavering desperately / up the screen, beating, insane, / behind the geranium." The plant resembles a small tree and holds up ten clusters of blossoms, of a color so special Carruth can't name it exactly: "Isn't there a color / called 'geranium'?" The plant dates back to the writing of his poem, shortly after his marriage, when he bought it as a seedling for nineteen cents in a supermarket. Now, "so thick, leathery-stemmed, / and bountiful with blossom" it secures the hot, dark night—the moth now rests, clinging, as the nearby brook "talks."

Stephen Dobyns strikes a fresh, original variation on the motif. His cat is no fluffy darling, but rather the agent for a small girl's innate cruelty. In "Getting Up" his wise child fools a yellow-eyed cat by extending a paper bird towards it where it reclines in its cat basket. The girl, naked, lies on her bed, holding the bird, wanting to know "what it's like to kill." Morning sounds. Coffee smells. Shortly she will leave for school, having finished her report on Argentina. At school, she'll be like all her friends, dressed similarly, all proceeding "through the civilized / unwinding of their day." Now, though, the interlude with her cat teaches her of the urge to kill, humiliation, and "the manipulation of power." With her lips set in a half-smile, as the feline leaps, the girl wins.

Yusef Komunyakaa's "Charmed," from *Copacetic,* turns a contretemps between a cat and a bird into a stunning of the necessity for violence, rendered in human terms. Once Fate proceeds, Komunyakaa subtly shows, it can't be deflected. The poet intervenes just as a cat is about to pounce on a bird. The cat's protest—the creature behaves as though Komunyakaa "had struck her with a stick"—is short-lived, and it proceeds once more to its quarry, which sits "perfectly lost / like a flower" waiting. The incident triggers a memory: once Komunyakaa interceded in a vicious fight between a woman and a man. Both turned against him. And now, with the bird waiting for death, and the cat intent, Komunyakaa again intervenes. He tries unsuccessfully to "shoo" the bird, then takes the creature up and feels its "small heart" fluttering. He realizes the bird won't sing, shuts his own eyes, places the bird on the ground, and walks away.

Snapshot Poems

T he snapshot poem may be inspired by an actual photograph or it may reflect a poet's attempt to create the illusion that his reader is leafing through an album, reading his poems almost as fast as if he were examining old pictures.

Faye Kicknosway's *Who Shall Know Them: Poems* is a "reading" of a famous Walker Evans photograph taken during the Depression, "Bud Fields and His Family." The stark arrangement (the wretched farmer, wife, two children, and mother-in-law, seated on a flaking metal frame bed, rickety chair, on a bare wooden floor) stares out from the brown book jacket with the force of a disreputable secret we wish would bury itself. Each figure, from the father stripped to the waist in the heat, the small son wearing only a striped shirt with his boyish genitals exposed, the older daughter with scruffed knees, soiled dress and haunting expression, the shoeless mother in her sagging dress with the hemline of her slip visible holding a sleeping little boy on her lap, the brutalized mother-in-law in her heavy workshoes, all gaze at us as though we are their photographer posing them for a picture that changes as we get set to snap it. There is no hatred in their eyes, rather a stunned wonder that they should be singled out for attention.

Kicknosway is far too fine a poet to produce a mere set of "readings" based on the photograph. Her "voice," or point of view, is that of a sharecropper daughter some forty or more years later, who considers that remote impoverished life, and relives many of her still intense frustrations. Kicknosway gives the lie to romantic notions of farm life—how sweet it was with the wimmin sittin' about makin' quilts with the menfolk fiddlin' and singin' spirituals and the good ole songs.

Another sequence of poems based on photographs is Richard Howard's "Homage to Nadar (II)" *(Lining Up)*. Opposite reproductions of the nineteenth-century French photographer's portraits of Delacroix, Millet, Corot, Verdi, Meyerbeer, Berlioz, Michelet, De Nerval, and France are poems in Howard's voice addressing each of the sitters from a modern perspective, with attention to their "readings" by Nadar.

Readers may also wish to turn to John Logan's much-praised "Three Poems on Aaron Siskind's Photographs," in *The Anonymous Lover*. All three are meditations on the visual properties of classical figures much brutalized by time. One particularly moving poem is on the torsos of a father and son: the son's entire upper body is missing, the father's arms are missing; both have been pocked and shattered.

Dave Smith also writes snapshot poems. In fact, they are among his best poems. In "The Perspective and Limits of Snapshots," he critiques a "crosswater shot" by one Aubrey Bodine, a scene of oyster scows on a channel of the James River in Virginia:

> Clearly, Bodine is not
> Matthew Brady catching the trenchant gropes frozen
> at Fredericksburg with a small black box.

Bodine has excluded much—the Mennonite church, yachts, the pool at the country club. The snapshot freezes life. Bodine does not see the dog sniffing "trash fish" turning and loping up the hill

> . . . under that screen of poplars, behind fat
> azaleas that hide the county farm and the drunks
> pressed against wire screens, sniffing the James. . . .

My recent *Shaker Light* contains several poems in the snapshot mode, to assist in shaping the milieu of the mystic Ann Lee, founder of the Shakers, and her followers in America. The poems read chronologically, starting in 1774 with the arrival of the sect at a foreordained spot near Albany, New York, and ending in 1784 when Mother Ann died as the result of beatings she received at the hands of mobs. Since the Shakers were noted for their practicality (their furniture remains unsurpassed for functional and aesthetic values), it made sense to try to evoke this old-fashioned pragmatism in the forms of the poems themselves. I found the snapshot technique useful:

> Skyscape
>
> A wedge of silver
> ripped open, then covered.
> An orb, yea,
> but at once a seal
> round and milky.
> Indigo clouds
> flow over the harbor.
> The sun eats
> its own edge now,
> ever to live!

Here a shot of a Shaker deal table is a metaphor for the souls of Ann and her husband Abraham, souls then in harmony:

> Our souls
> are two broad deal boards
> oiled and stained
> set up to form a table.
> The jointure, planed,
> is well-defined.
> The tincture of the grain
> glistens with wax and turpentine.
> Euphonious morning light.
> The solid grains
> make scintillations doubly bright.

At dusk, again affirming weight,
they celebrate their solid state.
The soul doth shine and glisten:

> it loves its substance,
> it loves its tatter,
> it loves its woes, it
> loves its laughter.

Snigger Poems

The snigger poem (a variety of the comic book poem) has numerous practitioners. In New York, imitators of Kenneth Koch and Frank O'Hara lead the pack. The poet looks out on a maimed world of personal and communal disasters and, though feeling threatened himself, reclines and makes jokes (*jokables*—a form of *vocables*). The snigger poet is the sort who might point his pen at a quadraplegic tipped over in the street, an old lady afflicted with Alzheimer's lost in the center of a busy crossing, or a three-legged dog.

Such poets rarely spew their fun forthrightly, preferring to hide behind irrationally contrived images and black humor. This view is a variation on the existential idea that we are lost in a dark world where God is absent (if indeed such a personage ever was). Camus's old hero Sysyphus spent his interminable days pushing his boulder up the mountain, where, once at the top, the boulder rolled back, Sysyphus running hard to avoid being crushed.

By contrast, our snigger poet, at his worst, lassitudinously allows his muscles to slacken, laughing gently and suggestively all the way to his grave, or, to be more accurate, laughing gently and suggestively on the spot of chosen ground from which he will not move until rigor mortis freezes his lips into a final smirk. These are gigglers at destiny, cute boy and girl poets whose mouths should be washed out with soap. On the other hand, when these poems work they can be stunning; they may evoke a skeletal snigger, a background cacophony for a fearsome contemporary danse macabre. These poets remind one of those skeletons enjoying themselves in James Ensor's paintings . . . they participate in a final, grim mardi gras. Ensor's paintings jolt us into spirituality. These poems, when they work, may do that as well—but when they don't. . . .

One of the best writers of snigger poems is James Tate. In one poem (from *Absences,*), seeing-eye people (heh heh) take over and give the dogs a break by leading them around. People harness themselves and lumber over a mountainside. These are "see-through people" with only enough depth "to fall more/ or less forever." They have sad little dogs for friends, dogs born blind, unable to tell a swinging door from a snowcapped mountain. Tate's people lead these pathetic dogs, dragging them along through "terror then beauty," hoping to be able to discern the differences. They try to lend the unfortunate canines some of "the courage" the dogs loaned them so often when they could see. Alas, they waken each day to an "impenetrable darkness"; excuses for jumping "from one grave into / another" are everpresent. "Dog," of course, is "God" spelled backwards, and is typical of the sort of gentle humor preferred by the snigger poet.

Victor Contoski, writing abut teeth, in "Teeth," allows himself the luxury of a humorous snigger, a quasi joke meant to help us see through the hard times:

> If you are beaten long enough and hard enough
> your teeth will be knocked out.
>
> Then you can use them as chessmen:
> front teeth, pawns;
> back teeth, pieces.

To be fair, this is only one section of five in "Teeth." The others, though they present disasters (in a dream your teeth turn soft and fall out "like rotten cactus"), are no match for the bleak snigger of the chessmen section.

David Bromige, the expatriate Englishman who has lived in northern California for more than twenty years, has tried his hand at many verse modes (Spear the Holy Kingfisher, if you must! For in the end, we come to dust!). He loves puns, double-takes, and jokes, sometimes in the snigger mode, since unfortunates (for example, plague victims) occasion risibilities. Here are some samples from what appears as a prose poem, "Red Hats." "A pretty face is like a malady, and he was into nurses." "What a squirrel does with his nuts, he does with their opportunities." "They died of the plague. Now all were in the same cart, not long before the horse."

Stand-Up Comic Poems

At their worst, stand-up comic poems are no funnier than most of the so-called comedy routines one is subjected to at Laugh Stops and similar venues. Loquaciousness and a slangy, intimate tone pass for beauty and brains. The genre seems typically American—I can think of no European poet who writes these. They are akin to gab poems, the difference being that the latter seem delivered by a half-soused poet seated beside you at a bar; in the former, the poet delivers from a platform or stage, isolated from the audience. Both forms revel in boasting and the tall tale.

Mary Shanley hits the stand-up tone in a pair of poems in a recent issue of *Long Shot*. She riffs along using full caps for humorous effect. She's much too anxious to catch the Times Square shuttle:

THE RACE IS ON
I'M PICKING UP SPEED
GOT TO GET IN BEFORE THEY CLOSE THE DOOR
50 FEET . . . 40 FEET . . . 30 . . . 20 . . . 10 . . .
5 . . . 4 . . . 3 . . . 2 . . . OH THANK GOD!
I MADE IT!

In "The Death Walk," Shanley chatters on about death, as a stand-up comic might, delivering slightly amusing personal facts segueing to a zap-idea (death) intended to pull in an audience who like their comedy dark:

i awoke in great mood wednesday
had some extra money and was thinking
about how to spend it
when suddenly . . . it happened . . .
i remembered that i was going to die.

This unpleasant news hits her as she boards the subway. On the way to the Metropolitan Museum to "check out caravaggio," she develops a slangy comic touch:

so i'm on the lexington avenue local
and this security guard gets on at 14th street
he's so young and healthy looking
his shoes all shined . . . probably digs the shit
out of wearing a uniform . . . he's lookin so proud . . .

oh no!
look what's happenin
he's getting so pale
his face becomes a mass of wrinkles and bags
his hair turns white and starts falling out
and he shrinks 4 inches . . .

why does this have to happen when i ride
the subway?
why am i so obsessed with death?

Here comes the shift towards the denouement:

oh, i don't know . . .
maybe i should try meditating
so i can get to that still, quiet place within
i've heard rumors about . . .

yeah . . . and maybe when i get there
i'll have a revelation that death is
without a doubt, going to be the
best thing that ever happened to me . . .
and i'll start looking forward to it . . .

oh happy day! i'm gonna die!

Eliot Katz, the editor of *Long Shot,* writes similar poems. In "Thieves at Work" he parades himself most loquaciously and hiply as a self-conscious bloke who knows all about the "bummers of work," like coaxing numerous "long jet black strands" of human hair, three or four at a time, out of the printing press he's hired to run. How did those hairs get there? Is there some quasi-mystical tie-in with other hard-to-explain events? Events like a hundred dictionaries falling off the shelves of a book warehouse (another of his shitty jobs) and all opening to the page beginning with UFO; or like meeting a blind mental patient in the hall of the hospital who reports that he's Henry Miller—and hearing the next day that the real Henry Miller is dead; or like finding some letters (he worked sorting mail) from the county coroner marked "E. Katz." Good-hearted soul that he is, Katz knows that there are all sorts of factory and mine jobs worse than his, inducing worse "bummers."

A far more complex example of the stand-up comic poem is Joel Oppenheimer's "When What You Dream" (*Just Friends / Friends and Lovers,*). Oppenheimer maintains a comic's self-regaling, chatty tone but invests it all with a concept: the place of "impossibilities" in his life. What he writes is to Katz's efforts as Mort Sahl's best jokes are to Henny Youngman's. He insists you stay awake and avoid the superficial laugh, for the joke may just be on you:

i am concerned with impossibilities, the
old man walking too slowly across
second avenue, impossible notes from
impossible people
       "if the check comes
       you can give it to me
       or h- at the cedar bar
          j-"
i am concerned with impossibilities, the
way the sun crept slowly and steadily to the
fourth window. the dream is perfectible,
and sometimes everything else falls before it.

it/s that i/m getting old and tired i
would guess, gaining something in each
instance. in each crackling log we steal from
ourselves to throw on the fire we learn something:
it is burned up, it is consumed,
weigh the smoke and the ashes, you come up

with the weight of the log that has been
thrown in. the fire crackles merrily, damn it, it
is the least efficient fire i have ever
participated in, or warmed myself before.

start again. if the check comes—and what the
hell do i care for him anyhow, a friend of a friend,
and not even his friend anymore, walking out of
the drugstore with a forty year old whore on
his arm, fell for his horseshit: he/s waiting for
his check. and me, like a damn fool, i give it
to him, better to go to jail for forgery than
give him his check.

what does this have to do with it?
something about the dream, his
was the check, at least for last night.

and if i didn/t
know better i/d say brandy was good for the soul,
but perfections count for nothing, and the
imperfections are what i depend on.

Stodge

In *Castle Tzingal*, Fred Chappell writes "poetry stodge," or "costume poetry." Very little here seems to transpire in the poet's own psyche— he's busy being anachronistic. His monologues are spoken in various voices tinted by Malory, Shakespeare, Tennyson, and Browning. Such poems are pieces for a literary museum, and, I grant, not devoid of skill. Chappell, deft and flamboyant, is always on the surface. Not one character boasts a dram of life deeper than what one finds in comic books.

Chappell's setting is a medieval castle ruled by the mad king Tzingal, who beheads his wife's lover, brutalizes his lackeys, and is finally conflagrated by a crazy homunculus who was born in an alchemist's beaker. The lover is a troubadour. In a smart turn, Chappell allows that you can behead a poet but you can't stifle his song. The severed noggin continues to sing, wafting songs throughout the castle, driving the Queen mad and leading to the King's destruction. Death of a Round Table? Chappell smears on an olio of borrowed motifs. Here he borrows from *King Lear*: "I heard the bat and owlet squeak and whoop." His aged admiral is as pompous as Polonious: "I caused no murders, / Committed no crimes. To the very last / I carried out my battle plan. / All commanding officers must do the same." Queen Frynna echoes Browning's old bishop at St. Praxed's

Church, wondering if he is alive or dead. Chappell loves stodgy archaisms, words nipped from traditional literary viscera, such as "fulgurant night," "mammet," "grutch," "slurk," "malapert," "glaur," etc. Elsewhere I've called these "navel words." Chappell's figures are as boring as figures in a moth-eaten arras. There are also echoes of Tennyson's easier effects. Here, Chappell seems inspired by the famous "Dark House" of *In Memoriam*. Chappell's old admiral meditates on a snowstorm he once sailed through, the "foamsprent wave" driving against "a lonesome reef / Its full freight of grief. / And I cannot sleep. / And the wind cannot stop."

Suburban or Commuter Poems

Here, everything is decent, *fetisly* (as Chaucer said) arranged. All is nicely tooled, both in form and content. No cracked mirrors, no tacky furniture either of mind or setting. Sanitized, easy reading, easy feeling. Blandness is the norm. My quarrel with writers of the suburban commuter poem is that their renditions are so scrubbed and polished that they are merely germ-free soporifics.

A crown prince of the mode is Easterner Dana Gioia. Though *Daily Horoscope,* is his first collection, he is already much anthologized, and has appeared in a raft of conservative magazines, including *The New Yorker, The Threepenny Review,* and *The Hudson Review.* An excessive cover blurb by Frederick Turner avers that because so many of Gioia's poems "do what an entire novel might aspire to do," it is surprising "why people write or read prose fiction." Presumptuous? Gioia, incidentally, is a member of the American corporate world, as the publisher notes in a silly non sequitur: Gioia is an "executive with a major American corporation" and "lives with his wife outside New York City."

Most of Gioia's poems are so bland you can read them with one eye on the landscape whizzing past your New Haven commuter car and the other eye on the page. Gioia's ideal reader would seem to be a man on the go, a middle-aged yuppie who flirts with poetry (probably a taste acquired in some Eastern college). Though much in motion, he is essentially passive. He is also a traveler, and has observed shadows lengthening in the Italian *campagna.* He is superficially cultured and knows the obvious stories about a handful of classical composers: Haydn's wife lined her bakery pans with his music, and so on. He is most likely displaced—Gioia himself hails from southern California, and is capable of a facile Keatsian or Shelleyan sadness (O life! O time!), as he meditates on the past, on death, or on the vastness of nature. Further, since the poetry this commuter knows is largely from the past (his knowledge ends, say, with late Robert Frost) he likes forms that remind him of "real poetry"—nice tight little stanzas and end-rhymes of no particular distinction slipping forth with a flatulent ease. He also likes poems that make brief sallies into carpe diem emotions, with uplifting endings. Gioia has mastered the

poem of undisturbed waters. Reading these seamless orts you'll step off
your train in Manhattan or Boston knowing that all's right with the world.

Here's a suburban flash from William Heyen's placid "Fires," a four-
part meditation on George Catlin's paintings: though Catlin's West is
"dead," the same sun with its "unimaginable power" now "drives subur-
ban / and miraculous" through the homes in these neat California tracts.
The sun "flames" the tiger lilies, those "black-flecked, slashed vivid /
undiminished orange heads." And even the lowly geraniums burst with
"spots of red fire / as the open mouths of horses trapped in that other
world." This final image is pretentious.

William Zaranka's *Blessing,*; creates a delicious persona (probably
himself) whose views of life are almost always seen through suburban
glasses. These are motifs which also appeared in his fine earlier book *A
Mirror Driven Through Nature*. Here, in his G. E. kitchen, his hero
Blessing considers the impact on his family if the bomb should hit: he

> calculates numbers of megatons
> divided by family members,
> arriving at numbers
> of tons apiece.
> —It's roughly twenty.

First, there'll be a flash, followed by a shock, then another flash powder-
ing his wife's bones, melting his son Tommy's heart into "a sizzling lump /
on hot linoleum." Blessing imagines that he'll survive, huddled in his
bomb shelter, wearing his "sandbag hat, / eating canned shit."

He has a facility for shrinking his fears of planetary catastrophe to a
pygmy-size, something one assumes most sensitive suburban husbands
and fathers manage to do, becoming "the craning god / of the sky-
scrapers, / overlooking the car-crash." He's adept at seeing "what is not
his fault." He lacks the grace he sees in his leaping cat, a creature he
upsets by sinking into his "new bean bag birthday chair":

> Three circlings,
> two sniffs,
> one swift cuff
> with his unsheathed, panzer paw
> will not dispatch the sleek, tar-colored thing.

Nor does Blessing care much for the chair—it reminds him of his youth—
the "rock stars and opinions." The chair is too uncomfortably like his life.
He sits there floating "like a cork / in his own living room." His middle-
class marriage slowly falls apart. Suspicious, he "tails / his wife to the
Ramada," where he loses her in the parking garage. Zaranka comes up
with some satiric and funny images:

> He zeroes on the shack of the attendant,
> pans on an awning but cannot enter the den
> of his worst unmaking where,

bored with her franchise, she unzips
and is unzipped, laid on a made bed
and made whole without him.

His heart is an anchor falling
through floors.
His eye is a microscope over the wrestle
and thrash of their coupling,
sandwiched like sperm in a stack
of smeared slides.

James Schevill's "Neighbors" is a devastating look at suburban good-
neighborliness (*The American Fantasies: Collected Poems 1945–1981*).

Next door
In a shingle-sliding house,
With paint curling off like worms
In their crawling pace
Lives the neighbor whose guts I hate
With his miser-face.

His house
Is a jungle of mice and junk,
And he means to cut my property value
with his ugly mess
Of broken furniture, decaying wood,
Nothing to bless.

In the morning
He stakes out his property line
With a tall imaginary fence;
I feel barbed wire,
Though he only hammers sticks in the ground
With eyes of fire.

His little head
Sits on his neck like a grape,
And the rags of his clothes fill with dirt.
To treat him mean
I give laughing parties for my friends;
He watches behind a screen.

I think he was born
to live a hermit's isolation
And serve himself with trembling hands,
Trapped in a shell
Of darkness where cold air blows
No saving church bell.

But every time
I look at him with hate he changes,
His shoulders sag, his head sinks,
He decays with his house,
As I paint desperately to keep my house alive
And set traps for any mouse.

Patiann Rogers arranges pieces of Heaven into sanitized patterns, keeping a neat suburban household on matters metaphysical. In "The Pieces of Heaven" she's assisted by these jaw-breaking phrases (all taken from the first stanza): "congealing of axis and field," "simultaneous opening and closing," "hardening of moment," and "wholeness into infinity." She maintains a museum case (let's say it's set up in a well-appointed suburban study) containing "bison knees," squid and fern fossils, cottonwood dust, lionfish quills—all meant to induce the reader to think deep thoughts about "everlasting motion," "terror," "peace" and to help him fit together the scraps of Heaven into a single mystical piece. The thinking and the writing are all so comfortable, waxed, dusted, and polished.

Mckeel McBride in a poem called "A Blessing" meanders through some early morning suburban clichés, scribbles some highly starched sibilant lines, and turns cute, noting the "constellations" her keys make on the "polished sky of the dresser top":

The blue shadow of dawn settles
its awkward silks into the enamelled kitchen
and soon you will wake with me into the long
discipline of light and day—the morning sky
startled and starred with returning birds.

In a second stanza, she shows no evidence of feeling a thing as she spins out a series of dull phrases ("haloed gnat," "waterfall of dawn," "the silver lake of a coffee spoon").

Ellen Bryant Voigt, in "The Bat," lies in bed at night reading, aglow with family sentiments induced by the "mild evening" and a snug sense of peace: her children are sleeping in "adjacent rooms" (no tenement crowding here), occasionally crying out in their dreams. A bat interrupts her coziness. Her ideal family rises to beat the creature down, swinging repeatedly at "its rising secular face." They succeed and shovel the crittur out into the yard where their suburban cat "shuttles easily between two worlds."

Unlike poets who live in suburbia and seem to love it, Robert McDowell, in his *Quiet Money*, writes poems exposing the sterility of these lives. His middle-class failures are dismayed, neutered, and enamored of risk and violence, seeking compensation for the utter sterility of suburbia. In "The Disconnected Party," a speaker returns from twenty years in prison where he was sent for viciously attacking a boss who fired him. Seeking to renew contacts, he phones a former friend. When he can't get through, he locates the friend's suburban house, and breaks in, only to find a scene of drab chaos. He fears he has reached his own house. Unable to locate a cordless phone he remembers the friend owned, he is momentarily pained. When he finds it in a study he dials, but gets no signal. When a kitchen phone rings, he dashes for it, but is too late—the answering machine is already whirring. Parts of our lives once misplaced can't be called back, or won't call us back.

In "The Malady Lingers On," Bill Davis is reassured in the evenings on returning home to suburbia by seeing "Cat" in his picture window. He knows he's reached the right house. Nor does our yuppie obsession with health and fitness escape McDowell's scrutiny. In "Coed Day at the Spa," a male joins a workout with some Amazonian women. These women work hard:

> They do not pause between stations.
> They do not loiter round the fountain
> Taking in the sights. They do not care
> How much your jumpsuit cost or what you do for pay.
> Kisses, wine, and candlelight
> Result in cellulite and loathsome flab.
> They fight it, breaking themselves on incline boards,
> Shrieking like whistles blown in a closet.
> They rise like Lazarus and spread the word.

The women have no illusions about the men, and see the hero, so he imagines, as "one more Jupiter with microscopic prick / Who lifts to show his strength— / One big push and he's done." A woman tells him to give up smoking so he won't wheeze so much. She snidely asks him whether he usually shaves before his workout. "Do you?" he responds. That seems to turn her on: "She smiles like a spasm," and invites him to pump iron with her. He obliges, aware that she knows too well the "subtle art of shrinking men." She is "tireless" at curls, and on the bench press "cranks out twenty repetitions at 225." He can't keep up, despite the increase of neck and arm girth he's managed. Still, his arms, "once thin and flaky, / As chicken legs in a crock pot, bulge with terror." He submits, an overmatched victim, and lies down, while she hovers over him.

No institution better symbolizes suburbia than the supermarket. Allen Ginsberg's classic "A Supermarket in California" is wonderfully subversive of middle-class heterosexual values. Ginsberg hopes to resolve his "hungry fatigue," his headache (he's "self-conscious looking at the full moon"), and his loneliness. He enters and observes suburbanite families shopping—"Aisles full of husbands! Wives in the avocados, / babies in the tomatoes!" His fantasy glows: the produce area is crammed with peaches and "penumbras."

The visionary in him explodes: he spies Garcia Lorca near the watermelons. Next he sees Walt Whitman, "childless, lonely old grubber," prodding the meats in the fridge, "eyeing the grocery boys," and asking off-the-wall questions: "Who killed the pork chops? What price bananas? Are you my Angel?" Ginsberg pursues Whitman through the store, and feels guilt, imagining the pair being followed by a store detec-

tive. The twinge is momentary, and the visit becomes a dream fulfilled—
the two possess "every frozen delicacy," taste the artichokes, and never
pass a cashier.

Once again in the street, Ginsberg asks Whitman where they should
go: "Which way does your beard point tonight?" Will they stroll the entire
night "through solitary streets," both of them "lonely," passing "blue
automobiles in driveways," dreaming of "the lost America of love," until
they reach their own "silent cottage" of love and adoration?

Arthur Lane in *Dancing in the Dark*, takes a saturnine look at a
suburban event:

> living with the animals
>
> the man next door
> catches hummingbirds
> in a net; I don't know why.
> he's retired, and I think
> he may be bored.
>
> when he catches one
> he calls out in Italian
> to his wife, who tumbles
> helpless from the house,
> from the porch,
> (her fluttering hands),
> to scream at him
> and watch him
> stamping on the net
> in his driveway.
>
> he gets two or three a day
> and grins when I call him
> a son of a bitch.
> he asks me when I'm going to shave,
> when I'm going to chop my trees down:
> he tells me he'll outlive me.
>
> every day when we come home
> we find him in the garden,
> stealing olives, stealing lemons,
> looking in the windows.

James C. Kilgore's "The White Man Pressed the Locks" is a succinct
and devastating look at a suburban man rushing away from a black inner
city, locking the doors of his sedan so as to feel secure. Kilgore's image of
the two bodies, one black and blighted, the other white and commanding,
is unforgettable:

Driving down the concrete artery,
Away from the smoky heart,
Through the darkening, blighted body,
Pausing at varicose veins,
The white man pressed the locks
   on all the sedan's doors,
Sped toward the white corpuscles
   in the white arms
     hugging the black city.

Sylvia Plath Poems

That Plath was rich, beautiful, and blessed with a fine Eastern education, had Robert Lowell for her mentor, married one of England's leading poets, Ted Hughes, and was an impressive poet, made an enviable legend of her. Distressed with her life (she had two small children) in a not entirely dismal part of London (near Regent's Park), she succeeded in killing herself in February, 1963.

Staunch feminists, of course, see a pattern—the loathsome Nazi-type father of Plath's famous "Daddy" poem; Hughes the cruel and destructive husband. Robin Morgan in "Arrangement" (*Monster*), arraigns Hughes while not appearing to do so. She rages with the subtlety of a sledge-hammer, her intended victims the British and American male "literary and critical establishment" who deny, without saying it "in so many words," that Hughes murdered Plath. She deplores the "controversy" occasioned by Plath's references in her poems and letters to Hughes's "peccadillos." Morgan pretends to accept the establishment view—Plath's accusation that Hughes raped her was pure "metaphor." The law, after all, allows for a husband to "rape" his spouse both "in body and in mind." It's also "perfectly legal" for him to turn her children against her. He is free even to "malappropriate her imagery" and to censure whatever he pleases of her indictments against him. He may legally become her "posthumous editor," cashing in on her fame, continuing to pen his own inoffensive, "puerile, pretentious dribbles of verse." And one can hardly blame Hughes for "committing the perfect marriage" (as in *committing the perfect crime*) for a second time.

Didn't you know, Morgan asks, that Hughes's second woman, Assia Guttman Wevil, also committed suicide? They never formally married. Assia translated poems from the Hebrew, and like most women feared "losing her beauty." She appears in Plath's "Lesbos," and, "in time," like her predecessor Lesbia, chose suicide as the way out, and found "the oven's fumes less lethal" than a husband's love. As a "heroic" Jewish mother, Assia took her daughter, Shura, with her. "What a coincidence," Morgan declares, dismissing Hughes as "a one-man gynocidal movement."

Then Morgan seems to exculpate Hughes, probably in order to intensify her rage against him. The calm as they say, before the storm. . . . Plath was "clearly unbalanced" for writing "terrifying poems" about Hughes, and Guttman was surely mad for killing her daughter to keep Hughes from her. Morgan herself, she observes, will appear "patently unstable" for seeing both women as "sane as Cassandra, / or even for writing this in poetry, rather than / code."

With mock humility, Morgan asks permission to speak of the power brokers of the literary world—A. Alvarez, George Steiner, and Robert Lowell, "and the legions of critical necrophiles" who conspire to lament Plath's "brilliance" as they patronize her madness, "diluting her rage, / burying her in politics, and / aiding, abetting, rewarding / her perfectly legal executor." What Morgan says, she declares, though not libelous, is "merely dangerous" to say, since it's "perfectly legal . . . for publishers to be / men / or cowards, / or members of the same fraternity." Nor does Morgan, in a final fillip, spare women. "We . . . change our minds a lot," she observes, implying that the horrors perpetrated by males leading to Plath's suicide may be softened or ignored—"Who knows?" In the meantime, Hughes "has married again."

Terry Kennedy in "hot mama plath" (*Durango,*) reads Plath's suicide as an escape from both husband and the traumas of being a young mother:

hot mama plath

it came in the night
like a husband's wet dream
disguised as sleep
it strangled the seraph on your bones
the young monroe
opening and closing
like a brand new morning glory

the bay's siren howling
rushing into you like smack
penetrating the membrane
of your moth-thin wings   yes

trampling your first pencil case
full of the whore's disgust

the dirty cat boxes
the broken electrolux
the pipes pissing
under the sink
on the skull and crossbones cleansers   yes

day-old grease
a kind of lubricant
ugly as snot
hanging on the skillet

you weren't surprised

the window sill geranium blooming
red   through all of february
and march

you write
dear murderer
on a grocery list
bring bacon
forget the eggs
do not take me
to lourdes
to be baptized
in leper's gyzm
my prosthesis has not been invented yet!

from the beginning
you understood
                no this is not a movie you said
                not for god's sake a tv script

you let the room spin
like a player piano
rolling the dishes on the floor
the high chair tilting
mama! mama!
the rhythm stabbing
bludgeoning the feathery network of your words

sylvia
ms plath
blood as thick as sperm
covers every page

Anne Sexton's elegy "Sylvia's Death" (*Live or Die,*), has the impact of lean, harsh blows of grief delivered to the psyche. Sexton and Plath were, of course, intimate friends, and this elegy, one of the simplest in form of all Sexton's poems, must be read against that brief, intense history. (Sexton dates it February 17, 1963—the period of Plath's death.) Both poets talked "often" of the "death" they both craved—they imagined it as a "sleepy drummer, or a sadist," or "a New York fairy" (a touch of homophobia here?), who on earlier visits (both had attempted suicide) waited "under our heart, our cupboard." Sexton realizes that once one craves death, the "terrible taste for it, like salt" never leaves. Death, she says, is "*our* boy." Plath's death is "an old belonging, / a mole that fell out" of one of her poems. Sexton concludes with an apostrophe of profound sorrow and affection:

> O tiny mother,
> you too!
> O funny duchess!
> O blonde thing!

Diane Wakoski's lenghty "The Water Element Song For Sylvia" is a discursive elegy which interweaves the poet's various personal preoccupations with Plath's death (*The Collected Greed*). Wakoski's concluding insight is one few of Plath's poet-mourners state: that weeping for Plath is really a weeping for oneself. "Water," Wakoski writes, "in any form," is "life." Like Morgan, Wakoski's Plath is a woman cruelly abandoned by her man, who rather than face the lengthening humiliations of coming days, rather than "fall into that / weeping well / of abandoned women," chooses to "float away." The recurring theme running through this ten-page elegy resembles a Greek chant: "I wont wont wont / die," Wakoski declares, not for poetry, or "for anyone's pleasure," or for "a man who betrays me." Though she sees herself "as thin as a sheet of cellophane," and "dry and almost past tears," she is too "spiteful . . . angry . . . nasty . . . bitchy," and of "too common" a fiber ("I'm peasant bread, not a delicate white roll") for suicide.

An entirely different Plath poem, by Edward Butscher, author of the controversial biography *Sylvia Plath: Method and Madness*, which he is now preparing for a new edition, is an attack on a review of his book. The poem, outrageous, scatalogical, and humorous, pummels the *New York Review of Books* for having done a "sloppy grease job" on Plath, perhaps sanitizing her in the process. "Yoeman Noman" supplies his own physiological corrective. The work is from a long manuscript, "And Thus Spake Godfrey," as yet unpublished:

Letter to the Idiot Editor
of the
New York Review of Books

Your reviewer's sloppy grease job on Sylvia Plath was duly noted and deplored, deplored, I say. (*Necrophilia!*) An injustice has been perpetrated in the name of pedantic pederasty, which must be herewith corrected, withdrawn . . . to the point of anti-climactic last rites, if necessary. Hear the elm and see your dull footnotes for the unmatched galoshes (?) they certainly

(*sic*) are . . . a nice touch there, literary but never frivolous, yes, always . . .
(sic em) . . . Accentuate the negative and
                                    you will get the poet
                                    in between (sheets).
Gloved Sylvia ate stone statues
                            and shit a daughter out,
                            a son, academic degrees,
                            a rosary of maybe chains.
Loving scared the living
                            words out of her, rooks
                            in her eyes, the right
                            labels in her
                                    lithe, lethal, little lines:
she sucked off tornado Daddy
        in the sky, dear dead Daddy,
        martyring mama, a stillborn
        lie, didn't dribble a single
        drop of semen rage . . .

                    (get on her, with it)
     Other things, to wit, inside and outside of the pure poetry, prevailed: fire
for her teeth, for instance, a moor in her mind (where Emily laid the Lord to
rest), gnawing quartz grit into a pearl mountain, ghost towns, Unitarian
bells (tongueless), her round railroad heels breaking the bent back of every
ass-kissing, boot-licking ball-lugger in her Sunday School Bible Class back
home, you babbling biddy!
                            Bald bowl of a milk Muse,
                            wet as cum, round as balls,
                            sifted death from an ocean
                            of yellow kike flotsam:

                            she lived in her farm shoe,
                            went in our pants, ate her
                            children's soiled piping
                            clouds, laid herself
low, and filled
Cinderella's slipper
                    with blood of the lamb.
An eskimo pie, her twat was a trap, you diddle stick!

                            Never Yours,
                            O/O
                            Yoeman Noman, U.P.I.
                                    I. P. U.
P.S. why don't you castrati ever print any of mine pal's brilliant letters?

Tortoise Poems

Poets are either tortoises or hares. Their Aesopian progress towards a goal (the end of the poem) may wreak strange transformations: the tortoise may metamorphose into a hare along the way, or vice versa. Projective verse apologists have sufficiently explained how useful the hare is as an image for the poem racing helter-skelter through the open field toward its burrow and safety. The hare has energy, madness, a quick-spinning poetic life. The tortoise, plodding, takes his sweet time in a straight path. He may even stop to rest within the space of a single line of verse. This is what James Dickey does in *The Strength of Fields*.

Dickey is a most-decorated flying ace among American poets. He has retracted his poem-wheels and gone winging off into the blue sufficiently often to earn his place in the Poetry-Pilot Hall of Fame. And even if he never decides to publish another line, or rev up another engine, his reputation will be secure. *The Strength of Fields* contains some fifty pages of new poems and about forty of what Dickey calls "Free-Flight Improvisations from the Un-English," poems based loosely on a series of foreigners: Montale, Jarry, Po Chu-yi, Lautréamont, Alexiandre, and Yevtushenko. What interests me most is Dickey's own work—whether it contains new energies and new styles.

His "Haunting the Maneuvers" proceeds at a turtle's pace. During military maneuvers, Dickey finds himself "dead," lying on pine debris, observing the needles as they point, compass-like, toward the night sky. They seem whiter than his own skin. Great. But then Dickey's luminosity dissolves into sentimental rhetoric, staged and turtle-slow. Instead of shedding its clothes, as a good poem should, revealing itself specific and bare, this one hides in the swaddling of a stuffed military uniform.

The tortoise mode assumes two forms in Dickey's verse. First, we have such pompous and lugubrious phrases as "the quality of life," "better or worse," "death changed forever," "we can all be saved," and "of the renewing green"—chockablock phrases a tortoise making its slow progress down a beach might drop behind it. Second, we have a scattering of words and phrases over the page leaving double and even triple spaces between phrases and lines, designed to allow the tortoise of verse to have plenty of time to recoup its energies before creeping on to the next phrase. This is from the title poem of *The Strength of Fields*:

>   Hunger, time and the moon:
> The moon lying on the brain
>   as on the excited sea   as on
>   The strength of fields.

Readers wishing to pursue tortoise poetry further may want to investigate poems by Charles Olson, Larry Eigner, and Theodore Enslin.

Trapped Wife Poems

Few poets have written as potently of the trapped housewife as Heather McHugh. Her "Housewife" (*Dangers,*), should be sold in feminist bookstores. Right from the opening line ("I want to be whipped again"), the portrait of the exploited woman is devastating. Fortunately, McHugh is too expert a poet to allow the piece to snivel off into propaganda. The concluding image of the male (husband or son) taking off his metaphoric belt ready to whip her is both raw and complex.

I want to be whipped again. Whole day
on the floor, upon my knees, stripping
them clean, while men sleep
in a nearby room. Dying
to please, pleased
to die, I wait
for someone to wake
up. Grab a strap. Do me in.

Outside in fact
the day is soft and not
a killer. Children
and noises slip on it
without falling. Where
have I been.

After a week the scraps begin
to rot right in the sink.
Can't be hip doing dishes, baby, flipping
plates, stacking the rack. I might as well
have wanted to be born
black, as be free of these wishes. Now

a door slams open. They begin
to stumble out, awakening
to want, to shake the kitchen down,
break open cabinets. They grub
and rummage, and drop
the empty cups. I hear

the empty cups. I hear
a curse like a ketchup bottle hit
the tiles and I
start taking off, I do start taking off.
Already one of them
is playing with his belt
as if it were a sweet thought.
Already I have fought and felt

the long line of its coming true and my
own coming and, across
my back, my whole
life humming.

Van Gogh Poems

Few poems inspired by the painter Van Gogh are worth reading. W. D. Snodgrass and Anne Sexton have both written descriptive pieces on the painting "A Starry Night." Snodgrass actually mis-describes the picture. Robert Cooperman's "Van Gogh at the Asylum at Saint-Remy" presents the painter's memories of a dead brother. When he attempts to paint him, his own face emerges, "swallowed in color and bandages, / a pipe in his green mouth, / the lips thick as a body / bloating in the canal." Christopher Buckley (*Last Rites,*) writes a meticulously detailed reading of "Wheat Fields with Black Birds."

The most ambitious recent treatment of the Dutch painter's life and work is Peter Cooley's *The Van Gogh Notebook.* These fifty-six poems should excuse all future poets from tackling the subject again. Few of Cooley's poems match the intensity of their subject, though all are competently written. He's best when he writes in the voices of the painter's sitters. Like most poets who write about paintings, Cooley spends too much time recording details. When he seeks intensity, as he does in "Gauguin's Chair" he is absurd. Gauguin's "furies" are busy licking the cadmium, "touching it up to dance like yours. / Burnished with green, they feed on green and never will sit down."

To enhance her incredibly gloomy (almost absurdly so) "The Delicacy of Freedom," Mekeel McBride calls on Van Gogh to assist her. She sees the woebegone April morning as one of the painter's "freshly stretched" canvases before he starts to paint with his "terrible precision, / the paper-cut wings of a crow / against the wind-scoured sky. . . ." He's also adept at painting buds "unknotting, etc." Such writing has little to do with Van Gogh, and is only intended to elevate McBride's poem. Older poets would invoke God or some Muse; the modern poet invokes the shade of Van Gogh, Lorca, Whitman, Rilke, or Plath.

Harold Norse in *The Lone Poems,* employs references to Van Gogh to flatter a lover he's met in Amsterdam, a youth who attended a seminar Norse presented at a university. They made love "all night," and Norse is much turned on by the lad's "enormous gray luminous eyes." Next day, at the Van Gogh Museum, the youth (Richard) touches the glass frames of Van Gogh's drawings of peasants and declares they could be his grandparents. His family lives in Brabant, where Van Gogh's peasants lived, and they still dig potatoes. Suddenly, Richard is larger than life: his "applecheeked / Skin glows" and his "large eyes shine / With the flame of Rimbaud and Van Gogh." This sentimental note leads Norse to want to do even better, to "fix" the beautiful youth in his poem as "firmly" as the Dutch painter has fixed the boy's ancestors "in his immortal sketches." Norse adds, "I pray for this."

Vietnam Poems

Two anthologies provide the framework for discussions of poets writing about the Vietnam war. The first, edited by Robert Bly and David Ray in 1966, and published by "The American Writers Against the Vietnam War," was called *A Poetry Reading Against the Vietnam War.* The book was used for read-ins held at numerous college campuses and public halls during 1966. The back cover blurb reads: "The poets have not gathered to read propagandistic poetry, but to testify by the presence of their bodies on stage that they were opposed to the United States pursuit of the Vietnam War."

Bly and Ray organized the writers, the aim being "to encourage poets and students to take a public stand against the War, and to encourage read-ins at all major campuses." Among the chief participants were Bly, Robert Creeley, Lawrence Ferlinghetti, Robert Lowell, Louis Simpson, William Stafford, and James Wright. In addition to poems by several of the poets above, poems and short prose pieces were included by Abraham Lincoln, Walt Whitman, Robinson Jeffers, Siegfried Sassoon, Winfield Townley Scott, Sigmund Freud, Hermann Goering, President Kennedy, and I. F. Stone. e. e. cummings was to be generously represented, but Harcourt Brace refused permission, although the booklet was already printed. My edition contains blacked-out spaces "in mourning for the poems of E. E. Cummings [sic], for which permission was refused by Harcourt Brace." Further on, whole pages that once contained cummings's poems have been deleted.

Nor were the public read-ins the sum total of our poets' efforts against the war. Bly himself wrote powerful antiwar polemics: see his "The Vietnam War," a section made up of eight poems, including the superb "Counting Small-Boned Bodies," in *The Light Around the Body* (1967); and "The Teeth Mother Naked at Last" from *Sleepers Joining Hands* (1973). Denise Levertov also gave public readings, organized protests, and wrote poems. See her "From a Notebook: October '68–May '69," in *Relearning the Alphabet*, which winds its lengthy way to a call for revolution. Allen Ginsberg's "Witchita Vortex Sutra," *Collected Poems*, attempts to exorcise war demons.

The second book, *Carrying the Darkness: American Indochina— The Poetry of the Vietnam War,* was edited by W. D. Ehrhart in 1985. It completes the cycle (insofar as the consciousness of a people is ever freed from the nightmare of a particular war) by featuring poets who actually fought in Vietnam. This on-the-spot reportage is a match for the horrors of trench warfare evoked by the British poets of World War I.

Ehrhart, a U.S. Marine, served in the field in 1967 and 1968 as a battalion assistant intelligence chief. Readers will be familiar with his *The Outer Banks & Other Poems* and *To Those Who Have Gone Home Tired: New & Selected Poems*. In this new anthology, Ehrhart says that no one, either at the front or at home, was untouched by the conflict—simply living through those years made one a participant. "Here are poems by combat soldiers and draft resisters, living-room observers and full-time activists, men and women, whites, blacks, Native Americans and Asian Americans, young and old and in between." The emphasis is on young writers, those "who came of age during the Vietnam war," many of them veterans. The earliest, most visible work by a veteran was Michael Casey's *Obscenities*, which won the Yale Younger Poets Series for 1972. For whatever reasons, Casey declined to have his work represented here. Ehrhart includes a useful bibliography of anthologies of American war poems. Limitations of space prevented him from including more work by the older poets (he mentions Ginsberg, Ferlinghetti, and Ray) who were active then.

One of the finest poets among these veterans is John Balaban, who volunteered for alternative service as a conscientious objector and was a field representative saving war-injured children. His books *After Our War* and *Blue Mountain* both contain many Vietnam poems. Here is the opening of one of the most brutal:

After Our War

After our war, the dismembered bits
—all those pierced eyes, ear slivers, jaw splinters,
gouged lips, odd tibias, skin flaps, and toes—
came squinting, wobbling, jabbering back.
The genitals, of course, were the most bizarre,
inching along roads like glowworms and slugs.
The living wanted them back, but good as new.
The dead, of course, had no use for them.
And the ghosts, the tens of thousands of abandoned souls
who had appeared like swamp fog in the city streets,
on the evening altars, and on doorsills of cratered homes,
also had no use for the scraps and bits
because, in their opinion, they looked good without them.

D. F. Brown, a medic, evokes the fear, struggle, strain, and the gentle feelings men in extremity have toward one another. Here is a portion of "Eating the Forest":

It all depends on forty men
automatic rifles
grenades
faces painted green—
the man behind me is twenty feet away
circles join us, sandbagged

mines point from the spot
we guard with our lives
I keep count for them
the cases—malaria,
hepatitis, VD, purple
hearts, red marks
red marks we live
soak off into jungle
every day each man
the small, white antimalarial pill
fifty-two Mondays the big orange tablet
I have to go on
nothing got to die

He is poignantly honest in facing his own fears. Here is a passage from
"When I Am 19 I Was a Medic"

Each night I lay out all my stuff:
morphine, bandages at my shoulder,
just below, parallel, my rifle.
I sleep strapped to a .45,
bleached into my fear.
I do this under the biggest tree,
some nights I dig
in saying my wife's name
over and over.

W. D. Ehrhart writes vignettes with punch. A farmer tries to appease
both sides in the war and is brutalized by both. A fellow soldier dies, but
his surviving buddies won't miss him, since they'll be able to divide his
cigarettes. On a hideous patrol, "another night coats the nose and ears: /
smells of fish and paddy water":

Our gravel-crunching boots tear great
holes in the darkness, make us wince
with every step. A mangy dog
pits the stomach: rifles level;
nervous fingers hit the safety catch.

Telling civilians from Viet-Cong is impossible—women and children
fight, strapping grenades inside their clothes. Ehrhart, squinting down
his rifle, ready to "slowly squeeze the trigger," realizes that the only thing
in his young life he's ever hunted is other men.

Bryan Alec Floyd writes a series of portraits of fellow soldiers, most of
them dead. One is of a Sgt. Grandon Just, a marine, who finds a girl alive
after her village was napalmed, takes her to a hospital, and out of his
grief-stricken conscience attends to her:

And as he would come in,
Sung would hobble up to him
in her therapeutic cart,
smiling even when she did not smile, lipless,
her chin melted to her chest
that would never become breasts.

Bruce Wiegl served in the First Air Cavalry and was in Vietnam from 1967 to 1968. He has published four collections of poems, all well honed and elegantly cadenced. Despite the vividness of much of what he writes, excessive elegance deprives his work of the stench of the actual so present in Ehrhart, Balaban, Brown, and Floyd. Wiegl retells, as if from a distance, using phrases like "I was barely in country when . . ."; "All this time I had forgotten"; "In my dream of the hydroplane / I'm sailing to Bien Hoa"; and "In Vietnam I was always afraid of mines." Recollections are never as vivid as firsthand reports.

Certainly, Vietnam unleased poetic energies as no war had before for American poets. Even the Civil War, which smeared such nightmarish cicatrices over American psyches, didn't come close. We can hope that the accounts of these veterans will be so widely read and influential that as a nation we shall never experience a similar nightmare. Don't be too sanguine though, for as the smoke of Vietnam begins to fade, another fire seems about to burst into flame in Central America. Once again, poets are writing about their rage.

For a more expansive look at war as a general theme, see the entry "War Poems" below.

Violence and Horror Poems

No issues are more germane and reflective of our times than violence and horror. In the concluding decades of this beknighted century, we have invented things particularly our own: serial murder, drive-by killings, and random freeway assassinations. The simplest outing to the shopping center or to the theater may result in irreversible tragedy and death. Television and movie screens are rife with violence and horror. Heavy metal and punk rock music extol murder and sadism. Freeways bear maimed bodies and totaled automobiles. Such phenomena seem to demean and make callous our humanity. We drive past the latest bagged bodies with little more than a sigh, anxious not to be delayed. In our homes we secure our doors and windows with special double and triple safety locks, as we sit drinking coffee and reading the latest murder, torture, and rape news in the newspaper. No wonder that the recent episode of the California whales off Barrow, Alaska commands our attention. In their plight, the whales seem more human than we do, pristine and grand. Yes, violence is the religion of these times.

Despite the prevalence of these horrors, only now are poets beginning to confront them with any thoroughness. True, there have been verse models in the past: Odysseus slaughtering the suitors; Shakespeare's Edmund, Iago, Macbeth, and Richard the Third; Shelley's Cenci; Robert Browning's duke, Pompilia, and his laboratory murderer; Robert Frost's witch of Coos; Robinson Jeffers's Cawdor, and Karl Shapiro's "Auto Wreck." Stark indeed is John Donne's sonnet "Spit in my face you Jews," where filled with self-pity and mental distress he envisions himself as Christ's murderer. The poem reflects the paradoxical Christian mix of torture, violence, lingeringly painful death, compassion, and sacrifice:

> Spit in my face you Jews, and pierce my side,
> Buffet, and scoff, scourge, and crucify me,
> For I have sinned, and sinned, and only he,
> Who could do no iniquity, hath died:
> But by my death can not be satisfied
> My sins, which pass the Jew's impiety:
> They killed once an inglorious man, but I
> Crucify him daily, being now glorified. . . .

Many poets have devoted energies to writing about the greatest violence of all: war, from battles in Heaven to battles on earth. The host of young American poets who served in VietNam and report their raw horror in verse pay homage to Wilfrid Owen, Siegfried Sassoon, and Isaac Rosenberg of World War I, poets who by their visceral work changed writing about war forever.

Violence is a growing theme among American poets. Some write as a talismanic gesture; viz., to confront is to protect one's own life. Most see the issue as central to our time. Both groups must battle the prevailing notion that truly disturbing themes have no place in poetry. My own excursion into the psyche of a mass murderer, the seventeenth century Hungarian Countess, Elizabeth Bathory, who bathed in the blood of nearly seven hundred virgins as a way of maintaining her youth, *The Blood Countess*, disturbs many readers of the poems and viewers of the play.

No contemporary poet puts the issue subtly than John Ridland in "Ode On Violence", for he sees that violence transpires in quiet yet devastating ways. Since his poem has been long out of print, it appears here in its entirety. Ridland begins with a headquote from Julian Mayfield: ". . .the American mainstream, which is violence. . . ."

Ode On Violence

> It is violence by which the hammerheads find their places on the strings
>   and the delicate melody of Mozart winds into the mind,
>   so beautiful, and he was dead at 36

It is violence with which the typewriter letters
     slap this page, laying down commas and hyphens, periods
         ending the free and natural sequence of words,
and violence—twenty tons of it—by which the powerful press
     prints them, leaving fine marks frail as a spider's foot
         on paper that has been rolled through miles of violence

It is violence I use as I say to my two-year-old,
     Be quiet, Mummy is speaking to me,
         and violence she does not use as she replies, *Talking to Daddy?*

It is violence in the prison when the new kid, blond and fair, pink, soft-
     cheeked,

     is held down on bags of sheets in the laundry room
         to be raped by eight older men, all of them with wives and children
             all of them stung and beaten with violent self-denial

It is violence as this gentle water, barely sliding,
     shaves the fine mud-bank, carries the mud
         a little further, sanding the basalt with it,
             sanding down the landscape with grains of basalt

And violence as ice and seed split the granite, violence
     in the heart and veins, violence in the foot's balance, in the base of the
         spine
             where the muscles pull on their moorings with hundreds of pounds,
                 and violence between brother and sister, violence
                     in the gender wind-pipe of the helpless child vomiting,
                 violence in wind and tide, tree and moon,
             and violence under the sun, and in the brain
         where thinking wrenches on things to put them in order
     in a place where they did not naturally wish to be—
and violence. . .

and it is all violence, and what comes after violence?

Diane Wakoski's probing of violence throughout much of her work is
a major contribution. Her "Testament" (all of these poems are from
Trilogy) is steeped in premonition:

There is nothing in the world I have not feared.
Everything was alive eating me.
The shadows of the real things are as destructive
as the real things themselves.
I hate them all,
both the shadows and the things they stand for. . . .

In "Cock Fight," Wakoski explores the fascination of men with animal violence:

Silent men, in the night, stare at the spectacle, pausing
to light a cigarette, breathing tightly,
in accord with the lightning movement
of claw and beak,

Inhaling the tension of touch,
wishing the battle of the red bullets was their own
release. . . .

Here, in "After Looking At A Painting of the Crucifixion By An Unknown Master of the 14th Century," she considers the agony of the crucifixion and rebels against it as a personal threat:

The pain he felt
could not have had much to do with right and wrong.
The pain could not have been greater for him
than for those other two,
the thieves also hanging
by their own flesh,
gradually being ripped open
by the gravity that inevitably
pulls down.

Your painting makes me furious—
describing spiritual pain,
when the man was being literally torn open
with anaesthesia.
If he felt joy in that,
his mind was perverted:
are you describing the perversion of pain?

In "Love Poem" a murderer recalls a girl he has killed:

                    She is dead.
I cannot understand her hands.
They are like twigs; and the sun,
        it has died in her hair.
                    I love her and she is dead.
Tree, why are you trembling?
                    From her hands like twigs
                    and the dead sun in her hair.
I killed her, Tree;
I killed her.
                    The twigs scratched and the sun is like
                    the dead bodies of bees twisted in her hair.
Tree, where are your fingers?
                    On her hands and in her hair.

Since the sixties, Steve Richmond has quietly written and published poems that still await the recognition they deserve. He writes of a Los Angeles life seared by dope, booze, and incredible personal demons, in a private form called the "gagaku," a free-verse lyric form of direct statement inspired by shinto music which he listens to as he writes. Here, in *Gagaku*, a private demon visits him:

> the demons teeth I suddenly see
>   have little openings at the bottom of each fang
>   and multicolored liquid
>   drips

In another poem in the same collection a former lover wanders the Los Angeles streets wearing a dagger tied to her ankle. She'd earlier stabbed a rapist. Defecating demons

> now wipe themselves
> with pale blue "soft" toilet paper
>   now stab each other in heart
> a green and yellow blood drips
> over their nipples
> they have the chests of young men
>   rather hairless
>   and they laugh and weep simultaneously
>   as they stab. . . .

In an untitled poem, in *Wormwood Review*, no. 91, Richmond appears to feel that there are occasions when we escape our killers. He rescues an apparently dead monarch butterfly from a cat who is busily rubbing the insect into the ground. Richmond finds that after he tweaks the "dead uplifted wing" the creature flutters "up through / the branches of / a fig tree / gone and alive."

Another Los Angeles poet, Harry Northup, in *Enough The Great Running Chapel*, draws from the sexual and social violence he has seen and experienced in real life as well as in films (he has appeared in numerous films, including some by Martin Scorsese). Here is a passage from "Death Is A Great Experience, I Have Tasted One":

> Lorca led the bullfighter away & butchered the beast
>
> Lorca, said Death, I am ready to walk you've got heart
> What the cats in the ghetto say how much did he know
>
> Like he carries a piece & they say he's got heart
>
> He leaned his eyes back into horns I am on it now
> Lorca dug the cats in the ghetto, one imitated
>
> Brando & knew Death's secret, most fifty year olds
> They push their chest out & say I am still solid

Brando pushes the Death out & says I am relaxed
Death was always what went into a woman the man left

They say Lorca would do anything for money even write
Brando tore the rose bush out by its roots & knocked

Northup's six-part "I Cut Open My Mind In An Esso Station" reeks
of sexual and urban violence. This is the first section:

The black attendant removed the stitches
I cut open my mind in an Esso Station

Esso Stations are my favorite, clean toilets
It was the money I spent on tomatoes

I wanted the razor to cut her cunt
I hear them unfold their newspapers

I hear it now, fast knives through fire
Like red tomatoes, I love fresh meat

The way I live, I live alone
I know the cats sleep on pipes in the basement

I hear them unfold their newspapers
There is never any movement, still subways

A regular society, I love fresh cuts of cat
The testicles in your hand gag me

My marriage was a pretty red stove
A young blonde-haired man parks in front

He will knock on my door & ask for my cock
The door is locked, I'll ask the attendant

Todd Moore is currently completing a thirteen part epic poem on the
gangster John Dillinger. Once completed, this monumental poem will be
like no other. Its energy and style are incantatory. Much of Moore's earlier
writing, and he has been prolific, swelters and steams in small town
American violence and paranoia. Better than any poet I know he under-
stands obsessions with guns, the mindless machismo that leads to
punching out adversaries, the demeaning of woman, and a taste for
violent death. Life is always incredibly cheap. Moore's work, alas, is
largely ignored outside the rare circle of mimeo mags and small presses.
    In "lilburne lewis never," from *The Devil's Backbone*, Moore enters
the psyche of a murderer:

lilburne lewis never

gave blood a thought
when he sank his
axe into george's
neck that snap
of steel thru bone
felt more like
lopping off a
sapling than a
head then arterial
blood squirted
flag stone hearth
& log wall lilburne
didn't have to hit
him again but did
because of the blood george got
on his boots. . . .

In many poems, Moore sees the automobile as a lethal gun. In *Driving* a train hits a car:

as engine's
headlights
fill front
seat first
then all
that iron
piling thru
driver's
side every
thing coming
off clean
including
guy's head
& legs
off at knee
found 100
feet away
in weeds

kicking blood
into the wind

In this passage from *Dillinger: Dillinger's Faces* the gangster considers his face in a barroom mirror:

what is this face
I have shined on you
what is this shining
out from newspaper photos
snapshots & reward posters
who is that sonofabitch they'll
pay money for. . .
that fist of glancings
that thicket of bullets flying
out from eyes
& people's reactions to his face
please don't hit me
bunching into their wounds that pass for faces
please don't shoot me
spilling out of the scars they wear for eyes
their mouths open
the opening alone makes him think of the dead
their muted screams hang
like dark slabs of stone
retreat
behind the teeth
frightened animals
they only flutter
then flatten out for the long yell
. . .& that time a guy
got shot in the face
w/45 slug
hole thru the cheek
out the back of the head
had rearranged all the features
dislocated the nose
mouth shoved a little to the side
twisted
that effect given from close
range hole in flesh
powder burns
lips opening on teeth
like a dog
& can you go on like that
or w/out a face
at all
dillinger asking that
asking. . . .

No poet better anticipates the shape of poems to come than Jesse Glass, Jr. His vision of contemporary life is amazing. There seems no longer much rhyme or reason to life: one looks with eyelids peeled at new outrages and horrors. Glass is exceptionally well-read in earlier literatures, myth, history, and psychology, and incorporates elaborate materials from the past to illuminate the present. He writes with complete authority and loves figures who are larger than life, and through these persona sometimes gives us revealing glimpses of himself. His work, unfortunately, is hard to come by. He has published *Enoch, Worm, Man's Vows*, and is featured in Gary Blankenburg's new *Eclectic*.

In *A Most True Discourse Declaring the Life & Death Of one Stubbe Peter, Being A Most Wicked Sorcerer* (selections published in *Eclectic*, 1988), Peter is complete with bloody rack. He is also a doppelgänger for the contemporary poet who howls, rends, has diabolical sex, is both sadist and craving masochist, and finds himself on his own torture wheel. This passage is from "A Palace Built on Skulls":

> The Wheel clatters, turned by an iron glove. The Master sleeps in his private room that locks w/a triple lock. Comes at noon like a shy boy to eat the meat she burns, then leads her blushing, to her bed and there performs the strange deeds that give him pleasure—w/out speaking. No love words fall from that foul-smelling mouth, twisted into smiles. He is not like a man in all ways. His eyes do not see her when he probes inside to stretch her womb. And he will suddenly turn away and rip the covers with his small pale hands, eyeing her most savagely from beneath his brows. "Beat me!" he howls, & she must, with all her might, lay on w/ a bull's pizzle; he begs her to wrap herself in a pelt & bit him till he swoons. And she does, wondering as he whimpers at her feet.

Even the sexual act (in "White") for Stubbe Peter is a mammoth mix of necrophilia, endurance, and pain. The woman

> howled in
> his ear, bit
> his throat
> & impaled herself on his yard
>   now marvellously erect.
>   no pulse in
> her neck. cold,
>   no sweat fell
> from her brows.
>   cold.
> she rode him
> two days.
>
>   he cried out
>   under her blows
>
>   wanting to stop/
>   wanting more.
>
> & found that he could
>   tear her apart
>   like a doll

& she would spring together
   by diabolical art
& instantly be whole
& bleed
& dry & heal. . . .

In an unpublished poem "Nostalgia," a freaked out poet, on an "ordinary day," on the verge of insanity and violence, addresses his counterpart Faustus, thereby evoking both past and recent satanic forces:

. . . .
Where is human dignity, Faustus?
Now the hands of da Vinci's Grand Man
have dropped to cover the smallness of his cock,
& we are forced to sit in windowless rooms
intoning yay & nay
until we yawn.
The devil's forgotten to collect
his fee with a Renaissance boom & crash
or has collected it in more subtle fashion
surrounding us with well-behaved, triple-chinned devils
& radio talk show hosts
who court the applause of bank presidents
with their emphasis on nostalgic
retellings of the news. . . .
So fuck the world, Faustus,
step out from your casket
& grapple me down among the helices,
the meanders &
the spheres
I'm eager to trace the limits of your limbs
upon the miasmic air,
& pin you against the magma
of an office desk
& find my certainty in the
scabrous blessing of your
all-transfiguring scorn.

In another lengthy, powerful poem, "Mister Six," Glass writes a horror parable of our own times by presenting the Marquis de Sade imprisoned in the madhouse at Charenton. Here the sadist glories in memories of violated girls:

       . . . One was
Barely twelve, with a figure & face worthy
Of Titian's brush; one
Was sixteen—just as delightful; the next, a brunette,
Was nineteen; & the last, a strapping blonde of twenty,
Were each led forwd by separate attendants.

Ah! What delicious tears! & when he had finished,
The smallest girl, blood flowing freely as her screams,
Implored God to forgive us.

When de Sade arraigns God, the "Monster," for being an unmerciful "cosmic" ghost who fills earth with suffering and violence and then expects eternal adulation, Glass is arraigning our own sick Existential times. "Forget your Pater in the sky," says de Sade, "& look / Beneath your feet—for there resides the Truth."

De Sade fantasizes that once he is freed from Charenton he will again be a "man." His recollection of an earlier orgy guarantees that we know that he will not have changed. With entourage he climbs a mountain to a castle, moves through the iron gates, bowing his head so as not to disturb his coiffure on the nails studding the iron work:

After passing through twelve gates, crossing
Two moats, & crawling, by torch light,
Through four tunnels—(that were successively
Filled with water to make our retreat impossible)—
We climbed from the last tunnel into an enclosed
Courtyard. Two crones of about sixty years of age
Stepped from the shadows, & then, after Sbrigini signaled—
Advanced on their knees to us, whining & sniffing.
"Pinch them, kick them!" he shouted. "They want only your most violent
Greetings." & so we complied with our Host's
Suggestions. "Tie them up, the curs are ready for a beating."
"You there," Sbrigini whispered, "Give them a taste
Of French courtesy." And he handed me a bull's pizzle
Fairly six feet long. I plied their asses with it,
Making them scream while I cut their wrinkled hides
To the bone. By this time Sbrigini was surrounded
By four young men ranging in age from eighteen to twenty-four,
& an equal number of little girls, from nine to twelve
Years of age. The men took turns embuggering our gracious Host
While the little girls annointed their Master's prick
& led it to Omphale's vagina, which was now
Heated by the bloody spectacle that I was producing
For the company. . . .

As I have proposed, Glass, Northup, and Moore (I also include Patrick Mackinnon, Ron Androla, Nicola Manning, and Jay Doughtery here) indicate new and serious directions for poetry of the 1980's. They represent, at the very least, refreshing alternatives to the vapid and quiet experiential, first-person, reportage poem that now dominates nearly all of the journals, reviews, presses, and academic writing workshops considered to be our most reputable, I'll bet on Glass, Moore, et al. Put your money here too.

Voice Poems

Volumes could be written on the "voice" or "persona" poem as practiced by American poets. Here I shall merely sketch some of the varieties, and name some of the better-known poets who work in this way. Their generally acknowledged sire is Robert Browning, whose dramatic monologues are justly famous. One of Richard Howard's monologues is spoken by Browning on a last visit to his son Pen before his death.

Contemporary voice poems fall into two chief categories. First, there are those, generally short, in which the poet keeps him or herself at a distance from the speaker—the poet either fails to enter, or does not choose to enter, the other psyche. Second, there are those, generally book-length, in which the poet does manage to inhabit, or wear the skin of, the speaker.

One recent ambitious collection of monologues which falls into the first category is Pamela White Hadas's *Beside Herself: Pocahontas to Patty Hearst* made up of brief excursions into the minds of twenty-five females, all victims of male domination. Most had the grit needed for survival. The pitch of the book is polemical. The dullest poems are those about Betsy Ross sewing the flag, passionate for doltish George Washington; Patty Hearst, written as a quasi-recitative in the voices of Patty's family, kidnappers, and friends; and Carrie Nation, who is far more loquacious than her tale warrants. The best pieces are either fairly short or humorous. Anyone who has seen a daughter waste away with anorexia will be moved by the poem "Diary." The letters from a wife and her maid to Lydia Pinkham are hilarious and touching. Harriet Tubman, in dialect, also succeeds. Hadas' overall problem is that she seems too intent on making readers feel comfortable with what they already know. The result is a popular poetry, a sort of *People* magazine in verse.

In contrast, Adrienne Rich's "Paula Becker to Clara Westhoff", in *Dream of a Common Language,* is anything but superficial. Rich inhabits Becker's psyche without forcing the persona into a mold—the poem reads effortlessly and compassionately. Beneath it stirs Rich's rage over the difficulties met by these two women, one married to the poet Rainer Maria Rilke, the other married to the painter Otto Modersohn. Becker died in childbirth, after a hemorrhage, murmuring, as Rich reports, *"What a pity!"*

A most impressive series of voice poems is W. D. Snodgrass's *The Fuhrer Bunker,* a book-length series of monologues in the voices of Speer, Heinrici, Weidling, Bormann, Fegelein, Goebbels, Goebbels's wife, and Eva Braun. But there are problems, the chief being a general sameness of voice. The monologues are usually long—but the best ones (Hermann Fegelein, for example) are short. The cadences of succeeding lines border on the monotonous, a monotony not quite redeemed by the frequent end-rhymes and the well-turned rondeau (spoken by Magda Goebbels). While Snodgrass's technical skills are as much in evidence as ever, I rarely feel here that the master's voice has a real chance to be heard. He seems to strive for the manner and presence of a stageable work; as a result the voice is too often Shakespearean in language and timing. There is considerable fustian and staginess, elocution rather than deeply felt acting.

For other treatments of the voice poem, see John Berryman's classic *Homage to Mistress Bradstreet;* Richard Howard's various collections, especially his "Homage to Nadar" from *Lining Up;* Frank Bidart's *The Sacrifice,* which contains a chapbook-length monologue in the voice of the dancer Nijinsky; Ruth Whitman's *Tamsen Donner;* and my own treatments of the lives and psyches of the seventeenth-century mass murderer Countess Elizabeth Bathory; the English mystic and founder of the Shaker religion Mother Ann Lee; the nineteenth-century Bavarian king Ludwig II; the nineteenth-century Cornish vicar, mystic, and poet Robert Stephen Hawker; the American explorer Elisha Kent Kane; and the early Victorian painter Benjamin Robert Haydon.

War Poems

One historian determined that between 1860 and 1980 the world had seen 182 wars. Numerous poets from Homer onwards have written of these conflicts. Walt Whitman's "Drum Taps" was probably the first book to describe graphically the horror as it seared the individual soldier fighting during the Civil War. Whitman had not entirely abandoned a belief in patriotic glory, and believed that war generates intimacies between men impossible in peace time. It remained for poets of the Boer War and the First World War to mark the transition in literature from combat as abstract glory to war as an individualized horror.

During the Boer War the British imprisoned Boer civilians in camps, where between 16,000 and 26,000 women and children died—more than the number of soldiers killed during the entire war. In several other respects, this was an unpleasantly twentieth-century conflict. As one war correspondent wrote: "In Natal, war was divested of absolutely everything that once lent it meretricious glamour—no bright uniforms, no inspiring bands playing men into battle, no flags, no glitter or smoke or circumstance of any kind, but just plain primeval killing, without redemption." This nasty war was a war of trenches, hand grenades, dum-dum bullets, khaki uniforms, armored trains, and cut telegraph lines. Its guerrilla successes foretold a chain of similar applications, in China, France, Malaysia, Ireland, Vietnam, and Angola. In hindsight it seems prophetic that a large empire at its peak had such difficulty defeating a two-colony federation.

World War I was naively called "the war to end all wars," the "Great War," or the "World War"—as if there could never be others. We see it today as a war fought ferociously and with little justification, more for business and colonial rearrangement than specific ideals. An old saw in military history says that any given army always has the equipment and tactics ready to win the war that it has most recently participated in. A corollary to that is suggested by mustard gas and maxim guns: military applications of technology are always one war ahead of the ethical and intellectual considerations relevant to the use of that technology.

Approximately twenty-five thousand miles of Allied and Axis trenches snaked through western Europe, from the North Sea to Switzerland. These trenches were narrow corridors through the mud, filled with water, lice, rats, shell fragments, and human and animal (particularly horse) remains. Front-line troops lived as much as possible below ground. The poet Siegfried Sassoon, who was there, dryly commented: "The war was mainly a matter of holes and ditches." The British averaged seven thousand casualties per day. Paul Fussell, in *The Great War and Modern Memory,* quotes an unpublished manuscript by a British officer. While in the trenches, he reports that "it was a morbid but intensely interesting occupation tracing the various battles amongst the hundreds of skulls, bones and remains scattered thickly about. The progress of our successive attacks could be clearly seen from the types of equipment on the skeletons, soft cloth caps denoting the 1914 and 1915 fighting, then respirators, then steel helmets marking attack in 1916. Also Australian slouch hats, used in the costly and abortive attack in 1916."

Between eight to ten million people were killed in this war, and over twenty million were wounded. Given all this, the incredibly bitter tone of the British "war poets" Rosenberg, Owen, and Sassoon is not surprising. When Sassoon tried to place one of his poems in the *Westminster,* it was turned down because the editors felt it might "prejudice recruiting." Any general recognition of what these poets felt and wrote took a decade to arrive, and most of the classic prose works on the war did not appear until ten years had passed after the armistice—Remarque's *All Quiet on the Western Front* and Robert Grave's *Goodbye to All That* in 1928; Hemingway's *Farewell to Arms* in 1929; and Sassoon's *Memoirs of an Infantry Officer* in 1930.

The war consumed many of the very people who might have most tellingly recorded it: Brooke, Gaudier-Brzeska, Grenfell, Hulme, McCraw, Owen, Rosenberg, Seeger, Thomas—all were killed before November 11, 1918.

Nor was World War II to be outdone for horrors, with its concentration camps, the gargantuan losses of military and civilian lives (particularly by the Russians and the French), the internment of Japanese civilians and conscientious objectors in America, and the use of nuclear weapons for the first time on Hiroshima and Nagasaki. And then came the Vietnam conflict, which so wrenched and divided the American people. Our poets, interestingly, were almost universally opposed to the conflict, and, indeed, by launching rallies of poetry readings and speeches played a seminal role in concluding the war. Vietnam, perhaps because of the searing moral dilemmas and lack of clear-cut reasons for waging it, has generated more poems than any other American war. One sees the aftermath of its influence in the controversy over American policy in Central America; once again American poets are employing their pens in protest.

Since poems on war are so numerous, I shall here name some of the more visible ones written by American poets, listed war by war, without discussing them. Poems about the Vietnam War appear earlier. Readers may consult their libraries for war anthologies; one of the most recent is Jon Stallworthy's *The Oxford Book of War Poetry* (1984). I have been assisted in preparing "War Poems" by Charles Hood.

World War I

e. e. cummings: "i sing of Olaf glad and big," "my sweet old etcetera," "next to of course god america, i," "the bigness of cannon," and numerous love poems to French women
T. S. Eliot: "Triumphal March"
Amy Lowell: "Convalescence"
John Peale Bishop: "In the Dordogne"
Robert Lowell: "Verdun"
Harriet Monroe: "On the Porch"
Ezra Pound: "Canto XVI"
Carl Sandburg: "AEF," "Gargoyle," and "Grass"
Robert Frost: "Range-Finding"
Wallace Stevens: "The Death of a Soldier"

World War II

W. H. Auden: "September 1, 1939"
Gregory Corso: "Army"
James Dickey: Helmets and "The Firebombing"
Richard Eberhart: "The Fury of Aerial Bombardment"
William Everson: "The Raid"
T. S. Eliot: "Defense of the Island"
Thom Gunn: "The Corporal" and "Claus Von Stauffenberg"
Alfred Starr Hamilton: "Deign to Design," "Hold Fast Army Buttons," "It's Army Baloney," "the a.w.o.l. pacifist"
Anthony Hecht: "More Light! More Light!"
Edwin Honig: "Soldier"
Randall Jarrell: "Burning the Letters," "Death of the Ball Turret Gunner," "8th Air Force," "Losses," "A Camp in the Prussian Forest," "A Front," and "Prisoners"
Philip Levine: "The Horse: for Ichiro Kawamoto . . . survivor of Hiroshima"
Robert Lowell: "Christmas Eve Under Hooker's Statue"
Archibald MacLeish: "Memorial Rain"
Marianne Moore: "In Distrust of Merits"
Thomas Merton: "Epitaph for a Public Servant"
Howard Nemerov: "Redeployment" and "A Fable of the War"
Edward Oppen: "Armies of the Plain"

Kenneth Patchen: "How to Be an Army" and "I Don't Want to Startle You"
Kenneth Rexroth: "On a Military Graveyard"
Karl Shapiro: "The Conscientious Objector" and "Elegy for a Dead Soldier"
W. D. Snodgrass: The Fuhrer Bunker and "After Experience Taught Me"
Louis Simpson: "Carentan O Carentan," "Memories of a Lost War," "The
    Battle," and "The Heroes"
Richard Wilbur: "First Snow in Alsace"
James Tate: "The Lost Pilot"

The much ignored Alfred Starr Hamilton (I treat him at length in "National Treasures") writes anti-militarist poems, some of which appear in the only substantial collection of his work to date, *The Poems of Alfred Starr Hamilton*. The entire second section of *Poems*, subtitled "the a. w. o. l. pacifist," is irretrievably antiwar, though no poems are overtly propagandistic. In fact, most are so devious they make sense only in terms of the subtitle. This is one of the more overt pieces:

Peace—1934–1939

Gosh, it didn't last very Long.,
        It was proud gray deserted Feeling,
Come Comfortable out of a Fog—
                Too boot or to bootless and onto dry Martinis
            Until finally a dark brown taste
                            Set down in the back of its Mouth,
            Fog drifting away—we had to know what it was—
Being driven by war monsters

During wartime, the lovely homespun events of a seemingly trivial day are tarnished and threatened:

Peace Being

Morning's dishwashing isn't as golden to some,
If others have their afternoon's golden noonish
And golden sun's in east side's kitchen windows,
And golden suds, and golden suns's suds are rarer
In the morning's fresh and full of Saturday's dishpans,
Peace being, frying pans, that do belong, to be scraped,—
Truth is there are afternoon's Saturday children to be scraped;
Knees that are scraped, those that shine, those that are dirtier,
And heroes that hid behind fire escapes, those are dirtier than others,—
And sunshine in suds does live in the minds of golden mothers
Out of afternoonish golden west side kitchen windows,
Outlandishly, they couldn't be scraped, they can't be scraped,
They will never be scraped or cleaned or gilded forever

In "Deign to Design," a chilling sense of lost hope accretes around the image of a steel pin, possibly a part of the soldier's rifle:

If
it's
a
steel pin

It
isn't
to
dig your grave with

If
it's
dug
already.

Lighter is this satiric comment on GI beer:

Even Himmler who'd accused us of rape
Gasped at ivy 3.2. American poisoning.

In this pair of poems, his personal bitterness is vivid; the Army has him
fast by the buttons:

It's Army Baloney

Is hatred baloney?
And getting one's teeth into it
And getting one's teeth out of it
And never forgiving any of them for any of it

Hold Fast, Army Buttons

Ironically, those are brass buttons
that are made of holdfast iron

Dumbfounded, those are brass knuckles
to have been tied to just straitjackets

Those are a tyrant's muscles
to your best vest buttons

He writes of World War I, which occurred during his boyhood:

Wilhelm's

Aw, why didn't you say pie and cake?
and pie in the sky
and a nickel in the slot, and to boot,
And that's all I had

At the bottom of my heart
That I needed another dime, and to boot;
Aw, why didn't you say half witted?,
And wanted the feathers put back on the owl, to loot,
That old Father Wilhelm had ordered a lot
And had turkey and pie and a heart,
An owl for a nickel shot out of the whole slot

He satirizes parades celebrating wars and a stupid citizenry ("class hysteria") incapable of comprehending what they huzzah for:

(just after the war with the Kaiser)
NOONDAY TRUMPETS

Why, they are musical giants who came to town!
One blew the trumpet louder than all the rest!
Another one shook the neighborhood with what wonderful laughter;
I laughed and I cried when I heard of them coming;
An elephant most certainly shall have been leading the procession.
That had been a beast of silence and ingratitude
That had hovered over us like a brooding cloud for days.
But they cleared the atmosphere;
And rattled our china closets.
They came to a halt!,
And played, and played to a brooding silence that has ever been.
Another one who blew the trumpet louder
Can have tickled the ribs, said to the bannisters, and asked for mercy;
Another one of my age rode downstairs to meet the clown.
There can have been such an ingrained ingratitude—
By now the elephant was as delighted as ever;
I listened to the music clearer than ever before;
I laughed and I cried for joy.
Others waved back at another clown;
They stayed at a halt!
That had been a town that for days
and days had forgotten what wonderful laughter!

  (before, that has been a state of class hysteria,
  but no state of mind at all.)

George Oppen was among the few American poets of World War II who participated in actual combat. Echoes of his experience appear in central portions of the forty-part title poem of his collection *Of Being Numerous* (1968). The reticence for which he is known is also present—he eschews heroics, and jingoism, nor does he seem much concerned with evoking for civilian readers the harrowing life of soldiers on the European front. He arraigns the president and the militarists for the defenseless civilians bombed and burned in raids. Helicopters reflect the atrocities of "the casual will."

In "Route" (from *Of Being Numerous*), Oppen writes a lengthy prose account of his experience near the Battle of the Bulge, and recalls how citizens of Alsace joked about "digging holes." *Faire une trou* assumed grisly connotations for them. Alsatian men, knowing they were to be drafted into military service by the Germans, would tell their families they were leaving to dig a hole for themselves—and often that hole became death via car-wreck, so anxious were they to avoid fighting for the Germans.

These passages lead Oppen to reflect on the conduct of men in war:

> We are brothers, we are brothers?—these things are
> composed of a moral substance only if they are untrue. If
> these things are true they are perfectly simple, perfectly
> impenetrable, those primary elements which can only be
> named.

Water Creature Poems

The denizens of oceans, lakes, streams, and ponds have always excited poets. The archetypal image for rescuers and sustainers of human life is biblical—Jonah's whale, along with the miraculous loaves and fishes.

Among older poets writing on this theme were William Blake ("Behemoth and Leviathan"), Alfred Tennyson ("The Kraken"), Matthew Arnold ("The Forsaken Merman"), Robert Browning ("Caliban upon Setebos"), A. C. Swinburne (the shark-leviathan image from "Hymn to Proserpine"), Walt Whitman (the tormented fluke-splashing whale of "Song of Myself"); D. H. Lawrence ("Whales Weep Not!"); and William Carlos Williams ("The Sea-Elephant").

More recent are Elizabeth Bishop's "The Fish" and her less well-known but even better "At the Fishhouses"; Mary Oliver's "Mussels"; Robert Bly's "The Dead Seal Near McClure's Beach"; Laurence Lieberman's lavish and energetic display of life on a coral reef seen from the point of view of a sea-diver, "The Coral Reef"; James Dickey's "The Movement of Fish"; Daryl Hine's "The Trout"; James Merrill's "The Octopus"; Robert Morgan's "Bass"; Marianne Moore's "The Paper Nautilus"; Edward Field's "Giant Pacific Octopus" (which transmogrifies into a lovely boy anxious to make love with all his arms); and Charles Bukowski's "the catch."

James Hejna's "Fish Teach Him About Violence" reflects the scientist-poet's speculations on the evolution of forms and human error:

> The human error comes in, accounting
> for different head sizes in the same carton.
> —a random newspaper clipping

No wonder amphibians evolved!
Piled in the market are so many fish
heads with mouths that could pouch
a frog's ancestry (fish have changed little).
Far less competition was to be found
in Devonian swamp-forests of cycads and ferns.
Once they could digest arthropods, nothing stopped
the move inland to a three-chambered heart,
limbs and lungs, cockroaches taken by surprise, virtually
licked off the stalks of thin-stemmed horsetail.
No true magic, only tricks: evolution—
from out of the water, the structural
requirements of limbs, feeling the head
to turn about the body.

Out of the water, caught in nets and pithed,
Rana pipiens, your niche is no longer secure.
    I knew a hotel at St. Charles Place and Boardwalk;
    The publicity postcard was labelled, "Section of Lobby."
    Davenports. Loveseats. Armchairs. Venetian blinds.
Left and right auricles. Pancreas. A thigh rigged
to a power supply and the threshold voltage
for a kick graphed on a revolving drum.
There is no question of the eventual loss of habitats.
The Sahara advances; swamps fill in and die.
What selective pressure does man exert on himself?
Looking back, I find I fell in love with a girl
who singed my hair with a Bunsen burner—
God! I want to be fossilized . . .

West Coast Poems

Among American cultural centers San Francisco alone rivals New York as a center for poetry. Los Angeles, Seattle, Port Washington, Portland, Santa Cruz, Stanford, and San Diego are much less brilliantly lit centers, though not without their special ambiences. What San Francisco lacks in publishers, awards, organizations, relics of the hair and bones of dead poets, and statues to famous poets, it more than makes up for with verve, daring, and its own special brand of brains. Ever since the mid-fifties when the New York Beatnik expatriates Allen Ginsberg, Gregory Corso, and assorted drelbs piped their way to San Francisco, displacing an indigenous Bay Area poetry scene—Madeline Mason, Robert Duncan, James Broughton—San Francisco has been a magnet for hirsute, dope-ingesting, "far-out" poets.

Much of what transpires in the Bay Area today is almost entirely disregarded on the East Coast. Such highly visible San Francisco poets as Robert Duncan, Lawrence Ferlinghetti, and Michael McClure love the city so much they are content to be better known in Europe than in New York. This seems true also of the horde of good but lesser poets who hardly bother to look up from their parchments to glance east. San Francisco is as cozy, nourishing, and self-contained as a vixen's den, all weatherized with golden hair, ivy leaves, and sumac and eucalyptus fronds. Poets live out entire lives there, satisfied to appear in local poetry-reading venues, to publish their books in limited editions (which they may hawk on Telegraph Avenue in Berkeley), and to luxuriate in San Francisco's reputation as the American city most "on the edge."

Within that hallowed area between the Golden Gate and the Bay, factions do exist. There are the older poets and their followers—Duncan, McClure, Gunn, and Broughton. A North Beach group clusters over espresso at the Vesuvius or some other nearby spot, chanting "Beatitudes" to one another, gazing through their hair, speaking through their beards, scribbling odes and free-verse missives on the backs of napkins and torn shopping bags. The current guru of the scene is Jack Hirschman, the longtime radical and still very much a political activist. There is a Noe Valley poetry world just over the hill from Castro centered around Small Press Traffic, a bookstore with one of the largest supplies of poetry books and journals in the country. Finally, there is the San Francisco State Poetry Center, with one of the largest collections of video and casette tapes and films of poets anywhere.

The most visible new faction, and one with Eastern overtones, consists of the "language poets," known for their "snubbery" of all poetries that don't click with theirs. Initiated by Easterners Charles Bernstein and Barrett Watten, the cult is the second influx of note to hit San Francisco from New York—the Beats were the first. Marjorie Perloff devotes much energy to writing up her enthusiasms for these poets. *Temblor* and *Sulfur* specialize in them. These poets are pretty much ignored by *The American Poetry Review*, the writing programs, and the Poetry Society of America, and their books are seldom reviewed in major Eastern magazines.

An important presence unifying all Bay Area scenes is *Poetry Flash*, containing the best reviews, interviews, and calendar listings devoted to poetry in the United States. Joyce Jenkins and Richard Silberg are in charge. Interviews and features (not only of Bay Area poets) are of primary importance.

Across the bay in Berkeley, the University of California poetry scene is as conservative as any on the East Coast. What special poetry occurs in Berkeley does so away from the University—in Jack Foley's reading series on Telegraph Avenue, and at Cody's Bookstore. There is also Marin County, where whatever happens seems to have a lot of money behind it—conservative poets are welcome; no hirsute, exclamatory, irreverent, scatalogical scribblers need apply.

Just north of San Francisco lies Bolinas in a lovely cove. During the seventies poets flocked there, seeking cheap rents (or no rents) and a "community" impossible to sustain in San Francisco or Berkeley. Before long the town was known as the hepatitis capital of the West Coast—

homeless poets, hippie vagabonds, dogs, and an assortment of flower children and other free spirits carelessly deposited their feces on the beach, creating a disastrous health hazard. The best-known poet there was Robert Creeley.

The only threat to San Francisco's domination of West Coast poetry comes from Los Angeles, an area that has matured much culturally over the past few years. A clear Los Angeles tone appears in its verse, visible in the pages of William Mohr's recent anthology *Poetry Loves Poetry:* Holly-wood, Beverly Hills, the glorious beaches, tanned people, the Gucci-level dope, the plethora of vivid rock and punk groups, the lotus, the nymph, the hustler, and the columbine. While L.A. has a vigorous poetry center (Beyond Baroque, in Venice), it lacks a major journal.

White Poems

L et's fantasize about the sources of poetic inspiration. Let's imagine blood-red beef filets dripping and glistening with saliva-inducing juices, a sort of wonderful "sillion," to use Hopkins's word, shiny with protein. Let's imagine that beside those life-sustaining, protein-rich filets there are white daisy petals, swan breasts smothered in chestnut sauce, candied pear blossoms, blanc mange, luna moth wings, or nitre scraped from the ceilings of a guru's cave. White doesn't excite us much, whether as food or as poetry.

A brilliant "white" poem, however, is Robert Frost's "Design," a tour de force investigating the thematic materials of a white spider, a white moth, and a white heal-all flower. To lack redness, I am saying, or to lack tint, is to come off as pallid, precious, and ineffectual—muslin and gauze, not beef on the hoof.

Gerard Malanga's "Rosebud" is rife with easy phrases: "frozen with silence," clouds crossing moons "in the distance," "the invisible wind," "the life of the one real dream." I understand that during his "Rosebud" days, Malanga consciously entered his white night of the soul period (as distinguished from the practice of other mystics, who achieve transcen-dence via a dark night of the soul). Dressed in mystic white he appeared as a pure non-body meditator who delivered whitening mystical poems. He was a poet caught up in his own whiteness.

Pallor abounds. If Malanga's world were more substantial, he'd fill the landscape with limpid, glassy Pre-Raphaelite pools, surrounded by narcissi, white roses, and pale lilies, all meant to induce perfect white-ness. There's a winsome purity about it all, as though a lovely angel with somewhat bedraggled though still iridescent wings tumbled from the sky, can't return, and remains on earth with snow, pale pebbles, and gentle regrets. In his poem "snow voices swirling," the title is the most vital moment. The sentimental words flag where a telling image might have hinted at some profound feeling: "inside," "a silence is hiding," "all i need / it's here in this silence."

A master of the white poem was Wallace Stevens, with W. S. Merwin close behind him. Read Stevens's "The Poems of our Climate" (a white bowl is "cold, a cold porcelain, low and round, / With nothing more than the carnations there"); "On the Manner of Addressing Clouds"; "On the Surfaces of Things"; and "The Curtains in the House of the Metaphysician."

W. S. Merwin, in *Writings to an Unfinished Accompaniment*, creates a Puvis de Chavannes world of washed tones and misty languor. His technique is so fluent and polished you forget what he is saying, marveling at his brilliance. His tone is always somewhat formal, *grave* (in the French sense), seldom humorous, and never offensive. There is almost no color here, and hardly any detail, except for vaguely rendered bandages, clouds, asters, worn brick surfaces, a paw print, smoke, gold, a doorstep, a crack in a wall. At least fifteen of these poems have mountains, and almost as many have clouds, lights, doors, and windows (both shut and open). None of these (including dogs, his favorite animal) is clearly seen. He gives us "cloud," say, and leaves us to determine whether it is cumulus, sagging with rain, or cirrus. To my mind, an image ordinarily suggests something concrete, a thing seen, felt, smelled, or tasted. Just as an egg in a basket represents something more than breakfast, an image carries one or more concepts with it. Merwin's typical image leaves the visual possibilities almost entirely open. This is typical of white poetry.

One of his favorite images is "light," an image calculated to gratify readers seeking to generate white feelings of a transcendental sort. Light, Merwin says, is special, since it is "the true hunger." In "Dogs" (yes, "God" spelled backward) note the "Happiness is a warm puppy" echoes. "Loneliness" (one of the whitest of all tags)

> . . . is someone else's dog
> that you're keeping
> then when the dog disappears
> and the dog's absence
> you are alone at last . . .
> but at last it may be
> that you are your own dog
> hungry on the way
> the one sound climbing a mountain
> higher than time

If we are "the one sound" climbing the mountain (are we also one hand clapping?), our lives are minuscule existentialist acts. Our strain does not equal what Sisyphus endured; climbing a mountain, packless, bookless, can be debilitating, and especially if the mountain is colorless and abstract. The need for struggle of some kind is implicit.

Shelley's idea of beauty, in its origins and combinations, is similar. Shelley took the image of a forest lake: bubbles begin at the bottom and effervesce almost soundlessly to the surface. These bubbles escape, combine with other bubbles emanating from other lakes and from all living matter, and finally form a symphony of life in the universe. In their highest ascension these sounds reach the One, the All. Well, this may not be good science, but it fosters good art. And it still does, as Merwin's poem "Gift" shows. He moves from a pure Shelleyan statement to a prayer uttered by the speaker (Merwin?) in his loneliness.

The Shelleyan symbols (and even the Shelleyan language) reveal Merwin's sources, and his place in a long tradition. Merwin's mountain is "shadowless." It is the Romantic poet's mountain, seen as the Ideal bathed in full lambency. Night also appears, and silence—the alembic for Shelley's mystical awareness. He summons the Eternal, and the morning—the Romantic symbol of refreshment. These are all considerable "gifts" to Merwin, who expresses his gratitude in a surprisingly pure Shelleyan prayer:

> I call to it Nameless One O Invisible
> Untouchable Free
> I am nameless I am divided
> I am invisible I am untouchable
> and empty
> nomad live with me
> be my eyes
> my tongue and my hands
> my sleep and my rising
> out of chaos
> come and be given

I call this white writing, not poetry.

Another poet specializing in white poetry is Theodore Enslin, whose *Songs Without Notes* is a gathering of airy trails, leaf-notes, and white verses, which go far toward the end goal of presenting readers with empty pages. A wearying didacticism accompanies Enslin's minimalism—self-imposed isolation seems to engender a tedious malady among many American poets.

These forty-eight poems are brief and compressed. They might have been scribbled in berry juice with a turkey quill on birchbark, or brushed down with gray ink on rice paper. Many are mere whispers (Enslin likes the word) meant to turn in one's mind and be lingered over. As with Malanga and Merwin, specific details are largely absent—the reader must flesh out Enslin's abstractions on his own. Such white poems eschew color, dramatic emotions, and reflect little energy beyond pallid flickers wrought through meditation. Enslin is the James McNeill Whistler of contemporary American verse, a poet of white washes and pastel tints.

Poem 9 is almost entirely whitened off the page. There's nary a scrap of color for latching one's imagination to. The culminating abstractions "essence / and immanence," flatulent concepts, are led up to by these equally neutral concepts: "place," "space," "figure," and "object."

In one sense the ideal white poem is the empty page itself. Perhaps it's a matter of degree. I wait for the spiritual brush before which Enslin meditates to burst into flame.

A fine poem by Gary Metras, "The Contradiction of White" (*Destiny's Calendar*) is a reminder that white poems may transcend their built-in limitations. He's writing of white-walled nunneries and mental hospitals:

> When every wall is white
> there is a darkness where no one looks.

A praying nun evokes much dark/light play:

> There is light in the words to match
> the hour of death. Her room is white
> in anticipation of death.
> She kneels like the black "L"
> in Light, in Love.

As she ages, her prayers "blur" in her heart:

> Walls become indistinguishable
> except for the spot where the window
> tempts. It shines without halo,
> is a silk dress never worn.

When prayer is "diffused," a shadow falls out, a "last piece" unsuited to fit the final "sculpted hole in the puzzle." So, in asylums, "pale walls . . . meet / in dark corners / where white is a complexion of the mind." And as aging parents pray in a church, "watching the white ceiling arch back on itself / until vision is clothed in shadow," death is "postponed another year." Metras' style is *unwhitened*—Malanga's, Merwin's, and Enslin's are not.

A triumphant poem of whiteness is Lawrence Ferlinghetti's "White on White" (*Endless Life: Selected Poems,*). The assembling of white objects is original, and at first the reader is unaware that what seems a tour de force will exfoliate with meanings. Clues are present from the start: a sea creature "eats light / straining the ocean for its phosphorus." "Present time" is a mere "white dot" in space. The white sand in the hour glass is running out. Geography expands—to African white sand dunes, Siberian snows, sperm-white seas, white moonlight through which "aluminum stars wheel about noiselessly / over quivering earth." Something expansive and momentous is at hand.

The agent of truth is a white angel hovering over a railway platform where a train of boxcars waits filled with "three billion people," all the inhabitants of the earth, refugees from "a torn village." Placards go up, as white searchlights pierce the night looking for raiding planes. "*No pasaran / Go back Wrong way.*" The angel moves its gossamer wings, "breathing the light white air," air which seems an anarchistic "freedom." Human liberty, Ferlinghetti says, is never free (men crave to be governed). A white phoenix rises from pinion smoke, bearing a secret we can't decipher:

And the "white sphinx of chance"
still holds its tongue
on the desert roads of the future

Wise Child Poems

Too many poems on children are blatantly sentimental and, if the child belongs to the poet, self-congratulatory. The worst of these likely take their cue from the famous passage in Wordsworth's "Ode: Intimations of Immortality," giving a thoroughly saccharine reading of babyhood:

> Behold the Child among his newborn blisses,
> A six-years' Darling of a pygmy size!
> See, where 'mid work of his own hand he lies,
> Fretted by sallies of his mother's kisses,
> With light upon him from his father's eyes!

Robert Lowell's "Home after Three Months Away" flirts with sentimentality. Though the poem does not make this clear, the reader assumes that Lowell has returned from a stay in a mental hospital. His joy at bathing with his small daughter is convincing. She's "dimpled with exaltation." Lowell is forty-one—he's added a year during his absence. He's reassured when his daughter performs the usual ritual, dabbing her cheeks with shaving cream to start her dad on his beard. She's most playful. Dressed in sky-blue corduroy,

> she changes to a boy,
> and floats my shaving brush
> and washcloth in the flush. . . .
> Dearest, I cannot loiter here
> in lather like a polar bear.

Gary Snyder's "The Bath," in which he shares a sauna with his young son, is loving and intimate. The steam is rich, and as he observes Kai's body he is moved:

> Kai's little scrotum up close to his groin,
>   the seed still tucked away, that moved from us to him
> In flows that lifted with the same joys forces
>   as his nursing Masa later,
>   playing with her breast,
> Or me within her,
> Or him emerging,
>
>   *this is our body. . . .*

Another moving poem of a father with a child is Robert Bly's "For My Son Noah, Ten Years Old" (*The Man in The Black Coat Turns*). Here Bly juxtaposes his own aging with the aging of physical objects (the lumber pile, an old tree, the barn) and the on-going of creatures who have no awareness of human time and death:

> The horse steps up, swings on one leg, turns its body,
> the chicken flapping claws onto the roost, its wings whelping and
>   walloping. . . .

This "kind man" cools his rage, moves to the table where his son is drawing:

> when you sit drawing, or making books, stapled, with messages to the
>   world,
> or coloring a man with fire coming out of his hair.
> Or we sit at a table, with small tea carefully poured.
> So we pass our time together, calm and delighted.

Peter Cooley's "For Alissa" does not avoid the adventitious and sentimental. Eight-year-old Alissa is a charmer, with dancing topaz eyes, and is always in motion. She was from her mother's womb untimely ripped (I wish Cooley hadn't made this facile allusion, yet another instance of academic sleaze):

> Who from her mother was ripped
> before her time and clung to Death
> three days until he fell.

Far more original is Elizabeth Ann Socolow's "Men in the House, Summertime After A Swim." She comes upon her adolescent sons naked for the first time since they were babies—and remembers their "scabby knees and boysex" as she helped trundle them into their pajamas. Now, six or seven years later, they come in from a swim and she sees their "penises thick and sudden, crowned / in the wide nests of hair." Her wonder becomes something of a vision:

> It happened by accident—
> maleness sprung from me,
> *and* seeing it, again—
> a whale on the horizon,
> the enormous presence
> altering the water
> for miles.

At times when poets write of their own childhood, their wee selves come off as precocious. Maura Stanton, for example, in "Childhood", recalls lying on her back reversing her house so that the floor became the ceiling. Life was simplified, for all the rooms turned empty, with the normal ceiling light now a glass globe standing in the middle of the floor. Family life going on below her was so cluttered and dismaying she "dizzily" returned to "her perfect floorplan / Where I never spoke or listened to anyone."

D. H. Lloyd's "Dusk" falls flat on its chubby face, done in by kiddie cuteness. Lloyd with his son in a park considers a sunset, and informs the kid that no words can describe its "beauty." His son's rejoinder? "'It looks like . . ./ God got ice cream all over his face.'"

Much more ambitious (and better) is Michael Waters's "Remembering the Oak" (*Not Just Any Death*). Waters believes that his kid has done odd, almost metaphysical things, and that since one of these events occurred near a pine tree, lake, or mountain, there must be a real time-and-theme connection between parent and child. Waters' son has hammered a series of nails into an oak tree to facilitate the squirrels in their climbing. I don't doubt for a moment that the kid did it, though it is a precious. There's a Christ image too—the son has been "hammering his own stubborn / nails into boards, sweating / like Christ in the sun, thumbs blackening. . . ." Waters hopes that someday when the son is grown he will remember this moment when Eternity zapped the oak tree, the father, and the son:

> The nails climbing the trunk
> like furious locusts,
> The father
>
> Who held his fist like the first
> spring leaf, who remains
> rooted like memory
> in the earth.

The generic baby in Joyce Carol Oates's "Baby" p. 209) develops into something of a cutely dimpled, pink, delicate swollen sausage suffocating its mother. It behaves like a mother-devouring organism. Oates is deft and original: the clambering child resembles "a plump wattled purse," coming towards mommy. And the child grows

> . . . enormous with the calendar.
> Cherub-fat, quivering thighs and buttocks,
> snorts of laughter escape you at the sight.
> Wet wide lips, a carnivore smile, *Love me*.

All poets who write sentimental poems about their children should be required each dawn to face east and recite Weldon Kees's "For My Daughter." Kees, you will recall, wrote what seemed to be a parody of such poems. The poet W. B. Yeats hoped to give his daughter, uneducated, a role as the centerpiece of a rich gentleman's life, where all would be "ceremonious." Beneath his daughter's "innocence of morning" Kees discerns death-hints, chilling winds, snarling seaweed, "night's slow poison," a "foul, lingering death" in a war, "the slim legs green." He imagines her as "the cruel" bride "of a syphilitic or a fool." Then comes the famous twist:

> These speculations sour in the sun.
> I have no daughter. I desire none.

Workshop Poems

This malady is a difficult one to pin down; there are so many symptoms. In Rita's Dove's "The Fish in the Stone," chosen by Helen Vendler to represent Dove's work in the *Harvard Anthology*, several signs appear. First, the subject seems contrived—a fish in a stone (a fossil, I assume) appeals to the poet. She's obliged in line one to inform the object with some keen feeling, to show that the object matters. But what does she do? She grabs another workshop device, the pathetic fallacy. Her fish not only would like to "fall" from the stone "back into the sea," but he's something of a philosopher—"analysis" wearies him, he's tired of "small / predictable truths." These high-flown, pretentious sentiments, are ludicrous. Such strained momentosity passeth in workshops for profundity.

Since she has no keen feelings of her own to impart, Dove persists in the pathetic fallacy: he wearies "of waiting / in the open, / his profile stamped / by a white light." This is more workshop business—easy symbolism. "White light" has to be high on a list of facile symbols, and the ensuing "silence" depicting how the ocean "moves and moves," as a poetic device, is far more obvious than the proverbial nose on one's face.

Our fossil (the species of fish is never identified—that might occasion some homework) now arrives at a piece of great wisdom, in the guise of a gift to us "the living": by finding himself locked in stone, he's failed. He's not greatly distressed though, since he "knows to fail is / to do the living / a favor." Wait, we're not finished. The true workshop poem must conclude with some imagery fireworks. No matter how quick the fizzle, there must be a shower of sparks. The more vague and undecipherable the image, the more amazed will other workshop denizens be.

Dove sets off a pair of Roman candles—an ant engineering "a gangster's funeral" and a scientist stroking "the fern's / voluptuous braille." These candles dazzle, and they fizzle as well. Why ant and scientist behave as they do, Dove's fish knows. I'll leave you, dear reader, to supply your own interpretations. Perhaps, when the fish casts "his / skeletal blossom," as he does in the fifth stanza, he has some idea that he too will be studied to further human knowledge. Yet, that doesn't fit too well with Dove's early reading that her finny bit has wearied of analysis and "small predictable truths." I can easily imagine a slow writing workshop spending a good half hour or more on a critique of this one.

While you're busy with Vendler's *Harvard Book of Contemporary American Poetry,* thumb back to the selections by Jorie Graham and feast yourself on more workshop poems. She is almost shockingly bad. "The Geese" begins with a line as spavined as any of the worst written by Matthew Arnold: "today as I hang out the wash I see them again, a code. . . ." It's geese, of course, that the housewife is watching. "Sometimes" (a nicely vague workshop word, useful for softening down any vigorous assertion) she fears the "relevance" of the birds, and comforts herself with things at hand—spiders imitating "the paths the geese won't stray from." The poem goes off into dull abstractions. In "Over and Over Stitch" this woeful line appears: "the bushes have learned to live with their haunches." This is a triple-whammy pathetic fallacy—bushes not only have human consciousness but possess animal haunches. As if this weren't enough, Graham proceeds with other fatuous pathetic fallacies: "The hydrangea is resigned / to its pale and inconclusive utterances." "The tobacco leaves / don't mind being removed / to the long racks." "Mind" begins with a facile image of rain drops as an "unrelenting, syncopated / mind."

Greg Kuzma has written a devastatingly perceptive critique of creative writing in today's colleges and universities, "The Catastrophe of Creative Writing" (*Poetry,* September 1986). He describes better than anyone else has the attributes of the workshop poem. The occasion was a visit by Martha Collins, Director of the Writing Program at the University of Massachusetts, Boston, to the University of Nebraska, where Kuzma teaches. Collins gave a public reading, and it was this event that helped Kuzma crystallize his thoughts.

Workshop poems, he says, "are about nothing much at all except maybe the problem of their own existence." He demonstrates what he means by examining Collins's "Several Things" from her book *The Catastrophe of Rainbows.* Her poem, he finds, "pretends to be about creative writing, but itself entirely lacks a "sense of necessity or urgency." Such poems "risk nothing" and offend no one. They are impersonal, since being personal reveals feelings and also implies responsibility for those feelings. The "quintessential workshop poem," cool and dispassionate, stimulates more cool and dispassionate workshop poems. Kuzma traces these anemic modes to John Ashberry (who stresses "nondeterminacy"), recent work by Donald Justice (probably Collins's teacher at Iowa), and Mark Strand. These poets "lack resolve," and inspire poems lacking in passion, poems that make "little maneuvers" for a self in a totally arbitrary world.

One of Kuzma's examples is a poem by Collins about a Doberman left outside to freeze. The poem is called "Snow":

Five years ago a Doberman froze
in the yard next door to her parent's yard.
From the kitchen window they watched it arch,
trying to touch itself with itself,
until one day it walked away

from the house to the open part of the yard
and made a nest in the snow.
That was the day they had meant to complain. . . .

For Kuzma this poem discourages empathy and action—the only action people take is to react. They have their brandy by the fire, indifferent to the dog's misery as it curls into the smallest possible space to avoid freezing. Collins remains unaware, Kuzma says, of any "guilt she ought to suffer for having been uninvolved."

He finds a similar regrettable distancing in Collins's "In Argentina," inspired (if that is the word) by the famous movie in the 70s in which a woman was supposedly "snuffed" on screen. Collins succeeds here in making her college literary audience feel guilty without taking any position on the matter herself. This is another "trick" of the workshop poem: "The poet herself is not involved with the world, or unwilling to engage anything or to risk anything, and this truth will surely become obvious to the reader or to the audience. But this development, which would then be damaging to the poet, can be averted if the audience is made to direct criticism at itself for its own greater failure in the face of the world's causes and opportunities."

You Poems

This much abused mode turns on these notions: first, the "you" addressed is dead but remains prescient, and thus can hear what's being spoken here on earth. Usually there's some unfinished business—hatred toward a departed family member or a friend dead by suicide or accident. Second, the "you" is still on planet Earth but is absent—possibly a lover who has split after a lover's quarrel. These poems become expressions of wish-fulfillment ranging from self-pity to ecstasy. In both forms the poet's ego is paramount.

Michael Ryan's "Winter Drought" displays the inherent difficulties in this kind of writing. Ryan begins by doing what many of these poets do when writing to someone dead—they assume that the addressee can read or hear the poem, and they also insist on giving information to "you" that "you" would obviously know. Here Ryan reminds P.K. that he (P.K.) first cut his wrists and throat and then lived through three months "of hospitals and talk." Later, "you" stole your dad's car and drove it into a bay. The cops found the car three days before they discovered your "bloated and frozen" body, bequeathing to your friends a "terrible final image." Obviously, while P.K. doesn't require this information, we readers do, and Ryan might have inserted it as a headnote, freeing him to face the issue of his own feelings about his friend.

We soon discover that P.K. was a mere acquaintance. "You were nearly nothing to me—a friend / of a friend, a pushy kid who loved poetry." Yet, Ryan reports, recently, while on a walk he often takes across a wintery field, "you rose abruptly from the undercurrents of memory." The slackness of this line is typical, I fear, of this poem generally. The whole seems "written" and not much "felt" until the close. There is one fine moment though, as Ryan finds his memory "dredged in a steel net" as he approaches the spot where the accident occurred, a spot he'd never seen:

> . . . amid boat noise
> and ocean stink, your corpse
> twisting as if hurt
> when the net broke the surface
> then riding toward me, motionless
> pale blue against the water's black.

Ryan senses that the "you poem" must do more than review information from the past.

Margaret Gibson's excursion into this mode, alas, does not fare well. "Catechism Elegy," a letter to dead parents, is narcissistic ("I"s abound in piles, much as flies and wasps drop on rural Midwestern windowsills during the winter) and filled with pretentious literary turns of phrase: "the rude intent of our silence," "the sting of death hummed in our daily bread," "a radiance that ripened," etc. One unhappy image almost dissuades me from continuing—she sees the parents "as deeply as years" (again the fancy literary turn) curving their "parenthesis" around her, demanding answers to questions she imagines they gave her to answer. What are these questions? Generalized personal destiny questions, such as "Where's your sister?" "Where are you?" "Who are you?" "What have you done?" Again, if the dead folks are alert spirits, they should be smart enough to know the answer to these questions.

On the other hand, Lynn Emanuel creates an original "you poem" while still indulging in the tacky convention of telling "you" what you already know. I assume that the person addressed is Emanuel's mother, who as a girl was taken by her rake of a father to California. She loved the progress of the train over the landscape, "that trail of noise and darkness / Hauling itself across the horizon, / Moths spiraling in the big lamps." She loved "the oily couplings and the women's round hats / Haunting all the windows." The father liked "fast black minks," and on the occasions he left her behind in hotels, she observed his women parading before windows, drinking, naked. She "discovered lust," and knew that some day she would be "on its agenda,"

> Like the woman who drank and walked naked through the house
> In her black hat, the one you used to watch
> Through a stammer in the drapes.
> In that small town of cold hotels, you were the girl in the dress.
> Red as a house burning down.

Another successful poem is Marge Piercy's "Burying Blues for Janis". Piercy does not waste time addressing news to Joplin she would already know. The poem is crammed with energy, conveying Joplin's incredible impact on one fan:

> Your voice always whacked me right on the funny bone
> of the great-hearted suffering bitch fantasy
> that ruled me like a huge copper moon with its phases. . . .

Joplin's "downtrodden juicy longdrawn female blues" fired Piercy's distaste for the "rat race of men" and her own unwillingness to follow through Joplin's ostensible message for female behavior:

> You embodied the beautiful blowzy gum of passivity,
> woman on her back of the world endlessly hopelessly raggedly
> offering a brave front to be fucked.
> That willingness to hang on the meathook and call it love. . . .

Ray Carver in "Your Dog Dies" addresses "you" as a means of stepping off to the side of his own pain in handling the demise of the family's canine, his daughter's favorite pet. The distancing provided by the second person pronoun, and the presence of a dumb, numb tone of almost a Dick and Jane simplicity, produce irony, undercutting as they do the poet's distress:

> it gets run over by a van.
> you find it at the side of the road
> and bury it.
> you feel bad about it.
> you feel bad personally. . . .

"You" buried the creature in the woods, "deep, deep." Your poem is so good "you" are almost happy the dog died. Winsome. You try a new poem, one about writing a poem about the death of a dog. You seem to get carried away, until you are interrupted by a woman screaming "your name, your first name, / both syllables, / and your heart stops." You keep on writing, and she continues screaming: "you wonder how long this can go on."

John Hollander with his usual elegance of form and phrase employs "you" in a generic sense to write a sixteen-liner (four quatrains) on "you"'s departure, a departure either real or imagined. In "A View Out the Window," the departure occurs without glitter or fanfare, with no clinging "pearl of cloudy promise" for the future. Is the sailing simply temporary, to a "warmer port" for a holiday, or is the sailing a permanent rupture, on "a great unreturning ship"? The image, probably imagined by the speaker through his window, turns "dull pigeon gray" rather than white, as "your steamer" dissolves, smeared against the horizon.

List of Primary Works

The following bibliography lists those collections and anthologies where poems receiving more than passing notice may be found and is intended to assist readers who may wish to explore individual authors further. Whenever poems appear in an anthology rather than in a volume of a single poet's work, to save space we have abbreviated the titles of these recurring anthologies; a full list of these books follows. Poems appearing in journals are pinpointed as to the volume, number, and year of those journals. Here are the anthologies most often cited and referred to, with their codes:

ALCATRAZ: *Alcatraz*, ed. by Stephen Kessler, Santa Cruz, 1984, 1985. Appears irregularly.

BREAD: *The Bread Loaf Anthology of Contemporary American Poetry*, ed. by Robert Pack et. al., Hanover & London, University Press of New England, 1985.

CONTROVERSY: *A Controversy of Poets: An Anthology of Contemporary American Poetry*, ed. by Paris Leary and Robert Kelly, Garden City, Doubleday & Co., Inc., 1965.

GENERATION: *The Generation of 2000, Contemporary American Poets*, ed. by William Heyen, Princeton, Ontario Review Press, 1984.

GEOGRAPHY: *A Geography of Poets: An Anthology of the New Poetry*, ed. by Edward Field, New York, Bantam Books, 1979.

HALPERN: *The American Poetry Anthology*, ed. by Daniel Halpern, New York, Avon Books, 1980.

KENNEDY: *An Introduction to Poetry*, sixth edition, ed. by X. J. Kennedy, Boston & Toronto, Little, Brown and Co., 1986.

LIGHT: *The Light From Another Country: Poetry From American Prisons*, ed. by Joe Bruchac et. al., Greenfield Center, NY, Greenfield Review Press, 1984.

MEN TALK: *Men Talk: An Anthology of Male Experience Poetry*, ed. by Elliot Fried and Barry Singer, Eugene, Pacific House Books, 1985.

NAP: *New American Poets of the 80's*, ed. by Jack Myers and Roger Weingarten, Green Harbor, Wampeter Press, 1984.

NEW: *The New American Poetry: 1945–1960*, ed. by Donald M. Allen, New York, Grove Press, 1960.

NETWORKS: *Networks: An Anthology of San Francisco Bay Area Women Poets*, ed. by Carol A. Simone, San Francisco, Vortex Editions, 1979.

NEWS: *News of the Universe: Poems of Twofold Consciousness*, ed. by Robert Bly, San Francisco, Sierra Club, 1980.

OPEN: *Open: Four Anthologies of Expanded Poems*, ed. by Ronald Gross and George Quasha, with Emmett Williams, John Robert Colombo and Walter Lowenfels, New York, Simon and Schuster, 1973.

PLP: *"Poetry Loves Poetry": An Anthology of Los Angeles Poets*, ed. by William Mohr, Santa Monica, Momentum Press, 1985.

PM: *The Postmoderns: The New American Poetry Revised*, ed. by Donald Allen and George F. Butterick, New York, Grove Press, 1982.

POETS ON: *POETS ON: TENTH ANNIVERSARY REPRISE*, Chaplin, CT, vol. 11, no. 1, 1987.

POULIN: *Contemporary American Poetry*, third edition, ed. by A. Poulin, Jr., Boston, Houghton Mifflin & Co., 1980.

STREETS: *The Streets Inside: Ten Los Angeles Poets*, ed. by William Mohr, Santa Monica, Momentum Press, 1978.

VENDLER: *The Harvard Book of Contemporary American Poetry*, ed. by Helen Vendler, Cambridge, Harvard University Press, 1985.

VIETNAM: *Carrying the Darkness: American Indochina—The Poetry of the Vietnam War,* ed. by W. D. Ehrhart, New York, Avon Books, 1985.

VOICE: *The Voice That is Great Within Us: American Poetry of the Twentieth Century,* ed. by Hayden Carruth, New York, Bantam Books, 1971.

YAP: *The Morrow Anthology of Younger American Poets,* ed. by Dave Smith and David Bottoms, New York, Quill, 1985.

21 + 1: *21 + 1: American Poets Today,* ed. by Emmanuel Hocquard and Claude Royet-Journoud, Montpellier Cédex, France, 1986.

List of Authors and Works

Ai, *The Killing Floor*, New York, Houghton Mifflin, 1979

Androla, Ron, "Johnny Cash" in *Bogg* 52, 1984

Antler, "Factory" in *Last Words*, New York, Ballantine, 1986

Arguelles, Ivan, "Shafts of Agony" in *Caliban*, no. 1, 1986; "Nikki I Am Still Talking To You" in *pieces of the bone-text still there*, Portland, OR, Sky Dog Press, 1987

Arnold, Matthew, "A Summer Night"

Ashbery, John, *Selected Poems*, New York, Viking Penguin Inc., 1985

Baker, David, "Running the River Lines," YAP

Balaban, John, *After Our War*, Pittsburgh, University of Pittsburgh Press, 1974

Barnes, Jim, *A Season of Loss*, W. Lafayette, Purdue University Press, 1974; "An Interview with Jim Barnes," by Heinz Woehlk, in *Paintbrush: A Journal of Poetry, Translations, and Letters*, vol. 13, nos. 25 & 26, Spring & Autumn 1986

Bass, Ellen, Untitled Poem in *NETWORKS*

Beckman, Madeleine, "Rosie" in *New York Quarterly*, no. 28, 1985

Bell, Marvin, "Trinket" in *The Antaeus Anthology*, New York, Bantam, 1986

Bernstein, Charles, "Surface Reflectance" in *Temblor*, no. 2, 1985;"Type" in *21 + 1*

Berrigan, Ted. *So Going Around Cities: New and Selected Poems 1958–1979*, Berkeley, Blue Wind Press, 1980

Berry, Wendell, *Farming: A Handbook*, San Diego, Harcourt Brace Jovanovich, 1971; "The Snake" in *GENERATION*

Berryman, John, *Homage to Mistress Bradstreet and Other Poems*, New York, Noonday Press, 1970

Berssenbrugge, Mei-Mei, *21 + 1*

Bertolino, James, *Precinct Kali & The Gertrude Spicer Story*, St. Paul, New Rivers Press, 1981; *Are You Tough Enough for the Eighties?*, St. Paul, New Rivers Press, 1979

Bidart, Frank, *The Sacrifice*, New York, Random House, Inc., 1983

Bishop, Elizabeth, *The Complete Poems*, New York, Farrarr Straus & Giroux, 1965

Blackburn, Paul, "The Slogan" and "The Once-Over" in *PM*

Blauner, Laurie in *Graham House Review*, no. 7, 1984

Blazek, Douglas, "The Factory at Bensenville" in *Alcatraz*, no. 2, 1984

Bloch, Chana, "Magnificat" in *NETWORKS*

Blumenthal, Michael, *Sympathetic Magic*, Huntington Bay, New York, Water Mark Studio, 1980

Bly, Robert, *The Light Around the Body*, New York, Harper & Row, 1967; *The Man in the Black Coat Turns*, New York, Doubleday & Co., Inc., 1981; *Sleepers Joining Hands*, New York, Harper & Row, 1973

Bogen, Laurel Ann, *Do Iguanas Dance Under the Moonlight*, Los Angeles, Illuminati, 1982

Bottoms, David, "The Desk" and "The Copperhead" in YAP

Braverman, Kate, *Lullaby For Sinners: Poems 1970–1979*, New York, Harper & Row, 1980

Brinnin, John Malcom, *The Sorrows of Cold Stone: Poems 1940–1950*, New York, Dodd, Mead & Co., 1951

Bromige, David, "Red Hats" in *Boxcar*, no. 1, 1983

Broughton, James, *A Long Undressing*, New York, The Jargon Society, 1971

Broumas, Olga, *Pastoral Jazz*, Port Townsend, Copper Canyon Press, 1983

Brown, D. F., "Eating the Forest" and "When I Am 19 I Was A Medic" in *VIETNAM*

Browne, Michael Dennis, "Mengele" in *Iowa Review*, vol. 16, no. 1, 1986

Bryan, Sharon, "Big Sheep Knocks You About" in YAP

Budbill, David, *Pulp Cutter's Nativity*, Woodstock, Countryman Press, 1981

Bukowski, Charles, *At Terror Street and Agony Way*, Los Angeles, Black Sparrow Press, 1968; *Burning in Water, Drowning in Flame*, Santa Barbara, Black Sparrow Press,

1977; *The Days Run Away Like Wild Horses Over the Hills,* Los Angeles, Black Sparrow Press, 1969

Butscher, Edward, Child in the House, unpublished; "Letter to the Idiot Editor of the New York Review of Books," unpublished. Manuscripts in collection of the editor

Carruth, Hayden, "August First" in *Brothers, I Loved You All: Poems 1969–1977,* New York, The Sheep Meadow Press, 1978

Carter, Jared, "Digging" in *Georgia Review,* vol. 36, no. 1, 1982

Carver, Ray, *Ultramarine,* New York, Random House, Inc., 1986; "Your Dog Dies" in *YAP*

Casey, Michael, *Obscenities,* New York, Warner Books, 1972

Chandonnet, Ann Fox, *Auras, Tendrils,* Moonbeam, Ontario, Penumbra Press, 1984

Chappell, Fred, *Castle Tzingal,* Baton Rouge, Louisiana State University Press, 1984

Christensen, Paul, *Weights and Measures: Selected Poems,* Huntington, University Editions, 1985

Clampitt, Amy, "Grassmere" in *Paris Review,* no. 91, 1984

Clinton, Michelle, *High Blood Pressure,* Los Angeles, West End Press, 1986

Cochran, William, "Doing Chores" in *Abraxas,* nos. 25 & 26, 1982

Codrescu, Andrei, *Selected Poems: 1970–1980,* New York, Sun, 1983

Coleman, Wanda, "6 AM & Dicksboro," "Eyes Bleed Pictures," Tales of a Black Adventurer," and "San Diego" in *PLP*

Collins, Billy, *Pokerface,* Los Angeles, Kenmore Press, 1977

Collins, Martha, *The Catastrophe of Rainbows,* Cleveland, Cleveland State University Press, 1985

Connell, Richard, in "Letter from the New World" *Open*

Connellan, Leo, *The Clear Blue Lobster-Water Country,* San Diego, Harcourt Brace Jovanovich, 1985; "Amelia, Mrs. Brooks" in *The New York Quarterly,* no. 32, 1987

Contoski, Victor, *Broken Treaties,* New York, New Rivers Press, 1973; "The Liar" in *Caliban,* no. 1, 1986

Cooley, Peter, *The Van Gogh Notebooks,* Pittsburgh, Carnegie Mellon University Press, 1987; "For Alissa" in *NAP*

Cooper, Dennis, "David Cassidy Then" in *Idols,* New York, Sea Horse Press, 1979

Cooperman, Robert, "Van Gogh at the Asylum at Saint-Remy" in *Mid-American Review,* vol. 4, nos. 1 & 2, 1984

Corn, Alfred, *Notes From A Child of Paradise,* New York, Penguin Books, 1984

Cortez, Jayne, *Coagulations: New and Selected Poems,* New York, Thunder's Mouth Press, 1984

Craig, Ray, "Sacramento" in *Contact II,* vol. 7, nos. 38–40, 1986

Creeley, Robert, *For Love: Poems 1950–1960,* New York, Charles Scribner's Sons, 1962

Crenner, James, "Young Hormones Madrigal" in *Iowa Review,* vol. 1, no. 1, 1986

Cruzkatz, Ida, "Selma: In Memoriam" in *Samisdat,* vol. 37, no. 3, 1983

cummings, e. e., *Collected Poems,* New York, Harcourt Brace & Co., 1938

Dacey, Philip, "Wild Pitches" in *NAP*

Dana, Robert, "Victor" in *Iowa Review,* vol. 16, no. 1, 1986

Daniels, Jim, *Places / Everyone,* Madison, University of Wisconsin Press, 1985

De Frees, Madeline, "Gallery of the Sarcophagi: Heraklion Museum" and elegy on Richard Hugo in *Graham House Review,* no. 7, 1984

Dickey, James, *The Strength of Fields,* New York, Doubleday & Co, Inc., 1979

Dickey, William, "Chickens in San Francisco" in *New Letters,* vol. 50, nos. 2 & 3, 1984

Dorn, Edward, *Recollections of Gran Apacheria,* San Francisco, Turtle Island, 1974; "For the New Union Dead in Alabama" in *PM*

Doubiago, Sharon, *Hard Country,* Minneapolis, West End Press, 1982

Douskey, Franz, "History of Night" in *Georgia Review,* vol. 36, no. 1, 1982

Dove, Rita, "Geometry" and "The Fish in the Stone" in *Vendler;* "Planning the Perfect Evening" in YAP; "Weathering Out" in *Agni Review,* no. 22, 1985

Dubie, Norman, "The Funeral" in *YAP*

Duncan, Robert, *Roots and Branches*, New York, New Directions, 1969

Dyak, Miriam, "Poem in Taurus" in *Yellow Silk*, no. 8, 1983

Ehrhart, W. D., "Hunting" in *VIETNAM*

Emanuel, Lynn, "Of Your Father's Indescretions and the Train To California" in *YAP*

Endrezze-Danielson, Anita, "Helix Aspersa" in *Poetry Northwest*, vol. 23, no. 4 (1982–1983)

Enslin, Theodore, *Songs Without Notes*, Austin, Salt Lick Press, 1984

Erlich, Gretel, "A Way of Speaking" and "A Sheeprancher Named John" in *YAP*

Eshleman, Clayton, "Apotheosis" in *Caliban* no. 1, 1986; *Fracture*, Santa Barbara, Black Sparrow Press, 1982; *Hades In Manganese*, Santa Barbara, Black Sparrows Press, 1981

Everwine, Peter, "a Short Novel" in *New Letters Reader Two: An Anthology of Contemporary Writing*, ed. by David Ray, Chicago and Athens, Swallow Press, 1984

Faulkner, P. W., "Medieval" in *Poetry Motel* 9, 1987

Ferlinghetti, Lawrence, *Endless Life*, New York, New Directions, 1981

Field, Edward, *Variety Photo Plays*, New York, Grove Press, 1967; *New and Selected Poems*, Riverdale-on-Hudson, The Sheep Meadow Press, 1987; "Night Song" in *MEN TALK*

Finch, Roger, "A Death Wish" in *Croton Review*, no. 98, 1985

Fincke, Gary, in *Graham House Review*, no. 7, 1984

Fisher, David, *The Book of Madness*, Cambridge, Applewood Press, 1980

Floyd, Bryan Alec, "Grandon Just" in *VIETNAM*

Forbes, Calvin, "M. A. P." and "The Other Side of This World" in *YAP*

Forché, Carolyn, *The Country Between Us*, New York, Harper & Row, 1977

Ford, Michael C., "The Homosexual" in *MEN TALK*

Fort, Charles, "Something Called a City" in *Georgia Review*, vol. 36, no. 1, 1982

Frost, Robert, "A Blue Ribbon at Amesbury" in *The Poetry of Robert Frost*, New York, Holt, Rinehart, and Winston, 1969

Fussell, Paul, *The Great War and Modern Memory*, New York, Oxford University Press, 1975

Gallagher, Tess, *Willingly*, Port Townsend, Graywold Press, 1984

Galler, David, "Meyer Levine" in *TriQuarterly*, no. 68, 1987

Gardner, Eric, "He Has A Noose" in *Poetry Motel* 9, 1986

Gerber, Dan, *Departures*, Fremont, MI, Sumac Press, 1973

Gibb, Robert, "March" in *Graham House Review*, no. 7, 1984

Gibson, Margaret, "Catechism Elegy" in *YAP*

Gildner, Gary, "Letters from Vicksburg" in *Blue Like the Heavens: New & Selected Poems*, Pittsburgh, University of Pittsburgh Press, 1984

Gildzen, Alex, *The Avalanche of Time*, Berkeley, North Atlantic Books, 1985

Ginsberg, Allen, *The Fall of America: Poems of these States 1965–1971*, San Francisco, City Lights, 1972; *Collected Poems 1940–1980*, New York, Harper & Row, 1986; *Planet News*, San Francisco, City Lights, 1968; *White Shroud: Poems 1980–1985*, New York, Harper and Row, 1986

Gioia, Dana, *Daily Horoscope*, St. Paul, Graywolf, 1986

Giorno, John, "Leather" in *OPEN*

Giovanni, Nikki, "Revolutionary Dreams" in *GEOGRAPHY*

Gizzi, Michael, "Avis" in *21 + 1*

Glass, Jesse, Jr., *Enoch*, Adelphi MD, Ewe Press, 1981; *Worm*, Kawabata Press, Cornwall, England, 1983; *Man's Vows*, Black Mesa Press, 1983; "Stubbe Peter" in *Eclectic*, Brooklandville, MD, Electric Press, 1988; "Nostalgia" and "Mister Six" in manuscript

Glaze, Andrew, *The Trash Dragon of Shensi*, Providence, Cooper Beach Press, 1978; "Reality Street" in manuscript copy sent to editor; *Earth That Sings: On the Poetry of Andrew Glaze*, ed. by William Doreski, Houston, Ford-Brown & Co., 1985

Gluck, Louise, "Mock Orange" and "The Mirror" in *YAP*

Goodman, Michael, "Little Neck Bay" and "The Testimony" in *Prairie Schooner*, vol. 60, no. 3, 1986

Goodman, Paul, "Long Lines" in *VOICE*

Graham, Jorie, "At Luca Signorelli's Resurrection of the Body," "The Geese," and "San Sepolcro" in *VENDLER The End of Beauty*, New York, Ecco Press, 1987

Gregg, Linda, "Marriage and Midsummer's Night" in *NAP*

Grenier, Robert, "Kansas" in *21 + 1*

Grosholz, Emily, "On the Untersberg: *Salzburg*" in *Southwest Review*, vol. 71, no. 3, 1986

Gross, Ronald, "Ice Cream Cone" in *OPEN*

Gullans, Charles, "Local Winds" in *Southern Review*, vol. 18, no. 2, 1982

Gunn, Thom, *The Passages of Joy*, London, Faber & Faber, 1982

Gwynn, R. S., *The Narcissiad*, New Braunfels, TX, Cedar Rock Press, 1981

Hacker, Marilyn, *Taking Notice*, New York, Alfred A. Knopf, 1980; *Assumptions*, New York, Alfred A. Knopf, 1985

Hadas, Pamela White, *Beside Herself: Pocahontas to Patty Hearst*, New York, Alfred A. Knopf, 1983

Hagedorn, Jessica, *Pet Food & Tropical Apparitions*, San Francisco, Momo's Press, 1981

Halpern, Daniel, *Seasonal Rights*, New York, The Viking Press, 1982

Hamilton, Alfred Starr, *The Poems of Alfred Starr Hamilton*, New York, The Jargon Society, 1970

Hamill, Sam, *The Nootka Rose*, Portland, Breitenbush Books, 1987

Harper, Michael, *Dear John, Dear Coltrane*, Pittsburgh, Pittsburgh University Press, 1972

Hass, Robert, *Field Guide*, New Haven, Yale University Press, 1973; "In Weather" in *GENERATION*

Haxton, Brooks, *The Lay of Eleanor and Irene*, Woodstock, Countryman Press, 1985; "Breakfast Ex Animo" in *Poetry*, vol. 160, no. 2, 1982

Healy, Eloise Klein, "There Are No Words For The Sexual Acts of Lesbians," "What It Was Like The Night Cary Grant Died," and "Wood, A Love Poem"—the first two poems are unpublished, the third appears in *STREETS*

Heaney, Seamus, "Punishment" in *POETS ON*

Hecht, Anthony, "Lizards and Snakes" in *CONTROVERSY*

Hejinian, Lyn, "The Person" in *Temblor*, no. 4, 1986

Hejna, James, all poems are unpublished. Copies are in the editor's possession

Hennessy, Eileen, "The First Clue" in *The New York Quarterly*, no. 32, 1987

Hense, Jeru, "Anarchist Heart," in *Blue Light Review*, no. 7, winter 86/87

Hershon, Robert, *The Public Hug: New & Selected Poems*, Baton Rouge, Louisiana State University Press, 1980

Heyen, William, "Fires" in *NAP*; *Lord Dragonfly: Five Sequences*, New York, Vanguard, 1981; "The Berries" in *NAP*; "Post Mortem: Literary Criticism" in *Poetry*, vol. 138, no. 1, 1981

Hickman, Leland, *Tiresias: Great Slave Lake Suite*, Los Angeles, Momentum Press, 1980

Higgins, Dick, *Pattern Poetry: Guide to an Unknown Literature*, Albany, State University of New York Press, 1987; *Poems Plain and Fancy*, Station Hill Press, 1986

Hirsch, Edward, "For The Sleepwalkers" in *YAP*; *Wild Gratitude*, New York, Alfred A. Knopf, 1986

Hirshfield, Alaya, in *Quarterly Review of Literature*, vols. 12 & 13, 1981 & 1982

Hitchcock, George, *The Wounded Alphabet: Poems Collected and New 1953–1983*, Santa Cruz, Jazz Press, 1984; *Losers Weepers: Poems Found Practically Everywhere*, Santa Cruz, Kayak Books, 1969; (with Robert Peters): *Pioneers of Modern Poetry*, San Francisco, Kayak Press, 1967

Hollander, John, "A View Out the Window" in *Southwest Review* vol. 71, no. 3, 1986; "Hidden Rhymes" in *Antaeus*, no. 44, 1984

Holthaus, Gary, *Circling Back*, Layton, UT, Peregine Smith, 1984

Hongo, Garrett, *Yellow Light*, Middletown, Connecticut Wesleyan University Press, 1977

Hood, Charles, "Red Sky, Red Water: Powell on the Colorado," forthcoming Sun/Gemini Press (Tucson)

Howard, Richard, *Lining Up,* New York, Atheneum, Inc., 1984

Howe, Susan, "Heliopathy" in *Temblor,* no. 4, 1986; "Speeches at the Barriers" in *21 + 1.*

Hudgins, Andrew, "From Commerce to the Capitol: Montgomery Alabama" in *Iowa Review,* vol. 16, no. 1, 1986

Janik, Phyllis, *No Dancing, No Acts of Dancing,* New York, Bookmark Press, 1982

Jarrell, Randall, "Next Day" and "The Woman at the Washington Zoo" in *VENDLER*

Jeffers, Robinson, "Science" in *News; Cawdor and other poems,* New York, Horace Liveright, 1928

Jerome, Judson, *The Village: New and Selected Poems,* Baltimore, Dolphin-Moon Press, 1987

Joans, Ted, "Knee Deep," "To Fez Cobra," and "Zoo You Too" in *GEOGRAPHY*

Jones, Daryl E., "The Hotstrip" in *TriQuarterly,* no. 68, 1987

Jones, LeRoi (Baraka), "For Hettie" in *NAP;* "Horatio Alger Uses Scag" in *GEOGRAPHY*

Jones, Rodney, "Thoreau" in *YAP*

Jong, Erica, "The Buddha in the Womb" in *YAP*

Joy, Donna, "Finches, moths, herons," in *The New Yorker,* vol. 58, no., 66, May 24, 1982

Justice, Donald, "Elegy for Cello and Piano" in *Iowa Review,* vol. 16, no. 1, 1986

Kamenetz, Rodger, *Nympholepsy,* Dryad Press, 1985

Katz, Eliot, "Naming the Red Juice" and "Thieves at Work" in *Long Shot* vol. 4, 1986

Kees, Weldon, "For My Daughter" in *Collected Poems,* Lincoln, University of Nebraska Press, 1960

Kelley, Robert, *The Alchemist to Mercury,* Richmond, The North Atlantic Press, 1981; "To Her Body Against Time" in *CONTROVERSY*

Kennedy, Terry, "hot mama plath" in *Durango,* New York, The Smith, 1978; *Heart, Organ, Part of the Body,* San Francisco, Second Coming Press, 1981

Kessler, Stephen, *Poem to Walt Disney,* San Francisco, Man-Root Press, 1977

Kicknosway, Faye, *Who Shall Know Them,* New York, Viking Press, 1985

Kilgore, James C., "The White Man Pressed the Locks" in *KENNEDY*

Kim, Chungmi Kim, *Selected Poems,* Los Angeles, Korean Pioneer Press, 1982

Kinnell, Galway, "December Day in Honolulu" in *Halpern;* "Duck-Chasing" in *VOICE*

Kizer, Carolyn, "The Worms," *Midnight Was My Cry: New and Selected Poems,* Garden City, Doubleday, Inc., 1971

Knight, Etheridge, *Born of A Woman: New & Selected Poems,* Boston, Houghton Mifflin & Co., 1980

Knott, Bill, "Childhood: the Offense of History" in *Caliban 1,* no. 1, 1986

Koch, Kenneth, "Sleeping With Women" in *PM*

Koertge, Ron, "Adults Only!" in *Diary Cows,* Los Angeles, Little Caesar Press, 1981; "I Never Touch My Penis" in *MEN TALK; 12 Photographs of Yellowstone,* Los Angeles & Fairfax, Red Hill Press, 1976

Koestenbaum, Phyllis, "Blood Journey" in *NETWORKS*

Kogawa, Joy, "July in Coaldale" in *Contact II,* vol. 7, nos. 38–40, 1986

Komunyakaa, Yusef, *Copacetic,* Middletown, Connecticut Wesleyan University Press, 1984

Kooser, Ted, *A Local Habitation and a Name,* San Luis Obispo, CA, Solo Press, 1974; *The Blizzard Voices,* Minneapolis, The Bieler Press, 1986

Kumin, Maxine, *Our Ground Time Here Will Be Brief: New and Selected Poems,* New York, Viking, 1982

Kuzma, Greg, "The Catastrophe of Creative Writing" in *Poetry,* vol. 148, no. 6, September 1986, 342–354; *Of China and of Greece,* New York, Sun Press, 1984

"La Loca" (Pamala Carol), "You Should Only Give Head To Guys You Really Like" and "Kiddie Shows I Used to Watch" in forthcoming collection to be published by City Lights Press

Lally, Michael, "Lost Angels" in *PLP*

Lane, Arthur, *Handing Over,* Winter Haven, Kenmore Press, 1984; *Dancing in the Dark,* Pasadena, Kenmore Press, 1977

Lea, Sydney, "Coon Hunt Sixth Month (1955)" and "Old Dog, New Dog" in *YAP*

Lee, Deborah, "Haiku for Leah" in *Contact II,* vol. 7, nos. 38–40, 1986

Leithauser, Brad, "The Ghost of a Ghost" in *YAP*

Lepson, Ruth, "Sleeping on the Couch" in *Helicon Nine,* no. 16, 1986

Levertov, Denise, *Relearning the Alphabet,* New York, New Directions, 1970; *Poems Nineteen Sixty to Nineteen Sixty-Seven: Including Jacob's Ladder, O Taste & See, The Sorrow Dance,* New York, New Directions, 1983

Levis, Larry, "Winter Stars" in *YAP*

Leyland, Winston, ed. of *Gay Sunshine Interviews,* vol. 1, 1978, and vol. 2, 1982, San Francisco, Gay Sunshine Press; ed. of *Angels of the Lyre,* San Francisco, Gay Sunshine Press 1977

Lieberman, Laurence, "The Tilemaker's Hill Fresco," *APR.* Jan 1982

Lifshin, Lyn, *Kiss the Skin Off,* Cherry Valley Editions, 1985

Lim, Shirley, "Pigeons" in *Contact II,* vol. 7, nos. 38–40, 1986

lloyd, d. h., "dusk" in *MEN TALK*

Locklin, Gerald, *Toad's Sabbatical,* Los Angeles, UPC Press, 1977; *Pronouncing Borges,* Stockton, as *Wormwood Review,* no. 67 [1977]; *Scenes From A Second Adolescence and Other Poems,* Long Beach, Applezaba Press, 1979

Logan, John, *The Anonymous Lover: New Poems,* New York, Liveright, Inc., 1973

Logan, William, "Debora Sleeping" in *YAP*

Looney, George, "The Last Vision of Light" in *Prairie Schooner,* vol. 60, no. 3, 1986

Lowell, Robert, "For Sheridan," "Home After Three Months Away," and "Waking Early Sunday Morning" in Vendler; *For Lizzie and Harriet,* New York, Farrar, Straus and Giroux, 1973; Ian Hamilton, *Robert Lowell: A Biography,* New York, Random House, 1982

Lummis, Suzanne, "Breasts" and "Death Rings Marilyn Monroe," unpublished. Manuscripts in editor's possession

Lynn, Catherine, "Fuck" in *Pearl,* no. 4, 1987

Macdonald, Cynthia, *(W)holes,* New York, Alfred A. Knopf, Inc., 1980

McDowell, Robert, *Quiet Money,* New York, Henry Holt & Co., 1987

Mackey, Nathaniel, "Ghede Poem" in *Eroding Witness,* Urbana, University of Illinois Press, 1985

MacLeish, Archibald, "Ars Poetica" in *An Introduction to Poetry,* sixth edition, ed. by X. J. Kennedy, Boston, Little Brown & Co., 1986

Malanga, Gerard, *Rosebud: Poems by Gerard Malanga,* Lincoln, MA, Penmaen Press, 1975

Mannes, Marya, "Satyr" in *New Letters Reader Two: An Anthology of Contemporary Writing,* ed. by David Ray, Chicago & Athens, Swallow Press, 1984

Mariani, Paul, "Lines I Told Myself I Wouldn't Write" in *YAP*

Mathis, Cleopatra, "Night Storm" in *Graham House Review,* no. 7, 1984

Matthews, William, "Loyal" and "Nurse Sharks" in *YAP*

McBride, Mekeel, "A Blessing" in *YAP;* "The Delicay of Freedom" in *Poetry East,* no. 17, 1985; "The Will to Live" in *NAP*

McClure, Michael, *Dark Brown,* San Francisco, Haselwood Books, 1967; "Jean Harlow and Billy the Kid" in *Star,* New York, Grove Press, 1970; *The Beard and Victims: Two Plays,* New York, Grove Press, 1985; "April Arboretum" in *New Directions,* no. 49, 1985; *September Blackberries,* New York, New Directions, 1974

McCombs, Judith, *Against Nature,* Paradise, CA, Dustbooks, 1979

McCord, Howard, *Selected Poems,* Crossing Press, 1975

McDaniel, Elizabeth, *Sister Vayda's Song,* Hanging Loose Press, 1982

McGrath, Thomas, *Passages Toward the Dark,* Copper Canyon Press, 1981; *Letters to an Imaginary Friend (Parts III & IV),* Port Townsend, Copper Canyon Press, 1985

McHugh, Heather, *Dangers,* Boston, Houghton Mifflin, Inc., 1982

Mackinnon, Patrick, *Walking Behind My Breath,* Duluth, No Press, 1986

McMichael, James, *Four Good Things,* Boston, Houghton Mifflin, Inc., 1982

Merrill, James, *From the First Nine: Poems 1946–1976,* New York, Atheneum, Inc., 1982; *The Changing Light at Sandover,* New York, Atheneum, Inc., 1983

Merwin, W. S., *Writings to an Unfinished Accompaniment,* New York, Atheneum, Inc., 1973

Metcalf, Paul, a review of Alicia Ostriker's *Writing Like A Womam* in *Alcatraz,* no. 3, 1985

Metras, Gary, *Destiny's Calendar,* Richmond, Vt., Samisdat, 1985

Metzger, Deena, "Crimes Against Soft Birds" in *STREETS*

Meyer, Thomas, *The Bang Book,* Highlands, NC, The Jargon Society, 1971; *the Umbrella of Aesculapius,* Highlands, NC, The Jargon Society, 1975; *Sappho's Raft,* Highlands, NC, The Jargon Society, 1982

Mezey, Robert, "Couplets" in *Iowa Review,* vol. 16, no. 1, 1986

Middleton, David, "Sirens" in *Southern Review,* vol. 18, no. 2, 1982

Miller, Walter James, "He Thinks On Bowling" in *Croton Review,* no. 8, 1985

Minarik, John Paul, "basic writing 702," in *LIGHT*

Minty, Judith, "Prowling the Ridge" in *GENERATION*

Mitcham, Judson, "Do A Young Sleepwalker," in *Graham House Review,* no. 7, 1984

Mitchell, Susan, ["Boone"] in *Ironwood,* no. 21, 1983

Moore, Marianne, "Enough" in *Harper's,* vol. 269, no. 1611, August 1984

Moore, Todd, *Glitch,* West Orange, NJ, no publisher listed, no. date; *D.O.A.,* Belvidere, IL, Crawlspace, 1982; *Dillinger,* 13 vols., Erie, Kangaroo's Court, 1986–

Morgan, John, "The Bone-Duster" in *Quarterly Review of Literature,* vo. 21, 1980

Morgan, Robin, *Monster,* New York, Random House, 1972

Motion, Andrew, "A Lyrical Ballad" in *Paris Review,* vol. 26, no. 91, 1984

Muske, Carol, *Sky Light,* Garden City, Doubleday, Inc., 1981

Niatum, Duane, *Songs for the Harvester of Dreams,* Seattle & London, University of Washington Press, 1981; editor of *Harper's Anthology of 20th Century American Native American Poetry,* New York, Harper & Row, 1988

Niedecker, Lorine, *From This Condensery: The Complete Poems of Lorine Niedecker,* ed. Robert Bertholf, New York, The Jargon Society, 1985

Norse, Harold, *The Love Poems: 1940–1985,* The Crossing Press, 1986

Northup, Harry, *Enough the Great Running Chapel,* Los Angeles, Momentum Press, 1982; "Listening to Savoy Brown at the Santa Monica Civic" in *STREETS*

O'Connell, Richard, "Letter from the New World" in *OPEN*

O'Hara, Frank, *The Collected Poems,* New York, Alfred A. Knopf, 1971

Oandasan, William, "The Presence" in *The Greenfield Review: American Indian Writings,* Greenfield Center, NY, Greenfield Review Press, 19

Oates, Joyce Carol, "Baby" in *GENERATION;* "High-Wire Artist" in *Southern Review,* vol. 18, no. 2, 1982

Ochester, Ed, "Changing the Name to Ochester" in *MEN TALK*

Olds, Sharon, *Satan Says,* Pittsburgh, University of Pittsburgh Press, 1980

Olson, Charles, "The Praises" in *VOICE*

Oppen, George, *Of Being Numerous,* New York, New Directions, 1968

Oppenheimer, Joel, *Just Friends and Lovers: Poems 1959–1961,* New York, The Jargon Society, 1980

Orr, Gregory, "Concerning the Stone" in *HALPERN;* "Gathering the Bones Together" in *GENERATION*

Ostriker, Alicia, "The Pure Unknown" in *Hudson Review,* vol. 34, nos. 3 & 4, 1981 & 1982; *Writing Like A Woman,* Ann Arbor, University of Michigan Press, 1983

Oyama, Richard, "mochi" in *Contact II,* vol. 7, nos. 38–40, 1986

Pack, Robert, "Father" in *CONTROVERSY*

Parlatore, Anselm, "The Mecox Poems," unpublished. Manuscript in possession of the editor

Peacock, Molly, "She Lays" in *Shenandoah*, vol. 32, no. 3, 1981

Perchik, Simon, *Who Can Touch These Knots*, Metuchen, Scarecrow Press, 1985

Perelman, Bob, "Coda" and "Sentimental Mechanics" in *Temblor*, no. 4, 1986

Peters, Robert, *The Sow's Head and Other Poems*, Detroit, Wayne State University, 1968; *Shaker Light*, Greensboro, Unicorn Press, 1988; *What Dillinger Meant to Me*, New York, Sea Horse Press, 1982; *The Blood Countess: Elizabeth Bathory of Hungary*, Cherry Valley, NY, Cherry Valley Editions, 1987; *Celebrities: In Memory of Margaret Dumont*, Berkeley, Sombre Reptiles Press, 1981; "The Heniad" in *The Brand-X Anthology of Poetry: A Parody Anthology*, ed. by William Zaranka, Cambridge, Apple-Wood Books, 1981; *The Great American Poetry Bake-Off*, first, second, and third series, Metuchen, Scarecrow Press, 1979, 1982, 1987; *The Peters Black and Blue Guide To Current Literary Journals*, first, second, and third series, Scarecrow Press, 1979, 1982, 1987; *The Peters Black and Blue Guide To Current Literary Journals*, first, second, and third series, Paradise, CA and Cherry Valley, NY, Dust Books and Cherry Valley Editions, 1983, 1985, 1987; editor, The Collected Poems of Amnesia Glasscock (John Steinbeck), San Francisco, Man-Root Books, 1977

Pfingston, Roger, "love your bones" in *New Letters Reader Two: An Anthology of Contemporary Writing*, ed. by David Ray, Chicago and Athens, Swallow Press, 1984

Phillips, Dennis, "This plain to the sea fog" in *Temblor*, no. 4, 1986

Phillips, Robert, *Running on Empty*, Garden City, Doubleday & Co., 1981; *The Pregnant Man*, Garden City, Doubleday & Co., 1978

Piercy, Marge, "Burying Blues for Janis" in *GENERATION*

Pinsky, Robert, "Fairyland" in *APR*, vol. 11, no. 1, 1982; "The Unseen" in *Ironwood*, no. 21, 1983

Piper, Janet, "Vista" in *Iowa Review*, vol. 16, no. 1, 1986

Plath, Sylvia, *The Collected Poems*, ed. by Ted Hughes, New York, Harper and Row, 1981

Plymell, Charles, *Forever Wider*, Metuchen, Scarecrow Press, 1985

Poulin, Al, Jr., "Cock Man" in *Outlaw*, nos. 4 & 5, 1984

Pound, Ezra, *Selected Poems*, London, Faber and Faber, 1927

Prado., Holly, "By Seasonal Odor" in *PLP.*

Radin, Doris, "Rivka Has a Man's Head" in *Helicon Nine*, no. 16, winter 1986

Ransom, John Crow, "Here Lies A Lady" in *Selected Poems Third Edition, Revised and Enlarged*, New York, Alfred A. Knopf, Inc., 1952

Rasula, Jed, "The Tent of Times" in *Sulfur*, no. 12, 1985

Ratch, Jerry, *Hot Weather: Selected Poems*, Metuchen, Scarecrow Press, 1982

Ratner, Rochelle, *Practicing To Be A Woman*, Metuchen, Scarecrow Press, 1982

Ray, David, *The Touched Life*, Metuchen, Scarecrow Press, 1982

Ray, Judy, "Ten Stations of the Sweet Briar Lake" and "Writing in Virginia" in *Helicon Nine*, no. 16, 1986

Reiss, James, *The Breathers*, New York, Ecco Press, 1974

Rios, Albert, "I Would Visit Him in the Corner" and "In the Woman Arms of the Ground" in *YAP*

Rich, Adrienne, *Dream of A Common Language: Poems 1947–1977*, New York, W. W. Norton, 1978

Ridland, John, *Ode On Violence and Other Poems*, Martin, TN, Tennessee Poetry Press, 1969

Robbins, Doren, *Sympathetic Manifesto*, Van Nuys, Perivale Press, 1987

Robertson, Kirk, "My Father" in *MEN TALK*

Rogers, Patiann, "Justificatiion of the Horned Lizard" in *NAP*

Rosen, Kenneth, "The White Egret" in *NAP*

Rothenberg, Jerome, "Blood River Shaman Chant" in *Sulfur*, no. 10, 1984

Rutsala, Vern, *Walking Home from the Icehouse*, Pittsburgh, Carniege-Mellon University Press, 1981

Ryan, Michael, "Winter Drought" in *NAP*; "You Can Thank" in *In Winter*, New York, Holt, Rinehart and Winston, Inc., 1981

Sallee, Wayne Allen, "What I saw From My Window" in *Blue Light Review*, no. 5, winter 85/86

Santos, Sherod, "The Evening Light Along The Sound" in *NAP*

Schevil, James, *The American Fantasies*, Athens, Ohio University Press, 1981

Schmitz, Dennis, "uncle Lucien" *Field*. fall 1981

Schwartz, Delmore, "Baudelaire" in *VOICE*

Sexton, Anne, *Transformations*, Boston, Houghton Mifflin, Inc., 1972; *Live or Die*, London, Oxford University Press, 1961

Shanley, Mary, "The Death Walk" and "Times Square Shuttle" in *Long Shot* vol. 4, 1986

Shapiro, Karl, "Auto Wreck" in *New Selected Poems*, Chicago, University of Chicago Press, 1987

Sheck, Laurie, "The Annunciation" in *Iowa Review*, vol. 16, no. 1, 1986

Shelton, Richard, *Selected Poems: 1969–1981*, Pittsburgh, University of Pittsburgh Press, 1982

Sheridan, Michael, "Shooting the Loop" in *NAP*

Shiffrin, Nancy, *What she could not name*, La Jolla, La Jolla Poets Press, 1987

Shore, Jane, "A Clock" and "A Luna Moth" in *The Antioch Review*, vol. 45, no. 1, 1987

Simic, Charles, *Dismantling the Silence*, New York, George Braziller, Inc., 1971

Simon, Maurya, *The Enchanted Room*, Cooper Canyon Press, 1987

Smith, Dave, "The Perspective and Limits of Snapshots" in *YAP*; "Under the Scrub Oak a Red Shoe" in *GENERATION*; "Careless Love" in *Poetry*, vol. 147, no. 5, February 1986

Snider, Clifton, "George Practices the Sitar" and "John Lennon's Erotic Lithographs," unpublished

Snodgrass, W. D., *The Fuhrer Bunker*, Brockport, Boa Editions, 1977; "A Flat One" in *CONTROVERSY*; "Cock Robin's roost protests from (W. D.) (Mr. Evil)" in *Word and Image*, vol. 2, no. 1, 1986; "Mother and The Child" (as S. S. Gardons) in *NEW*

Snyder, Gary, *A Range of Poems*, London, Fulcrum Press, 1966, contains *Riprap* and *Myths and Texts*; *Turtle Island*, New York, New Directions, 1984

Socolow, Elizabeth Ann, "Men in the House Summertime After A Swim" in *New York Quarterly*, no. 32, 1987

Soto, Gary, *Black Hair*, Pittsburgh, University of Pittsburgh Press, 1985

Speer, Laurel, "A Movie Script of Paradise Lost" in *Crab Creek Review*, vol. 33, no. 3, 1986

Spender, Stephen, "Auden's Funeral" in *Antaeus*, no. 44, 1982

Spicer, Jack, *The Collected Books of Jack Spicer*, ed. by Robin Blaser, Santa Barbara, Black Sparrow Press, 1980

Spivack, Kathleen, *The Beds We Live In*, Metuchen, Scarecrow Press, 1986

St. John, David, "The Orange Piano" in *NAP*

Stafford, William, "One Home" and "The Farm on the Great Plains" in *VOICE*; "Some Things the World Gave" in *Iowa Review*, vol. 16, no. 1, 1986

Stanton, Maura, "Childhood" in *YAP*: "Good People" in *NAP*

Stern, Gerald, "Fritz" in *HALPERN*

Stevens, Wallace, *Harmonium*, New York, Alfred A. Knopf, 1953

Still, James, *The Wolfpen Poems*, Berea, Berea College Press, 1986

Stokes, Terry, *Sportin' News*, Memphis, Raccoon Books, Inc., 1985

Stoloff, Carolyn, *A Spool of Blue*, Metuchen, Scarecrow Press, 1983

Stone, Arlene, *The Double Pipes of Pan*, Berkeley, North Atlantic Books, 1983

Strand, Mark, "Keeping Things Whole" in *VENDLER*

Stryk, Lucien, *Collected Poems, 1953–1983*, Athens, Ohio University Press, 1985

Swander, Mary, "Doc" in *Iowa Review*, vol. 16, no. 1, 1986

Swann, Brian, *The Middle of the Journey*, University of Alabama Press, 1982

Sward, Robert, *Poems: New and Selected 1957–1983*, Toronto, Aya Press, 1983

Taggart, John, "The Rothko Chapel Poem" in *Temblor*, no. 1, 1985

Tanaka, Ronald, *The Shinto Suite: Opus 2*, Greenfield Center, NY, Greenfield Review Press, 1981

Tate, James, *The Lost Pilot*, New Haven, Yale University Press, 1967; *Absences*, Boston, Little Brown, 1972

Thompson, Phyllis, "What the Land Gave" in *Quarterly Review of Literature*, vols. 12 & 13, 1981–1982

Tichborne, Chidiock, "Elegy, Written with His Own Hand in the Tower Before His Execution" in *An Introduction to Poetry*, sixth edition, ed. by X. J. Kennedy, Boston, Little Brown

Towle, Tony, "Works on Paper" in *Poetry*, vol. 125, no. 6, March 1975

Trachtenberg, Paul, *Making Waves*, Cherry Valley, NY, Cherry Valley Editions, 1986; *Short Changes For Loretta*, Cherry Valley, NY, Cherry Valley Editions, 1982; *Mercury Tea*, Mansfield, TX. Latitudes Press, 1988

Troupe, Quincy, *Skulls Along the River*, Berkeley, I. Reed Books, 1984

Updike, John, *Facing Nature*, New York, Alfred A. Knopf, 1985

Upton, Lee, "The Wives" in *Connecticut Poetry Review*, vol. 3, no. 1, 1984

Urdang, Constance, "Lizard" in *The Poetry Review: The Poetry Society of America*, vol. 1, no. 2, 1983

Van Walleghen, Michael, "The Age of Reason" in *Iowa Review*, vol. 16, no. 1, 1986

Vangelisti, Paul, *Air*, Los Angeles and Fairfax, Red Hill Press, 1973; "Villa," unpublished: "Los Alephs" in *Temblor*, no. 5, 1987

Villanueva, Alma, three poems in *Alcatraz*, no. 3, 1985

Voigt, Ellen Bryant, "The Bat" in *YAP*

Wagoner, David, *Landfall: Poems*, Boston, Little Brown, 1986

Wakoski, Diane, *Trilogy*, Garden City, Doubleday & Co., Inc., 1974, includes *Coins and Coffins* and *The George Washington Poems; Dancing on the Grave of A Sonofabitch*, Los Angeles, Black Sparrow Press, 1973; *Smudging*, Santa Barbara, Black Sparrow Press, 1972; *The Collected Greed: Parts 1-16*, Santa Barbara, Black Sparrow Press, 1984; *The Magician's Feast Letters*, Santa Barbara, Black Sparrow Press, 1982

Waldman, Ann, *Fast-Speaking Woman & Other Chants*, San Francisco, City Lights, 1975

Wantling, William, *San Quentin's Stranger*, Paradise, CA, Dustbooks, 1976

Warren, Robert Penn, *Chief Joseph of the Nez Perce*, New York, Random House, 1982

Waters, Michael, *Not Just Any Death*, Boa Editions, 1979

Welch, Lew, "After Anacreon" in *NAP*; "Wobbly Rock" in *PM*

White, Steven F., *For the Unborn*, Greensboro, Unicorn Press, 1986; *Burning the Old Year*, Greensboro, Unicorn Press, 1984; editor for *Poets of Nicaragua, 1916–1979*, Greensboro, Unicorn Press, 1982, and *Poets of Chile 1965–1984*, Greensboro, Unicorn Press, 1986

Whiting, Nathan, *running*, New York, New Rivers Press, 1974

Whitman, Ruth, *Tamsen Donner: A Woman's Journey*, Cambridge, Alice James Books, 1977; *The Passion of Lizzy Borden: New and Selected Poems*, New York, October House, 1968

Wiegel, Bruce, "Sailing to Bien Hoa" in *Darkness*

Wieners, John, *Behind the State Capitol: Or Cincinnati Pike*, Boston, Good Gray Poets, 1975

Wilbur, Richard, *The Poems of Richard Wilbur*, New York, Harcourt Brace Jovanovich, 1963

Wild, Peter, *Cochise*, Garden City, Doubleday & Co, Inc., 1973

Williams, C. K., *Tar*, New York, Vintage Books, 1983

Williams, Jonathan, *Get Hot or Get Out*, Metuchen, Scarecrow Press, 1983

Williams, William Carlos, *Selected Poems*, New York, New Directions, 1949

Wong, Nellie, "When I Was Growing Up" in *Electrum* no. 33, 1984

Wright, Charles, *The Other Side of the River,* New York, Vintage, 1984; *The Venice Notebook,* Boston, Barn Dream Press, 1971

Wright, James, *Collected Poems,* Middletown, Connecticut Wesleyan University Press, 1972

Yamada, Mitsuye, *Camp Notes,* San Francisco, Shameless Hussy Press, 1976; *Desert Run: Poems and Stories,* Latham, NY, Kitchen Table Press, 1988

Yates, David C., "Making Bread" in *POETS ON*

Yau, John, *Corpse and Mirror,* New York, Henry Holt and Co, 1983; "All This Changing Trouble Luck and Suddenness" in *Sulfur,* no. 17, 1, 1986

Young Bear, Ray A., "Nothing Could Take Away the Bear-King's Image" in *Sulfur,* no. 10, 1984

Young, Geoffrey, "Elegy" in *Sulfur,* no. 12, 1985

Zaranka, William, *A Mirror Driven Through Nature,* West Lafayette, Sparrow Press, n.d.; *Blessing,* Denver, Wayland Press, 1986

Zimmer, Paul, *Family Reunion: Selected and New Poems,* Pittsburgh, University of Pittsburgh Press, 1983

Index